CHARTISM AND SOCIETY

CHARTISM AND SOCIETY:
An Anthology of Documents

edited by

F. C. MATHER

BELL & HYMAN
London

HOLMES & MEIER PUBLISHERS, INC.
New York

First published in 1980 by
BELL & HYMAN LIMITED
Denmark House
37–39 Queen Elizabeth Street
London SE1 2QB

First published in the United States of America 1980 by
HOLMES & MEIER PUBLISHERS, INC.
30 Irving Place
New York, N.Y. 10003

Library of Congress Cataloging in Publication Data
Main entry under title:

Chartism and society.

Bibliography: p.
Includes index.
1. Chartism – History – Sources.
I. Mather, Frederick Clare
HD8396.C49   1980   322'.2'09   80–15587
ISBN 0–8419–0625–4 (Holmes & Meier)

British Library Cataloging in Publication Data
Chartism and Society
1. Chartism – Sources
I. Mather, Frederick Clare
322.4'4'0941   HD8396
ISBN 0 7135 1114 1 (Bell & Hyman)

Typeset by Computacomp (UK) Ltd,
Fort William, Scotland
Printed in Great Britain by
Redwood Burn Limited, Trowbridge & Esher

Contents

Abbreviations

Econ. H.R.	*Economic History Review*
EHR	*English Historical Review*
H.O.	Home Office Papers (Public Record Office)
IRSH	*International Review of Social History*
L.D.O.S.	Lords Day Observance Society
L.W.M.A.	London Working Men's Association
N.A.U.T.	National Association of United Trades
N.C.A.	National Charter Association
N.S.	New Series
P.R.O.	Public Record Office

Preface

The starting point of this volume, which is intended for students and the general reader, was the need, stated by Asa Briggs in *Chartist Studies*, to fit Chartism 'into British history as a whole'. Historians have often portrayed it as a cause distinct: visionary and born out of due time. Its central purposes were, it is true, at the time unattainable, and there lay the cause of its failure. Chartism, however, was not a sect but a popular movement. Its devotees expressed themselves on a variety of issues, local, national, international, ranging from how the town's gas supply should be administered to the principles of British foreign policy. Committed to a specific legislative programme, they took account of the realities of the political system, and employed methods overlapping those of other parties in the state. Moreover, because it rested on a broad spectrum of the British public, the Movement displayed, more frequently than has been supposed, attitudes embedded in society at large, and responded to changing social conditions. It is with the outward dimension of Chartism that this collection is concerned. The aim is to show how Chartists behaved towards others and how others behaved towards them, and to recapture the authentic spirit of the Movement by letting its friends and opponents speak for themselves.

Aware of the objections which may be raised to reproducing documents in part rather than in their entirety, the editor judged that the need for representative sampling justified this, more especially as, in many instances, only a portion of the document was relevant. Where necessary, however, he has endeavoured to indicate the content of the missing portions in the introductory note or in bracketed inserts within the text. Interference with illiterate texts and with archaic spelling and use of capitals has been kept to a minimum needed for intelligibility.

In writing the Introduction and notes the editor has been able to draw heavily on the published work of several generations of scholars, but certain themes await definitive treatment, and the collection is, in these respects, intended to open rather than to close the study of the subject.

Transcripts of Crown-copyright records in the Public Record Office appear by permission of the Controller of H.M. Stationery Office, viz. on pp. 120–6, 141–6, 168–9, 172–3, 174, 175, 176–7 and 178–80. For authority to reproduce extracts from the Ms. Volume, 'The Chartist Movement in Derby, 1841: Original Correspondence' (pp. 220 and 299–301) my debt is to Derbyshire County Library: Derby Local Studies Library.

In seeking and assembling material for this volume I have been helped by many librarians and archivists, especially by the staff of the Public Record Office and of the British Library, by Mr. D. R. Webb, Reference Librarian of the Bishopsgate Institute Library, and his staff, and by the staff of the Central Libraries of Birmingham, Bradford, Manchester and Sheffield, Leeds Library, Derby Local Studies Library, Dr. Williams's Library, the British Library of Political and Economic Science, University of London Goldsmiths' Library, the Institute of Historical Research, and Southampton University Library.

I am indebted to my wife and to Miss Phoebe Bankart for proof reading and the construction of the Index.

For the interpretation in the Introduction and notes the editor bears sole responsibility, but he wishes to acknowledge the large contribution to his thinking made by undergraduate and postgraduate students of the University of Southampton through theses, dissertations, and participation in the Special Subject seminars which he has been privileged to conduct over many years. To those students this book is humbly dedicated.

F. C. MATHER

Introduction[1]

[1] The figures in brackets in the Introduction refer to parts and sections in the collection of documents.

The Chartist Movement

Chartism, as portrayed by the historians, has a distinct and recognizable shape. It was a national political movement, summoning delegates from various parts of the country to conventions in London, forming associations with articulated rules and constitutions, and operating a dedicated and powerful press. The avowed object of this activity was to procure the enactment of the Six Points of the People's Charter (I, 1), but of greater long-term significance was the social basis on which it rested. Though a handful of professional men, unrepresentative of their order and headed by an equally uncharacteristic Irish squireen, contributed ideas and initiatives out of all proportion to their number, the agitation was sustained, and in large measure shaped, by the energy and enterprise of ordinary working men. Nothing quite comparable had ever previously been attempted in Britain from so humble a social stratum. Indeed, Dr. J. T. Ward is, no doubt, warranted in the claim that Chartism was 'the first great working-class political movement in the history of the world.'[2]

The pattern of events may be briefly sketched, for it has been surveyed in detail elsewhere. In London and some provincial centres of the North there had been an independent agitation for universal manhood suffrage during the struggle for the Great Reform Bill. When only the Whig Bill passed, working men concentrated for a while on more limited objectives—improved trade union organization, the ten hours bill for textile factories and abolition of the stamp duties on newspapers. From about 1836 onwards dissatisfaction with Whig policies and subsequent Whig inertia engendered a mounting criticism of the 1832 act. Under the

[2] *Chartism* (London, 1973), p. 11.

impact of recruiting drives by Feargus O'Connor, a discarded Irish M.P., and later by the London Working Men's Association, radical societies were formed in the provinces and in Scotland. The impetus to focus reforming inclinations upon a single national endeavour came from Birmingham.[1] There the middle-class leaders of the revived Political Union, tiring of the Melbourne government's refusal to concede currency reform or allow the possibility of amending the Reform Act, and lacking confidence in the determination of their own order, 'choked with pride, jealousy and servility', turned to enlist the aid of working men throughout the country in a new mass movement. The model was that of 1830–32, but the aim this time, adult male democracy. Thomas Attwood sounded the tocsin at the Council of the Union on 19 December 1837. Soon his colleagues were planning the institutional framework of what was to become the first Chartist campaign—a National Petition, which came to embody five of the six points of the (L.W.M.A's) People's Charter (Attwood's prejudices excluded equal electoral districts), an elective Convention, and a National Rent to finance the movement. Emissaries were despatched far and wide. With the relatively well paid skilled artisans of the L.W.M.A. rapport was quickly established, and by August–September 1838 the National Petition and the People's Charter were being widely adopted, even in the factory districts of Lancashire and the West Riding hitherto preoccupied with resisting the introduction of the New Poor Law. The adhesion of the children of the industrial revolution, which was encouraged by Feargus O'Connor, added numbers to the cause, but also introduced a desperate note, fanned mainly by the wild ex-Methodist preacher Rayner Stephens. This sat uneasily with the calculating pressurizing of the Birmingham group, and boded trouble for the future. Even so, with the rallying of the North, Chartism in its completeness was given birth.

The record of the movement during 1839 was heroic, but in terms of achievement barren. Probably nothing could have induced the Reformed Parliament to adopt universal suffrage, etc. at a stroke, but, as Dr. Kenneth Judge[2] has shown, the Chartist Convention, which sat from

---

[1] For a recent demonstration of the importance of the Birmingham Political Union in launching the Chartist Movement, see Carlos Flick, *The Birmingham Political Union and the Movements for Reform in Britain, 1830–39* (Hamden, 1978) espec. Chap. VII.

[2] 'Early Chartist Organization and the Convention of 1839'. *IRSH*, Vol. XX, 1975, pp. 370–97.

February to September, failed to give a lead in such elementary matters as organizing missionaries and collecting the National Rent. The Birmingham leaders abandoned the Convention after little more than three weeks, alienated by methods which Stephens did more than the relatively diplomatic O'Connor to promote. For the rest of 1839 the movement lacked a clear focus of direction. Intense militancy developed in the industrial areas early in the year, but it was not used constructively and only led to arrests, which weakened Chartism. The Petition, with 1,280,000 signatures, was discussed by the House of Commons on 12 July and rejected. The Convention called a general strike (the 'Sacred Month') to compel a reconsideration, but almost immediately rescinded its appeal. The year ended in a series of planned but badly co-ordinated local outbreaks which extended into the January of the following year. Of these the march of 4,000 Welsh miners and ironworkers on Newport on 4 November was the most dramatic.

Chartism never recovered the popular support which it commanded in 1839. The average weekly sales of its principal newspaper, the *Northern Star*, fell from 36,000 in that year to 12,500 in 1842, and did not rise above 12,000 in the next great year of excitement, 1848,[1] (though annual averages mask short period fluctuations). Nevertheless, the movement was quick to regain momentum, and in some important respects made good the deficiencies of 1839. The Manchester conference of 20 July 1840 gave Chartism for the first time a permanent organization, the National Charter Association, resting at the local level upon an elaborate hierarchy of classes, wards and councils, and directed by a compact executive. Feargus O'Connor did not plan the association. The delegates who launched it were new and obscure men. James Leach, an operative, claimed the credit for the idea.[2] But the resourceful Irishman, assisted by the journalistic resources of the *Northern Star*, soon established for himself the position of informal leader of the Chartist movement, though not, as yet, a member of the executive. O'Connor was not the dictator which he has been represented to be. His editor, the Rev. William Hill, was allowed to criticize his policies in the columns of the *Star*. He nevertheless committed a grievous error by his vigorous proscription of Education Chartism, Christian Chartism and Teetotal Chartism in April 1841. Perhaps he was sincere in his plea that

[1] J. A. Epstein, 'Feargus O'Connor and the Northern Star'. *IRSH*, Vol. XXI, 1976, pp. 51–97.
[2] D. Jones, *Chartism and the Chartists* (London, 1975), p. 70.

the specialized emphases of these movements were destructive of Chartist unity; the effect of his action, however, was to create an open schism between Lovett's National Association—founded in 1841 to establish schools, adult education centres and libraries—and the N.C.A. The dissidents, who aimed to forward the Charter by raising the moral stature of working-men, were popularly known as 'New Move' Chartists. They were soon to be drawn into the ambit of the middle-class inspired Complete Suffrage movement of 1841–42. In the latter year Chartism rose to a new peak of intensity. A National Petition for the Six Points was presented and negatived on 2 May. Three months later the Chartist leaders became involved in a widespread strike movement in the manufacturing districts, which began as a wage dispute, but was subsequently harnessed to a demand for the People's Charter. These 'Plug Plot' disturbances led to a fresh wave of prosecutions which damped down Chartism.

Through the middle 'forties the Chartist movement persisted, but with a lower level of support. Reviving trade brought a shift in working-class interests away from politics and towards the direct pursuit of economic betterment through trade-unionism, consumers' co-operation and factory reform. Chartism was obliged to adapt to the trend. Individual Chartists and the *Northern Star* helped the miners to organize their Miners Association of Great Britain. In April 1845 O'Connor launched his ill-fated Land Plan for settling working men upon the land in colonies of smallholdings. Contrary, however, to the impression conveyed by older histories, such as those of Hovell and West, the movement was not, except for the Land Plan, bereft of ideas. Some Chartists established contacts with European revolutionaries through bodies like the Fraternal Democrats and the Peoples' International League; others turned to registration of electors as a means of building up a nucleus of Chartist sympathizers in the House of Commons. The Revolutionary year 1848 brought a revival of hopes that the original objects of Chartism might be carried. A further Petition for the Six Points was conveyed to the House of Commons on 10 April to the accompaniment of a demonstration, which in nervous breasts raised fears of an overthrow of government. The day passed peaceably for the most part, and the Petition was discredited by the revelation of forgeries. That, however, was not the end of the movement. A National Assembly met during the first half of May, to carry the Charter by an appeal to the Queen. When it had failed, a new wave of tumultuous demonstrations and disturbances stirred the capital and certain provincial centres at the end of the month. A more sinister note was struck, as Chartist extremists spent the summer organizing themselves and plotting insurrection. They drew closer to the Irish Confederates resident in Great Britain, in a web of intrigue designed to aid the very real rebellion which was being planned in Ireland. All this could not disguise the fact that Chartism was falling apart. Feargus O'Connor and some of his associates joined the household suffrage wing of the middle-class reformers in the National Parliamentary and Financial Reform Association established in 1849, while Julian Harney converted the executive of the National Charter Association to an explicitly Socialist programme in the following year. Though the energies of working men went increasingly into trade-unionism and co-operation during the 1850s, Harney's supplanter Ernest Jones kept an enfeebled, though sporadically reviving, Chartist agitation alive until 1860.

Some Problems of Definition

Beyond the familiar contours of the narrative, the search for the essence of Chartism becomes problematical. The difficulty stems from the immense diversity of the movement, which, as Dr. Judge affirms, was 'deficient in natural unity'—'a coalition of many different radical associations and personalities with a multiplicity of varied experiences, traditions and beliefs.'[1] Contemporary observers and historians have been led therefore to varying interpretations of its relationship to society at large. Four overlapping assessments have been made. In the first place the movement has been seen as a response to distress. 'Impatience, engendered by fireless grates and breakfastless tables', wrote Hovell, 'was the driving force of much northern Chartism.'[2] Secondly there was the romantic Tory view, expounded by Disraeli in the parliamentary debate on the first National Petition, which denied to Chartism a 'strictly economical' basis but ascribed it to 'an apprehension on the part of the people, that their (established) civil rights were invaded' by a 'government by the middle classes'.[3] Nostalgic reaction against bourgeois aggression, conducted under the patronage of a Tory aristocracy, has also featured in a more recent explanation of the Chartism of the unskilled.[4] On the other hand, historians sympathetic to

[1] op. cit.
[2] M. Hovell, The Chartist Movement (Manchester, 1966), p. 118.
[3] Hansard, Parliamentary Debates, 3 ser., Vol. XLIX, pp. 246–7 and 250.
[4] R. N. Soffner, 'Attitudes and Allegiances in the Unskilled North, 1830–50' IRSH, Vol. X, 1965, pp. 429–54.

the labour movement, especially Marxists, view Chartism in a forward-looking perspective: as an expression of independent, or, in some cases, 'revolutionary' working-class consciousness. As these have contributed much to the writing of Chartist history in the twentieth century, the movement is often presented as a forerunner of the Labour Party, if not as a harbinger of the destruction of capitalism. A fourth interpretation emphasizing Chartism's affinities with nineteenth-century Liberalism, rather than with Labour, has been recently propagated, notably by Drs. Brian Harrison and Patricia Hollis.[1] These assessments must be examined in turn.

Chartism as a Distress Movement

Though its title deeds were drafted by relatively comfortable artisans and middle-men in London and Birmingham, Chartism could not have flourished as a mass movement without economic hardship. A map of the distribution of National Charter Association localities in 1841, compiled by Dr. David Jones, shows, London apart, a concentration on the industrial districts, more especially on those involved in the manufacture of textiles: South East Lancashire, the West Riding of Yorkshire, Wiltshire, the East Midland counties of Nottingham, Leicester and Derby. Gammage confirmed that more than half the localities represented in the 1848 Convention were likewise situated in the textile districts.[2] There the economic stimuli were primary. A Stockport Chartist leader observed: 'The great distress is the cause of our discontent—if the wages were what they ought to be, we should not hear a word about the Suffrage.'[3] The evidence of Richard Pilling, a poor mill hand, proves how real the deprivation could be (V, 1d). But what was the cause? There are no firm grounds for asserting that the industrial revolution, which transformed the conditions of life for workers in the basic industries, depressed the material living standards of working men. Space is not available to survey the protracted academic controversy which has been conducted on this issue, but a recent contribution by Professor M. W. Flinn, based upon a study of most of the available data for wages and commodity prices, suggests that the purchasing power of a working man's wages rose rather than fell, at

[1] 'Chartism, Liberalism and the Life of Robert Lowery'. *EHR*, Vol. LXXXII, July 1967, pp. 503–35.
[2] Jones, *op. cit.*, p. 9; R. G. Gammage, *History of the Chartist Movement, 1837–54*, (London, 1969), p. 301.
[3] C. Godfrey & J. Epstein, 'Notes on Sources: H.O. 20/10: Interviews of Chartist Prisoners 1840–41'. *Labour History Society Bulletin*, No. 34, Spring 1977, pp. 27–34.

least from the closing years of the Napoleonic Wars onwards. Down to the mid-1820s real wage gains may have ranged up to an average of 2–3 per cent per annum. After that progress continued at a much slower rate, being less than 1 per cent for the second quarter of the nineteenth century.[1] It is impossible to be sure whether the improvement, which relates only to the earnings of workers in full-time labour, was offset by a long-term rise in the overall percentage of unemployment.

Material comfort cannot be judged solely by the nominal wage packet, the market price of goods, and the level of employment. It is agreed that working men suffered much, during the Chartist period, from oppressive systems of employment and living conditions: from excessive hours of labour, from the exploitation of women and children in industry, from long contracts, truck payments and bad housing. Authorities on such matters have usually insisted that these abuses formed an inheritance from the past, that they remained at their worst where small factories, indirect employment or domestic outwork survived, and that a slow and uneven improvement occurred in early-nineteenth century Britain. Professor Eric Richards has argued that from about 1820 onwards industrialization diminished rather than increased the participation of women in economic life,[2] though this would not now be rated wholly as progress. National figures drawn from the census returns show a marginal decline in the number of persons per inhabited house in the period 1821–41, with an even more marginal increase from 1841 to 1851. But, while Nottingham spawned a multiplicity of 'excellent artisan houses' erected in the new suburbs during the 1820s and 1830s, the back-to-back dwellings in the town centre, where the framework knitters and twist hands lived, displayed little improvement down to 1850.[3] In general, working men profited only to a very limited extent from industrial expansion before the People's Charter was drafted. Their gains were held back by the pressure of a rising population on a still limited area of food supply and by the heavy dependence of early growth on the multiplication of economically weak handicraft producers, whose services remained essential on account of the uneven progress of technology. In respect of material goods and conditions, however, no general deterioration resulting from the industrial revolution can be

---

[1] 'Trends in Real Wages, 1750–1850'. *Econ H.R.*, 2.ser., Vol. XXVII, 1974, pp. 395–411.

[2] Eric Richards, 'Women in the British Economy since about 1700'. *History*, Vol. LIX, October 1974, pp. 337–57.

[3] S. D. Chapman ed., *The History of Working-Class Housing. A Symposium*, (Newton Abbot, 1971), p. 211, and Chap. IV. passim.

proved. The causes of the distress component in Chartism must be sought in more specific factors.

Most immediate in their operation were those stemming from the vagaries of the food supply and the fluctuations of the business cycle. Both were significant, but the latter gained in importance relative to the former as the Chartist period progressed. Chartism was launched too late to be goaded by the collapse of the American trade in 1837, which, in any case, produced less dislocation of output in the cotton industry than was once supposed, owing to the resilience of the home market.[1] The impetus to the mass movement, which arose late in 1838 and in 1839, came initially from the poor harvest of 1838, the third of its kind in succession. At that time North-West Europe as a whole was becoming collectively deficient in bread grains, and a serious subsistence crisis could well have developed had not the repeal of the Sliding-Scale Corn Law in 1846 encouraged merchants to import from more distant areas of supply. As it was, wheat prices reached 81 shillings a quarter in January 1839, the highest price since December 1818.[2] A secondary stimulus, which developed early in 1839, was the short-time working in the cotton industry, concerted by the masters to checkmate an American speculation in raw cotton prices. It was the deflationary effect of high corn prices and protracted grain imports, together perhaps with the continued expansion of industrial capacity beyond the point where trade had started to deteriorate that produced in 1842, as a booster to the Second National Petition and the 'Plug Plot', one of the severest depressions of the nineteenth century. Then many mills closed entirely and unemployment reached astronomical proportions: 60 per cent of the factory operatives of Bolton, over 50 per cent of the mechanics and shipbuilders of Dundee.[3] Chartism's fresh emergence into the limelight in 1848, out of the shades of the middle 'forties, owed less to purely economic factors than before, being strongly influenced by revolutionary political developments on the continent of Europe and in Ireland. But the distress factor again operated, particularly in the form of heavy unemployment early in the year, as the business cycle, which had been characterized by substantial long-term investment in railways at its peak in 1845, entered upon its trough. Sharp recovery of the leading

[1] R. C. O. Matthews, *A Study in Trade Cycle History* (Cambridge, 1954), p. 137.

[2] A. D. Gayer, W. W. Rostow & A. J. Schwartz, *The Growth and Fluctuation of the British Economy, 1790–1850*, (Oxford, 1953), Vol. I, p. 276.

[3] Matthews, *op. cit.*, pp. 138–9, 144, 214–17; E. J. Hobsbawm, *Labouring Men*, (London, 1965), pp. 74–5.

trades dated, however, from about the middle of June, and was perhaps more responsible than the government's counter-measures for taking the heat out of Chartism.[1]

Severe trade depressions linked to a developing crisis in the nation's food supply exacerbated all particular hardships, and forced together discontents at certain times. They do not, however, provide the entire cause of the distress underlying Chartism. Conditions prevailing in particular trades must also be examined. 'The whole working class', wrote Frederick Engels, 'is behind the great Chartist assault on the middle classes ...'[2] In reality, the movement exhibited a wide distribution among trades, combined with a heavy concentration on certain occupational groups. Economically weak elements figured more prominently than those which were strong, but moderate distress was more conducive to political action than extreme destitution, recent loss of status more than unaltered misery. It is impossible to be more than impressionistic about the Chartist rank and file, but two useful studies of the nominations to the General Council of the National Charter Association, as published in *The Northern Star*, have lent precision to our knowledge of the local leadership. Dr. David Jones has analyzed 853 nominations from localities in England and Wales generally in 1841; Dr. Iowerth Prothero, 430 nominations for London alone in 1841–43.[3] Though there is room for further work on these sources, both to extend the period of national coverage and to compare the representation of trades in Chartism's leadership with the importance of those trades in the labour force as a whole, the findings may be provisionally summarized.

Two categories stand out. Firstly, the outworkers in the large-scale industries. In Dr. Jones' study, 130 'weavers' headed the list of nominations. Framework knitters, based on the East Midland counties, came fourth, with 33 nominations, wool-combers ninth, with 17. The vast majority of trades listed had fewer than 5. Handworkers, who laboured in their own homes, or in small domestic workshops, on materials put out by a merchant employer or his agent, were the principal victims of the industrial revolution. On account of the unevenness of the technological breakthrough of the late eighteenth

[1] Gayer, Rostow & Schwartz, *op. cit.*, I, pp. 304, 339–40.
[2] F. Engels, *The Condition of the Working Class in England*, trans. W. O. Henderson & W. H. Chaloner, (New York, 1958), p. 258.
[3] Jones, *op. cit.*, pp. 30–2; I.Prothero, 'Chartism in London', *Past and Present*, No. 44, 1969, pp. 76–105.

century, a vast expansion of their numbers had been the concomitant of economic growth in the half century or more after 1780. Their services were needed to prepare, or afterwards to manufacture into goods, the yarn which emerged from the cotton and worsted mills. As recruits to these trades were often casual workers or children trained by their fathers, the supply of labour could not easily be regulated, and wages fell. The discomfiture was completed when steam-driven machines began to take over the processes hitherto left to the handworkers. This at first intensified protest but eventually extinguished it by liquidating the victims. The cycle affected different outwork trades in varying degrees and at diverse times. Dr. Duncan Bythell has made us aware of the differences of remuneration in the cotton industry between the relatively comfortable workers in handloom factories, who netted about 10 shillings per week or more in the late 1830s, and the mass of unskilled cottage weavers, often women and children, whose individual earnings could be as low as 4 shillings per week.[1] There can be little doubt, however, that from some point between the 1790s and the 1830s the fortunes of most outworkers had declined, and that the decline was often catastrophic. In some instances, as in the case of the Spitalfields silk weavers,[2] it was so crushing as to inhibit participation in the Chartist movement. This, however, was a rather special case, related to the peculiar social structure of the metropolis. In most instances, up to the time of the Chartist movement, the experiences of outworkers tended rather to aggravate than to eliminate political activity. It has been argued, admittedly, that by the beginning of Chartism, cotton handloom weavers had so contracted before the advances of the power loom as to constitute a minor element in cotton's labour force, resident outside its main industrial belt.[3] But the fact that the names of weavers occur in the nominations to the N.C.A. Council from such typical cotton towns as Ashton, Oldham, Stockport, Bury, Stalybridge and Manchester, suggests that hand-loom weavers exerted an influence out of proportion to their reduced numbers. Some of the nominees, it is true, may have been powerloom-weavers, but these, like Richard Pilling (V, 1d), were often ex-hand workers, influenced politically by their former life style. Moreover, other types of depressed handworker were either, like the stockingers, hardly affected by factory machines during the Chartist

[1] *The Handloom Weavers*, (Cambridge, 1969), pp. 133–4.
[2] D. J. Rowe, 'Chartism and the Spitalfields Weavers', *Econ H.R.*, 2 Ser., Vol. XX, 1967, pp. 482–93.
[3] Bythell, *op. cit.*, pp. 221–2.

period, or, like the wool-combers, challenged by them only in the later 1840s, when their will to fight was increased, not diminished.

The second group prominent in N.C.A. nominations was from the humbler skilled trades. Skilled artisans in general were raised above labourers and outworkers by a recognized status and by their use of trade-union organization to maintain apprenticeship and shore up incomes. They were, nevertheless, a very heterogeneous element. Some, like the mechanical engineering crafts, were products of the new technology, but in Chartist times the vast majority still pursued traditional small-scale handicrafts, where the line between master and men was thin. They differed also in economic strength. To club them together as an 'aristocracy of labour' can be misleading. Though there were 'aristocrats' in many skilled occupations, e.g. the London compositors, the goldsmiths, the watchmakers and the body-makers in the coach-building establishments, with incomes in excess of about 35/- per week by mid-century, most artisans did not earn more than 30/- seventeen years later.[1] At the bottom of the scale marginal artisans shaded imperceptibly into outworkers. Dilution, stemming basically from the influx of surplus labour in a country with a rapidly rising population, threatened various crafts during the three decades after the withdrawal of state support for apprenticeship in 1814, but fell with particular force on shoemaking and tailoring, where the few 'honourable' workmen were undercut by expanding forces of sweated labour engaged by unscrupulous 'slop masters' paying low wages for long hours.[2] These were the trades from which most nominations were obtained. In Jones' analysis 'shoemakers' came next to 'weavers' with 97, and a further 30 'cordwainers' and 13 'boot- and shoemakers' appeared in the list. 'Tailors' came third with 58. Prothero's study for London yields similar results—shoemakers leading by a firm head and tailors coming third.[3] Both samples reveal a significant proportion of middle-grade artisans, notably building workers, who earned about 30/- per week in London, less in the provinces. These, however, were fewer relative to their numbers in society.[4] Moreover, the London list shows a weak representation of the true metropolitan labour aristocrats: the

---

[1] John Burnett, *Useful Toil*, (Harmondsworth, 1974), pp. 260–2.

[2] See E. P. Thompson & E. Yeo ed., *The Unknown Mayhew*, (London, 1971), *Passim*.

[3] *Op. cit.*

[4] The ratio of nominations to adult male workers in England and Wales enumerated in the 1841 Census was 1:3552 for building workers; 1:1101 for shoemakers; 1:1497 for tailors.

compositors, printers, watchmakers and jewellers. These, however, figured more prominently in the London Working Men's Association, which, if atypical of London Chartism, played an undeniably large role in launching the Chartist movement nationally.

Though distress was a prime inducement, economic factors alone do not explain the special role of artisans in Chartism. By their dependence on skill, however rudimentary, such men were predisposed to use the opportunities for self-education which their control of their own time made available. Private reading and attendance at mechanics' institutes or at the meetings of obscure literary associations of working men, such as Lovett discovered at Newport market, nourished political convictions. This was a path followed by practitioners of weaker trades as well as by those of the stronger, as the career of Robert Knox, the slater, displays (V, 1b). It is not always clear, moreover, that skilled tradesmen became radicals because they were artisans. Sometimes the converse was true. R. G. Gammage confessed that it was a desire for 'personal independence', a common attribute of radicals, that made him a shoemaker.[1] William Cuffay seems almost the classic case of a distressed tailor who became a physical-force Chartist, but his politics were rooted in family experience: escape from West Indian slavery (V, 1c).

It must be emphasized that many workers other than those in the two key groups participated in the Chartist movement, especially in its early stages. Lancashire factory operatives supported Rayner Stephens, joined the Radical Association, and attended the great Chartist demonstration on Kersal Moor on 24 September 1838. Many were dismissed by their employers for so doing.[2] The list of processionists to Kersal Moor provides an indication of the wide range of trades represented (VII, 1). South Wales coalminers were Chartist activists at Merthyr Tydfil for some years after the failure of the Monmouthshire rising.[3] Generally, however, support for the cause was too patchy and ephemeral to warrant the assumption of a united mass movement. Even in the industrial counties of Northumberland and Durham the response was modest, and the region was only of importance to the national agitation for a few weeks in the summer of 1839.[4] Agricultural labourers, the largest single component in the labour force, and also one of the weakest

[1] Op. cit., pp. 387–8.

[2] The Northern Star, 18 August and 29 September 1838.

[3] Angela V. John, 'The Chartist Endurance: Industrial South Wales, 1840–68'. Morgannwg: The Journal of Glamorgan History, XV, 1971, pp. 23–49.

[4] D. J. Rowe, 'Some Aspects of Chartism on Tyneside'. IRSH, Vol. XVI, 1971, pp. 17–39.

elements in English society, contributed very little to Chartism. The pervasive interest of the middling and lower artisans and the stalwart support of outworker groups stemmed from the vulnerability of these classes to declining status or insecurity: factors specially conducive to the movement's being.[1]

Chartism and the Defence of Civil Rights

Chartist political theory was a blend of the destructive, slate-cleaning approach of Thomas Paine, who confessed to be 'contending for the rights of the living' against 'the manuscript-assumed authority of the dead',[2] and an older radical tradition which looked to the past as a guide to the present. There was tension between the two, but the latter predominated over the former. It did so because it was more deeply rooted in the mentality of the people. Before the French Revolution and the dissemination of *The Rights of Man*, Major John Cartwright, the idol of the popular reformers, had taught that annual parliaments and equal electoral districts were ancient practices. His most recent biographer insists that he 'helped to shape the policies which were to influence the mainstream of British radicalism until the middle of the nineteenth century.'[3] Thus Chartists believed that universal suffrage was a feature of the English constitution until the reign of Henry VI (I, 4a). For the English poor, traditionalist loyalties were not completely out of touch with reality. When the People's Charter was published, older people might recall an age when, as E. P. Thompson has shown in an article of seminal importance, food rioters appealed for legitimation against middlemen to the prejudices of magistrates and to the pronouncement of a chief justice in 1795 that forestalling and regrating remained an indictable offence at common law.[4] Another form of legitimation, the eighteenth-century 'myth of the freeborn Englishman', joined zeal for liberty to chauvinism. In Chartist times xenophobia softened, and there was a growing sense of the solidarity of peoples against their rulers (III. Passim). The latest study of Chartist internationalism, however, confirms

---

[1] For a more detailed assessment of the distribution of Chartism among trades see my 'Chartism'. *Historical Association Pamphlet*, G.61, (London, 1972), reprint, including the Postscript. C. Godfrey, 'The Chartist Prisoners, 1839–41'. *IRSH*. Vol. XXIV, 1979, Pt. II, pp. 189–236, has an important analysis of the occupations of many Chartist prisoners, based on official sources. It reveals a wide distribution combined with a predominance of the traditional artisan and outworker trades.

[2] G. A. Williams, *Artisans and Sans-Culottes*, (London, 1968), p. 14.

[3] J. W. Osborne, *John Cartwright*, (Cambridge, 1972), pp. 18–19.

[4] E. P. Thompson, 'The Moral Economy of the English Crowd in the Eighteenth Century'. *Past and Present*, No. 50, February 1971, pp. 76–136.

that outside London, the current did not run deep. Chartist speeches and editorials retained a conviction that it was better to be English than to be foreign, and European royalty and Continental systems of centralized government remained particular objects of animadversion. Peter Murray McDouall, whose background was distinctively provincial, defended himself at the Chester Assizes in 1839, by predicting 'a train of evils which is calculated to level down the fundamental principles of the constitution, and the few remaining privileges of the people, in the new and arbitrary ideas of centralization, copies from the despotic governments of France, Prussia and Russia.'[1]

Appeal to an ancient constitution did not guarantee acceptance of the constitutional arrangements of the present. Underlying the demand for the Six Points of the People's Charter was an uncompromising theory of equal political rights and popular sovereignty. An editorial in the *Northern Star* affirmed early in 1841: 'The Crown, the Ministers, and the Parliament, are all trustees for the nation; they have peculiar privileges delegated for the sake of the prosperity of the country, not for their own sakes' (I, 2). Hence, even the moderate physical-force leaders in the 1839 Convention, Feargus O'Connor and Bronterre O'Brien, held that in the last resort the authority of the House of Commons might be superseded either by the Convention's declaring its own sittings permanent and assuming the role of an anti-parliament or by a march of the men of the North on London to constitute a parliament of their own.[2] The more extreme Julian Harney, in a speech at Newcastle which the *Northern Star* declined to print in full, did not hesitate to urge that the marchers should throw honourable members into the Thames (I, 6a). These opinions should not all be taken seriously. Chartism's avowed objective was to reform the House of Commons not to supplant it, and when the moderate 'physicals' proposed anti-parliaments, their intention was to apply a threat which would coerce the House into adopting the National Petition. The fact, however, that these suggestions could be advanced is indicative of a confrontation, not perceived to be soluble by ordinary constitutional means, between a powerful movement of the Queen's subjects and the nation's legislature. Chartist awareness of the conflict was most acute in the early years. It was in 1842 that O'Connor remarked: 'We have no chance whatever from the House of Commons.

---

[1] Henry Weisser, *British Working-Class Movements and Europe, 1815–48*, (Manchester, 1975), pp. 89–91, 164–8.
[2] T. M. Parssinen, 'Association, Convention and Anti-parliament in British Radical Politics, 1771–1848', *EHR*, Vol. LXXXVIII, July 1973, pp. 504–33.

Our Charter must be carried out of the House before it is even temperately discussed within.'[1] The sense of alienation was later reduced a little by that leader's endeavours from 1844 onwards to create a party of 20 Chartist M.P.s by proceedings in the registration courts (I, 6c), by the developing links between Chartism and the Radical member Thomas Slingsby Duncombe, and after the 1847 election by O'Connor's own presence in the House.

By and large, however, Chartists displayed little concern to upset the institutional structure of British government. The Rev. Joseph Barker's plea for 'the entire abolition of the present constitution'[2] was atypical of the movement. In the 1830s House of Lords reform was a middle-class interest, thrust on the London Working Men's Association in June 1837 by Daniel O'Connell.[3] A hostile pamphleteer declaimed in 1848: 'Chartism—at least Chartism such as it is preached in Fitzroy Square—is nothing else but Republicanism.' 'A favourite theme with the Chartists is the inutility of a Queen.'[4] Such remarks, however, are misleading if applied to the movement as a whole. Some Chartists, it is true, claimed the title of republican, using it to describe their journalistic ventures, e.g. *McDouall's Chartist and Republican Journal*, Linton's *Republican* and Harney's *Red Republican*. In its allusions to the monarchy the Chartist press was unenthusiastic, chiefly on account of the attendant expenditure. Sometimes it attacked the monarchical principle. 'When the ancient kings touched the people, that they might thereby cure the king's evil', observed the *Chartist Circular*, 'it was customary for one to say, "the king hath touched thee, and may God cure thee;" to the latter part I say, amen.'[5] Even so, criticism of Queen Victoria was relatively mild. Bronterre O'Brien's *Southern Star*, after disparaging her short and unqueenly appearance and her preference for foreigners, added: 'Take our word for it, good reader, you have a sovereign of whom you may be proud; and whose reign will form one of the brightest portions of British history.'[6] Chartist republicanism remained, for the most part, academic (I, 5a) and historical, encapsulated in a broader opposition to oligarchical government, and played a secondary role in the movement as a warning

[1] *The Northern Star*, 7 May 1842.

[2] *The Reformer's Companion to the Almanac*, No. 11, September 1848.

[3] D. J. Rowe ed., *A History of the Working Men's Association from 1836 to 1850*, by George Howell, (Newcastle, 1970), pp. 77–8.

[4] *What the Chartists Are. A Letter to English Working-Men*. By a Fellow Labourer (London, 1848).

[5] *Chartist Circular*, 24 October 1840.

[6] *The Southern Star*, 12 July 1840.

to the upper classes of what might happen if the demand for the People's Charter was frustrated. Its devotees never succeeded in raising the dethronement of the Queen to the status of a live political issue, nor did they try very hard to do so. McDouall asserted in May 1841 that Parliament's resistance to the Charter was turning the movement against the crown and the established church[1] but four months later, when he lectured at Derby, he was criticized by a Socialist listener for not going far enough, in particular for not pointing out that 'the time was fast approaching when we should dispense with both Kings and Queens ...'[2] Such restraint owed much to the influence of Feargus O'Connor and the *Northern Star* newspaper, which was exerted against republicanism as it is normally understood, on successive occasions, e.g. in February 1841,[3] in October 1844 (I, 5b), and again in 1847.[4] More important, perhaps, in their effect, were long-term changes in the tone and in the constitutional function of the monarchy, which rendered that institution less a bone of contention for the Chartists than for radicals living under Victoria's three predecessors. In the Convention of 1839 there were 'smiles' but there was no firm opposition, when R. K. Douglas moved an adjournment to watch the state opening of parliament (I, 5c). Chartism was, at heart, a very English movement.

One feature of the constitution evoked from the Chartists unfeigned admiration, viz. the rule of law. Discussing the case of Hansard v. Stockdale in July 1839 the *Northern Star* supported the Court of Queen's Bench in its decision to uphold the demands of the law of libel against the privileges of Parliament. It even had words of praise for the judicial system: for trial by jury, for the fairness of judges like Lord Denman, and for the determination of Englishmen to resist the encroachments of prerogative and privilege (I, 3).

There was enough respect for the constitution in Chartist circles to make credible the claim that the movement was, in part, a reaction against revolutionary administrative changes, sincerely believed to violate established civil rights. The Poor Law Amendment Act of 1834 was held by some of its opponents to contravene 'the old *forty-third of Elizabeth*, that charter of the poor of England.'[5] According to an ex-

---

[1] *McDouall's Chartist and Republican Journal*, 1 May 1841.
[2] Report of lecture on 16 September 1841. Ms. volume, 'The Chartist Movement in Derby, 1841. Original Correspondence'. Derby Public Library.
[3] *The Northern Star*, 27 February 1841.
[4] Weisser, *op. cit.*, p. 153.
[5] Dorothy Thompson ed., *The Early Chartists* (London, 1971), p. 136.

Chartist, Joseph Rayner Stephens deliberately courted arrest and trial in order that its legality could be tested in the Courts.[1] The same suggestion was advanced in the *Northern Star* at the time (I, 4b). A professional police force was likewise regarded as 'French' and unconstitutional by men who still believed that disorder should be handled by the *posse comitatus* called out by the Sheriff as in ancient times. Nothing, in fact, drove the Convention of 1839 to greater fury than the proposal considered by the government early in the year to introduce a centralized police force into the English counties (I, 4c) or the use which was later made of London 'Peelers' to restore order in the provinces. In the North of England the Rural Police, instituted originally under an act of 1839, were denounced at first as 'blue bottles', 'blue idlers' and 'blue drones'. Their actions, as well as those of forces operating under the Municipal Corporations Act and various special acts, and of the Metropolitan police detachments, were countered by fierce local resistance of a violent kind. Most of this was non-political, provoked by the exertions of the police to impose new standards of orderliness upon communities habituated to a rough and ready way of life. The constables broke up customary gatherings of the poorer inhabitants in the streets and interfered with beershops and rumbustious sports and festivities. Local Chartists may have given direction to the anti-rural police riots at Colne in 1840—though the evidence is circumstantial—but, when on 4 July 1839 the Birmingham magistrates used metropolitan policemen to suppress a Chartist meeting in the Bull Ring, not only did a serious riot ensue, exacerbated by dislike of the police, but the excitement aroused by the incident reverberated through the movement (IV, 3). In language which led to the imprisonment of its secretary, the Convention denounced the policemen concerned as 'a bloodthirsty and unconstitutional force from London'. Though working men formed the core of the opposition to the new police, they could find justification in the example set by the Queen's troops, who also clashed with the police, when off duty, at Hull and at Leeds; also by 'respectable' farmers and tradesmen, who hurled abuse at the constables for appearing at the Lancaster races.[2] In 1839 a Shoreditch vestry remonstrated against the detachment of Metropolitan policemen to the country on grounds of interference with 'the old constitutional plan of quelling riots by magistrates reading the Riot Act,

[1] T. M. Kemnitz & Fleurange Jacques, 'J. R. Stephens and the Chartist Movement'. *IRSH*, Vol. XIX, 1974, pp. 211–27.
[2] R. D. Storch, 'The Plague of the Blue Locusts'. *IRSH*, Vol. XX, 1975, pp. 61–89.

using the local civil force, and if not sufficient, to call to their aid the military.'[1] It was little more than half a century since men with the authority of the Middlesex and Surrey justices had thought it 'a dangerous innovation and an encroachment on the rights and security of the people' to propose a police force for the whole metropolitan district.[2]

When every allowance has been made for the lingering of notions of a time-honoured constitution and of ancient laws, it is scarcely possible to deny that Chartist pronouncements upon these subjects were largely out of date. The laws which they decried were based on current statute, and eighteenth and nineteenth-century lawyers knew that statute could amend the law. Probably the Chartist case was to some degree propagandist, but it also reflected a distrust of change. The first three reformed parliaments engendered a spate of reforms subverting institutions which had endured for centuries: the Poor Law Amendment Act, the Municipal Corporations Act, the Civil Registration Act, the Rural Police Act. All were informed by the Benthamite philosophy which aimed to impose standardized uniformity and remote governmental control on a land where, for nearly two hundred years, local authorities had been allowed to go their way. Like the middle-class reformers who later constituted the Anti-Centralization Society, the Chartists had a healthy distrust of centralization, which they regarded as incompatible with liberty (I, 7c). McDouall even regretted the passing of the Anglo-Saxon heptarchy.[3]

Concern for the preservation of civil rights was also very much an issue in the Chartists' confrontation with the government in 1839, 1842 and 1848. In April 1839, when pikes were being amassed by supporters of the movement in the provinces, the Convention affirmed its belief in the constitutional right of the people to possess arms (I, 4d). The claim was valid in the abstract, but it was circumscribed by the requirement that weapons should not be accumulated for an illegal purpose such as disturbing the public peace.[4] At Stockport, Ashton-under-Lyne and elsewhere the police ransacked the houses of local Chartists for stores of arms. The power could not, however, be exercised lightly. After the Mansfield riots of 1839 a local Chartist brought a successful action against a magistrate for illegal search of a house; and the Home Office

[1] F. C. Mather, *Public Order in the Age of the Chartists* (Manchester, 1959), p. 107.
[2] T. A. Critchley, *The Conquest of Violence* (London, 1970), p. 88.
[3] *McDouall's Chartist and Republican Journal*, 29 May 1841.
[4] Lord John Russell's Letter to the Magistrates in Sessions etc. on the Preservation of the Peace in Disturbed Districts; 1839 (179) XXXVIII.

declined to pay the defence costs on the grounds that the search warrant
failed to set out the illegal purpose for which the arms were kept.[1]

In Chartist eyes the government was guilty of trampling on civil
liberties in the counter-measures which it took against them. They
accused it of striving to put down public meetings 'by proclamation
which was not law',[2] and were quick to assume, when witnesses who
had been accomplices were produced against them in the courts, that
there had been a government plot to trap them into violence by the use
of *agents provocateurs*. The criticisms were misplaced. The glosses put
on the Royal Proclamation against Torchlight Meetings (December
1838) and on the subsequent Proclamation (May 1839) condemning
certain Chartist assemblages held by daylight, in correspondence
between the Home Office and the magistrates (IV, 8/Ia), show that the
intention was to apply the Common Law definition of illegality, viz. that
the meeting must be 'calculated to excite alarm and endanger the public
peace.' Then and in 1848 (IV, 8/Ib & d) discrimination was exercised as
to time, place and circumstances before condemning an assemblage as
unlawful. The *Northern Star*'s quip that by that definition 'little boys
who carry about Guy Fawkes, and let off a cracker, are guilty of felony'[3]
cannot be squared with the pronouncement of Judge Alderson at
Vincent's trial at Monmouth that 'the opinion of rational and firm men,
men of reasonable capacity and understanding and of reasonable
firmness' must be the criterion of whether there was a threat to the
peace.[4] It is true that, in times of the greatest excitement, both Whig and
Tory governments sometimes stretched the law to permit a general
assault on large open-air meetings (IV, 8/Ic), but if their conduct is
viewed over a long period, ministries can be seen to have been
responding with growing severity to challenges, not initiating offensives.
In any case the Home Office's weak control of the local authorities and
the differences of view as to tactics between the military commanders
and the civil power, especially when General Napier held the Northern
Command, would have rendered any conspiracy against the democratic
cause impossible to implement.

We may conclude that a concern for civil liberties played a part in
launching Chartism through resentment of the New Poor Law, and was
even more important in sustaining the pitch of the agitation in 1839. The

[1] Memorial of Duke of Portland and Others, 7 November 1840. H.O. 40/55.
[2] Speech by William Lovett in the Convention. *The Northern Star*, 18 May 1839.
[3] *The Northern Star*, 14 September 1839.
[4] Report of Proceedings Against Vincent and Others, 2 August 1839. H.O. 40/45.

view, however, that there was a commitment to the traditionalist elements among the higher orders in a bid to hold back the bourgeoisie, is more questionable. Chartism was not just anti-middle class; it was not less opposed to the aristocracy. To be sure the movement inherited from the Ten Hours' and Anti-New Poor Law agitations, which were to a far greater extent conducted under upper-class patronage, leaders with Tory backgrounds and of a paternalist cast of mind, e.g. J. R. Stephens and Matthew Fletcher (V, Ia). Stephens believed not in the Six Points but in an ordered society with 'the rich bearing the burdens of the poor and the poor bearing the burdens of the rich.'[1] But the violent methods urged by the Tory radicals severed them from the party led by Peel and Wellington. Lord Francis Egerton, a prominent Conservative landowner in South Lancashire, stirred the Home Secretary against Stephens' campaign in the winter of 1838–39.[2] Furthermore, as the case of Stephens makes clear, a Tory was unlikely to remain for long a Chartist unless he became something more than a Tory. Dr. Tholfsen has rightly observed that Chartism was 'an intensely class-conscious movement directed against all forms of deference and subordination.'[3] The decision, prompted by O'Connor, to support the Tories at the polls in 1841 was largely tactical: to display Chartist strength by tipping the balance against the precariously positioned Whigs (VI, 3). Though generally anti-Whig, the movement was often critical of the Tories. 'He knew their power, their rule, and had tasted bitterly of their cup of poison', observed O'Connor in the Convention in April 1839.[4] Even the paternalist blandishments of Young England failed to draw. O'Connor made a passing bid to cultivate this coterie in the winter of 1844–45 (VI, 5a), but the feudal overtones of the movement repelled sincere democrats (VI, 5b).

Chartism as an Expression of Class Consciousness

No facet of Chartism is more difficult to treat objectively than the movement's relationship to social class. Current historical scholarship is sharply divided both on the broader issue of whether a coherent working class then existed and on the narrower problem of whether Chartism echoed class awareness. The questions are related but not

[1] Kemnitz and Jacques, *op. cit.*

[2] Lord Francis Egerton to Lord John Russell, 14 December 1838. H.O. 40/37.

[3] Trygve R. Tholfsen, *Working Class Radicalism in Mid-Victorian England* (London, 1976), p. 85.

[4] *The Northern Star*, 20 April 1839.

identical, for the Chartist movement was not the whole working class—
how representative it was falls within the area of debate—and may,
therefore, have been, ideologically speaking, more compact than that
class. Nevertheless, one's view of the character of Chartism cannot but
be strongly influenced by whether one is ready to accept Mr. Edward
Thompson's now classical judgment that by the time of the Reform Bill
struggle the English working class was 'no longer in the making' but
already 'made'.[1] Differing opinions have been advanced. Lord Briggs, for
example, has cited evidence from 1846 that the labouring population
was considered to be divided into several classes,[2] while Henry Pelling,
from his knowledge of labour movements half a century or more later
has concluded that it is 'a mistake ... to speak of a homogeneous
"working class" in Britain at any time before the later nineteenth
century.'[3] The division is not simply between Marxists and non-
Marxists. Non-Marxist historians, such as W. L. Burn[4] and Trygve
Tholfsen,[5] have often presented the 1830s and 1840s as an age when an
intensely militant labour movement, acting under Owenite and Chartist
leadership, frightened the aristocracy into fortifying their country
houses. Some, however, notably Professor A. E. Musson, have stressed
the already limited and sectional character of trade-union objectives and
methods at that time.[6] The debate is complicated by a lack of agreement
on what is meant by class. Is it a tangible reality capable of exact
measurement in terms of income bracket, occupation, relationship to
control of the means of production, or even of marriage ties between
families and residence in certain localities? An approach to class based
on one or more of these assumptions has been adopted by G. D. H. Cole,
Professor Eric Hobsbawm and Dr. John Foster. In recent years,
however, a growing body of opinion has followed Asa Briggs and E. P.
Thompson in making awareness of class and of the habits of class the
true touchstone. Class has been regarded as the embodiment of certain
traditions, experiences and values which have been held in common.
Thompson put this succinctly, '... class itself is not a thing, it is a

---

[1] E. P. Thompson, *The Making of the English Working Class* (Harmondsworth, 1968),
   p. 887.
[2] Asa Briggs ed. *Chartist Studies* (London, 1959), p. 4.
[3] H. M. Pelling, *A History of British Trade Unionism* (Harmondsworth, 1963), pp. 13–14.
[4] *The Age of Equipoise* (London, 1964).
[5] *Op. cit.*
[6] A. E. Musson, *Trade Union and Social History* (London, 1974), espec. Chaps. I & II;
   'Class Struggle and the Labour Aristocracy, 1830–60'. *Social History*, October 1976,
   pp. 335–56.

happening.'[1] By these historians the essence of the working class has been found, not in an economically homogeneous layer of social stratification, but in working-class consciousness, working-class culture, response to discrimination against the working-class.

With these ambiguities unresolved, the question 'Was Chartism a class movement?' cannot be answered with an unqualified 'Yes' or 'No'. Certainly Chartists talked the language of class. It is difficult to improve on Mrs. Dorothy Thompson's restrained appraisal: 'Chartism was pervaded by a sense of class—both a positive sense of identification and a negative hostility to superior classes—which was stronger than perhaps existed at any other point in the nineteenth century'.[2] The capacity of one section of the labour force to identify with others was often the *sine qua non* of the movement's existence. David Rowe has argued tellingly that the Spitalfields silk weavers were restrained from playing an active part in London Chartism in 1839 by their social isolation,[3] and it seems to be agreed that the impersonal, anonymous character of life in the metropolis presented an obstacle to London Chartism, which could not have been overcome but for the existence of numerous small trade societies supplying the contacts by which unity was eventually forged.[4] Conversely there were areas of the provinces where a successful mass movement of workers in the dominant industry depended for leadership on outward-looking members of other occupational groups. Thus in Leicestershire, down to 1846, the framework knitters were led politically by artisans, tradesmen and small masters rather than by members of their own order.[5] A similar situation could be found elsewhere, but the presence, among the leaders, of men who, on one assessment, could have been described as lower-middle class, serves as a reminder that the working class which Chartism represented did not correspond exactly with the wage-earner category. In the yet semi-industrialized England of the 1830s and 1840s there were still many small producers, employed and self-employed, who were conscious of the interests which they held in common.

---

[1] Thompson, *The Making etc.*, Postscript, p. 939.

[2] D. Thompson ed., *The Early Chartists* (London, 1971), p. 14.

[3] D. J. Rowe, 'Chartism and the Spitalfields Silk-weavers', *Econ.H.R.*, 2 Ser., Vol. XX, 1967, pp. 482–93.

[4] I. J. Prothero, 'London Chartism and the Trades' *Econ.H.R.*, 2 Ser., Vol. XXIV, 1971, pp. 202–19.

[5] J. F. C. Harrison, 'Chartism in Leicester' in A. Briggs ed., *Chartist Studies* (London, 1959), Chap. IV.

Identification expressed itself in self-reliance. Even those Chartists who were disposed to accept help from well-intentioned members of the middle classes usually insisted on having it on their own terms or at least with substantial concessions to their point of view. William Lovett and the foundation members of the London Working Men's Association were profoundly suspicious of leadership from the higher orders of society, whether proffered by middle-class radicals like Daniel O'Connell or by high-born champions of the people such as Feargus O'Connor. Their aim was to help the humblest to be themselves. It went back to the times of the London Corresponding Society, when at the meetings of Francis Place's division each member was chairman by rote and all were expected to say something.[1] By Chartist times this democratic emphasis was well-established in the provinces. In an address congratulating J. A. Roebuck on his remarks in the House of Commons, asserting equal rights and avowing himself 'a DEMOCRATIC REPRESENTATIVE OF THE PEOPLE', the Carmarthen Working Men's Association felt it necessary to add: 'They rejoice, however, at the acquisition of your abilities in their cause, but they feel that it is on themselves and on their fellows, and on the progress of intelligence, they have principally to rely'.[2] John Collins, the Birmingham shoemaker, voiced the psychology of this attitude at the Complete Suffrage Conference in April 1842: '... if there be one thing more humiliating than another—more soul-degrading, it is to be compelled to do a thing at which your mind revolts, and yet to do that act as if it was of your own free will'.[3]

This aspiration embraced something more important than class rivalry: the foundations of democratic government itself. But the Chartists were unquestionably involved in a persistent quarrel with the higher orders of society. This was not merely over their being excluded from the franchise, though committed Chartists cared deeply about that. It was also concerned with the quality of life which they were obliged to live, with the social arrangements, with what Carlyle called 'the condition of England question'. That was the sense in which the *Northern Star*, under the editorship of Julian Harney, insisted that 'political institutions are merely to be regarded as the *means* to an end, that end being the happiness, prosperity, and independence of all classes, but especially of that class whose labour produces the wealth of the

[1] Thompson, *The Making etc.*, pp. 169–70.
[2] Address of the Working Men's Association at Carmarthen to J. A. Roebuck, 11 February 1837. Lovett Collection, Birmingham Public Reference Library, p. 56.
[3] Quoted from Tholfsen, *op. cit.*, p. 98.

country'.[1] Harney was a Socialist, and most Chartists were not. But the moderate, moral-force journal *The Charter* also held that 'Chartism, or the proper representation of the people in Parliament is but the means to an end'.[2] Most adherents of the movement, however great or however small the transformation in society which they wished to effect, agreed with the Knaresborough Working Men's Association that 'the primary cause of all the evils under which we labour is Class Legislation'.[3] This formula, vague and adaptable as it was, supplied the characteristic theme of many Chartist discourses and addresses.

Chartism was not, however, the homogeneous, razor-sharp instrument of class warfare identified in Marxian analysis. That it was not such for most of its history is evident from the fact that in 1851 Ernest Jones strove to turn it into a workers' party based on economic self interest, thinking that previously it had been 'too theoretical and not practical enough'.[4] As a class movement it suffered four limitations. In the first place it did not represent the whole working class or even the entire labour movement. The gap between the industrial and political wings of labour remained until the end of the period. It is true that the trade unions, which had survived the débâcle of 1834 in an attenuated form, sent representatives to early Chartist demonstrations (VII, 1), but in 1839 they tended to withdraw their support, alienated by the growing physical-force tone of the political movement,[5] and recoiled from a 'Sacred Month' or general strike for the Charter (VII, 3). Successive attempts were made in the ensuing years, mainly from the Chartist side, to re-forge the links. There was the bid, encouraged by McDouall in 1841, to plant N.C.A. branches among the trade societies (VII, 4), the help given by Chartists and the Chartist press to the struggling Miners' Association of Great Britain founded in 1842, the interest shown by the National Association of United Trades and various bodies of trade delegates in political reform during 1848 (VII, 7), Harney's Democratic Conference of 1850 and Jones' Labour Parliament of 1854. Success, however, was limited. The unions remained preoccupied with basic shop-floor problems of wages, hours and control of entrance to their trades. Already there were craft unions like the Journeymen Steam

[1] *The Northern Star*, 18 March 1848.
[2] *The Charter*, 1 September 1839.
[3] Tholfsen, *op. cit.*, p. 90.
[4] John Saville, *Ernest Jones: Chartist* (London, 1952), pp. 171–4.
[5] Kenneth Judge, 'Early Chartist Organization and the Convention of 1839', *IRSH*, Vol. XX, 1975, pp. 370–97.

Engine and Machine Makers' Society, which anticipated by more than a decade the sectional and exclusive policies ascribed by the Webbs to the so-called New Model Unions of the 1850s and '60s.[1] Such bodies normally kept aloof from politics, though during the abnormally depressed years of the early 1840s workers in the iron trades of Manchester, the hammermen and the mechanics, who were involved through machine-making in the misfortunes of the cotton industry, decided collectively to join the National Charter Association (VII, 5). It is true that the trade union movement of the 1830s and 1840s also included societies of weaker tradesmen, such as the tailors and shoemakers, which were more prone to support the general union styled the National Association of United Trades, and favoured overall remedies for their trade grievances, which sometimes involved state action—e.g. minimum wage legislation and public works to absorb the surplus labour by which their standards were threatened. Such bodies were much more likely to have connections with Chartism.[2] N.C.A. branches were frequently formed out of their members, and sometimes met at the regular house of call. Amidst the revolutionary excitement of the year 1848 certain local meetings of trade delegates in London and Manchester raised the cry for 'a full, free, and complete representation of the entire people in the Commons House of Parliament' (VII, 7). The Miners' Association of Great Britain also showed some sympathy with Chartism after the failure of its strike policies in 1844, entertaining O'Connor at its Wakefield Conference and hearing an appeal from W. P. Roberts to support the Land Plan.[3] It should be remembered, however, that these unions were only partly concerned with forwarding the political movement. Most of their energies went into rectifying trade grievances, as did almost the whole of those of the larger and more powerful unions. Chartists often launched Co-operative stores (VII, 9), but the Co-operative societies usually preferred to develop along independent political lines, and Co-operation, as patronized by Edward Vansittart Neale, the Christian Socialist, was denounced by Ernest Jones in the later stages of Chartism (VII, 10).

A mass labour movement under Chartist leadership cannot, therefore, be assumed to have existed in early-Victorian England. Something of the

[1] See Musson, *op. cit.* Chaps. I & II, for the diversity of trade-union aims during the Chartist period.
[2] I. J. Prothero, 'London Chartism and the Trades', *Econ.H.R.*, 2 Ser., Vol. XXIV, 1971, pp. 202–19.
[3] R. Challinor and B. Ripley, *The Miners' Association* (London, 1968), p. 228.

kind began to develop in the Manchester district under stress of the excitement of the 1842 'Plug Plot', when a parliament of trade delegates assembled in the town, and started to direct the strike of various kinds of workers towards a political objective. But the policy provoked dissension among the turnouts, some of whom wished to keep to the trade dispute which had provoked the outbreak, and the government quickly crushed the movement. This interpretation differs from that of Dr. John Foster, who has claimed that by the late 1830s and early 1840s a permanent subordination of all sections of the working population to radical control had been achieved.[1] His conclusion refers primarily to Oldham, where, in 1842, he maintains, the local leadership had been converted to striking for the Charter by the rank and file.[2] My inference from accounts in *The Manchester Guardian* of meetings at Stockport, Stalybridge, Ashton and Macclesfield is that there was much hesitation and division at grass roots level as to proclaiming the Charter to be the object of the strike.[3] Had not the Home Office intervened decisively at the crucial point, a mass movement, fusing Chartism and some elements of trade-unionism, might have developed more effectively in August 1842 than at any other time in the period.

A second weakness of Chartism as a class movement was that its social ideology lacked coherence. Inspired by Owenite or Romantic models its apologists often talked the language of total reconstruction. Like the London Working Men's Association in an initial address they aspired 'to probe our social evils to their source' or proclaimed, as Lovett and Collins did in *Chartism: A New Organization of the People*, that the aim of the movement was 'the regeneration of all'. But the advocates of such opinions often aimed to achieve their objects principally through some individualistic project of self-education or self-help. Embedded in the cause was a deep respect for the individual and his rights. The poet W. J. Linton's 'radical vision' of each individual's realizing 'the most perfect beauty of which his nature is capable' exemplifies this.[4] One old North-Country Chartist sharply repudiated the charge of levelling.[5] On the positive role of the state in the reformation of society Chartists found no agreement. The powerful O'Connor, always a strong individualist at

---

[1] *Class Struggle and the Industrial Revolution* (London, 1974), p. 146.

[2] *Ibid.*, pp. 116–17.

[3] See further T.D.W. and Naomi Reid, 'The 1842 "Plug Plot" in Stockport.'' *IRSH.*, Vol. XXIV, 1979, Pt. I, pp. 55–79.

[4] Tholfsen, *op . cit.*, p. 100.

[5] Benjamin Wilson, *Struggles of an Old Chartist* (Halifax, 1887), pp. 13–14.

heart, deemed his own Plan for settling urban workers on the land a better sanitary reform than any that the government could devise (II, 5, Comment). Moral-force Chartists sometimes professed a modified individualism, combining freer trade with a better provision for the poor, public-health reform and public works to cure unemployment (II, 1a). On the Left there was a Chartist Socialism, committed to the nationalization of land, mines and fisheries and to the establishment of state credit for working men, and public markets which would supersede the middleman. Bronterre O'Brien's National Reform League was the main organ of these principles (II, 1c). Its ideas were not incorporated into the official programme of Chartism until 1850–51, by which time the movement had passed its best. It is a mistake to suppose that generally Chartist proposals for the renovation of society marked a decisive break with the political approach of previous English radicals. The consequences of parliamentary reform had to be spelt out, of course, in terms of social benefit; so, however, they had been in Part II of Paine's *Rights of Man* and in Cobbett's notion of reform as a prelude to an attack on fundholders and placemen. The crucial question is how far an old analysis in terms of distress resulting from the parasitism of those who benefited from state revenues or who, as Thomas Spence pointed out before the end of the eighteenth century, monopolized the nation's land, had been replaced by a new analysis, which envisaged manufacturers' and middlemen's profits as the truly damaging exploitation. In Chartism the new had appeared but the old had not been driven out. P. M. McDouall, a central figure in the N.C.A., was a severe critic of factory 'slavery' and 'the exactions of the master manufacturer' (II, 2), but he also inveighed against the taxes appropriated by the aristocracy from the labourers, and described the Charter in old-fashioned language as a 'lever in our hands to pull down the old house of corruption and build a nobler house'. His claim that it 'cannot operate at all without securing permanently to all classes in society, the blessings of a cheap government ...' shows how far he was from an *étatiste* ideology.[1] Probably he was not the only Chartist for whom an attack on class legislation concealed an uncertainty about what to put in its place.

Ambivalent views on social policy connect with a third weakness: the want of a single, identifiable class enemy. As G. D. H. Cole explained, 'for Marx, in relation to contemporary advanced societies, only two

[1] *The Northern Star*, 20 May 1848; *McDouall's Chartist and Republican Journal*, 10 April 1841. For these references and their interpretation I am much indebted to Mr. Pattrick Frean, a graduate of Southampton University who is preparing a thesis on McDouall.

classes really counted—bourgeoisie and proletariat'.[1] Hence at any one time conflict was sharp and definite. The Chartists, however, faced two enemies at once—a retreating but still strongly entrenched aristocracy and the rising middle classes. Though contemporary writers and historians have often emphasized the movement's hostility to the latter, animosity towards the aristocracy and its preserves, the Church and the Army, continued strong within it (V, 2a). McDouall mercilessly pilloried that class as 'drones' and tax-eaters. Ernest Jones in *Notes to the People* (1851–52) compared its members unfavourably with the rich plutocrats: 'At least, the moneyocracy do SOME work for their plunder. The aristocracy are lazy, useless, ground-encumbering idlers'.[2] He was not consistent in this evaluation. A little earlier he had written: '... I hate the lords of gold even more than I hate the lords of land'.[3] But in a lecture at St. Martin's Hall in November 1856 he held forth against the hereditary aristocracy and the laws of primogeniture, settlement and entail, which enabled it to lock up the land and keep it uncultivated.[4] Joseph Barker of Wortley was obsessed by hatred of 'the accursed Aristocracy' and vigorously denounced the inheritance laws in his journal in 1848.[5] It is true that the Chartists also inveighed with great bitterness against the middle classes. Bronterre O'Brien in a letter to McDouall's *Journal* in July 1841 denounced the avarice of the 'MONEY MONSTER', which 'makes you poor in the midst of wealth of your own producing'.[6] With searing invective that same periodical flayed 'the methodist tea dealer' and 'high church shopman' for making tea out of sloe, fern and hawthorn leaves.[7]

Nevertheless, the middle classes were opposed less consistently than the aristocracy. In the early stages of the movement they were treated by the moderate moral-force men as reluctant allies, who should be persuaded to recognize their common interest with the workers, and support the Charter (V, 2a). Much of the criticism which was later levelled against them was for their political role in underpinning unpopular Whig legislation and in helping to put down Chartism by force in 1839 rather than for their economic role as profit mongers (V,

[1] G. D. H. Cole, *Studies in Class Structure* (London, 1968), p. 12.
[2] *Notes to the People*, Vol. II, (London, 1852), pp. 845–6.
[3] *Ibid.*, Vol. I, p. 186.
[4] 'Hereditary Landed Aristocracy'. Scrapbook of Newspaper Cuttings on Ernest Jones Chartist, Manchester Central Reference Library Archives Department, Ms. f. 923. 2–J. 8.
[5] *The Reformers' Companion to the Almanac*, No. 4, April 1848.
[6] *McDouall's Chartist and Republican Journal*, 17 July 1841, pp. 126–7.
[7] *Ibid.*, 8 May 1841, pp. 44–5.

2b). Moreover, the Chartists were not undiscriminating in handling the concept of a 'middle Class'. Master manufacturers and other large capitalists were singled out for particular animadversion, being designated 'moneyocracy' or 'money lords' so that they might share the obloquy of the aristocracy. But class-conscious Chartists from O'Brien in 1837[1] to Ernest Jones in the early '50s (V, 2d) recognized that those of the middle classes who were immediately dependent on the custom of working men (i.e. some farmers and shopkeepers) should be whipped in as allies. Collaboration with advanced middle-class reformers in suffrage movements which stopped short of the People's Charter, in substance or in name, however, was a sensitive area in Chartist politics. Because of the differing shades of opinion as to the desirability of it, the issue sometimes proved to be disruptive of the unity of Chartism. (For attempts to unite with middle-class reformers, see Part VI, 1, 4, 7 & 8).

Fourthly, Chartism lacked the will to lead a genuinely revolutionary mass movement. Historians have long recognized the division of Chartists into moral-force and physical-force camps. Recent discussions of the movement's strategies have presented a more complex picture, distinguishing three or four groupings classified by the amount of pressure they would apply to government. It has been shown that the most influential of the supposed physical-force leaders—the big 'O's, O'Connor and O'Brien—relied not on force but on the threat of force to carry the Charter, and continually tempered their intimations of future violence with present injunctions to keep within the law and avoid 'premature outbreak'.[2] To be sure there were also those who worked in an uninhibited way for armed insurrection—Rayner Stephens, who first popularized in Chartism the policy of arming the people, Julian Harney, who in 1839 wished to employ the proposed general strike to spark off a revolution on the French model, Thomas Cooper in 1842, Peter Bussey, Richard Marsden and others. Some even plotted rebellion. Alexander Somerville claimed to have been introduced to a 'Secret Committee of War' about the time of the 1839 Convention. McDouall, who had cast himself for the lead, was said to have inspected Woolwich Arsenal to see how it could be captured.[3] Dr. John Taylor, another Scottish medico, with the mien of a romantic hero, was involved in plans to raise a revolt

[1] Alfred Plummer, *Bronterre* (London, 1971), p. 74.
[2] T. M. Kemnitz, 'Approaches to the Chartist Movement: Feargus O'Connor and Chartist Strategy', *Albion*, Vol. V, 1973, pp. 67–73; Parssinen, *op. cit.*; Plummer, *op. cit.*, pp. 92–3, 99.
[3] Plummer, *op. cit.*, pp. 107–8.

in the North of England in support of the Newport rising later in the year.[1] There was more backstairs conspiracy and enrolment of members in National Guards in the late spring and summer of 1848, when the Chartists were in touch with the Irish Confederates (IV, 1b & 7). Again McDouall was party to it. But the numbers involved were minimal, and the timing was poor, the most determined plotting occurring after the great bursts of enthusiasm for Chartism had passed—i.e. in the winter of 1839–40 and in the months June–August 1848—instead of being undertaken in advance to take advantage of crises when they occurred. Physical-force extremism was by no means an unmixed asset to the creation of a mass movement behind Chartism. The 1839 Convention found it an obstacle to recruiting working-class support in Scotland and in parts of Southern England.[2]

If there was a serious danger of bloodshed and destruction in early Victorian England it was not because the Chartists headed a united movement bent on the overthrow of government, but because in the tinder-dry climate of an underfed land the slightest brush between the people and their employers or between the people and the authorities at the local level might escalate into a national confrontation. This was the danger of which General Napier, a judicious observer, was most conscious: '... I lay down as an axiom, and our first greatest principle', he wrote, 'that the queen's troops must not be overthrown anywhere, because the effect in the three kingdoms would be fearful. If only a corporal's guard was cut off it would be a "total defeat of the troops" ere it reached London, Edinburgh and Dublin; and before the contradiction arrived the disaffected, in the moral exaltation of supposed victory, would be in arms'.[3] In avoiding such encounters, and in containing them when they occurred, the machinery of public order had a crucial role to play. Unfortunately, when the expertise of a professional police force was not widely available, amateur magistrates, furnished with troops or with borrowed police detachments, could, with difficulty, restrain, and might more easily provoke (IV, 3 & 5). The precipitancy of the Birmingham magistrates in suppressing a Chartist meeting in the Bull Ring in July 1839, like the inertia of the South Lancashire justices and millowners in August 1842, when their towns were invaded by crowds

[1] The best study of this is A. J. Peacock's fascinating *Bradford Chartism, 1838–40*, University of York Borthwick Papers No. 36.
[2] K. Judge, *op. cit.*
[3] W. Napier, *The Life and Opinions of General Sir Charles James Napier, G.C.B.*, (London, 1857), Vol. II, p. 14.

bent on turning out the factories, did more than the Chartist leaders to generalize discontent.

Chartism and Liberalism

The nineteenth century was an age of rapid change and shifting political alignments. As a label in politics, therefore, the name 'liberal' was used at successive stages in two quite different ways. In the eighteen thirties it was bestowed not on a party but on a corpus of middle class provincials (e.g. Edward Baines of Leeds and Mark Philips of Manchester) who were inspired by the ideas of Jeremy Bentham and the Classical Economists. Usually they attended Nonconformist chapels, and favoured continuing administrative and financial reform. Freer trade was their watchword, education their prescription for the masses, corporate reform their charter. They gave a not undiscriminating allegiance to the Whigs in parliament, but their radical left flank was apt to rebel against aristocratic Whig inertia over Corn Law repeal and the secret ballot. A quarter of a century or more later the term 'Liberal' came to be applied to a coherent political party which formed at the parliamentary level in 1859 by the fusion of Whigs, Radicals and Peelites, and rapidly acquired in the country a following drawn from 'a new cheap Press, Militant Dissent ... and organized labour.'[1] This distinction must be borne in mind when discussing the relationship of Chartism to Liberalism.

Traditional labour history has assumed a sharp discontinuity between the working-class movements of the 1830s and 1840s, among which Chartism was both pre-eminent and characteristic, and those of the 1850s and 1860s, which fed into the emerging Liberal party. Surveying the history of English trade-unionism the Webbs stressed the transition from revolutionary general unions to the 'New Models' with their industrial pacifism and provision of friendly benefits for their members. This has since been generalized into a concept of ideological *embourgeoisement*: a surrender of working-class independence and working-class values to the dictates and standards of capital. Foster in the study of Oldham and other towns cited above conceives of 'liberalization' as part of a process whereby capitalist authority was reimposed and the vanguard of the mass movement of the workers, which had existed in Chartist times, was isolated.[2] On the other hand,

---

[1] J. Vincent, *The Formation of the Liberal Party, 1857–68* (London, 1966), p. 257.
[2] *Op. cit.*, Chap. VII and Postscript.

much historical writing during the last forty years has demonstrated that working-class attitudes changed less than they were once believed to have done as the second quarter of the nineteenth century gave place to the third. It is true that arbitration and conciliation were more strongly advocated on the industrial front from the 'fifties onwards and that platforms were more freely shared with middle-class spokesmen in the revived parliamentary reform agitation of the 'sixties. This, however, was largely because the capitalists were willing to concede more than most of them had offered twenty or thirty years earlier. It can now be seen that there was no capitulation by the workers to the economic philosophy of the middle classes, no abandonment of strikes or of apprenticeship restrictions in the interests of a free labour market. Politically, the workers continued to voice their own independent claims to the vote through the manhood suffrage associations of the 1860s and the Reform League of 1865 against middle-class advocacy of household suffrage or less.[1]

The contrast mellows still further when it is recalled that elements of the subsequent Liberal consensus were already present in Chartism. A growing body of historians, including Brian Harrison and Patricia Hollis, D. J. Rowe and Trygve Tholfsen, have identified the areas of overlap between Chartism and Liberalism. Mention has already been made of one of these—the animosity towards the aristocracy which Chartists shared with the Anti-Corn Law League. To a certain extent religion furnished another. David Jones has estimated that no fewer than forty clergymen sympathized with the Chartist movement, and supported it by lecturing, loaning chapels, and presenting books and money.[2] They were principally Dissenters. In some localities, such as Leicestershire and Nottinghamshire and in Wales, Nonconformist preachers, lay or ministerial, furnished Chartism with leadership. But it would be a mistake to connect the causes too closely. Some Chartist leaders were rationalists like Hetherington and Watson, as was Richard Carlile, who hovered on the fringes of the movement (VIII, 2b). Moreover, the Chartists founded churches of their own, held out-of-door camp meetings and ceremonially buried their own dead, using the occasion to preach a social gospel, which did not gain much ground in conventional Nonconformity until after 1880 (VIII, 8). Temperance (II, 3), belief in state-provided, unsectarian education (II, 4a), and hostility to

---

[1] R. V. Clements, 'British Trade Unions and Popular Political Economy, 1850–1875'. *Econ.H.R.*, 2 Ser., Vol. XIV, 1961–62, pp. 93–104; Tholfsen, *op. cit.*, pp. 315–25.
[2] *Op. cit.*, p. 50.

the Established Church, supplied the chief links between Chartism and the advanced Liberal Dissent of mid-Victorian times. Chartists detested the Church of England as an aristocratic institution (VIII, 1). They demonstrated at its Sunday services in the summer of 1839 (VIII, 2), and called for the disestablishment and disendowment of the Church, for the abolition of tithes and church rates and for the provision of free and compulsory state education, in the programme adopted by the Convention of 1851. Here were anticipations of the later exertions of the Nonconformist-supported Liberation Society and National Education League.

Parliamentary reform, too, furnished some common ground. A depressing fact, which the Chartists had to recognize, was that the solid core of middle-class opinion in the two generations after the 1832 Reform Act was no more prepared than the aristocracy to concede universal suffrage in harness with the other points of the People's Charter. Jealousy for its own newly won privileges and fear of the economic objectives of the masses took care of that (V, 3a). Only a minority of extreme radicals, mainly drawn from the ranks of Political Nonconformists, was prepared to go to the length of supporting all the Six Points in the Complete Suffrage movement of 1842, and almost all in the National Alliance of 1847. (VI, 4 & 7, Comment). During the 1840s, however, liberals of a more representative kind, stung by the resistance of aristocratic administrations, Tory and Whig, to the plea for Corn Law repeal and cheap government, offered to assist in effecting electoral reforms of a moderate character. There was collaboration with the Chartists in Wakley's and Duncombe's move to repeal the ratepaying clauses of the Reform Act in 1847 (VI, 7) and with some Chartists, including O'Connor, in the Parliamentary and Financial Reform Movement for household suffrage etc. in 1850 (VI, 7, Comment). Despite Ernest Jones' sustained but failing efforts to preserve the distinctness of the working-class political movement in the 'fifties, the eirenic disposition of the Reform movements leading to the 1867 Act can be traced to developments in later Chartism.

Chartists also shared with middle-class reformers a sensitivity to offences against the freedom of the individual at home and abroad. The L.W.M.A. conferred with the radical M.P.s, Roebuck and Molesworth, to protest against Whig proposals to set aside constitutional rights in Canada in 1837.[1] The protest which Lovett and Hetherington organized

[1] G. Howell, *A History of the Working Men's Association from 1836 to 1850*, with introduction by D. J. Rowe (Newcastle, 1970), pp. 67–9.

in 1844 against the security opening of letters sent through the Post Office stirred liberal consciences inside and outside Parliament, and moral-force Chartists worked with Richard Cobden and various Benthamite radicals to free the press from the newspaper stamp duty from 1849 onwards.

One especially important shared assumption between Chartists and many middle-class Liberals and Radicals was an acceptance of the ethic of self improvement. The belief that, in the words of J. Wood, a member of the National Charter Association, Chartism 'must represent the best intelligence, and the best morals of the people'[1] was very widely held within the movement. It was not confined to the teetotal, education and Christian wings, typified by Henry Vincent, William Lovett and Arthur O'Neill respectively, though it formed the basis of all three. Consequently it was not abandoned when O'Connor exorcised these movements in April 1841. In the early 1850s Ernest Jones' *Notes to the People* issued again the temperance call, 'Raise Chartism from the Pothouse.' (II, 3). The founding of halls, where lectures on Science, Political Economy and Literature were given and Libraries and reading rooms were located, and the establishment of Chartist Sunday Schools for teaching all kinds of useful knowledge under the broad umbrella of the N.C.A. (II, 4c) had been afoot during the preceding decade in various Northern towns.[2] The underlying motives were various. Tholfsen has cited examples, from Leeds, Birmingham, Bradford and elsewhere, in which the supporting case was argued in the spirit of assertiveness against the higher classes on the assumption which Harney held so firmly that 'Knowledge is power'.[3] But the desire to advance the Charter by demonstrating to others that working men could conform to accepted standards of respectability, and could therefore be trusted with the vote figured prominently in Lovett's and Collins' *Chartism: A New Organization of the People*, and was also expressed by more class-conscious Chartists like Hick of Leeds.[4] This was an appeal to consensus values, for the more sensitive of the Utilitarian Liberals, men like Samuel Smiles, were already beginning, while Chartism lived, to urge popular education, not simply as a means of reconciling working men to their miserable lot but as an aid to genuine freedom and independence. These

---

[1] *Notes to the People*, Vol. II, (London, 1852), p. 890.
[2] Brian Simon, *Studies in the History of Education, 1780–1870* (London, 1960), pp. 243–76.
[3] Tholfsen, *op. cit.*, pp. 103–7.
[4] *Ibid.*, p. 105.

steadily pursued their aim of moral elevation through the mechanics institutes of the 1820s, the provident societies of the 'thirties and the temperance organizations of the 'forties,[1] calling upon working men, as Place's friend, the American James Roberts Black, did from 1834 onwards, to unite for their own self-improvement.

This concern stemmed from a further conviction which the Chartists shared with early Victorian Liberals—optimism rooted in the thinking of the eighteenth-century Enlightenment as expressed by the Marquis de Condorcet. Macaulay's belief in inevitable progress, Samuel Smiles' conviction of the march of the human mind towards self-control and self-emancipation found an echo in the work of William Lovett and John Collins. Of the light of intellectual enquiry which they sought through educational Chartism to diffuse, these wrote that 'the spark once struck is inextinguishable, and will go on extending and radiating with increasing power ...'.[2] Harney, at the other end of the political spectrum, affirmed with equal assurance midst the revolutions of 1848 that 'the rule of the bourgeoisie is doomed; like Belshazzar they have been weighed in the balance and found wanting, and their kingdom will be given to the Proletarians.'[3]

It must be stressed, however, that the power of these common elements to unite the middle- and the working-class components of the reform movement was not realized until after Chartism was dead. Chartism was one of the streams which fed into the consensus Liberalism of the 1860s, and one can now see why it could do so without complete loss of consistency. With the middle-class Liberals of their own golden age, however, Chartists were more often in disagreement than in agreement. Collaboration was most in evidence during the early formative stages of the movement in 1836–38 and in the declining phase from 1842; far less so when the campaign was at its height. It was more apparent at the local level, where Chartist town councillors slid into 'establishment radicalism', pressing for cheap rates and better sanitary conditions,[4] than in national politics, where the two sides quarrelled over Corn-Law repeal and Household Suffrage. The campaign for the People's Charter was separated from contemporary Liberalism both by class and by ideology. Distrust of the middle classes,

---

[1] *Ibid.*, Chap. IV.
[2] W. Lovett & J. Collins, *Chartism: A New Organization of the People*, with introduction by Asa Briggs (Leicester, 1969), p. 1.
[3] *The Northern Star*, 26 February 1848.
[4] Jones, *op. cit.*, pp. 93, 177–8.

especially of the large capitalists, repeatedly inhibited Chartists of all
kinds from attaching themselves to movements initiated by those groups
and from accepting compromises on the suffrage question propounded
from above. These suspicions, rooted in economic distress and
resentment of the exclusive privileges of the £10 householder conferred
by the Act of 1832, softened from the middle 'forties onwards. Trade
improved, the strength of the militant outworkers declined, and
experience taught the lesson that, without allies from outside the
working classes, the Chartists had but little chance of advancing towards
their political objectives.

On the ideological level the Liberals of the 1830s looked to
Benthamism, which, despite the efforts of its more benign practitioners
to humanize it, remained a coldly scientific creed, impatient of familiar
custom, authoritarian yet committed to a freedom of the labour market
which told against protection of adult workers. They also appealed to a
version of Political Economy case-hardened by the difficulties of the
period of, and after, the French Wars. Chartism was the heir of an older
tradition, carried over from the eighteenth century by Major John
Cartwright and sharpened by Tom Paine in the 1790s. This claimed
universal suffrage and other democratic reforms on grounds of history
or of natural right. Bentham, by contrast, despised tradition, and
ridiculed natural and imprescriptible rights, calling them 'Nonsense on
stilts'. Though his disciples usually called for an extended franchise, they
qualified the demand by insisting on at least a minimum of literacy for
voters. The ideologies clashed in the economic sphere even more than in
the political. From the time of the publication of the second part of
Paine's *Rights of Man*, with its proposals for a graduated income tax and
welfare benefits, natural rights had been made to yield conclusions
which were unacceptable to the individualistic middle-class reformers of
the early nineteenth century. If most Chartists were not constructive
Socialists, the continual harping in their lectures and articles on such
anti-capitalist themes as the evils of competition, the damage effected by
machinery (II, 2), the inquity of the burden of the National Debt (II 1c),
the notion that labour was the source of all wealth (II, 1b), aroused
suspicions that they were hostile to property rights. Here, too, the gap
narrowed in the third quarter of the century by modifications of view
adopted, not only by the labour leaders, but by the Political Economists
and employers.

In fine one is left with a paradox. Chartism made an assertion of
working-class separateness, unique in nineteenth-century Britain for its

magnitude and its intensity. As such it arose from particular pressures upon working men, economic, political and cultural, which eventually slackened, and were not bound to recur. Even so when the efforts to create an independent workers' party in the country were renewed from the 1890s onwards, memories of Chartism served to sustain them.[1] But the Chartist movement also has its place in the slow evolution of popular radicalism from its eighteenth-century origins to the Gladstonian Liberal party. Of Robert Lowery, the North-Eastern Chartist, who, like Henry Vincent, plunged, after his break with the O'Connorites, into temperance lecturing jointly with Nonconformist radicals, Asa Briggs has written: 'He found many allies among ex-Chartists.'[2] Even the class-conscious Ernest Jones ended, as Harrison and Hollis have pointed out, as radical candidate for Manchester in the general election of 1868.[3] The Liberal consensus which emerged in the 1860s was broad enough to enable former Chartists to take up a position on its left wing without repudiating their erstwhile principles. Facts of chronology render it probable that more Chartists were absorbed into the Liberal party than survived to become late-nineteenth century Socialists. But whether the contribution of their movement to the former cause was more important than their legacy to the latter is a question not simply of history but of values.

[1] E. P. Thompson, 'Homage to Tom Maguire', *Essays in Labour History in Memory of G. D. H. Cole*, ed. A. Briggs and J. Saville (London, 1960), Chap. VIII, pp. 287–9.
[2] Lovett and Collins, *op. cit.*, intro. p. 21.
[3] Harrison and Hollis, *op. cit.*, in which numerous other examples are given of ex-Chartist Liberals.

PART I

Chartism and the Constitution

1. *The Programme of Reform*

(The People's Charter was published as a draft parliamentary bill on 8
May 1838. Though the initial proceedings were taken at the 'influential
meeting' in the British Coffee House, Cockspur Street, Charing Cross,
when a committee consisting of the 'subjoined' Radical M.P.s and
members of the London Working Men's Association was appointed to
draw it, the task of preparing the document fell mainly to William Lovett
and Francis Place. The following broadsheet summarizes its demands.)

'THE SIX POINTS OF THE PEOPLE'S CHARTER.

1. A VOTE for every man twenty-one years of age, of sound mind, and
   not undergoing punishment for crime.
2. THE BALLOT.—To protect the elector in the exercise of his vote.
3. NO PROPERTY QUALIFICATION for Members of Parliament—
   thus enabling the constituencies to return the man of their choice, be
   he rich or poor.
4. PAYMENT OF MEMBERS, thus enabling an honest tradesman,
   working man, or other person, to serve a constituency, when taken
   from his business to attend to the interests of the Country.
5. EQUAL CONSTITUENCIES, securing the same amount of
   representation for the same number of electors, instead of allowing
   small constituencies to swamp the votes of large ones.
6. ANNUAL PARLIAMENTS, thus presenting the most effectual
   check to bribery and intimidation, since though a constituency might
   be bought once in seven years (even with the ballot), no purse could
   buy a constituency (under a system of universal suffrage) in each
   ensuing twelve-month; and since members, when elected for a year
   only, would not be able to defy and betray their constituents as now.

*Subjoined are the names of the gentlemen who embodied these principles
into the document called the "People's Charter," at an influential meeting
held at the British Coffee House, London, on the 7th of June, 1837:*

Daniel O'Connell, Esq., M.P.	Mr. Henry Hetherington.
John Arthur Roebuck, Esq., M.P.	Mr. John Cleave.
John Temple Leader, Esq., M.P.	Mr. James Watson.
Charles Hindley, Esq., M.P.	Mr. Richard Moore.
Thomas Perronet Thompson, Esq., M.P.	Mr. William Lovett.
William Sharman Crawford, Esq., M.P.	Mr. Henry Vincent.

W. COLLINS, PRINTER, "WEEKLY TIMES" OFFICE, DUDLEY.'

(From Volume of Lithographs and Broadsheets, 'Chartism and Reform',
Bishopsgate Institute)

2. *The Underlying Principle*

(Feargus O'Connor's *Northern Star* was the chief press organ of the
Chartist movement. An editorial on De Tocqueville's *Democracy in
America* (published 1835–40) propounded a basic tenet of English
working-class radicalism in the early nineteenth century, that true
political authority was delegated upwards by the people. Belief in the
sovereignty of the people figured in the thought of English reformers like
Obadiah Hulme, James Burgh and Major John Cartwright in the
eighteenth-century commonwealthman tradition before the French
Revolution, but was popularized by Thomas Paine, whose *Rights of Man*
first appeared in March 1791. Paine's ideas were influential in Chartism,
especially with the radical Left of the East London Democratic
Association, formed in 1837 by Julian Harney and others.)

'THE FIRST PRINCIPLES OF GOVERNMENT
... We would regard the subject in a more general and useful form, by
the light of reason and experience, hanging our faith on the individual
opinion of neither this person nor that. From one principle alone, we feel
convinced, may be deduced every rational and true proposition relating
to a democratic government—and that principle is:

"The people are the source of all power."

Is this assertion well founded? Let us try it by the common, yet
excellent, hypothesis of a transition from a state of nature to a state of

society. Men first unite together for protection and mutual advantage; they feel the necessity of having some head, or leader, to controul the vicious and reward the meritorious; they, therefore, *by the general voice, and for the general good*, invest one or more of their fellow-beings with superior authority; these persons, thus privileged, may admit others to their councils, and to a share in their power; but yet this alters not the source of that power; it must, if traced up, be found to spring originally from the people, the public, the nation at large.

From the establishment of the above truth flow many valuable maxims. First. All who are affected by this power are entitled to a voice in its creation. This assertion, so strongly supported by reason and common sense, receives additional strength from the supposition, on which we are proceeding; for, how can we conceive a body of men, just associated from a state of wild nature, *all equal, all free*, delegating a power to one individual above the rest, for the government of *all*, without at the same time believing that he was nominated and elected by *all*. To aver the contrary would be absurd and contradictory to that self-interest which reigns so powerfully in the human mind.

Secondly. Power springing from the people must be responsible to the people. In other words, the channels must be referrable to their source. We cannot fancy that any men would be such fools, and so blind to their own advantage, as to delegate unlimited and irresponsible authority to any individual as to say, "Cut off our heads, spoil our property, ruin the country; we give all into your hands; we throw ourselves upon your generous mercy; we reserve no license of revocation to ourselves".

The Crown, the Ministers, and the Parliament, are all trustees for the nation; they have peculiar privileges delegated for the sake of the prosperity of the country, not for their own sakes.

Thirdly. Any power exerted to the disadvantage and detriment of the country at large is illegal, and without any authority. The people do not confer strength for their own injury, but for their own good; they do not furnish weapons for their own destruction, but implements for their preservation; they limit the power of their rulers to the wants of the ruled; they bestow it for the general prosperity, and, therefore, there is no power delegated for injury and injustice. Many more important corollaries might be deduced, but these are sufficient for our present subject. Well, then, what government approaches most nearly to these necessary qualities of a free constitution? Under the now existing forms we have no hesitation in giving the palm to a republic; but if our constitution, in its mixed monarchical form, were to be rendered sufficiently democratic; if every member of the State had a voice in its public affairs; if Universal Suffrage prevailed, and the whole people were, in truth, recognised as the legitimate source of all power, then we believe the requisite advantages would follow, that their delegates would be responsible to the nation at large, and exert their powers, thus bestowed, for the good of the whole community.

Let the whole country; let every class then be assured of this, that in the present age and the present character and opinion of the nation, the only means of avoiding a republic is by infusing the true spirit of rational democracy into our constitution, and giving to every Briton his rights as a human being, and his privileges as a freeman.'
(*The Northern Star*, 2 January 1841)

3. *The Rule of Law*

(The case of *Stockdale v. Hansard*, which came before Lord Chief Justice Denman and three other judges in the Court of Queen's Bench in 1839, originated in a decision of the House of Commons to order the printing of documents in which Stockdale was accused by the inspectors of prisons of having published obscene books circulated in Newgate gaol. Stockdale sued the parliamentary printer for defamation, whereupon Hansard entered the defence that he had acted on the order of the House of Commons, a court superior to any court of law and a body which was the sole judge of its own privileges, of which the right to publish defamatory matter was one. Finding in favour of the plaintiff, Queen's Bench ruled that the House of Commons alone could not change or dispense from the law, nor were its resolutions as to the extent of its privileges beyond scrutiny by other courts. The *Northern Star*, in an editorial, applauded this judgement, thus showing that Chartists respected the rule of law, however frequently they might criticize the legislature and the courts. The particular privilege denied by the Court— freedom to publish papers, even when defamatory—was made good to the House by the Parliamentary Papers Act of 1840.)

'PRIVILEGE *versus* LAW

... If we regard this contest as merely relating to the present case of libel, we shall see on the one hand, the Commons enraged because they are not allowed to cast foul imputations on Englishmen according to their fancy; and on the other, the Judges determined to show them that they shall not violate the laws with impunity. The Legislators desire to have the power of destroying the fair character of any that may be obnoxious. The reputation of man, which is generally dearer to him than life, is to be sacrificed at their pleasure. They claim a right to libel, and declare it their own especial privilege to vilify all men.

What is the common sense, and what is the law of the case? Reason tells us it is absurd that any class of mankind should be invested with the power of blackening the fame of their fellow-beings; that a portion of the community should be exempt from the punishment, which they themselves have declared against libellers; that they should prohibit offences, and yet reserve a right to be the offenders; that in fact they should declare that to be a crime in others, which they hold to be innocent, when committed by themselves; that they should declare actions to be illegal, and yet legalise them for their own advantage; that they should make laws, and break them.

Established law supports common sense on this subject. It is true there are a mass of decisions, formed in the reigns of tyrants, and in the times of obsequious, cringing lawyers, which declare the Parliament to be almost *omnipotent*, and De Lolme, only looking at one side of the question, has most unwarrantably asserted that the English Parliament "can do anything but make a woman a man, and a man a woman." These were the arguments adduced by Sir JOHN CAMPBELL. But on the other hand, there are also the *dicta* of upright judges, who have declared the power of Parliament to be undoubtedly limited; and what is much stronger, all former decisions of a contrary nature may be looked upon as overruled by the resolutions of the two houses *themselves*, whereby it was established in 1763, that "writing and publishing seditious libels were not to be entitled to privilege, and that the reasons on which that case proceeded, *extended equally to every indictable offence*".* Now, all libels are indictable offences, and therefore by the admission of the Legislature itself, they have been resolved to be excluded from privilege. The law of libel, as it now stands, is a blot upon our code, but surely the makers, or those who have the power of altering it, have no right to complain, when they suffer by its operation. WILKES was expelled from the House for a libel; it would be an excellent plan to follow the precedent, and to expel the *whole lot* for this libel, which all acknowledge. The present dispute, however, should be also regarded in a much more extensive view. It is a struggle between the privileges of a particular body, and the laws of a whole nation. On its issue depends whether the House of Commons shall be allowed to declare itself above all law? If this be admitted, Parliament, under the mask of privilege, may invade the liberties of England, and may break down those barriers, which have been raised for her defence by the patriotic among our forefathers. Some may say the Commons represent all, and therefore that their privileges are the rights of all. We deny that they are a national representation, but even if they were, we would rather limit their power within certain, defined bounds; for we are convinced that the people can always assert their own rights, and that it is better to trust to the fettered authority of any branch of the Legislature, than giving it boundless power, to put faith in the generosity, with which it may be used.

Why are the Commons to be exempt from law? If the statutes of their own making be just, they surely need not object to be ruled by justice; unjust, the fault is theirs, and they deserve to suffer. The best guarantee that we possess for the enactment of good laws, consists in the fact, that they will affect those by whom they are made. Laws should not be made for a few, but for the whole nation, and their violators, of whatever rank or class, should be equally punished. What respect or obedience do law-makers expect to be paid by others to their statutes, when they themselves are the first to break them.

Wherever a power is conferred above the laws despotism exists, and birth is given to the strangest anomalies. The Monarch is not above, but is subject to, the laws, for by them he is made, and by their force he wears the crown. He takes an oath, that he will rule according to law, and whenever he violates this oath, he breaks the trust reposed in him, and has no longer any right to that situation, which he attained on condition of being faithful thereto. The Judges are not above the laws, for they swear that they will be guided and ruled thereby. The *Parliament is not superior to the laws*, and it is the essence of presumption in them to advance so monstrous a claim.

Let no one ever forget the admonition of the great and patriotic Chief Justice Lord Holt, that "the authority of Parliament is from the law, and as it is circumscribed by law, *so it may be exceeded*; and if they do exceed those legal bounds and authority, *their acts are wrongful and cannot be justified any more than the acts of private men.*"†

We have no fear for the result of this question; we feel assured that no class or individual will be suffered, with impunity, to violate the law made for all. For Lord DENMAN we entertain the highest respect. However much we may dislike his politics, we consider him one of the most consistent, straight-forward, and independent men of his party. We feel that he will not be deterred from doing his duty, but that, if necessary, he will imitate his illustrious predecessor, Sir EDWARD COKE, who, when asked before the privy council, whether he would resist the supremacy of the Royal prerogative, boldly replied, in the presence of JAMES the FIRST, "*That he would do that which should be fit for a Judge to do*". The duty of a Judge is to render justice equally and impartially to all; to be biassed neither by party nor by power; to be independent in principle and determined in courage; not to be dazzled by authority, nor awed by threats; to punish ALL violators of the law, whether rich or poor; and to adopt for his motto, the words of Magna Charta—"*Nulli vendemus, nulli negabimus aut differemus rectum vel justitium*". To no man will we sell, deny, or delay, that which is just and right.

The liberties of this country can never be entirely destroyed while trial by Jury exists, while the Judges maintain the true spirit of justice, and while Englishmen assert the supremacy of laws, sanctioned by their power, over the oppression of privilege and the extortion of prerogative.'

* Com. Jour. 24th Nov., Lords' Jour. 29th Nov.
† L. Salk. 505.

(*The Northern Star*, 2 July 1839)

4. *Ancient Rights*
(a) To the Points of the Charter
(Peter Murray McDouall, a Scottish surgeon who practised at Ramsbottom, was a leading figure in the Executive of the National Charter Association in 1841–42. His *Chartist and Republican Journal* lasted for only a few months. The claim that universal suffrage persisted until the reign of Henry VI is a political 'myth', significant not for its truth but for its influence upon the radical movement. It derives from the statute of 1430, which determined that the county voter should be in future a forty shilling freeholder. Annual parliaments were indeed ordered by statutes of 1330 and 1362, but not always held.)

'REMAINING RIGHTS OF THE PEOPLE
WHEN we look back to the Saxon Institutions and laws founded as they were, upon the principles of the Charter, even to equal division of the empire, and the appointment of a Parliament for each division; when, from Henry of Huntington, an old writer, we likewise learn that "*King Sigebert growing incorrigible, the great men and the* PEOPLE *assembled* TOGETHER *in the beginning of the second year of his reign, and deposed him with unanimous consent*".

When we refer to the still more democratic system under Alfred, and likewise the practice of holding annual parliaments as late as the reign of Edward the Third; finally, when we look into the statutes enacted by

Henry the Sixth, we discover that he was the first king who put any restrictions on the exercise of Universal Suffrage; and, consequently, when we perceive the great body of society in the year 1841, utterly deprived of the franchise, and possessing no influence over laws, rulers, or taxes, what other question possesses more importance than the one put at the head of this article? We are told there are common rights belonging to the people, such as the right to meet in public to discuss grievances, and petition for their removal. The meetings have been dispersed and tyrannised over by the police; complaint has been prohibited by royal proclamation, and our petitions would have been far more effectual if sent to the king of the Cannibal Islands. Trial by jury has been converted into a farce, and the right to possess and use arms, if necessary, has been denied by the magistrates, and punished by the judges. ...

[In the paragraph omitted the writer deplores the labourer's apathy towards the invasion of his rights, which is fostered by the complexity of the law and the prevailing poverty.]

The first inhabitants of this country were known as the early Britons. Sir Henry Spelman, an antiquary, who lived in the year 1600, informs us "*that the Britons had their common council or parliament, which they called Kyfr-y-then, from their laws being framed in that assembly.*" All warriors, wise men, and all who did service to their country were members of this primitive parliament, which not only made laws, but likewise elected leaders, generals, and kings. Cassibellan, who led the British against the invading Romans, was elected by that assembly; which also, on the retreat of the Romans from the island, invited the Saxons to aid them in opposing the Picts and Scots.

Thus, at the very beginning of our history, the great principle of the Charter was admitted, and republicanism, in reality, practised; for, who was Cassibellan but the people's general? and what the Kyfr-y-then or law-giving assembly but the people's parliament.

Worth, service, and duty were at the bottom of those congresses of the early Britons, and merit, capacity, and popular approval were all taken into consideration before such men as Cassibellan could start into elective power. What is of greater importance too, is, that the parliament retained the legislative and executive powers instead of transferring both, for ever, from their hands, by fixing upon one family, and one set of domestic tyrants. These rude ancestors of ours ought to teach us wisdom, and at their tombs we must seek instruction.'

(*McDouall's Chartist and Republican Journal*, 8 May 1841)

(b) Against the New Poor Law

(The Poor Law Amendment Act of 1834 radically overhauled the machinery of poor relief in England, ousting the parish from its traditional role and introducing poor-law unions centrally controlled by a national Commission. This was designed to prepare the way for systematic deterrence of able-bodied pauperism by the application of the workhouse test. The extent to which the test was enforced varied in practice from area to area, but the threat to introduce it into Lancashire and Yorkshire in 1837–38, when distress was acute, engendered sharp resistance to the new authorities by the populace. Joseph Rayner Stephens, a Methodist minister at Ashton-under-Lyne, who had been disowned by the Wesleyan Conference, counselled violent obstruction of proceedings taken under the new Act, which he regarded as contrary to the established law and constitution. Stephens was arrested by a Bow Street runner on 27 December 1838, and tried at the Chester Assizes in the following August for addressing an unlawful meeting at Hyde. The ensuing comment was written while the proceedings against him were still under consideration. Though Stephens was never a true Chartist, his view that the New Poor Law was unconstitutional was shared by those who were. R. J. Richardson, a Salford Chartist, speaking at Brighton, claimed that commissions such as the Board of Poor Law Commissioners contravened the Bill of Rights, which condemned 'the late commission established for Ecclesiastical purposes, and all other commissions of the like nature.' He further maintained that the Board's power to build union workhouses by drafts on the Exchequer Loan Commissioners ran contrary to the provisions of the 'Bill' that the King 'should not levy taxes without consent of Parliament.')

'THE REV. MR. STEPHENS

Considerable anxiety has been manifested by many of our readers to know the result of the "appearance" of the Rev. J. R. STEPHENS in the Court of Queen's Bench, on Friday: we give it elsewhere from the *Times*; also, abstracts of the Three Indictments. ...

In reference to the indictments, we copy the following remarks from the *Times*:— "It is clear from the perusal of these indictments, that the Government has abandoned their original intention to prosecute Mr. STEPHENS for a conspiracy to resist the operation of the Poor Law Amendment Act; this great constitutional question is studiously evaded. Two of the indictments contain no mention at all of the Poor Law or the Commissioners; the third merely includes 'the Poor Law Commissioners' in a catalogue of sundries in the loosest and most general terms. It is evident that the law officers of the Crown have dissuaded the Home Secretary from the hazardous attempt to bring this matter into a court of law. The expressions positively sworn to by the witnesses from Leigh, in reference to Poor Law Guardians, etc., are all omitted in the indictment. It will be recollected that previous to Mr. STEPHENS'S committal at the close of the second examination, Mr. BRANDT, on behalf of the prosecution, distinctly stated 'that it was their intention to indict the defendant for conspiracy, along with others, for resisting the laws, especially those relating to the Poor Law Amendment Act'. As it is well known that Mr. STEPHENS'S agitation has been confined to an opposition to that measure, to the abuses of the factory system, and similar social grievances to which the people are subjected, independent of all reference to, or connexion with, any questions of forms of government or party politics, it will scarcely serve the turn of the Poor Law Commissioners and their Home Secretary, to evade the only matter at issue between themselves and Mr. STEPHENS, by the paltry manouvre they have played off in this much-talked-of prosecution. Mr. STEPHENS has said strong things. He has recommended the people to resist, and advised them to arm. He has declared it to be the right and the duty of the people to possess arms, and under certain circumstances, and on certain conditions, to use the arms they so possess. But these conditions and circumstances all have reference in Mr. STEPHENS'S arguments to the principle and practices of the Poor Law Amendment Act. He may be wrong; he may be guilty; and if guilty he ought to be punished. But the question of his error and guilt has to be proved. It is a grave and solemn question—not merely to the defendant himself, but to the country at large. The public were led to expect the discussion and legal settlement of this question by means of the state prosecution entered into against Mr. STEPHENS. The attempt now to evade it altogether will fill the public mind with unqualified disgust and contempt. To call a torch-light meeting illegal which was held before the Home Secretary's letter to the magistrates, and before the Royal proclamation against such meetings was issued, which was peaceably conducted, and which terminated without any indication of riot or disturbance, is worse than trifling.

Men of all parties will unite to condemn such a procedure, and will conspire to denounce the conduct of a Government so persecuting and malignant in its spirit. To make Mr. STEPHENS talk of arms in connexion with the objects of the so-called 'National Convention', is cowardly as well as base.

Of all the exhibitions, and they are not a few, of their imbecility, meanness, and cowardice, this is the very worst. To convict Mr. STEPHENS upon such charges, sustained by such evidence, would

damage them and their 'Commissioners' infinitely more than his acquittal in a *bona fide* prosecution upon the original charge. We are much inclined to think that it would be better for Mr. STEPHENS, when brought to trial, to enter a solemn protest against the whole proceedings, to refuse to enter upon any defence, from which indeed he is virtually debarred by the framing of the indictments, and at once boldly dare the Government to pursue their own course, leaving Parliament and the country to say whether such a procedure can be tolerated in a free state; if it can, there is an end of public liberty; the subject is left without protection as to personal freedom, or life itself, and lies at the mercy of an unconstitutional Board of Commissioners, backed by the Government of the day.

It ought not to be overlooked in this prosecution that all the witnesses to the Hyde and Ashton indictments, with scarcely an exception, are mill-owners and others, whose conduct Mr. STEPHENS has frequently had occasion to bring before the public in his addresses upon the abuses of the factory system.'''
(*The Northern Star*, 4 May 1839)

(c) Against a Professional Police
(Though a quite well-staffed professional police had existed in London from 1829, and in some large provincial boroughs after 1835, the English counties continued to be served by amateur constables chosen by the court leet or parish vestry and supplemented in the towns by paid deputies and corps of watchmen. Early in 1839 the Whig government started to collect the opinions of the county magistrates on the expediency of establishing county forces under their own control, and in March a Royal Commission appointed three years earlier reported in favour of a more centralized plan. These proceedings led to the following debate in the Chartist Convention on 18 March. Other newspapers, including the *Morning Chronicle* and the *Charter*, ascribed to Dr. Fletcher advice to resist the new police with bludgeons, but the *Northern Star* with characteristic caution suppressed this. Four months later the government, to counter intensified Chartist unrest, hurriedly introduced a weak and unsatisfactory Rural Police bill, which became law.)

'GENERAL CONVENTION
Monday, March 18th.
RICHARD MARSDEN, Chairman.
WILLIAM LOVETT, Secretary.
... Mr. SANKEY then brought on his motion for an address to the citizens of London, relative to the threatened Rural Police Bill. He

observed that this system was first tried in Ireland, whose chains England assisted to rivet, or, by her apathy, allowed others to do, and that now it seemed something like retributive justice that it should be tried upon herself. (Hear.) Ireland had been for a long period the nursery in which the future legislators of England were sent unfledged to develop their powers of mischief. (Cheers.) We had examples of them in Castlereagh, Peel, Stanley, Lambe, Glenelg, Levison, Gower,[1] Wellington, Morpeth, and others; they had introduced a system of rural police into Ireland, and now in the full maturity of guilt they came to fasten the vile system upon England. (Hear.) These men in Ireland were originally called *Peelers*, in honour of their originator, Sir Robert; and I may mention (said Mr. Sankey) that the Right Honourable the late Mr. Sawrin, Attorney-General, opposed the system (Tory though he was) upon the ground that it was unconstitutional. It was at first proposed to appoint stipendiary magistrates, and a police in each county. This was done, but gradually the magistrates either obtained or usurped the power, the whole power of appointing the policemen, and now the Lord Lieutenant of Ireland is in fact the independent general of an army appointed by himself, commanded by officers chosen by himself—and the whole subject to him alone, for, let what might be said, I maintain them to be nothing less than an army organised, equipped, armed, divided into horse and foot, and in every respect a military force, at the command of one man, a despot, because wholly irresponsible. (Hear, hear.) The orders given to the police were disgraceful; they were nothing else than by *every means to make acquaintance with the servants towards obtaining a knowledge of family affairs.* (Hear, hear.) It had, indeed, been said that such was not the object, but who would or could believe they had any other? (Hear, hear.) It had been proved that within these few years the police of London had been put upon another footing, and now was infinitely more efficient, (indeed was acknowledged to be so) than the metropolitan police. Why, then, change so good a system? Why take away the management of their own concerns from men who had shown themselves so capable of conducting them? (Hear, hear.) It was done, forsooth, under the pretence of relieving them of so much trouble in the same way as was proposed with regard to relieving Bishops of attendance in the House of Lords—(hear, hear, hear)—it was, in other words, to deprive them of their rights. (Hear.) They had no other

---

[1] Lord Francis Leveson-Gower, Chief Secretary to the Lord Lieutenant of Ireland, 1828–30.

object than to carry out that vile system of centralization, which they had been gradually drawing around the country, and having deprived Englishmen, by the most insidious means, of the reality of their freedom, now to take from them even the semblance of freedom. (Hear.) It is our duty, therefore, to come forward to the assistance of our London brethren, and protest against this measure. (Hear.)[1] A system of *gend'armerie* may be a very good one for personal security, but public liberty should be too dear to risk for it. (Hear.) I must state, however, Mr. Chairman, that even this personal security is not a necessary consequence of such a system, for I have, during my residence in France, been made aware that on one occasion, when a murder had been committed, a person was taken, tried, condemned, and executed under the auspices, and by the evidence, of the police; another and another murder, to the number of four, were perpetrated and in like manner punished, when the whole were ultimately discovered to have been perpetrated by the police, and legal murders added by a conspiracy against others. (Hear.) The system would not stop here at the first step, as in France, from which it was borrowed, and where a man, when drawn for the militia, even when not called upon to act, was yet not permitted to leave that part of the country for five years, so would it be in England. Passports secured obedience abroad, and passports would be had recourse to at home. Since the Whigs had been in power, they had struck more and deeper at the liberties of Englishmen than the Tories, throughout the whole of their career—(hear, hear):— and I detest the Tories as much as any man can do. (Hear.) But this now proposed was one of the most infamous and barefaced attempts which ever had been attempted to be perpetrated against a nation's rights—(hear, hear);—and must be met, in its very first step, with determined opposition. (Hear, hear). I have no objection to a police force properly chosen, and put under proper controul—chosen by Universal Suffrage, and officered by themselves. (Hear.) There was a force something of this kind in Scotland, although chosen by the ten-pounders, and it worked so well as to shew that, if more fully carried out by a more extended constituency, it would answer all purposes. (Hear, hear.) Every individual in the executive should consider himself as a servant of the public. (Hear, hear.) Mr. Sankey sat down amid loud cheers by proposing an address, which we shall present to our readers next week.

Mr. O'CONNOR said that, in seconding Mr. Sankey, he would have

[1] For the background of this allusion see Part I, 7c.

but little to do, as that gentleman had sufficiently shown the propriety of the measure he advocated; but he could not help adverting to one or two circumstances. [The rest of O'Connor's speech was merely concerned with two specific instances of collusive abuse of justice by the police and magistrates of Ireland] ...

Mr. WHITTLE thought that there could not be doubt of the unanimity of feeling upon this point, and it was of such deep importance that the opinions of everyone ought to be known on it. (Hear.) He did not agree with Mr. Sankey that even if we had Universal Suffrage, any police would be advisable—its introduction was the first step to a despotism, and its general adoption synonymous with one. The old English law was that the Sheriff should call out the force of the country, and that force consisted of every male person in it. (hear.) Its object was to prevent the expression of the people dying under starvation [sic]. O'Connell, himself, is the prime aider and abettor in this infamous scheme—for infamous it is inasmuch as they are divided into horse and foot. Armed and equipped like soldiers, who keep their hats on in courts of justice, whose evidence is considered of more weight than anyone else, and some of whom he had seen to strike witnesses in open court. (Hear.) Mr. Whittle then amid loud cheers quoted the opinion of Lord John Russell, as under—"The force which shall be employed in the final overthrow of English liberty will not be a standing army; it will not march down to Westminster and dismiss the House of Commons, it will assume the guise of a guardian of order; it will fight no battles but with the body of the people, and shed no blood but that of labourers and mechanics. It will not establish a single despotism, but will uphold the tyrannical power to a host of corrupt senators, and half a million of local petty despots." Mr. Whittle after a very eloquent appeal sat down amid loud cheers.

Mr. RICHARDSON was glad to have an opportunity of speaking on this subject; Government thought the people of this country wanted protection; this was true; but not such protection as that Government would offer, the protection which wolves give to sheep, and calls the dissent it has made a peace. (Hear, hear.) The Government had departed from the ancient Constitution; and in direct ratio as they had so done, so had the people sunk deeper and deeper in misery. (Hear, hear.) ...

Dr. JOHN TAYLOR said, I have heard Mr. Sankey allude to the *gend'armerie* of France, and while I concur with him in the very great importance of this measure, I will strengthen his instance of the manner in which the police conspire by merely stating that in the year 1827 and

1828, when the Jesuits were anxious to find an excuse for consolidating their power by increasing the only force which, from a long system of bribery, they could rely on, the *gend'armerie*, by several regiments, endeavoured to withdraw the attention of the public from their insidious schemes, by endeavouring to create an alarm, in consequence of the number of murders and robberies which were committed at night in the streets of Paris, and the continuance of which they pretended called for increased police power. Belonging, as I did, to a society for watching these men, and opposing their influence over Charles the Tenth, I had occasion to traverse the streets at all hours, and never met with anything like a murderous attack. In two of the only five cases which came before the tribunal of police correctionable, and in one which went even to the higher tribunal, the police in disguise were found and proved to be the parties instigating to the affray, and taken in the very act, by the activity of the committee to which I belonged. (Cheers.) In order to keep up the panic, they had actually got dead bodies from the hospitals of La Petre and L'hotel Dieu, at which I was then a student, and having inflicted on them some wound of a knife or blow, they exposed them in the dead house, called *La Morgue*, as pretended proofs of the danger. Such are the means which a tyrannical government always adopts, such it will adopt with you, and this bill is the first step to it. (Hear.) You may submit to it in the South of England—the men of the North, I tell you will not. (Hear.) I know the men of Newcastle better. I know the men of Winlaton, of Carlisle, of Sunderland, and Wigton, and before such a system can be put in force there, you will hear of many a bloody struggle; and when all else has failed and England is subdued, every valley in Scotland shall be a battle-field, the union with England repealed, and the country one smoking desert ere such a force be permitted to exist. (Loud cheers.)

Messrs. NEESOM and PITKE[I]THLY followed on the same side, the former showing the vagabond conduct of the police at the Calthorpe Street meeting,[1] the latter read a letter (we think from Sutton-in-Ashfield) intimating that thirty of the metropolitan police had been sent down, nobody knew for what, and that they had so little to do, that hitherto they had been obliged to occupy their time in playing at snowballs and breaking windows.

---

[1] The Cold Bath Fields affray of 13 May 1833, when a Metropolitan policeman was stabbed to death. See G. Thurston, *The Clerkenwell Riot* (London, 1967).

Mr. CARPENTER made an excellent speech which we regret we cannot give at length, but which we must allude to as containing a very remarkable fact, viz. that the London police were never complained of when in an inefficient state, and the only reason he could now suppose why they were so anxious to interfere with the city police, which was confessedly on the most effective scale, was that the present Lord Mayor had employed the police under his command to see justice done to the poor and the starving, when the Devil Kings of Somerset House, and the coldblooded guardians wished them to starve in the streets. But he thought the motion might have gone a little further, and as London was the most corrupt corporation in the world, and did not deserve to be attended to, he would move an amendment only in so far as that the address should include the other counties mentioned in the proposed infamous bill. (Hear, hear.)

Dr. MACDOUALL seconded the amendment and took occasion to remark that Dr. Taylor was right when he said that no such bill should ever be permitted to affect Scotland. (Hear, hear.)

Dr. FLETCHER said that Mr. Macdouall had just remarked that if the people of England should submit to this bill, the men of Scotland would resist it. He (Mr. F.) would tell Mr. Macdouall that the men of the North of England would be as prompt to resist this invasion of their liberties as the men of Scotland could be. When the project first assumed a tangible form in the letter of Lord John Russell to the magistracy, the men of his own town, Bury, gathered to the number of 1500 without any public notice, and declared that no armed police should ever be introduced into their town. He agreed with Mr. Carpenter that this was a Rural Police Bill, but he must differ from that gentleman's opinion that the fact of seven counties submitting, if such should be the case, would justify the assumption that the rest of England would submit. The South had submitted to the New Poor Law, but Lancashire, Yorkshire, and the North of England generally, had declared their determination to resist, and they had effectually resisted. That law was not in virtual operation in any part of Lancashire. He was glad to see timid slaves, who were aiming this blow at our rights, shrink from their avowed intention to begin with Lancashire. He had been at some pains to teach the people of his district their right to resist violence from a peace officer. If they had used moral resistance against the New Poor Law, it was for the Government to say what kind of resistance this measure would be met with, but calmly and advisedly heard, and resisted it would be.'
(*The Northern Star*, 23 March 1839)

(d) The Right to Arm

(From the closing months of 1838 onwards, rank and file Chartists began to equip themselves with pikes and, to a lesser extent, with firearms. Recent scholarship[1] has blamed J. R. Stephens for launching them upon this foolish course, which resulted in the arrest of the leaders and the sowing of dissensions within the ranks. The debate in the Convention on 9 April 1839 shows, however, the pertinacity of the claim that arming was allowed by law.)

'MR. RICHARDSON brought forward the motion of which he had given notice long previously, and only delayed because so many members were absent, and he thought the question of such vital importance as to demand a full attendance. (Hear.) His motion was to have a committee to draw up a case to be submitted to Council [sic], relative to the power of the people under existing laws to provide themselves with arms, and as he (Mr. R.) thought this, the question of questions, the subject to which the minds of all were turned, both the government and the people, and it was of the utmost importance that the people should know exactly the ground upon which they stood. (Hear, hear.) The subject could no longer be blinked and it was with a view of putting the Convention in complete possession of the subject, that he was induced to bring forward this motion. (Hear.) Among the authorities cited by Mr. R to show the advantage and propriety of arming the people as the best guarantee for the liberties of a country, were many of the most celebrated amongst the patriots, generals, and statesmen of ancient and modern times. We would only particularly allude to Aristotle, Cicero, Sir Walter Raleigh, Fletcher of Salt Down, Major Cartwright, Marchmont Needam, Sir John Fortescue, Brackton, Alland Matthew of Westminster, Queen Elizabeth, Algernon Sidney, Sir W. Jones, Sir Wm. Blackstone, Sir Wm. Temple, Wilkins, Harrington, Hume, Dr. Johnson, Dr. Gilbert Stewart, the Earl of Liverpool, Cobbett, Granville Sharp, Arthur Young, Selden, Lord Coke, Locke, Trenchard, Bacon, Burnett, and Prynne, all of which spoke in unequivocal terms as to the fact that the possession of arms was the best proof of men being free, and the best security for their remaining so. Mr. R. then went into the legal authorities for the people arming themselves, and proved most satisfactorily, at once, his own knowledge of the constitutional history of his country, and the perfect right which belonged to the people to

---

[1] T. M. Kemnitz and Fleurance Jacques, 'J. R. Stephens and the Chartist Movement', *IRSH*, Vol. XIX, 1974, pp. 211–27.

prepare themselves for the worst. He observed that the laws were in themselves so complicated, and so hard to be understood, that it was impossible to avoid being subject to prosecution and indictment. (Hear, hear, hear, and cheers.) Yet not one of those laws denied the constitutional right of Englishmen to be armed; and until they took the advice of Sir William Jones, they would never be safe. Sir William Jones said that every man should have a strong firelock in his bedroom. (Hear, hear.)

The following are some of the acts to which Mr. Richardson alluded:—

Wilkins' Leges Angelo Saxoniae [sic].

The Year Bookes.

The 13 Edward I., by which constables were bound to inspect the arms of the people twice a year, and present defaulters.

The Statute of Winchester, which commanded every man to have arms in his house.

The 13 Henry IV., by which justices, Sheriffs, etc., were empowered to call for the assistance of all knights, gentlemen, yeomen, labourers, servants, and apprentices, above the age of 15, who were bound by the Statute of Winchester to have arms.

The 33 Henry VIII, by which every man was bound to possess himself with such arms as were then in use, and if a labourer had not arms, his master was bound to find them, and stop the value out of his wages.

The Act of James declaring that there was no necessity for having arms, but the propriety was not doubted.

The Bill of Rights, which declares that the subjects which are Protestants may have arms for their defence, according to their condition, and as allowed by law.

The 1 Geo. I., commonly called the Riot Act.

The Yeomanry Cavalry Act.

Dundas's Act.

The Game Laws.

The Six Acts.

In conclusion Mr. Richardson said, that there was no act of Parliament, nor any clause of any act of Parliament, which gave power to any magistrate, any justice of peace, any commander, or any Lord Lieutenant to call out the soldiers upon any occasion whatever. (Hear, hear.) The law only allowed of the calling out of the *posse comitatum* [sic] of the kingdom. (Hear.) At the present time the magistrates were acting contrary to law when they called out the troops on any occasion whatever. (Hear, hear.) If the people were in possession of their arms, Government would never dare to propose such a law as the New Rural Police Bill or the Poor Law Amendment Act. (Hear.) And, until Government knew that the country had availed themselves of their undoubted privilege, the statute-book would remain sullied by these blood-stained Acts. (Hear, hear.) He (Mr. R.) was not in favour of secret arming, neither, on the other hand, was he in favour of a display of arms at public meetings: yet he wished it to be known to the Government that they were armed, and he would even say that he had no objection to a Registration Act, provided it was founded upon the principle of the 33 Henry VIII, which allowed the undoubted right of men to be armed. (Hear, hear.)

MR. BRONTERRE O'BRIEN seconded the motion.

DR. FLETCHER moved as an amendment—"That we should not take any legal advice on the subject, but that this Convention is fully convinced that all constitutional authorities agreed in the undoubted right of the people to possess arms." (Hear, hear, hear.)

Dr. MACDOUALL seconded the amendment, because it would be like throwing a doubt upon the right of the people, if they took the advice of any lawyer on the subject. (Hear, hear.)

MR. HARNEY had intended to move an amendment to the effect that a committee of six should be appointed to draw up an address to the country, shewing their right to possess arms. He would, however, for the sake of unanimity, support Dr. Fletcher's amendment.

MR. BRONTERRE O'BRIEN defended the line of conduct proposed by Mr. Richardson, as being useful in shewing the people the authority on which they were acting.

MR. O'CONNOR thought that O'Brien had mistaken both the law and the prophets, and the proposal to take legal advice would be dangerous as placing them, in some measure, at the mercy of a lawyer, who might be a rogue, and perhaps succeed in arming the people with a halter round their necks. (Hear.) Let the opinion be what it might, it would not, however favourable, add ten stand of arms to those now in use, and if unfavourable, they would have to go to work with a halter round their necks. (Hear, hear.)

MR. HUSSEY followed on the same side, because both he and Mr. Richardson had all along been telling the people of their right to arm, and it would look a little singular if they now went to a lawyer to ask if what they had been saying were true. (Hear, hear.)

MR. DUNCAN supported Mr. Richardson.

MR. SANKEY supported the amendment of Dr. Fletcher.

MR. LOVETT would support the original motion.

MR. HALLEY ridiculed the idea of arming, because even if we were armed, we were not in a position to take any steps to obtain any good. He supposed they would next have a commissariat department and drill sergeants. (Loud cries of "Oh, oh, oh.") Very few of the country had yet joined them (Cries of "Oh, oh," and "Question".) Very few had signed the petition ("No, No," from every quarter.) He would have nothing to do with any thing but moral means, and he did not consider the entertainment of this question one of them. He moved the previous question, which, after long delay, found a seconder in MR. BURNS, who said that he did so, not from any fear of speaking of arming, but because he thought the time for considering the question would be after the petition had been presented.

MR. CARDO repudiated the opinion of Mr. Halley, that the speaking of arming had done havoc in the North (Hear, hear). He had been through a great part of the North lately, and he could assure the Convention that it was quite the reverse. (Loud cheers.)

MR. ROGERS had learned the doctrine of the rights of man in the school of Major Cartwright, and had continued in the same view to the present day. He did not think that, properly speaking, the Convention had any thing to do with the matter; the country had armed itself independently of the Convention, and would continue to do so, therefore he would support the previous question. (Hear, hear.)

MR. CARPENTER would not approve of getting quit of the question by moving the previous question, and being opposed to the motion he would support the amendment.

MR. COLLINS supported the previous question.

MR. DEEGAN spoke in favour of the amendment.

MR. MOORE thought the amendment of Dr. Fletcher pregnant with mischief, and would therefore support the amendment.

MR. RIDER AND MR. MARSDEN could assure the Convention, that so far as the cause was now concerned, it mattered very little whether the motion of Mr. Richardson were carried or not, for they were quite sure the country would care very little for the opinion of any lawyer whatever. (Hear, hear.) Mr. Marsden knew that in one street alone, twenty muskets had been procured.

MR. RICHARDSON replied at some length, and with great minuteness, when the votes were taken.

The following was the state of the votes:—

For Mr. Richardson's motion, 4; for the previous question, 6; and for Dr. Fletcher's amendment, 19.'

(*The Northern Star*, 13 April 1839)

5. *Monarchy versus Republicanism*

(a) Speculative Republicanism

(The *English Chartist Circular* was a short-lived experiment in cheap but educative journalism. A weekly, originally priced at one halfpenny, it ran only from 1841–2. It was the organ of teetotal Chartism, part of the moderate wing of the movement, which broke with O'Connor in April 1841 and continued in alliance with middle-class reformers. From such a quarter, the article which follows affords impressive evidence of the survival of theoretical republicanism among the self-educated artisans, who so much fashioned the intellectual culture of Chartism, but it also demonstrates how far its authors were from advocating the republican cause as a practical political issue.)

'MONARCHISM AND REPUBLICANISM CONTRASTED

A monarchy is in itself a state which no one can contemplate with any patience or satisfaction. Live under a monarchy you may, and live under it in peace and submission, because we may consider it as our duty so to conduct ourselves, as not to disturb the peace of the society of which we form a part, but to yield an entire approbation to its institutions; to submit one's capacity to all its follies and its anomalies, *that*, in our opinion, is not possible for an honest and a sensible man to do.

It would be no very difficult matter to prove that whenever monarchies deviate into republics they always do so to the improvement and elevation of mankind, and to the bettering of the condition of the human beings whom such change concerns. It would not be difficult to prove also the converse of this proposition, which is that whenever republics merge in monarchies, the human race in those monarchies suffer a deterioration, and the people become more wretched and debased. Now we are not arguing in favour of republics, for two reasons. *Firstly*, because it would ill become us living under a monarchy to hold such opinions. *Secondly*, because if we were to hold such arguments our readers would not attend to them. No! our opinions are merely speculative, and are rather taken up as amusing objects of meditation than as matters on which we hope to convince. We assert it, aye! and we are ready to maintain the opinion, too, against all, that when monarchies deviate into republics, they render men happy, and when republics deviate into monarchies, they render them wretched. Nay! we will go further than that and assert, that monarchies, are political machines, are the mere *commencement* of civilization, and that all monarchies must—if the human race advance in improvement—end in republics. These are facts we lay down, and it only remains for us to prove the truth of our opinions. It will be admitted, we presume, that the ancient states of Greece and Rome began in the establishment of pure tyrannies, and afterwards deviated, when the people became more improved, into republics. Republics were then the offspring of improvement in those countries; and if this conclusion be not allowed, we know not what other can.'

(*The English Chartist Circular*, Vol. I, No. 3, c. February 1841)

(b) Practical Republicanism: A Division of Opinion

(Thomas Cooper, the Leicester Chartist, once the most fervent of O'Connor worshippers, was already estranged from his Chief when he left Stafford gaol in May 1845, after serving a sentence of two years imprisonment for seditious conspiracy during the Plug Plot. A private letter penned by Cooper, which was critical of O'Connor, had been maliciously shown to Feargus by Jonathan Bairstow, a renegade disciple of Cooper. O'Connor responded by accusing Cooper publicly of a design to overthrow him. Cooper riposted in kind. When, just before his release, he received an invitation from the secretary of the Shakespearian Brigade of Chartists to return to Leicester as a leader, he published his reply in the form of a blistering pamphlet. In this he explained the grounds of his own criticisms of O'Connor. This extract from it relates primarily to one of these: a lecture delivered by the latter at Newcastle-upon-Tyne on 9 October 1844 entitled 'Chartism v. Republicanism'. Afraid of some undefined but anticipated bid from outside to turn the flank of Chartism from its original purpose, O'Connor had attacked the American system of four-yearly presidential elections as being unstabilizing and republicanism as being liable to 'degenerate into licentiousness'. While not arguing a positive case for English royalty, he claimed that what mattered was to vest power in the whole people, not to substitute an elective head of state for an hereditary one. He made it clear that to accept the name 'Republican' would draw down on the Chartists 'another ten years of reckless prosecutions and persecutions'.[1])

'... I remember, perfectly well, that in that letter I termed Mr. O'Connor a "rash and vindictive man." I thought him "rash" for attempting to thwart Crawford's motion for "Stopping the Supplies", and for lecturing

[1] *The Northern Star*, 19 October 1844. I am indebted to Dr. D. J. Rowe of the University of Newcastle-upon-Tyne for this reference.

against Republicanism, at Newcastle-on-Tyne. The latter act of his, especially, roused me. You all know my preference for a Republic to a Monarchy. I do not want us to go back to the feudalism of the Middle Ages: I am for advancing. You all know that I have declared again and again, in your market place, that I would not give a fig for the Charter, if I did not believe it would lead to our entire deliverance from Kingcraft and priestcraft; to the grand Community; the universal Brotherhood; the diffusion of such *real* Equality that none should be privileged to revel in splendour while others starve; none should claim the land exclusively for theirs, but the entire soil become the heritage of the whole People; none should be exempt from labour of some kind, and, consequently, labour itself, by being equally and generally shared, should become mere exercise, especially now science is so rapidly disclosing to mankind the means of existing without the bodily slavery that has degraded the human race for ages. I repeat, *you know* that these are my views: Mr. Buchanan and Mr. Campbell, the Socialist lecturers, know that these are my views, for they found that my views and theirs were identical on all these points, in the discussion that I held with them, in the Amphitheatre, and which turned out to be *no contest*.

Now, it seemed to me, that in lecturing against Republicanism, Mr. O'Connor was undoing what Paine and Owen, and a host of enlightened spirits had been aiming to do, for long years. I was alarmed at this. How could it be otherwise, with the views I entertain; with the sentiments that have been growing in me, I may say, almost from childhood? I became a Republican in opinion at 14 years of age, and my preferences for a purely democratic form of government have strengthened with years. Was it likely I could read of O'Connor's attacking this, my favourite doctrine, and not feel excited? Was it likely, that, with my views, I could fail to think he was doing a real injury, instead of a good, to the cause of Liberty, (the cause for which I am in a dungeon), by this course of procedure? And then, can any one wonder that a poor solitary, suffering from numerous afflictive causes, should write with some degree of sharpness, under such a belief? ...'

[The remainder of the *Letter* fastens upon O'Connor's obstruction of Sharman Crawford's scheme to give teeth to the Complete Suffrage movement by blocking essential government.]

('A Letter to the Working Men of Leicester', by Thomas Cooper, Stafford Gaol, 12 March 1845; Howell Collection, Bishopsgate Institute.)

(c) The Young Queen Victoria Through Chartist Eyes

'DID YOU EVER SEE THE QUEEN?

YES. The first time and the last time I ever saw her was when she went down in February, 1839, to open the Parliament of do-nothings. On that very day I took my seat in the Parliament of the workers, the old Convention. Craig, of Kilmarnock was in the chair, and Douglas, Hadley, Salt, and Pierce* of Birmingham, were sitting at the head of the table. I mention their names on account of a rather extraordinary circumstance which took place. There was apparent anxiety on the part of these men to hurry over the proceedings on that day, and I recollect that O'Connor and O'Brien were moving resolutions, etc., which were likely to protract the sitting to late in the afternoon, when Douglas rose to move an adjournment. His chief reason for so doing was because the queen was going down to open Parliament at two o'clock and some of the members would be anxious to see her. A murmur arose amongst the members, some smiled, some laughed outright, others, the very few however, remonstrated. "Did you ever see the queen?" was the prevailing question amongst the strangers.

I felt a slight desire to see her myself, not because I was curious to witness the folly of John Bull, or look at a child's show. No. I had a far higher object in view. I wanted to witness her reception amongst the people, and thereby be enabled to test the public mind as to its folly, gullibility, and loyalty.

No one in the Convention made a counter motion to that of Douglas, and I think, without voting, we agreed to adjourn. What have become of those sight-seers now? Of these men, who for the sake of looking at a toy, actually suspended the business of the workman's Parliament. The moment that its displeasure was expressed through the medium of a proclamation, they fled and outran even the long-legged attorney-general. I walked slowly down towards the Horse Guards after we had dissolved the Convention, and I was really surprised to see the stream of passengers flowing in its usual current, past Charing Cross and up and down Fleet-street, as if nothing remarkable was going on. The hackney coachmen were on the stand as usual, their bare bone hacks were quietly nipping the hay from the bundle hung at their heads, the coal-heavers were taking their drowsy walk into the gin palace, and I saw one street-sweeper who had even time to lean on his broom and blow his nose. Well, I thought, as I walked along, this is cockney loyalty, is it? I was more than ever impelled onwards. I encountered a line of policemen

---

* Pierce is since drowned in New Zealand

extended across the street above the Horse Guards, to prevent the passage of coaches, carts, etc.

This was the first evidence of the neighbourhood of royalty. On I went and I saw a crowd of persons extending from the gates of the Horse Guards, across the street; they were lined within with policemen and several of the Guards were mounted, and stationed on either side of the gateway.

The crowd could not be more than three or four deep, including the policemen; and so little notice did they attract, that the stream of passengers flowed on either side of the street, as if they were well aware that a ceremony was going on with which they had nothing to do, and about which they never inquired. "Have a stand, sir," said a ragged orangeman, carrying his box under his arm. I could not see over the heads of the people, therefore I said to him, "What is your charge?" "Sixpence, sir." "Well, put it down, I'll have a sixpenny look at the queen, any how." Down went the box and up I mounted, just as the show began. First there came an officer, prancing on a horse, and seemingly sweating at a great rate, but nobody could tell the reason why the poor fellow was thus punishing himself and the animal he rode. I wonder whether he would be so valiant before an enemy, or so anxious to "move on." Then came more soldiers looking very fierce, as if they had got a good breakfast, and were working for a better dinner. Out came six horses next, all covered with harness and gilt brass, and looking as if they were better fed and housed than the majority of on-lookers; at the head of each, on one side, walked a footman, whose only business seemed to be to cover his silk stockings and pumps with mud. "By the Holy Father," said an Irishman beside me, "there is work for the washer-woman, bad luck to you, you overgrown moth; does your mother know you are out? Hard feeling to you, you big-bellied thief; murder alive, look at the gould on the coach." All eyes were directed to the coach which the six fat horses dragged out from beneath the gateway. Coach after coach followed, and a most vinegar expression seemed to adorn the face of the working men near me. "Who pays for all this finery," said a decent looking artisan at my side; a great powerful coal-heaver swung round his slouched hat, "who pays, did yer harsk? why who but sich like as me and you," and three or four coal-heavers gave a great chuckle at the supposed ignorance of the inquirer. "We could do with less I think." "It would be better for Old England," said another fustian jacket, "if the damned German crew had been sunk in the channel." "Aye, the curse of Cromwell on every mother's son of

them." "Or rather another Cromwell to go down to the house instead of
the queen," remarked I, extremely delighted with the deep seated
discontent expressed by my neighbours. Several looked up at me with a
doubting glance, but it was only for a moment. "You are right." "Aye,
by G—d, that's it," said several. "Here comes little Vic.," said several.
Now was the great test to be applied. Out came the soldiers, then the
horses, then the state carriage, like a great big candlestick, in the centre of
which was stuck our young queen, as yellow as a penny candle, and
about equally as attractive. Three hats, in truth not more, were raised, a
ghost of a cheer sounded like the expiring whine of a dying kitten. The
poor thing looked as if she wished to please, or wanted a cheer. The mass
of hats were nailed to the heads of the wearers; every mouth was sealed.
Meantime, as the heavy machine lumbered on, a deep murmur arose.
"More taxes." "Give us bread." "Where is the Charter?" And as the
carriage went on, one deep and terrible voice arose, hoarse and loud
above all, "Damnation to the hellish Poor Law."

The queen started, turned her head quickly round, she looked
fluttered: she passed on. I descended from my orange box. "Vic., Vic.,
the taper of loyalty is put out," and walking away, I thought of her with
compassion. "Poor thing, and you, you a child, and a girl too, are
destined to wield the sceptre, when millions are on the move, and the
surge of a revolution is even seething the footstool of thy feeble throne.
God help thee, for thou art not so much to blame as the system which
supports thee, and the fools that have put thee where thou art." This was
the first time I saw a queen: I hope it may be the last.'
(*McDouall's Chartist and Republican Journal*, 3 April 1841)

6. *Parliament and Parliamentary Elections*
(a) Chartists and Anti-Parliament: the Short Cut to Power
(The view that the people of England might circumvent a corrupt and
recalcitrant parliament by electing delegates of their own to legislate in
its place went back to Paine and other radicals of the late eighteenth
century. Sometimes, as in the 'legislatorial attorneys' plan of 1819, it was
envisaged that the people's representatives would demand admission to
parliament itself. Early Chartism developed this idea. In June 1837, just
before the general election on the accession of Queen Victoria, Bronterre
O'Brien unfolded his hustings plan, whereby the unenfranchized masses
would muster at the nomination of parliamentary candidates in the
constituencies and secure the adoption of Chartist leaders by show of
hands. Disregarding the subsequent poll, in which only electors could
participate, the popular candidates would then present themselves at

Westminster. How they would establish themselves there was a question which O'Brien, a moderate, did not choose to face. Probably he aimed merely at a demonstration which would frighten the government. At a meeting on Town Moor, Newcastle-upon-Tyne, on 20 May 1839, called to approve the ulterior measures proposed by the Convention, the extremist Harney propounded a clear-cut solution. Fortunately, it was never adopted, but the General commanding the troops in the Northern district laid plans to intercept any march on London from the provinces, in the Derbyshire valleys. The *Northern Star* prudently omitted those portions of Harney's speech which recommended violence against M.P.s. The account which follows is taken from the *Northern Liberator*.)

' ... MR. RUCASTLE, chemist, moved the third resolution, which he regretted had not fallen into abler hands. He was glad to see that, in spite of intimidation, they had come forward in such force. Mr. R read the resolution as follows:—

"That should the Convention deem it necessary in the event of a general election, to have Chartist candidates put in nomination for every county and Borough in the United Kingdom, this meeting pledges itself to carry out, as far as possible, this recommendation of the Convention. [seconded John Blakey] ..."

MR. HARNEY spoke in support of the resolution. He was received with a loud and long cheer. That cheer told him that they loved him still. This was indeed a glorious spectacle; the true representatives of the people had called upon the men whom they represented to come forth in their strength, in their might, and in their majesty, and declare, in the face of heaven, that themselves and their children should be free. He had to propose one of the most important resolutions that could be submitted to them. It was this—That, in the event of a general election, would the people of England elect their representatives as their fathers elected them? ("We will.") They were to call upon every man to vote by holding up their right hands—and those representatives were not to be sent to London as a petitioning body—the question he wished to ask them was were they prepared to elect their representatives and carry them into the House of Commons. The £50 of expense was only move the first; were they prepared to make move the second? (Loud cheers, and shouts of "We are, we are".) How would they do it? To send those representatives singly would be to send them to destruction. When they would knock at the door of the House they would be told that they had no business there, and that no one was admitted there except on business; and if their representatives knocked a second time they would be apt to have their brains knocked out. Let them have nothing to do with the poll except the vote of every man present was recorded—let them be satisfied with a show of hands. Let the shopocrats go to the poll, and, if they liked, let them send their representatives to London; the people should also send theirs, or, rather, they should take them there, for fear of any mistake. The men around him had been kind to him (Mr. H.)—they had shown him much hospitality, and, in return, he could not do less than invite them to London. (Loud cheers.) There was plenty of room for them there—there were fine houses in the West End, and they would have nothing to do but "knock and it should be opened unto them." (Loud laughter and cheers). But they would require to go with a well armed body-guard; that was the only way to ensure an entrance into the Commons' House. Perhaps what he said was not constitutional—perhaps it was—for he had heard much of the British Constitution, and, like Paine, he never could find out what it was.

" 'tis this, 'tis that, 'tis t'other thing.

'tis everything, 'tis nothing."

If the working men elected their representatives, they must see them safely into the House of Commons, through the Horse Guards, down Parliament Street, and into the old House of Corruption itself; and if, when they arrived there, they found that the Shopocrats' nominees had taken up the place, he would say to these fellows "Make way for better men!"—(loud cheers)—and, if they did not, he would say let them be kicked out, or, if they were hot enough for a "skrimmage", it might do them good to get a cool ducking in the Thames. (Tremendous cheers.) Were they prepared to carry out the resolution? (Yes, yes.) Were they tired of the present House of Commons, or rather he should call it House of Thieves? Were they prepared to support the humble individual who stood before them if he put up for their suffrages? Were they prepared to support Taylor?—Would they support Lowery? Would they support the brave Scotchman who had that day stood before them?—(To each of these interrogatories a loud affirmative was responded, followed by tremendous cheers.) Well, then, he believed the days of the present house were almost numbered, and that the Convention would shortly be in office in its stead. The difference of opinion that had once existed in that body had all disappeared: there were in it neither physical force or moral force men, but a shade between the two—they were physico-moral-force men. The people had learned them their duty, and here they were prepared to do that duty, whatever might betide. (Loud cheers.) He was pleased at their removal to Birmingham, as London was a rotten place, and would be till the rottenness was cleared out by the energy, virtue, and determination of the country, and, more especially, of the men of the North. Let them be determined to have their rights, peacably if they could, forcibly if they must. He was one who said but little, but it might be well understood that he meant a great deal more than he said.

"God is our guide from field, from wave,

From plough, from anvil, and from loom:

We come our country's rights to save—

To break the slumber of the tomb.

We will—we will—we will be free,

Our sacred watch-word liberty!"

(loud and long cheering.)—The chairman then put the resolution which was carried by acclamation.'

(*The Northern Liberator*, 25 May 1839)

(b) Chartists at the Polls, 1841

(Though the 1832 Reform Act established a mainly middle-class electorate, the Chartists possessed some direct voting potential. In some large towns, where the rateable value of property was high, the ten-pound householder qualification brought in working men, while others qualified as ancient right voters. A parliamentary return for 1866 estimated that 26 per cent of the borough voters were working class.[1] In strongly working-class communities like Oldham[2] the votes of small shopkeepers, publicans and farmers could be influenced by exclusive dealing. At the general election of 1841 the Chartists endeavoured to test their strength. O'Connor advised them to support the Conservatives against the Whigs, but in some constituencies candidates stood in the Chartist interest, with results described in a sympathetic source.)

'CHARTIST CANDIDATES AT ELECTIONS.

The Chartists of Great Britain have made a constitutional effort to carry their point; but, we are sorry to say, in consequence of the want of a well defined plan to act upon, aided by sound legal advice in the elections, they have not been able to carry on the good work in an organised and effective manner. The squabbling of leaders has contributed in no small degree to weaken the masses! and the personal denunciations, and scurrilous language used in many towns by over-zealous and mistaken friends, have done much to injure our cause. Such has been the amount of odium incurred by the Chartists in consequence

[1] J. Vincent, *The Formation of the Liberal Party 1857–1868* (London, 1966), p. 105.
[2] See J. Foster, *Class Struggle and the Industrial Revolution*, pp. 52–6.

of their foolish demonstrations in many places, that it has been a matter of considerable difficulty to procure even movers and seconders of Chartist candidates at elections. The letters we have received from various places upon this subject, convince us that, if the unenfranchised really wish to succeed, they must be more sparing in their denunciations and abuse of that class who almost exclusively possess the votes. Whatever we may think of the conduct of the middle class towards the poor unenfranchised slave class, we must bear in mind that we have an object to gain; that object is, a Radical change in the representation of the people in the Commons' House. This can only be attained by one of two courses—*argumentum adjudetium*, by an appeal to the common sense of mankind; or *vi et armis*, by force of arms. By appealing from the hustings to the electors present in behalf of the non-electors present and absent, we discharge one of the noblest duties of a patriot; but, as the law now stands, we require two ten-pound voters before we can avail ourselves of the opportunity of appealing to our fellow-countrymen in behalf of the poor and unrepresented. In many places the Chartists have been unable to procure two ten-pound voters, who possess sufficient nerve, to come forward upon a hustings to propose candidates in opposition to the yelling, hisses, groans, and other factious disturbances; or who could afterwards bear up against the odium and persecution that generally follows the nomination of Chartist candidates. Under these circumstances we ought to be very chary in our steps, and as politic in our views as will render the powers that be subservient to our purpose. In Northampton, P. M. McDouall stood forward in the Chartist interest, and obtained 176 ten-pound votes; this was not a step, but a stride towards the attainment of our grand object. How was this effected, may be asked? Why, by the calm and dispassionate reasoning of Collins and Vincent, who have from time to time visited them, and not by fiery denunciations and terrible anathemas calculated to destroy every hope of success, and every chance of making progress. Let Northampton be a lesson to the people of the manufacturing towns in the north of England. In Marylebone (London), W. S. V. Sankey, Esq., obtained 76 votes of honest ten-pounders; and we are confident that, if the vote by ballot had been in force, even with the present suffrage, Sankey would have gained many hundred more votes. In Aberdeen, R. Lowery contested the election in the Chartist interest, and secured the support of 30 ten-pound voters. In Banbury, Henry Vincent gloriously contested the pocket-borough of the Marquis of Bute; and by his honest, manly, and temperate course, secured a number of votes. In Glasgow Mr. Mills contested the election against Whig and Tory, and succeeded in recording 314 honest ten-pound votes. J. Moir withdrew from the contest. These are the only boroughs contested by Chartists, except Hull, contested by our old friend the Colonel; who, we are sorry to say, from some strange cause or other, lost the election. We fancy he made himself too sure of Hull, which induced him to refuse several places where he might have been returned. We believe Dundee would have returned Colonel Thompson, had he been here in time, in preference to the hermaphrodite politician they have now for an M.P. We would enjoin the independent voters of Northampton, Marylebone, Aberdeen, and Banbury to form from their number a Registration Committee, in their respective towns, to watch the march of events, and employ them in securing those who are in the least inclined to support the cause of Universal Suffrage: register them if they are qualified, and keep them constantly in tow, that they may be ready at a moment's notice to poll for a good man; preserve them from the polluting breath of faction, and the contaminating touch of Whig and Tory gold, and let independence and purity of election be their guide, and success will ultimately crown their efforts.'

(Richardson Newspaper Cuttings, Manchester Central Reference Library)

(c) The Registration of Voters Movement[1]
(In 1843 Sir James Graham's new English Registration Act transferred appeals in disputes over the registration of electors from the House of Commons to the Court of Common Pleas. The Court signalized its new jurisdiction by a sequence of decisions interpreting the £10 franchise in a liberal sense. This encouraged the Chartists to follow the parliamentary parties and the Anti-Corn Law League into the battle for political power through the electoral registers. On 21 May 1844 the Executive Committee of the National Charter Association issued an address announcing a plan to return twenty Chartist M.P.s at the next general election by 'attending to the Parliamentary and Municipal Registry, and raising a Missionary Fund.' Edmund Stallwood became General Registration Secretary and local Registration Committees were formed. The intention was that the desired 20 M.P.s should obtain the People's Charter by holding the balance between the two main parties in the House of Commons and by exploiting parliamentary procedures to hold up government business. Some initial success in increasing the

[1] In writing this comment I have benefited from a University of Southampton undergraduate dissertation by R. I. Megan entitled 'English Radicals and the Movement for the Registration of Voters, 1832–48'. For the interpretation of events I must myself bear the responsibility.

ratepayers on the electoral roll was reported, principally in London. But, although a more co-ordinated initiative was taken in August 1846, as the fall of Peel's ministry increased hopes of a general election, a mainly apathetic response was still encountered. The movement suffered from being launched at a time when Chartism was in the doldrums. Nevertheless, by the act of initiating it, O'Connor was forced to admit that the franchise established in 1832 did not wholly prevent a working-class movement from resorting to ordinary parliamentary procedures.)

'CHARTISTS
REGISTER!   REGISTER!!   REGISTER!!!
REVISING BARRISTERS' DECISIONS

A return of the appeals from the Courts of the Revising Barristers to the Court of Common Pleas, pursuant to the Act 6th and 7th Victoria, cap. 18 (the new English Registration Act), shows that the total number of appeals, including both counties and boroughs, has amounted to thirteen, on the hearing of which the judgement of the Court was pronounced in favour of the appellants in only three cases, and for the respondents in ten.

No order respecting the payment of the costs of any of these appeals has been made by the Court of Common Pleas, it not having appeared that any of the cases were frivolous or vexacious.

The following points relating to cities and boroughs are amongst those decided:—

1—"That any number of rooms in a building, such rooms being each of £10 annual value, and let separately to different occupiers, is sufficient to confer a qualification.

2—"That the name of such occupiers, being inserted in the rate-book jointly with that of the landlord, is sufficient rating, and the payment of the rates by the landlord is sufficient payment on the part of such occupiers.

3—"A servant occupying a house not used for the purpose of his employer's business, but occupied by him for his own use, the rent being paid by him in his services, is held to be tenant, and entitled in respect of such occupation.

4—"The payment of rates by the landlord, in consideration of services performed by the occupier, who is rated, is held to be a sufficient payment by the occupier himself.

5—"A cowhouse or stable, of sufficient value, will give a qualification.

6—"Property situated in a borough, and of a description that will not give a qualification for the borough, will, if it be such as is required for county voters, confer on the owner the right of voting for the county.

7—"In cases of successive occupation of different premises, the voter must have all such premises as are required to make up the twelve months' 'occupation' inserted in the list of voters.

8—"Delivering to the post-master's managing clerk the duplicates and objections, for the purpose of posting, stamping, and comparing, is a delivery for the purposes of the Registration Act, to the postmaster.

9—"Where a servant rents a house belonging to the master, but which he is permitted to occupy only for the more efficient discharge of the duties of his situation, there is no relation of landlord and tenant, and he will be disqualified from voting in the borough in which such house is situated.

In addition to the committees announced in the *Star*, a Registration Committee sits every Wednesday and Friday, at the Golden Lion, Dean-street, Soho; and one for the Tower Hamlets at the Standard of Liberty, Brick-lane, Spitalfields. Every information afforded on application to EDMUND STALLWOOD,

General Registration Secretary,

  Executive Office,

    243½ Strand, London.'

(*The Northern Star*, 25 May 1844)

'THE ST. PANCRAS REGISTRATION AND ELECTION COM-MITTEE TO THE CHARTIST PUBLIC AND WORKING CLASSES GENERALLY

Friends and Brothers,

In August last year your representatives met in Convention at Leeds delegated by you for the especial purpose of devising and recommending for your adoption such plans for future agitation as they in their wisdom might consider to be the best calculated to ensure the enactment of the People's Charter.

With the important questions that occupied their deliberations, and their wise decisions thereon, you are already cognisant, therefore we will not here enumerate them, but proceed to state that the object of this address is to call your serious attention to that which we consider to be the most important of their recommendations, viz., "That a determined, energetic, and united effort be made to return to the House of Commons at the next general election ten or twelve stern, incorruptible, and unflinching advocates of the people's cause. Men imbued with democracy and patriotism, whose spirits, burning with freedom's sacred fire, would fearlessly expose and denounce the wrongs, and never rest until they had wrung from the tyrant factions those equal and inalienable rights which are justly due to the sons of labour".

We contend that this is neither visionary nor utopian, but sound and good policy, and as we fully agree with Brother Wild of Mottram, that "The House of Commons is the place for the discussion and promulgation of our principles, and that the Charter cannot become law until our lawmakers are made to understand it," we therefore hail it as the best and most practical plan that can be propounded.

That this noble project might be efficiently carried out, the Conference also recommended that Registration and Election Committees be forthwith formed in every city, borough, town, village, and hamlet, and likewise that a central committee be elected to sit in London to concentrate and direct.

The central committee has been elected, they have met week after week, they have drawn up and printed for general circulation, addresses and forms of claims for registration, and they have solicited your cooperation. The utility, the magnitude, the vitality of the question has been urged on your attention through the columns of our democratic organ, and, although four months have elapsed since the Convention met, yet the central committee have not received any communication or support from you, excepting an application from the Glasgow friends for a quantity of addresses ...

We are prepared to do our part with the greatest alacrity, but, until we ascertain what amount of support we are to expect from such places as Manchester, Leeds, Nottingham, Birmingham, Sheffield, etc., we feel a diffidence in exerting our energies, therefore, let us at once understand each on this matter. Let there be no delay. The general election will soon be here. Let us be prepared. Let us not have the soul harrowing and heart burning reflection, that had we been united and energetic we could have conquered. Away then with apathy. Rally round the committee, and agitate! agitate! agitate!

Signed on behalf of the committee,

WILLIAM FARRIS, Chairman.

JOHN ARNOTT, Secretary.'

(*The Northern Star*, 12 December 1846)

7 *Local Government*

(Benjamin Wilson of Skircoat Green near Halifax was a working man who joined the Chartist movement in, or before, 1839. Employed successively as a farm worker, bobbin winder, weaver, wool comber, railway navvy and quarryman, he earned over several years wages averaging less than nine shillings per week. The bid of the working classes, which he describes in the two following passages, to intervene effectively, first in the politics of Skircoat township, and then in the municipal affairs of Halifax, after that town was incorporated as a borough in 1848, was not without precedent elsewhere. As early as about 1812 the radicals of Oldham began to establish over the township vestries and other organs of local government a stranglehold which lasted for about a quarter of a century, and was used to paralyze action against riots and industrial violence. This is admitted to have been 'somewhat exceptional',[1] but a more responsible interest in local issues was present in Chartism from the beginning, and became increasingly influential as the movement progressed. In the middle and later 'forties Chartists scored notable successes in capturing the offices of overseer, churchwarden, constable and surveyor, and became town councillors in a number of boroughs. The strength of municipal Chartism should not be over-estimated. At Leeds, one of its strongholds, there were never more than seven or eight Chartists at any one time out of a council of sixty-four members, and they were mainly small tradesmen, not working men.[2] But the phenomenon had its value. By harnessing the hitherto untamed energies of primitive democracy in the hearts of the people to existing workable institutions, it helped to build up representative local government in Britain.)

(a) Township Politics

'The bulk of the people, particularly the working classes of Skircoat, took no part or interest in the township's business. Though they had been struggling to have a voice in national affairs, they did not see the importance of local affairs, which were left in the hands of a few rich men, who took a deep interest in national affairs as well. The first vestry meeting I attended would be about the year 1843; I was the only working man present—working men scarcely ever attending those meetings then; there being about twelve gentlemen present, comprised several of the largest ratepayers in the township. I felt uncomfortable, and wished I was nicely out. Mr. Robert Wainhouse was chairman, and when he put a motion to the meeting he looked on the table and said—"Carried unanimously, I suppose." The board of surveyors, numbering ten or twelve gentlemen, were appointed at these meetings, for the management of the highways. They always took care that the roads near

[1] J. Foster, *Class Struggle and the Industrial Revolution* (London, 1974), *passim*.
[2] J. F. C. Harrison, 'Chartism in Leeds' in Asa Briggs ed., *Chartist Studies* (London, 1959), pp. 90–1.

their own residences were kept in good repair, although the roads in other parts were in a wretched condition; great improvements were also made on private property for which the township had to pay. I travelled the roads regularly with a horse and cart for two years, and what I say is no exaggeration of the facts. The thing became so glaring that it began to open the people's eyes, as it had certainly opened mine; to be a political reformer was not all; there were other things requiring looking into besides those at London, and in this case the greatest requirement appeared to be a man with the moral courage to expose the surveyors' actions in their proper place. We had not long to wait, for a man to the front who was equal to the occasion, Mr. James Longbottom, who spent a great amount of time and trouble in the people's cause. The agitation now begun lasted some ten or twelve years, and the struggle was as fierce as any that I have ever witnessed in the political movement. It was several years before we could make any headway; the great amount of influence that was brought to bear against us was such as I had never anticipated, for actually numbers of men were brought to the meetings with their managers, and I have seen employers stand on the benches to see how their men voted. Seeing at last that this did not answer another trick was resorted to,—"a requisition was signed to call a public meeting to take into consideration the desirability of adopting the Small Tenement Act." If they could have carried this, landlords paying the rates of small occupiers would have deprived them of the right to attend meetings. Mr. Longbottom waited upon Mr. Thorpe and other gentlemen who had come [to] reside in Skircoat to attend the meeting held in the large room of the workhouse at Scarr Bottom, which was crowded; Mr. Geo. Haigh and Mr. Thorpe were both proposed and seconded as the chairman, and although the former declined, they were put to the vote when Mr. Thorpe was carried by ten to one. In consequence of numbers being unable to get in, the meeting adjourned to a larger room at the Copley Arms, which was also crowded, about three hundred persons being present. The Chairman called upon the requisitionists, but no-one came forward, and the Chairman said he hoped the thing would never be attempted again. Skircoat at this time was thinly populated, and sent one Guardian to the Union, for which office Mr. Longbottom was nominated, and after thoroughly canvassing the township we succeeded in electing him; he rendered good service to the poor people at the Union.'

(*The Struggles of an Old Chartist*, by Benjamin Wilson of Salterhebble, (Halifax, 1887), pp. 7–8; the work is undated but the date

1887 is assigned to it in the catalogue of the Leeds Central Reference Library, where the edition from which this and the following extract were selected, is held.)

(b) Municipal Elections

'The first Municipal Election for Councillors in Halifax took place in May, 1847. The late parliamentary election and the defeat of Jones and Miall left their friends in a fit state for the coming election, and it soon became evident that it was to be fought on party lines. Each side nominated the strongest candidates they could get. There was great excitement, and party feeling ran as high as if it had been a parliamentary election. Nicholl's Temperance Hotel in Broad Street was largely attended by Chartists, and we formed ourselves into a committee to do what we possibly could, more particularly in agitating the borough. Open air meetings were held in different wards, and addressed by Clisset, Straddling, and others. At the close of the poll the friends of Jones and Miall had carried all before them. Mr. Edward Akroyd, his brother Henry, and their uncle, Mr. Geo. Beaumont, were amongst the defeated candidates. In the evening, a black flag was hoisted from Nicholl's Temperance Hotel.'

(*Ibid.*, pp. 11–12)

(c) Anti-Centralization

(The occasion of this comment was a bill introduced by Lord Melbourne's government in February 1839 to unify the control of the police of the metropolis in the hands of Peel's Metropolitan Police. The authorities of the august City of London resisted the encroachment on their own separate police powers, and eventually procured exemption from the new act. While the struggle was in progress, the *Chartist* launched an attack upon the underlying principle of this and other Whig legislation. An organ of moderate moral-force Chartism, it expressed a sentiment, which was widely held in the movement. Feargus O'Connor and Peter Murray McDouall both denounced centralization, but some later Chartist-Socialists could see virtues in central control if combined with democracy. Ernest Jones proposed in 1854 that magistrates should be appointed by the state and paid by the people.[1])

'THE CENTRALIZATION SYSTEM

The good folks east of Temple Bar have shown a degree of spirit and resolution in the defence of their watchmen which has struck with dire

[1] J. Saville, *Ernest Jones: Chartist* (London, 1952), pp. 176–7.

astonishment the official lovers of centralization. It appears from the
report of the City Committee to which this subject is entrusted, that half
the corporate towns in the kingdom have made common cause with the
City of London and have required their representatives to vote against
the Bill.

We are not much in the habit of sympathising with the airs of
offended dignity, which are put on by the Gogs and Magogs of
Cockaigne. We do not believe in the absolute wisdom of the Court of
Aldermen, and we are heretics enough to doubt the infallibility of the
Lord Mayor. Taking the Magogians altogether, we believe them to be a
greasy-chinned, vulgar, guzzling crew, without a particle of taste,
sentiment, or liberality; but, nevertheless, we perfectly agree with them
in the propriety of their resistance to the new attack upon the
Corporations. The centralization which is so prevailing a Whig mania, is
nothing more than another word for despotism. The object of it is to
make Downing-street the centre, to which strings from every part of the
kingdom shall converge, so that the Minister may sit in his office and
manage the country as a showman does his puppets.

This centralization has long since been brought to perfection in
France. France has for years been governed by the telegraph. The
Minister for the time being is as absolute as a Turkish Bashaw, and the
KING has nothing more to do than to constitute himself his own
Minister in order to become as well established a tyrant as any Shah of
Persia or Rajah of India. This LOUIS PHILIPPE has done, and it will
take a revolution to displace him. Establish a similar system in England
and LOUIS PHILIPPE's example might be followed and carried out by
such a man as the King of HANOVER, if any unfortunate chance should
give him the opportunity.

Local governments have been looked upon, from the time of the
Romans down to our day, as the strongholds of liberty, and such they
have always proved themselves. We esteem it to be a positive proof
against the practical liberty of a people, that they are unable to appoint a
constable, light an extra lamp, or mend the paving of a street, except
through the intervention of the State. This is of the very essence of an
absolute monarchy; it is carrying the power of the State into minutiae
with which the State has no business to interfere—it is weaving a net
about us which cramps our every movement and restricts us in all
healthful exercise of our individual will.

There is little doubt that these things would be better done by the State
than they are ordinarily done by local boards; but the difference by no

means compensates for the loss of control over our own immediate affairs. There is little doubt that we should all enjoy better health if the State obliged us to go to bed every night at ten o'clock, and to arise at six; but we believe there are few who would care much for life, however healthy, under such restrictions. The liberty of a nation is in proportion to the unfrequency of the interference of the State. Every interference of the State, which is not absolutely necessary, is a palpable act of tyranny. Those who have resided in countries such as Prussia, where this centralization is complete, know well the great abridgement of personal comfort, and the constant and harassing inconveniences which arise from the frequent and unbending rules that are established for the regulation of trivial matters. The Whigs, who have surrendered even every pretence of that jealous affection for liberty by which their fathers were distinguished, are hurrying us fast along in this path. They are eager utilitarians, and would sacrifice the best safeguard against tyranny which we have, for the sake of an efficent policeman or greater regularity in the lighting of the gas-lamps.

It is quite time that this centralization system should be checked. The New Poor Law is an egregious instance of what it is likely to effect. The London Police Bill is to be followed by a Rural Police Bill, and that is to be followed by other schemes all of the same tendency, each calling into being several thousands of Government spies. John Bull had better arouse himself in time, or in a very few sessions a man will not be able to go out at his own door in the evening without finding some blue-coated spy near it, who will peep down his throat in order to let the people in Downing-street know what he has eaten for dinner'.
(*The Chartist*, 21 April 1839)

8 Conscription to the Militia

(At the beginning of 1846 the government was expected to introduce a bill authorizing the embodiment of the Militia, the traditional citizen army of the English counties chosen by ballot, which had been allowed to lapse during the long peace following the Napoleonic War. Formerly men between the ages of eighteen and fifty had been liable to serve or find substitutes. The reason for reviving the force was believed to be the hostility between Great Britain and the U.S.A. over the Oregon boundary dispute in 1845. Both the National Charter Association and Lovett's rival National Association regarded the proposal as arbitrary and unnecessary, and organized protest meetings in many places. The following is a report of one held by the former in the metropolis. Lord Aberdeen, the Foreign Secretary, in due course, settled the quarrel with America by compromise.)

'NO VOTE! NO MUSKET!
MEETING IN THE CITY OF LONDON

An overflowing and most enthusiastic public meeting was held at the City Chartist Hall, 1, Turn-again-lane, Farringdon-street, January 18th, to protest against the embodiment of the militia, on Sunday evening, at eight o'clock. Mr. William Dear, an old militia man, was unanimously called to the chair. He said he could not agree with the idea of embodying the militia at the present time, as it did appear to him to be done for no other purpose than that of putting down democracy in America—(hear, hear)—and he did not like the idea at any time of taking away the son, the prop, and even support, of an aged father or mother—(hear, hear)—or the new married husband from the young wife of his early and best affections; or the honest industrious man from his home, breaking up his business, and sending him forth to be, at least, a wandering vagabond on the face of the earth, dressed in the disgusting habiliments of a Government slave. (Loud cheers.)

Mr. T. M. Wheeler came forward, and read the following resolution, the reading of which was received with great cheering:

That in the opinion of this meeting the contemplated embodiment of the militia force is an act of tyranny towards the unrepresented classes of the community, violating the first principles of justice, and that it would stamp the working classes of this country with eternal infamy if they allowed it to be carried into effect without protesting against it by the strongest effort the law and constitution allows; and that this meeting further believes that the alleged cause for this tyrannic act, viz. the prospect of a war with America relative to the Oregon territory, is one in which their best interests are perilled, which can only tend to throw into confusion the dearest interests of the empire, and that they will not allow their family ties to be torn asunder, their domestic comforts to be invaded, and their liberty sacrificed, in order that their brethren in America may be slaughtered, and a fresh impulse given to despotism and misrule.

In moving the adoption of the resolution, he said, it was an approved maxim "That taxation without representation was tyranny, and ought to be resisted." If this be true, by what stronger name shall we designate the compelling of the unenfranchised to serve in the militia—(hear, hear)—in an ensanguined livery? and where was the man that would not blush, aye, even deeper than the scarlet coat he would be compelled to wear, to be placed in such a disgraceful predicament? (Loud cheers.) There was no necessity for going to war with America about the Oregon territory. If land was wanted, there was plenty to be had at home. (Great cheering.) At any rate, he was resolved not to be a militiaman; and if the giving vent to that assertion was treason, "he was proud to be a traitor, aye, and prouder still to be surrounded by so many hundreds of such "traitors". (Tremendous cheering).

Mr. D. W. Ruffy seconded the resolution, eloquently describing the militia force as a snare, designed to fill the regular army (which enlistment had failed to do) with tools of tyranny, leaving wives to become widows, children to become orphans, converting our youths into debauchees and blood shedders, taking them from their virtuous homes and callings, and sending them forth to spread desolation, rapine, and murder far and wide. (Great cheering). The resolution was put and carried unanimously amid the loudest applause.

Mr. Stallwood rose to move—

That a committee of five persons be elected by that meeting to aid and assist in getting up a demonstration against the proposed embodiment of the militia, and take such other steps as may be deemed necessary.

He said ... he trusted they would do something more than meet and hold up their hands for resolutions; he would not counsel violent resistance to the law, but nothing was ever obtained worth the having, except by moral daring. He remembered during the struggle for a free press, that his friend, Henry Hetherington, was charged with violating the law. "No," responded Hetherington, "I do not violate the law; I only give it the alternative, I must either have my paper stamped, pay a fine, or go to prison, and I prefer going to prison". (Laughter and cheers.) Now the result would be, that should any of his family be drawn, he should advise them to give the alternative; that was neither to serve, find a substitute, nor pay the fine in money—(loud cheers);—for he did think the man who disliked to become a *man-butcher* himself, yet would tempt another man through the means of his poverty to do so, was a mean, despicable scoundrel indeed (Great cheering.) It might be said your family exempts you. Yes, but some of that family would soon be of the age that the law set down for the period at which liability commenced, and his parental affection naturally made him desirous of protecting his children. He had instilled into their young breasts a natural hatred of blood-shedding, and he had no hesitation in saying that they would be found equally resolved with himself; and were it otherwise, he would discard them, disown them, were they ever to don the scarlet livery of a hired murderer. Far better, and much more honourable was it even to suffer the prison gloom than to have the crime of murder on their souls (Loud cheers.) ...

Mr. William Benbow said, he thought this delicate ground to tread on, he must say that he would rather fight *with the Americans* than against them. (Loud cheers.) A Militia Law was essentially British, and he held that every man should have the vote, and have arms in his hands, and also be taught the use of them; so that he might be enabled to protect that vote and their homes. (Loud cheers.) The law had been much distorted, and men had now been taught that they had "nothing to do with the laws but to obey them".[1] He was of the opinion that the people should act individually in this matter, to prevent their being taken hold of as conspirators against the law. (Hear, hear.) He was beyond the age himself, but he had sons that were liable, and if the suffrage was universal, and the war a just one, he would say to those sons, take your parts honestly, fight like Britons, and die, if needs be, like Grecians. (Loud cheers.) He was proud to see such meetings, and hoped that every man would act as became him in his individual capacity against the present iniquitous system. (Loud cheers.) He was of opinion that no faith could be placed in either Peel, Russell, or Morpeth. If you want your work well done you must do it yourselves. (Much cheering.) ...

Mr. Stallwood said that these meetings were called at a very fitting time, seeing that the matter will be brought before Parliament, and a short bill passed before the embodiment took place; it would, therefore, be their duty to memorialise the Premier, petition the House, and bother the Parliamentary representatives to support their memorials and petitions. (Cheers.) The resolution was unanimously adopted, and Messrs. Dear, Gover, jun., Dunn, Overton, and T. M. Wheeler, were elected the committee. A vote of thanks was then passed to the chairman, and the meeting separated, evidently pleased with its deliberations and the preliminary steps taken.'
(*The Northern Star*, 24 January 1846)

---

[1] An allusion to a remark by Bishop Samuel Horsley in a debate in the House of Lords on the Younger Pitt's repressive legislation half a century earlier.

PART II

Chartism and Social Reform

1. *State Intervention and the Rights of Property*
(a) Social Reform by Modified Individualism
(The *Charter* was issued on 27 January 1839. It was begun by the London trade societies in conjunction with William Lovett and other leaders of the London Working Men's Association. William Carpenter, a veteran of the unstamped warfare, was the editor. Though it built up a circulation of 5,000 in 1839, it was not a success, and went out of existence early in 1840, being merged into the *New Statesman.*[1] The branch of Chartism, for which it spoke, discoursed vaguely on 'equal social rights' for the working classes and the evils of 'exclusive legislation', but rarely expressed these ideals in a concrete programme. The extract given below is more than usually explicit. It reveals the viewpoint of a social reformer rather than a socialist, and shows acceptance of some of the leading postulates of Classical Political Economy, e.g. that wages were determined by the supply of and the demand for labour and that emigration ought to be encouraged.)

'POLITICS
HOW CAN THE CONDITION OF THE PEOPLE BE IMPROVED?
We have recently been told by Lord John Russell in a speech in the House of Commons, that we "ought not to encourage the hope that any change in the persons by whom the House of Commons is elected, or any change in the mode of election, would produce high wages, and a greater degree of comfort to the working classes."...

It seems to me that a Parliament resolved on consulting the interests of the many and not of the few, might, in an infinite variety of ways, increase the comforts and exalt the character of the human race ... And here I would premise that there is no probability whatever of carrying

[1] See M. Hovell, *The Chartist Movement* (Manchester, 1966), pp. 76–7; J. A. Epstein, 'Feargus O'Connor and the Northern Star', *IRSH*, Vol.XXI, 1976, pp. 51–97; Patricia Hollis, *The Pauper Press* (Oxford, 1970), pp. 119, 154, 308–9.

into effect any one of the measures about to be mentioned until the people are *really and truly represented.*

In the first place, then, I would beg leave to submit that a *repeal of the laws prohibiting the importation of food* from abroad, and a *repeal of all the TAXES upon articles of consumption,* would have the effect of making necessaries and comforts of every kind *more abundant,* and consequently of placing them more within the reach of all classes.

2. *That the poor, sick, and aged, might be better provided for.*

3. *That the people might be educated.*

4. *That justice might be brought within the reach of all, the laws and the administration of them being made more simple and reasonable.*

5. *That the dwellings of the poor might be made more wholesome and comfortable by public improvements; that their recreation and amusement might be effectually provided for; and that various encouragements and aids might be given to the provident and industrious.*

6. *And, principally, that employment might be MADE ABUNDANT,* the natural consequence of which would be "a FAIR DAY'S WAGES FOR A FAIR DAY'S WORK." The removal of the food monopoly would secure to the labourer the fruits of his earnings and prevent a rise in the price of necessaries corresponding with the improved means of the consumer. ... there cannot be good wages when the supply of labour greatly exceeds the demand. How to prevent the latter evil is the principal matter that now remains for consideration. In the first place the labour market may be relieved, to a very great extent, from *women and children*; for if the earnings of the head of a family be not sufficient for their support, let assistance be given by the public, in order that the children, instead of being put to work at a tender age, may be sent to school, and the wife be kept at home to attend to domestic affairs.

Secondly, it must be borne in mind that the cheapening of common necessaries will leave *more money to be expended on manufactured goods*; and, consequently, add vastly to our *home trade.* And the same effects will flow from an *increase of foreign trade, caused by the exchanging of our manufactures* for corn, meat, wine, wool, and other articles.

Thirdly, each trade and employment can be relieved, to a great extent, of its superfluous hands, by a *careful and judicious encouragement of emigration.* We find various parts of the earth admirably calculated for the abode of man, open to his choice. A few hundreds of thousands expended in erecting colonies would greatly increase the happiness of the human race both at home and abroad. No *expense* should be spared on the part of the government to establish colonies in a proper manner, in the most suitable situations. Everything should be provided for the *reception and permanent comfort* and security of the colonists. Instead of this these matters are left to private speculators, who are intent upon nothing but their own gain. New sources of commerce and trade—new marts for our manufactures—might be thrown open for us, and thus a double benefit be obtained, viz, a reduction of superfluity in the labour market at home, and a vast *addition* to employment.

Fourthly, great *public works* could be set on foot by the encouragement of the government, such as the making of suitable ports and harbours, and the bringing of millions of acres of marsh and waste lands into cultivation. This would create permanent employment. And to secure adequate remuneration for labour, peaceable combination to raise wages should be encouraged, instead of being repressed.

In fine, *it cannot be beyond human wisdom to secure employment for the people*, by these and other means. A *Parliament representing the working classes, and seeing that full employment is one of the most essential principles of national wealth, and having nothing to divert their attention from this paramount subject, will be determined that this essential shall not be wanting* ... REFORMATOR.'
(*The Charter*, 25 August 1839)

(b) A Chartist-Socialist's View of Property Rights

(Paradoxically Chartism also carried forward and adapted the advanced labour economics propounded in the 1820s by the anti-Ricardian Socialists—Thomas Hodgskin, William Thompson and other writers—who claimed for the workman the right to the whole produce of his labour. It was upon this interpretation of the labour theory of value that James 'Bronterre' O'Brien based the argument of the following passage. O'Brien was the most impressive social theorist in the Chartist movement. He wrote for the *Northern Star* in the early stages of its history, but broke with O'Connor over the Complete Suffrage movement, and for some years went into isolation. Though a strong Socialist, he gave primacy in his thinking to political reform by means of the People's Charter, for, as the passage shows, he believed that laws and government policy, engendered by the existing narrowly-based constitution, underpinned the exploiting system in a variety of ways.)

'PRIVATE PROPERTY

If all men are placed equal before the law—if the means of acquiring and retaining wealth are equally secured to all in proportion to the respective industry and services of each, I see no objection to private property. Every man has a right to the value of his own produce or services, be they more or less. If one man can and will do twice the work of another man, he ought certainly in justice to have twice the reward. But if his superior strength or skill gives him the means of acquiring more wealth than his neighbour, it by no means follows that he ought, therefore, to acquire a right or power over his neighbour's produce as well as his own. And here lies the grand evil of society—it is not in private property, but in the unjust and atrocious powers with which the existing laws of all countries invest it. If a man has fairly earned a hundred or a thousand pounds' worth of wealth beyond what he has consumed or spent, he has a sacred right to the exclusive use of it, if he thinks proper; but he has no right to use that wealth in such a way as to make it a sort of sucking-pump, or thumb-screw for sucking and screwing other people's produce into his possession. Sir John Cam Hobhouse, for example, has 60,000 £. in Whitbread's brewery. Now, supposing Sir John to have earned that money honestly, he has a right to use it, and live upon it, while it lasts; but he has no just right to make it the means of sucking 5,000 £. or 6,000 £. additional every year out of the public without a particle of labour or industry on his part. He has no just right to employ his money in usury or speculation. His money should not be allowed to grow money as cabbage grows cabbage, or weeds grows weeds ... Such are the effects of wealth as now administered. They result not from property, but from robbery—they are not rights of property, but wrongs on industry—they spring from bad laws—from depraved institutions. These laws and these institutions, instead of protecting industry from dishonest cupidity, have utterly sacrificed the former to the latter. The *employers* of labour and the *exchangers* of wealth are alone considered in the laws. The *producers* and active distributors are only thought of as slaves or criminals. Enormous fleets and armies are kept up to protect the merchants' gains. Enormous gaols and penitentiaries are kept up for the poor. Thus are the labourers forced to pay, not only for the protection of those who plunder them, but for the very instruments of their own torture and misery. Buonarroti considers all these results inseparable from private property. So did Babeuf—so did thousands of the French democrats of 1793—so do Robert Owen and his disciples of the present day. I think differently. I will never admit that private property is incompatible with public happiness, till I see it fairly tried. I never found an objection urged against it, which I cannot trace to the abuse, not to the use, of the institution. Assuredly, if men are allowed

to acquire wealth by all manner of nefarious means, and to afterwards employ that wealth more nefariously still, there must be public ruin and misery; but I deny that these are the necessary effects of private property. Usury, for instance, has destroyed all the nations of antiquity, and is now undermining all modern states; but is usury essential to private property? I deny it. But, then it is necessary to, and inseparable from commerce. I deny that too. It is, certainly, inseparable from commerce as now conducted; but I deny that an enlightened Government, representing all classes, would allow commerce to be conducted as it is now. I assert, that such Government would place commerce and manufactures upon a totally different footing from the present, and make the land the common property of all the inhabitants, and that, without any real or material injury to the existing proprietors. I hold, and I am sure I can prove, that such a dispensation of things is within the power of an enlightened Legislature, fairly representing all classes. I have no space to argue the question here, but assuming that I am right for the present, why should we conclude that private property is the inevitable cause of the evils alluded to, until the institution be fairly tried and tested?

JAMES BRONTERRE O'BRIEN'
(*The English Chartist Circular*, Vol. I, No. 18, c. May 1841)

(c) The Charter and Something More

(After the revolutionary excitement of 1848, as Harney and Ernest Jones broadened the objectives of the National Charter Association to include Socialism, and the individualist O'Connor drifted into irretrievable madness, O'Brien returned to the centre of the stage. The National Reform League for the Peaceful Regeneration of Society, of which he was President, and which served as a vehicle of ideas which had for some years been germinating in his mind, was proposed in September 1849. Though a small metropolitan society, whose members founded the Eclectic Institute, off what is now Charing Cross Road, it had close links with the N.C.A. and the Fraternal Democrats. Some of the undermentioned proposals, e.g. those relating to centralization of poor rates, settlement of the unemployed on the land, adjustment of the national debt and gradual nationalization of landed estate, found their way into the programme of the Chartist Convention of March-April 1851, organized by the Executive of the N.C.A. O'Brien kept alive in the middle years of the nineteenth century the cause of public ownership of land urged by Thomas Spence as early as 1775. Nevertheless, although Harney went further than O'Brien in urging that confiscation should be applied, O'Brien had to insist before land nationalization was included in the aims of the 1851 Convention.[1] More typical of Chartism was the vision of peasant proprietorship, which inspired O'Connor's Land Plan.)

PRINCIPLES OF BRONTERRE O'BRIEN'S NATIONAL REFORM LEAGUE

(as adopted by the National Regeneration Society, March 1850).

'1. A repeal of our present wasteful and degrading system of poor laws, and the substitution of a just and efficient poor law (based upon the original Act of Elizabeth) which shall centralise the rates, and dispense them equitably and economically for the beneficial employment and relief of the destitute poor. The rates to be levied only upon the owners of every description of realised property. ...

2. ... it is the duty of the government to appropriate its present surplus revenue, and the proceeds of national or public property, to the purchasing of lands, and the location thereon of the unemployed poor. ...

3. Pending the operations of these measures, it is desirable to mitigate the burdens of taxation, and of public and private indebtedness ... the more especially as these burdens have been vastly aggravated by the recent monetary and free trade measures of Sir Robert Peel. To this end, the Public Debt, and all private indebtedness affected by the fall of prices, should be equitably adjusted in favour of the debtor and productive classes, and the charges of government should be reduced upon a scale corresponding with the general fall of prices, and of wages. ...

4. The gradual resumption by the State (on the acknowledged principles of equitable compensation to existing holders, or their heirs) of its ancient, undoubted, inalienable dominion, and sole proprietorship over all the lands, mines, turbaries, fisheries etc, of the United Kingdom and our colonies; the same to be held by the State as trustee, in perpetuity, for the entire people, and rented out to them in such quantities, and on such terms as the law and local circumstances shall determine; ... the rental of the land ... would form a national fund adequate to defray all charges of the public service, execute all needful public works, and educate the population, without the necessity for any taxation.

5. ... a sound system of National Credit, through which any man might

---

[1] See especially Alfred Plummer, *Bronterre: A Political Biography of Bronterre O'Brien, 1804–1864* (London, 1971), Chap.X, *Passim*; the programme of the 1851 Convention, which should be compared with that of the National Reform League, is reproduced as an Appendix in J. Saville ed.. *Ernest Jones: Chartist* (London, 1952), pp. 257–63.

... procure an advance from the national funds arising out of the proceeds of public property, and thereby be enabled to rent and cultivate land on his own account. ...

6. That the National Currency should be based on real, consumable wealth, or on the *bona fide* credit of the State and not upon the variable and uncertain amount of scarce metal; ...

7. ... it is an important duty of the State to institute, in every town and city, public marts or stores, for the reception of all kinds of exchangeable goods, to be valued by disinterested officers appointed for the purpose, either upon a corn or a labour standard: the depositors to receive symbolic notes representing the value of their deposits: such notes to be made legal currency throughout the country, enabling their owners to draw from the public stores to an equivalent amount, thereby gradually displacing the present reckless system of competitive trading and shop-keeping. ...

Doubtless there are many other reforms required besides those alluded to; doubtless, we want a sound system of national education for youth, made compulsory upon all parents and guardians; doubtless we require a far less expensive system of military and naval defence than now obtained; doubtless, we require the expropriation of railways, canals, bridges, docks, gas-works, water-works, etc.; and, doubtless, we require a juster and more humane code of civil and penal law than we now possess. But these and all other needful reforms will be easy of accomplishment when those comprised in the foregoing proposition shall have been effected. ...'

(*The Northern Star*, 30 March 1850)

2. *Machinery and the Factory System*

(A point at which Chartist economic views diverged from those of the middle classes and the Political Economists concerned the effects of the introduction of machinery on the condition of the people. To Charles Knight, the publicist for the Society for the Diffusion of Useful Knowledge, these could be expressed in terms of cheaper consumers' goods and increased employment. Chartist commentators were principally hostile to machines, though some, like O'Brien, observed that, under different management these could have been made the means of relieving mankind of 'his primeval curse to live by the sweat of his brow'.[1] There were differences of degree in Chartist opposition. Some of the leaders of the movement contented themselves with observing that machinery in the hands of the capitalists promoted wage-cutting and

---

[1] Plummer, *op. cit.*, p. 87.

unemployment and helped to bring on a crisis of under-consumption. Often they suggested palliatives to mitigate these evils. Jonathan Bairstow, one of the most popular of the Chartist lecturers, speaking at Leeds in August 1840, proposed that the people should voluntarily accumulate wealth to purchase machinery for themselves and that there should be home colonization to drain off the surplus labour.[2] Other Chartist orators, such as J. R. Stephens and P. M. McDouall, delivered *carte blanche* denunciations of the factory system, as in the latter's speech to the Convention on 13 March 1839.)

'NATIONAL CONVENTION
WEDNESDAY
THE FACTORY SYSTEM

Dr. M'DOWELL rose to move "That the Convention do enter into a consideration of the Factory System of England, for the purpose of expressing a decided opinion on that system as it now exists." He considered this question one of very great importance; and one upon which the Convention should send forth its sentiments.—(Hear). The facts which he should lay before them were such as had come under his own personal observation as a medical man, and he felt it his duty to come forward and state them. At Ramsbottom (Lancashire), where he resided, he had visited 309 cottages; the furniture, in a great majority of cases, was of the poorest and meanest description; in some few instances, it was true, there was an appearance of decency and comfort, but the great majority were in the state he had described them. The most important evil that struck him was the smallness and want of space of the apartments in which the cottagers were crowded; this had a most unhealthy tendency. He found twenty-one families in which four individuals occupied but one bed; and in one instance thirteen persons were huddled together in the same room. When it was considered how the moral character of the people must be affected, by being thus crowded together without regard to sex or age, he thought it became a question of national importance. Upon an examination he found that these families did not, upon an average, earn more than 5s. per week; in many cases they came so low as 2s. 6d. Was it to be wondered at that there were very few of these who were not in debt? When he went to the cottages of the poor, he found in a great many instances they were without a morsel of bread. He had asked, first, how many workers; secondly, how many eaters, each family contained, and then how much

[2] *The Northern Star*, 15 August, 1840. Home colonization meant the settlement of the poor on disposable land either by private or by state purchase.

they received weekly as wages. In one house there were six males and three females; of these two only were workers; these two workers earned 17s. 6d. per week, with which they had to support nine individuals. They did not, however, receive the whole of this sum in money, 5s. 6½d. of it being subtracted for coals, rent, &c. and 2d. more for the support of a Sunday-school, being obliged to pay whether they sent their children or not. These deductions being made, left 11s. 7d. for the week, or 2½d. per head per day. He asked if that, at the present price of provisions, was sufficient to support a human being? As a medical man he denied that it was.—(Hear). But the master manufacturer made other extractions from his victims; he gave a nominal amount of wages, but paid, in fact, what he pleased. The condition of the factory slaves was not to be learnt by a government commissioner taking a tour through the manufacturing districts, and dining with their masters.—(Hear, hear.) The whole system had been established upon the most iniquitous robberies. One of the first efforts of the erectors of these factories was to get an infamous Government to hand over to their tender mercies the foundlings of an hospital. These they worked in such a manner, that, to say the least of it, it was murder. The hand-loom weavers had been reduced to a condition as abject as that of the Irish people. He remembered the period when the hand-loom weavers of his own country (Scotland) were in happy and prosperous circumstances; it was strange that he should come to Lancashire, and see the same devastation going on amongst the inhabitants of that district which he had witnessed at home. The factory system was not less physically than morally destructive of the population; could our armies be recruited, or our navies manned by the emaciated spectres of the factor[y]?—(Hear.) Not only were the constitutions of men ruined by the factory system, but women must be dragged from their domestic duties to satisfy the exactions of the master manufacturer. This was asking too much of human nature. He himself had seen a mother's milk whiten the floor of the factory when it should have nurtured her child.—(Hear.) Out of every thousand births five hundred of the children in the manufacturing districts died before they reached the age of five years—the remaining half were of the most squalid and miserable appearance; indeed, humanity could scarcely wish to see existence prolonged in such pitiable looking beings. In Ramsbottom one woman was engaged to look after four or five families while their parents were at work in the factories; thus the system tore the child from the breast of its mother and consigned it to the care of a stranger. He had seen in a factory the veins

of a woman's leg burst from the length of time she had been compelled
to stand at her work. This was the voice of nature, crying out "You shall
sooner die than work like this."—(Hear.) It was for his hostility to such a
system as this, and the one introduced by the New Poor-law Bill, that the
Rev. Joseph Rayner Stephens, as well as others, had become obnoxious
to our *wise and intelligent* Government.—(Hear, hear). Did it not
become them as Englishmen to say that this system should no longer
pollute the land?—(Hear.) During the hand-loom times, the
manufacturer could gain his living by working eight hours a day; but in
this scientific age he must labour twice as long for a less reward. Was it
not a natural inference that it was the purpose of God, by inventive
genius to lessen the necessity for human labour? He admired machinery
when its proper object was attained; the steam-engine and the power-
loom were both noble, wonderful, and beautiful inventions. If they were
enabled to live by working eight hours a day before their discovery, they
ought to be able to do the same now by working only four hours; but
how stood the fact? why, they had now to toil for 16 hours, as long
again as they did previous to their being known.—(Hear, hear.) Thus
were the very triumphs of intellect and science, instead of a blessing, a
curse to them; they had tended to swell the hoard of the capitalist and
strengthen the hands of their oppressors, instead of diffusing prosperity
and comfort amongst the mass of the people.—(Hear, hear.) The
working people of Lancashire were in a much worse condition at the
present time than even were the slaves of the West Indies; the black
slave-owner worked his slaves within the line of their physical
capabilities; he had an interest in preserving and improving the race,
which was a guarantee for his conduct. He worked his slaves in the same
way that a considerate farmer would his horses, and was careful of them
in like manner, because they were a valuable property. Our wise and
intelligent Government, while it ruined the slave owners of the West
Indies in its anxiety to abolish slavery abroad, permitted it to exist in an
aggravated form at home. He looked with considerable suspicion upon
philanthropists who travelled across the seas to find becoming objects
for their sympathies.—(Hear, hear.) It was time to look abroad when we
were free at home.—(Hear, hear, hear.) There was a far deeper and
deadlier stain upon England than upon the Indies, or upon America or
France.—(Hear.) But let their oppressors beware. The people were not
bloodthirsty, they were patient and enduring; but though patient and
enduring, they would not always remain so.—(Hear, hear.) In
conclusion, rather than submit to the present system, and behold our

countrymen crossing the Atlantic to find in other climes scope for their energies and remuneration for their labour, it would be better to put an end to it at any sacrifice. (On sitting down the speaker was cheered for several seconds. The speech, of which the above is necessarily but a faint outline, was the most eloquent and effective that has been delivered during the sittings of the Convention. In the delivery it occupied upwards of two hours.)'

(*The Chartist*, 16 March 1839)

3. *Chartism and Temperance*

(Chartists often met in taverns and beershops for want of alternative *venues*, and there were several drinksellers among the local leaders. From the outset, however, some were aware that drunkenness in working men undermined their political commitment and independence, and made Chartism and the Charter less acceptable to the middle classes and to women. A teetotal movement, closely linked to radical Nonconformity, had been gaining ground among the working- and lower-middle-classes of the North since 1833. Unlike the older and anti-spirits campaign, which was conducted under wealthy patronage, this exacted a pledge to abstain from all intoxicants, including beer, the working man's drink. Some of its leaders, such as Joseph Livesey, a Preston cheesemonger, supported universal suffrage and the secret ballot. When, therefore, Chartism was seeking the means of recovery from the disasters of 1839, Henry Vincent saw the answer in combining total abstinence and obligation to the People's Charter in a single pledge. This produced a crop of Teetotal Chartist societies early in 1841, and the attempt was made to form a National Teetotal Charter Association. O'Connor, who considered these developments to be destructive of Chartist unity, denounced them in the *Northern Star* in March–April 1841. After that the specific movement withered away, but both O'Connor and Ernest Jones continued to urge sobriety within the main stream of N.C.A. Chartism.[1] Advocacy of the cause in the latter's *Notes to the People* gave an impetus to the establishment of Chartist halls, to the holding of meetings in temperance halls, and even to the formation of Total Abstinence localities and societies in communion with the N.C.A. in 1852.[2])

'*Pothouse Localities*

Principles alone, however true and holy, are not enough to ensure adherence and respect for a popular movement. There is such a thing as degrading the best and noblest cause. The estimation in which that cause

[1] See Brian Harrison, 'Teetotal Chartism', *History*, Vol. LVIII, No. 193, June 1973, pp. 193–217, for a full discussion of the issues raised by Teetotal Chartism.
[2] *Notes to the People*, Vol. II, (London, 1852), pp. 728, 893, 926, 988.

will be held by the general public, and accordingly, the amount of adhesion it will obtain, depend upon the character of its standard bearers, the language of its advocates, and the places in which they meet. A great cause, like Democracy, must not be dragged down into the mire, but pedestaled aloft, on pure and spotless marble. Chartism has suffered terribly, from a deficiency in all three of these important particulars. I have to deal now with the third, and not the least essential of these points: the place of meeting. The advocacy of Chartism will "stink in the nostrils" of the many, as long as it meets in places such as those, which it now too often visits.

Raise the Charter from the Pot-house!

Do you suppose the thoughtful and self-respecting, or the respector of democracy, will go, and by his presence help to drag it down and desecrate it in the pot-house? We want the support and countenance of woman in our movement—for the Charter must become a domestic spirit, a tutelar saint, a household god, before it can arise a legislative power! And what shall make it so,—but the support of woman? That which does not emanate from the fire-side of a million homes, will have no lasting basis even amid the cheering of ten thousand platforms. It is woman that ever sways, more or less, the mind of man—it is woman that ever moulds the character of the child. And would you take your wives, sisters, and daughters, to the pot-house, among the reek of gin and porter, the fume of foetid pipes, and the loose ribaldry of incipient intemperance? Again, we want to instruct the rising generation. We want to make *children* Chartists, and then we shall be sure of having Chartist *men*. As the twig is bent, so the tree will grow. But, fathers and mothers! Is the pot-house a place to take your children to?—to inoculate them with vice—to give the example of drunkenness—to engraft the future curse upon their lives? As you value our cause, as you value our future, as you respect the truth, and as you love yourselves—

Raise Chartism from the Pot-house.

"But this is not always possible!" I hear them say, "There is no difficulty to him that wills"—brave axiom of the Gallic working-man, who swam to Kossuth's ship, because he was too poor to hire a boat! I deny that it is impossible, in any instance, to avoid the pot-house meeting. "Oh! but we can't afford to pay for a room!" Can't you? Then you pay nothing in the pot-house? You sit without calling for your pipe, or porter, or ginger-beer, or gin? Oh! no! Twenty men in the pot-house, meeting every week, spend on an average, 6d. each (some far more, some less), that is 10s. per week! Will you tell me that, in any town in England, you can't hire a decent room for *one evening weekly*, for TEN SHILLINGS the night? You might get it for the whole week for less than that. You might establish a reading-room in it—you might found a library—you might open a school—you might make it pay itself, and diffuse the blessings of knowledge and education from it, as from a centre—all which in the pot-house is impossible. All this you might do, if there were only twenty, aye! if there were only ten members in a locality. Don't say, then, "we must go to the pot-house—it's very bad we know—but we can't afford to house our principles respectably."

In the pot-house it is all loss and no gain—whereas the chartist-room might be made a self-supporting institution,—and if not, might be maintained at a cheaper cost than the pot-house degradation.

"All that is very well!"—I hear some of them exclaim—"It's very well for you to write this in your study, but if you knew the difficulties in our way, you would write otherwise. What shall we do, if we are just forming a locality, or if we number only four or five members? Surely, then, we can't afford to hire a room!"

Probably not. But, while you are only four or five members, can't you meet once a week, at a member's house? He's a sorry democrat who wont lend you the use of his parlour, or his kitchen, for two hours weekly. That's what you can do, if you are only four or five—and, when your friend's room grows too small to hold you, then you can afford to hire one, for it will cost you far less than the pot-house.

Raise Chartism from the pot-house! as you hope for the salvation of our movement, as you hope for the respect of men—as you hope for the consistent, worthy advocacy of our cause! Nine-tenths of the folly, bickering, contention, and treachery that have ever existed among us, were sown, nursed, matured and gathered in the pot-house—that fruitful hot-bed of madness, contention, eaves-dropping, and disgrace!

How check the evil? Firstly, by the good sense of the members.

Secondly, let all lecturers and apostles of the charter, when invited to lecture or attend a meeting, ask, "where is it to be held?" and if the answer is—"In a pot-house!" let *their* answer be—"Then I wont attend!"

Thirdly, let all local councils at once take steps to remove their locality from public-houses. 1852, whatever it turns out to be, must not find Chartism in the pot-house.

Before concluding, permit me to advert to another argument, used in favour of the pot-house. "The landlord is an influential man, and we should offend and lose him, if we didn't meet at his house!" If the landlord's democracy depends on how much money he can fleece you out of by half poisoning you with his noxious drugs, then the sooner you lose such democracy, the better. But I'll tell you what landlord's patriotism amounts to in nine cases out of ten: if they are not molested or frightened by the police, they are glad to get a Chartist locality for the sake of custom. In the competition among pot-houses, many of them are nearly bankrupt, and they pounce upon chartist prey as a forlorn hope to fill their empty tills. They vie with each other as to who shall get the lecturer that will "draw" the most—they interrupt the lecture with the ceaseless cry of "orders! gents! orders!" They drag down democracy to the level of any tight-rope, juggling, fiddling exhibition, that attracts an idle crowd around their bar—and almost all the "good" done by the lecture, is to fill the pocket of the speculating harpy. For as to instilling the principles of truth, I would not give much for the conversions made over the beer-pot and underneath the pipe. And all the while, our bold and gallant chartists will talk of "the kindness of the landlord, who *allows* them to meet in his house!"—the kindness of the landlord, who allows them to disgrace themselves for the purpose of enriching him.

Want of self-respect has been the great cause of inefficient organisation. Would you invite a Mazzini, a Kossuth, a Ledru Rollin, or, what is far, far more—a Barbes (Barbès), or a Blanqui—to come and lecture to you in a pot-house? No! Then if you have too much respect for the man to do so,—you ought to have too much respect for the cause, *which is far greater than the man who represents it.*

I repeat, the first step, if you would regenerate our movement, and regenerated it shall be, the world shall not find us, alone, wanting in 1852,—the first step if you would save our cause and guarantee our progress is

Raise Chartism from the Pot-house.'

(*Notes To The People*, Vol. II, London, 1852, pp. 623–25).

4. *The Education of the People*

(a) A Chartist Blue Print for National Education

(By granting £20,000 in 1833 against voluntary subscriptions for the erection of school buildings, the Whig government had taken the first great step towards the acceptance of state responsibility for popular education. How far the principle should be extended to include supervision by a government department and inspectorate, state responsibility for the training and payment of teachers, and the replacement of the schools run by the religious societies by a comprehensive state system, with attendance free and compulsory, was a live issue in English politics during the Chartist period. Public opinion was divided between a minority of Whigs and Radicals, anxious in various degrees to bring in the state, and a larger body of Nonconformists, who wished to proceed by extending the voluntary system. The London moral-force Chartists occupied an advanced position in the former camp, as the following extract from a diffuse address issued by the London Working Men's Association in 1837 shows. By 1851 what remained of organized Chartism was prepared to endorse the principle of 'national, universal, gratuitous and, to a certain extent, compulsory education' at the Convention in London.)

'We contend, therefore, that it is the duty of the Government to provide the means of educating the whole nation; for as the whole people are benefited by each individual's laudable exertions, so all ought to be united in affording the best means of developing the useful powers of each.

But how, it may be asked, are the means to be provided? We may reply, by asking how were the means provided for less worthy purposes? We remember that twenty millions were paid to compensate the owners of slaves for relinquishing their unjust traffic. That the means were provided for paying extravagant pensions, and for erecting useless palaces for royalty; and are still found to support an almost interminable list of idlers from year to year. Whence, too, we may enquire, came our means to war against freedom wherever it raised its head, and to assist all the despots in Europe to keep their people in ignorance and slavery? Were but half the anxiety evinced to train the human race in peace and happiness, as has hitherto been exerted to keep them in subjection to a few despots, abundant means would be afforded for the purpose.

But though we hold it to be the duty of Government to raise the means of education, by taxation or otherwise; to see it properly apportioned in the erecting of suitable and sufficient schools, and for superintending them so far as to see the original intention of the people carried into effect, we are decidedly opposed to the placing such immense power and influence in the hands of Government as that of selecting the teachers and superintendents, the books and kinds of instruction, and the whole management of schools in each locality. While we want a uniform and just system of education, we must guard against the influence of irresponsible power and public corruption. We are opposed, therefore, to all concentration of power beyond that which is absolutely necessary to make and execute the laws; for, independent of its liability to be corrupt, it destroys those local energies, experiments, and improvements so desirable to be fostered for the advancement of knowledge, and prostrates the whole nation before one uniform, and, it may be, a power of, despotism. We perceive the results of this concentration of power and uniformity of system lamentably exemplified in Prussia and other parts of the continent, where the lynx-eyed satellites of power carefully watch over the first indications of intelligence, to turn it to their advantage, and to crush in embryo the buddings of freedom.

We think, therefore, that the selection of teachers, the choice of books, and the whole management and superintendence of schools in each locality should be confined to a SCHOOL COMMITTEE of twenty or more persons, elected by *universal suffrage* of all the adult population, male and female. And to prevent local prejudices or party feuds from being prejudicial in the choice, the district for selecting the committee should be extended beyond the locality they should be called on to superintend. They should wholly, or in part, be elected annually; should give a public report of their proceedings, and an account of the money received and expended every six months, and be responsible at all times to the majority of their constituents.

We conceive that the *erection of Schools and Colleges should be at the expense of the nation*, and that the numerous endowments and charitable bequests given for the purposes of education would be justly devoted towards that object, as well as other lucrative branches of public revenue. That the whole application and management of them should be confined to a COMMITTEE OF PUBLIC INSTRUCTION, of twelve persons, selected by Parliament every three years. They should report annually, they should be responsible for all monies received and expended, and for the due fulfilment of all their duties, which duties should be publicly defined to them from time to time by Acts of Parliament.

We think also that *the whole expenses of conducting and keeping those schools in proper condition* should be provided for by *an annual rate*, to be levied by the School Committees in local districts; these districts to be divided, so as to embrace as nearly as possible an equal number of inhabitants, in order that all localities may share as equally as possible in the expenses and the advantages.

In order to provide competent and efficient teachers for those schools, NORMAL OR TEACHERS' SCHOOLS should be established in different districts throughout the country, in which gratuitous instruction should be afforded to a competent number of persons, who by their dispositions and abilities were fitting, and might wish, to become teachers. Those schools should be managed and conducted by competent professors of every useful branch of art and science, who should be responsible to the local committees, and to the Committee of Public Instruction for the time being. No teacher should be permitted to teach in any school who had not properly qualified himself in a Normal School, and could produce a certificate to that effect. We think that one of the most essential things to be observed in the education of those teachers, is to qualify them *in the art of simplifying knowledge*, of imparting it with effect, and kindness of disposition. Beyond these, we think there should be four different descriptions of schools :—

1st.   INFANT SCHOOLS, for children from three to six years old.

2nd.   PREPARATORY SCHOOLS, for children from six to nine.

3rd.   HIGH SCHOOLS, for children from nine to twelve.

4th.   FINISHING SCHOOLS, or COLLEGES, for all above twelve, who might choose to devote their time to acquire all the higher branches of knowledge. ...'

(*The Life and Struggles of William Lovett* (London, 1920), Vol. I, pp. 142–5)

(b) The Charter must come first

(Like Cobbett, however, many Northern Chartists experienced a difficulty which prevented them from throwing their full weight behind moves to increase education by state action. Their class consciousness made them distrustful of the content of the schooling administered by a government which working men could not control. The *Northern Liberator* for 28 September 1839 attacked Lord Brougham's plea for a national system of education as for 'a system of tuition which will make man see the beauties of *passive obedience and non resistance*.' Ernest Jones called for the writing of a 'democratic literature' for the young, to be used in schools.[1] As the *Northern Star* perceived, the difficulty was a secularized version of that of the Anglicans and Nonconformists, who quarrelled over state education. The churches, while insisting that education must be religious, could not agree on the national faith which was to be communicated. Like Disraeli, class-conscious Chartists could not agree that there was one nation.)

'NATIONAL EDUCATION

National Jackass! You may just as well talk of a national Jackass, a national pig, a national cow, or a national house [horse?], (indeed, better

[1] Saville, *op. cit.*, pp. 157–9.

the latter, as it is the national standard of intellect) as talk of National Education, or anything else national, till we have a nation. Would the discoverer of an uninhabited wild, call the wild a nation? No. There is no such thing as national institutions in England, therefore she has no pretensions to the name of nation. There is no national character; there is the machinations of necessity, brought on by misrule upon the one hand, and the retaliation of expediency upon the other. The English are neither morose, thankless, ungrateful, inconsiderate, or of naturally extravagant manner of luxury; they are not querulous without reason or vindictive without cause. Before you have anything national you must first have a nation and before you can have a nation you must have the best digest of the national will, as the only sure foundation upon which nationality can be erected. A people must have a Charter before they can have a nation. Get the Charter, and then call England the GREAT NATION, and any court in Europe will believe you; but now they laugh at you, and call your country a GREAT WORKSHOP.'
(*The Northern Star*, 10 October 1840)

(c) The Chartist Sunday School
(Whatever their differences concerning state education, Chartists could agree on the need to furnish instruction of their own to the common people and their children by voluntary initiative. The most elaborate and far-sighted plan was that devised by Lovett and Collins when in Warwick gaol.[1] O'Connor denounced this in 1841 for much the same reasons as he censured Teetotal Chartism, but the National Charter Association continued to provide teaching on a wide range of subjects through Chartist Halls and Sunday Schools, which were founded under its aegis. In December 1843 an N.C.A. Sunday School, meeting in the Carpenters' Hall, Manchester, instructed nearly 500 scholars in general knowledge and the principles of the People's Charter.[2] The following general plan for Chartist Sunday Schools appears in a letter arguing that national education must be taken up by the working people themselves as an alternative to sectarian schemes provided by the government and the churches.)

'PLAN
I advise that a committee should be chosen in every locality, who should make arrangements for the use of the Chartist meeting place for the

[1] W. Lovett and J. Collins, *Chartism. A New Organization of the People*, with an introduction by Asa Briggs (Leicester, 1969).
[2] *The Northern Star*, 2 December 1843.

purpose of establishing Sunday schools, both for children and adults, in which all kinds of useful knowledge should be taught, so far as the abilities of those engaged as teachers might enable them to proceed. The plan acted upon should be that of co-operative unity; the scholars in the higher classes acting in relation, and in such a manner as not to impede their own progress, as teachers of the lower classes; and if a plot of ground could be procured to be cultivated by the scholars, and the produce applied to their own advantage, so much the better; but in this the local circumstances of each school must decide the course to be pursued. In order to facilitate the cause, and secure unity both of plan and object, I advise that a society, to be called the "National Charter Association Sunday School Union", should be framed under the sanction of the Executive Council; and I beg to lay before you the following rules to be, if approved, generally adopted:—

1. That each school shall be called the Chartist Sunday School, in connection with the National Charter Association Sunday School Union, for diffusing sound and practical education amongst the working classes.

2. That each school shall be open for the reception of both children and adults of both sexes, and without reference to any sectarian religious creed.

3. That the superintendents, teachers, and other officers of each school shall be members of the National Charter Association, and that, should any of them withdraw from the said Association, such withdrawal shall be considered a resignation of the office held in connection with any Chartist school.

4. That each school shall be opened by singing a suitable hymn, and the offering up of prayer, and shall be closed also by singing.

5. That the Holy Scriptures shall in all the schools be used as a school book, the superintendents and teachers having a discretionary power in the choice of their particular portions they deem advisable to teach in the respective classes.

6. That no sectarian creed or catechism shall in any case be introduced, but that, instead thereof, every scholar shall be required to learn the Lord's prayer, the Ten Commandments, and the Christian Chartist Creed, as prepared by the Rev. W. Hill, and published in the Northern Star of April 3rd, 1841.

7. That as far as practicable all the scholars shall be instructed in reading, writing, arithmetic, and every branch of general knowledge; and especially in the practical application of information, so as to secure

the general prosperity and happiness of the domestic circle and the social state.

8. That if possible lectures on political, scientific, industrial, and entertaining subjects, shall be delivered every fortnight, on a week night, to which the scholars shall be admitted for one penny, and the public at such charge as may be deemed advisable; one half of the proceeds of each lecture to be given to the lecturer, as remuneration for his labour; and the other half to be divided into three portions, two of which shall be applied to support the current expenses of the school, and the remainder be paid over into the hands of a general treasurer, in aid of the objects specified in the two following rules.

9. The general committee of the union shall, as soon as circumstances will permit, form a depot of books of a general and useful character, including, not only school books of approved merit, but also such political, scientific, and other works, as may be deemed advisable for the formation of circulating libraries, one of which should be connected with every school in the union.

10. The committee shall, once in every three years, appoint a travelling agent or agents to visit all the schools, inquire into their general management, endeavour by their advice and assistance to rectify anything which may have got deranged, and in conjunction with the superintendents, teachers, etc. devise plans for future operation and extended usefulness ...

    I am, Brothers and Sisters, yours faithfully,

T. B. Smith

Leeds, April 8th, 1842.'
(*The English Chartist Circular*, Vol. II, No. 64)

5. *Public Health Reform*

(Though an earnest of better things to come, the first general Public Health Act, that of 1848, was itself an unsatisfactory measure. It established a weak General Board at the centre, leaving it to local initiative to decide whether local organs of sanitation should be set up. Much of the *Northern Star*'s criticism of the Act was justified. Corporately, however, Chartism had played no conspicuous part in the agitation preceding the Act, which was mainly an upper- and middle-class concern, though individual Chartist town councillors had furthered improvements in their respective boroughs. In a speech in the Commons on 16 March 1848 O'Connor had opposed his Land Plan to public-health reform. Claiming to have snatched men, women and children from 'the unhealthy lanes and contagious alleys', he affirmed: 'That was

the sanitary reform he looked for, better, far better, than any
government could realize.'[1])

'The Public Health Bill has, we suppose, at last been moulded into the
shape which fits it for public inspection, as a piece of legislative
workmanship. Its transmutations have been many and perplexing—a
sort of Parliamentary Proteus, which assumed new shapes even as you
looked at it. Since the 10th of February, when it made its first
appearance, under the title of a "Bill for Promoting the Public Health,"
down to the 27th of July, when it came out "a Bill as amended by the
Lords, intituled an Act for promoting the Public Health," it has passed
through six transformations, each of them involving the alteration of all
the old clauses and provisions, and the consideration of shoals of new
ones. There can be no doubt that this is mainly owing to the facile and
yielding temper of Lord Morpeth, who had the Bill in charge. A more
obstinate and determined man would have shut his ears to the countless
suggestions which poured in upon him from all quarters, and having
first satisfied himself as to the principle and machinery of the Bill, have
gone resolutely forward to his object. But Lord Morpeth is not cast in
that mould of statesmen. He may be said to "Stoop to Conquer," and,
perhaps, in this instance, looking at the multitude of interests that had to
be wrestled with and overcome, in the long run it was the best policy.
The tortoise has reached the goal at last—that is something to be
thankful for. A foundation, at least, has been laid for more effective
legislation hereafter.

In the progress of the measure through both Houses, it is generally
admitted that the Lords have shown themselves the most enlightened
and determined Sanitary Reformers; and that but for them the Bill
would ultimately have passed a mere *caput mortuum*, like many other
Whig measures, which, like Dead Sea fruit, fair and tempting to the
sight, crumbles into ashes at the touch. In fact, the Lords are removed
from the trade influences which operate on the minds of Members of the
other House, and can legislate on the subject of public health impartially.
They are not like Mr. Bright, personally interested in the provisions for
the prevention of smoke, and, therefore, they have not the obtusity of
intellect which prevents the honourable member for Manchester—that
capital of smoky chimneys—from understanding the meaning of the
term "opaque smoke". According to the amiable and innocent Mr.

[1] *The Northern Star*, 16 March 1848.

Bright, smoke is never "opaque" in itself, but merely seems so according as there is a black or a white sky in the background. You need not laugh, good people of Leeds, Bradford, Manchester, or Stockport, who are so familiar with "opaque smoke". This is the kind of stuff which may be safely talked to the squires, lordlings, and merchants, in the House of Commons, without much danger of detection. The secret of the opposition is that any attempt to compel the owners of mills to prevent the contamination of the air by the smoke belched forth from their tall shafts, involves expense. It is something, however small, that diminishes the per centage—that sacred idol, so devoutly worshipped, and, in comparison with which, public health and public well-being fades into insignificance. In addition to the owners of manufactories and steam furnaces, the owners of slaughter-houses, and persons connected with offensive trades, the shareholders of water-works—who coin one of the first necessaries of life into gold, and dole out water by the driblet—have all an interest in keeping things pretty much as they are, and preventing any interference with arrangements which yield them profit, however prejudicial to the community at large. The House of Commons is wonderfully sensitive to these influences, and had it not been that the approach of the cholera inspired a wholesome fear of consequences, it is probable that some of the Lords' amendments would have been negatived at last ...'

(*The Northern Star*, 12 August 1848)

6. *The Chartist Land Plan*

(The dominant social-reforming interest of the Chartists in the later stages of the movement was Feargus O'Connor's Land Plan. Its purpose was to settle working men on the land in two to four-acre plots with houses, on terms which would enable them to become small freeholders. The first practical steps were taken in 1845, when a Chartist Co-operative Land Society was launched, and the attempt was soon made to register it as a Friendly Society. The capital to be raised initially was to be merely £5,000. This was afterwards changed by a sequence of mutations into a more ambitious venture, the National Land Company, which obtained provisional registration as a joint stock company in June 1847. The proposal was now to raise £130,000 in shares of £1. 6s. each, payable in instalments. No one person was to hold less than two, or more than four, shares, but subscribers were to become entitled, on success in a ballot, to a plot proportionate in size to their shareholdings, to a house, and to some financial help in starting to farm. In return for this, the tenant was to pay to the Company a rental or interest payment, but a Land and Labour Bank was founded in conjunction with the scheme at the end of 1846, through which he could apply his savings to freeing his land from such charges. Underlying the plan was the assumption that land purchased by the Company would so rise in value under peasant cultivation, using spade husbandry, that it could be mortgaged to provide the means of acquiring further estates for subdivision. The Company purchased five estates, one at Heronsgate near Watford and the rest in the Gloucestershire-Worcestershire area, but settled only about 250 of its 70,000 members. It was financially unsound and based on false calculations of the agricultural potential of the holdings. When, unable to fulfil the costs of complete registration, O'Connor moved in May 1848 for a bill to bring the project within the scope of the Friendly Societies Act, Parliament responded by setting up a Select Committee, which pronounced the Company illegal. The Company was dissolved by act of parliament in August 1851. There has been much speculation by historians as to O'Connor's motives for launching this 'bubble', particularly as to whether he was reacting against industrial society in its totality or merely trying to strengthen the economic position of working men. His own explanations were not always consistent, but the following is what he told the Select Committee.)

'2439. Lord *Ingestre.* Will you be so good as to state to the Committee, as shortly as you can, what is the scope, and what are the general objects of the National Land Company?—I think the latter part of the question will embrace what otherwise might appear irrelevant. The cause of my first establishing this society was the conviction impressed upon my own mind, and which I had declared in writing and in speaking for several years, of the effect that free trade, when completed and carried out, would have upon the working classes of this country. I had heard it stated that when one channel was closed, another channel was always open for the industrious classes. I objected to the question of free trade from 1834, when I was in Parliament, and when I opposed it very violently, down to the time I established this society. During that time I had always made myself a part and parcel of the working class movement in this country, and in my own country. And I saw, during the time that I was taking part in those movements, that I was always jeopardized, and my life was endangered, when the men who were thrown out of employment called out ruthlessly, "Now we are hungry, come and lead us on." Then I was determined to befriend them, and when I was in York Castle I wrote six letters to the Irish landlords, in 1840, showing that their estates must be sacrificed and ruined if free trade was passed, if they did not subdivide them into small allotments. I showed them that they had come to the House of Commons for relief, which the House of Commons could not grant. I showed that the free-trade party were arguing that question upon enthusiasm, and complete fallacy, without the prudent and necessary concession being made to the landlord class, and the labouring class, as well as to the manufacturing class of this country; and for that reason, well knowing that railways would only be a temporary speculation, and that the workpeople engaged on them would again be thrown upon their own resources, I established this company. But I did not establish it as a mere speculative theory; I had tested it in some measure myself, for I had carried out the spade husbandry to as large an extent in my own country as any other person living in that country; and I found I could make the land produce three times as much by spade husbandry as I could by ploughed husbandry. Then in 1845, I determined to establish this company, and I established it at a conference of working men, called from different parts of the country; but from their not having any great interest in it, not many assembled. I showed the value of this plan in providing a market, better than the gin-palace or the beer-shop, for those who had small savings to carry to the labour field. When I first established it, I had no more notion of receiving 5,000 £. than I had of flying in the air. The people became, however, so fascinated with it, that the receipts went on at a speed which I had had no reason to contemplate. As soon as they had raised 4,000 £. it was determined to carry the plan into instant operation. I purchased the estate at Herringsgate, and my determination was then, as it is now, to give them an amount of aid-money, and charge five per cent upon the outlay. And when I am asked how that will realize the reproductive principle, my answer to that is, it will realize the reproductive principle with regard to land, precisely as it realizes the reproductive principle with regard to raw cotton, wool, coffee, sugar, or anything else; for it cannot be shown to me that the application of labour to the soil will lessen the value of the soil. Then the only thing I could possibly have to meet would be the aid-money of 30 £., in addition to what I expended upon the land. I then found that I could sell or mortgage the land, (or that, perhaps, selling it would be better,) and so I was led to believe that the reproductive system, as regards land, could be as well carried out as the reproductive system with regard to any raw materials on which a certain sum is expended to make it valuable, to sell again. I was aware that unless I could get Parliament to protect the industry and savings of the poor with the same scrupulous nicety that it does the savings of the rich, I should be always hampered with that question. I have yet to learn that the general expense upon an estate, that is, the expense of labour upon it, can deteriorate its value: and if I am asked as to the question of reproduction, I could easily show what I mean by that to this Committee, as I shall be able to elicit it from the overseer who has been with me from the commencement. And I would have it observed, that I am advocating the co-operative system, not the principle of communism. My plan is entirely opposed to the principle of communism, for I repudiate communism and socialism. My plan is based upon the principle of individuality of possession and co-operation of labour. What I mean by that is this, that if A. and B. are labourers, and B.'s field of wheat is not fit to reap, and A.'s field is fit to reap, then B. gives a day to A., and A. gives him a day in return. This sort of co-operative system is just what I want. I think I shall be able to show from this system of co-operation, if you admit that men must live in houses, that I can give a man a better house, built in a better style, and with better materials, with outbuildings, and two acres of good land, worth 40 £. an acre, at a less rent than a builder who builds a single house can give him the house alone for. Therefore, in fact, I put two acres to the house at less rent than the builder could give it at without the land. I found that during that period there was a very great outcry against working long hours of labour, and I found that those who were working those long hours were looking for a Ten-hours' Bill to protect them from excessive labour. I had always thought that it was a strong inducement to a man to work out his own salvation without parochial relief, or eleemosynary aid of any sort, to allow him to work as many hours as he chose, and to go to his own bed when he desired instead of going to the workhouse. And the result of my experiments upon this head has been this, that if I ask an allottee how many hours he works, he asks me what time it is light and what time it is dark; he works from daylight till dark. It is an admitted fact that labour is the source of wealth, and I believe it is the duty of every government to cultivate the usual resources of the country to the highest possible state of perfection. Then I think that a man working and having a regard for himself, every day in the year, will be much more likely to cultivate those resources to the highest state of perfection than a man working for another at so much remuneration. Then if I come to the question of reproduction, and I find a farmer with 100 acres of land employing two men and two boys, paying the interest of his capital out of their labour, able to educate his family, able to live, and either to extend his territory or to retire with something he has saved, then I say it is better that those men who have no surplus capital should be provided for out of their own labour than out of the poor-rates; and with this view I undertook this plan at Herringsgate. When I first commenced it, every one in the neighbourhood laughed and scoffed at it, because every one said it was impossible for a man to live on the production of two, or three, or four acres of land. But I met that fallacy thus: I said, "Show me the man that ever was born, or is likely to be born, that is capable of cultivating one acre of land to one-third part of its capability of producing; and if you contend that we are obliged to send to other countries for that produce which I say we can produce at home, then you are bound to show me the exact amount of land that a man can employ his labour profitably upon." My object is to show where the real value of my plan lies. There has been a very great opposition to it, and it is necessary for the Committee to understand the reason of its present constitution. I was determined to establish a settlement where the poor man could estimate the value of his own labour, below which he would not sell it in the market. At Herringsgate we commenced upon too large a scale, because the working classes of England when they hear of anything for their good, think that nothing can be too exalted, that nothing can be too stupendous or aristocratic, or superfluous to their wants.'

(Select Committee on the National Land Company, 3rd Rept., Mins. of Evidence, pp. 29–31; 1847–48 (451) XIII)

7. *Chartism and Women*

(a) Female Chartism

(Lucy Middleton has observed in a recent symposium that there were 'women supporters of the Labour movement twenty or more years before the modern Labour Party was born at the turn of the (nineteenth) century.'[1] Much earlier, in fact, Chartism marked out a special role for women, recognizing their power to mould the political attitudes of their children, the usefulness of their support in implementing the policy of exclusive dealing with pro-Chartist shopkeepers, which the General Convention endorsed in July 1839, and their unsparing devotion to the spadework of whatever cause they adopted. As T. C. Salt remarked in an Address 'To the Women of Birmingham', urging women to sign the National Petition: 'The agency of the Women sent the Missionary on his Christian pilgrimage; it redeemed the slavery of the Negroes! It has ever triumphed, and it shall now secure the most glorious and perfect of its victories.'[2] Chartists did much to awaken the political consciousness of women. It has been estimated that they formed at least eighty female Political Unions and Chartist Associations between 1837 and 1844.[3])

[1] Lucy Middleton, ed., *Women in the Labour Movement* (London, 1977), p. 22.
[2] T. C. Salt, 'To the Women of Birmingham, 16 August 1838'. Birmingham City Reference Library. F.3/358, 583.
[3] D. Jones, *Chartism and the Chartists* (London, 1975), p. 24.

'EAST LONDON FEMALE PATRIOTIC ASSOCIATION.
This association held its usual weekly meeting on Monday evening last, at the Trades' Hall, Abbey Street. After the regular business had been disposed of, arrangements were entered into for getting up the tea party. It was also resolved to publish the objects and rules of the association as follows :—

OBJECTS

1st. To unite with our sisters in the country, and to use our best endeavours to assist our brethren in obtaining Universal Suffrage.

2nd. To aid each other in cases of great necessity or affliction.

3rd. To assist any of our friends who may be imprisoned for political offences.

4th. To deal as much as possible with those shopkeepers who are favourable to the People's Charter.

LAWS AND QUALIFICATIONS OF MEMBERS

1st. All persons who are willing to subscribe to the foregoing objects, are eligible to become members of this association.

2nd. That the contributions shall be one penny per week.

3rd. That one half of the funds shall be appropriated to aid any of our brethren who shall be imprisoned for political offences, and the other half to assist any of our members who may be afflicted with illness, etc.

4th. That no money be voted for the payment of any bills or the relief of any person, without the sanction of the committee; five to form a quorum.

5th. That this association shall consist of females only.

6th. That no gentleman be admitted without the invitation of a majority of the members present.

7th. That any person wishing to lecture to, or address the association, shall signify the same in writing a week previous to the time, and the committee to report the same at a meeting of the members.

8th. That no person shall be allowed to lecture on religious subjects or on the marriage laws, except by the invitation of a majority of the members present.

9th. That the members be required to inform the secretary respecting the illness of any member, that the secretary may communicate the same to the committee, so that the case may be taken into immediate consideration.

10th. That the committee be empowered to give relief in all urgent cases as far as the funds from time to time will admit, and report the same at the weekly meeting.

11th. That this association hold their weekly meetings every Monday evening, to commence at eight o'clock and to conclude on or before ten. The foregoing objects and laws were unanimously agreed to, and adopted at a general meeting of the members, on the 16th September, 1839.'

(*The Charter*, 27 October 1839)

(b) Women in the Crowd

(Women workers formed a high proportion of the labour force in the English textile industries in the earlier nineteenth century. In the parish of Halifax at the 1841 Census worsted manufacture found employment for 3,241 women and girls as against 3,667 males. When the wave of strikes to restore wage levels and procure the People's Charter swept into the area in August 1842, the women were among the most militant.)

'MEETING ON SKIRCOAT MOOR

At two o'clock in the afternoon, a meeting of from ten to fifteen thousand people was held on Skircoat Moor. Three resolutions were passed, pledging the meeting not to return to work until the People's Charter became the law of the land; till their wages were advanced to the standard of 1840; and till a guarantee was entered into by the employers that they should be kept up to that standard. Loud shouts accompanied the passing of these resolutions. A deputation was then despatched to the magistrates to request them to release, that night, the prisoners who had been previously apprehended. After the more immediate business of the meeting was finished, the greater part of the immense multitude still remained encamped on the moor. A great number of them stretched themselves on the heather, in large circular groups, having a great many women amongst them, and several of these groups were singing Chartist hymns and songs, in which both men and women joined.

The snatches of conversation which might be heard amongst those groups were of considerable interest, as developing the spirit which animated them, which seemed to be that of firm determination. The women were extremely excited, and we heard several of them urging the men to rescue the prisoners who had been taken in the morning; one exclaimed, "If I wor a man, they sud'nt be long there;" another said "Ye're soft, if ye don't fetch 'em out to neet". These instigations from the women, who appeared from their dialect, to be chiefly Lancashire

women, who had marched with the men from the various Lancashire districts, were not without their effect, and they appeared to be gathering spirit and determination to make the attempt. Many of the men were armed with formidable bludgeons. At this meeting it was resolved to meet again at the same place, at six o'clock on Tuesday morning.'
(*The Halifax Guardian*, 20 August 1842)

(c) Chartism and the Women's Rights Movement
(Though Mary Wollstonecraft, Horace Walpole's "hyena in petticoats", had clamoured for the social emancipation of women in 1792, and William Thompson, the Irish landlord Socialist, argued for their political enfranchisement in 1825, it was not until about mid-century that the first stirrings of an agitation for votes for women could be detected here and there. Sheffield, which launched an Association for Female Franchise on 26 February 1851, was among the first to move. When the People's Charter was formulated, Lovett and his collaborators had received suggestions to include in it a call for women's suffrage, but had rejected these, not from any objection of principle, but from fear of inviting additional opposition to the Charter.[1])

'WOMAN'S RIGHTS

Though we abstain from inserting anything eugolistic (eulogistic) of our own writings, we think ourselves authorised to break through the rule in the case of our fair friends; but, especially, because the voice of woman is not sufficiently heard, and not sufficiently respected, in this country. The greatest test of enlightenment and civilisation among a people is the estimation in which woman is held, and her influence in society. Woman has an important mission in this country, and our fair friends in Sheffield shew themselves worthy of the task.

Women's Right's Association
84, Pond Street, Sheffield, Dec. 17, 1851.

Respected Sir,—A recent number of your "Notes to the People" was brought to our last meeting by one of our members, to consider that ably-written letter on "Raising the Charter from the Pot-house,"[2] and it was unanimously carried that a vote of thanks be given to you, and reply sent to that effect, for your advocacy of woman's influence; also to solicit your continued support; and in doing so, sir, we beg to state, or

[1] J. West, *A History of the Chartist Movement* (London, 1920), p. 83, drawing upon the preface to the third edition of the *People's Charter*, 1838.
[2] See above, II.3.

rather confirm your statements, that did our brothers but admit our rights to the enjoyment of those political privileges they are striving for, they would find an accession of advocates in the female sex, who would not only raise the Charter from those dens of infamy and vice from which so many of us have to suffer, but would with womanly pride strive to erase that stigma, which by the folly of our brothers has been cast on Chartism, not only by exercising their influence out of doors, but by teaching their children a good sound political education. This, sir, will never be done while men continue to advocate or meet in pot-houses, spending their money, and debarring us from a share in their political freedom.

 Signed on behalf of the meeting,

   ABIAH HIGGINBOTHAM, Cor. Sec.'

(*Notes To The People*, Vol. II, London, 1852, p. 709)

PART III

Chartism and External Affairs

(Chartism was mainly an insular movement, suspicious of foreign and colonial causes as being liable to deflect attention from the Charter. Had it not been such, O'Connor, who could usually sense the mood of the rank and file better than anyone else, would scarcely have written, as he did in the *Northern Star* in July 1847: 'Let Englishmen and Irishmen and Scotchmen work together for England, Ireland and Scotland—let Frenchmen work for France, Russians for Russia, and Prussians for Prussia. I will work only for home sweet home.'[1] From the earliest years, however, there was a creative minority, strongest in London, which sympathized actively with European revolutionaries in their struggles against autocratic regimes and foreign rule, criticized the oppression of colonial peoples by the British government, and attacked imperialist wars. Its transactions prepared the way for the International Working Men's Association formed in 1864. With the Irish nationalists the Chartists formed much closer links, especially in 1848, when the two parties demonstrated and plotted together for several months in the cities of Great Britain.)

1. *The 'Foreign Policy' Movement*

(Hatred of Russia increased mightily in Britain in the 1830s. It was nourished by that power's encroachments on the independence of Turkey in 1833, by the seizure of British ships, and by the clash of rival imperialisms in Persia and Afghanistan, where a threat to British India was discerned. English liberals, moreover, recalled the savage suppression of the Polish revolt in 1831. These animosities were compounded into a movement by David Urquhart, an eccentric British diplomat at Constantinople. In order to force a British naval execution in the Black Sea, he connived at the sending of a British vessel, the *Vixen*, to carry salt to the Circassian tribes, who were resisting the extension of Russian power on the North East coast of the Sea. Russia seized the ship in 1836, but the British Foreign Secretary, Lord Palmerston,

[1] H. Weisser, *British Working-Class Movements and Europe, 1815–48* (Manchester, 1975), p. 153.

compromised with St. Petersburg over the terms of compensation, and Urquhart was withdrawn. Conceiving the opinion that Palmerston was in the pay of the Tsar, Urquhart mounted a campaign in the press and on the platform against the government's neglect of British interests in the Near East. The Eastern crisis of 1839–41 furnished grist to his mill, for Palmerston intervened with Russia in a conflict between the Sultan and his rebellious vassal Mehemet Ali, pasha of Egypt, at the cost of alienating France. The Foreign Secretary's motive was to forestall unilateral action by Russia, but it was misrepresented as being pro-Russian. Urquhart was able to build up middle-class support, especially in Newcastle-upon-Tyne, where Charles Attwood, an ironmaster, the brother of Thomas Attwood of Birmingham, and William Cargill, a merchant, enlisted in the cause. Economic arguments against the high Russian tariffs and against Russian intrigues to the detriment of British trade in other parts of the world – France, Germany, Naples and the U.S.A.—figured prominently in the movement's propaganda. Such persuasives would not catch the Chartists, but the anti-Whig flavour of the campaign and the appeal to patriotism won over certain Chartist leaders from about the time of the ending of the first General Convention in September 1839. William Cardo, a Marylebone shoemaker, Robert Lowery of Newcastle, and John Warden of Bolton formed the nucleus of a Chartist 'foreign policy' group, which captured one major Chartist periodical the *Northern Liberator*. When Chartism recovered during 1840 from the collapse of the previous year, 'foreign policy' was put forward as one of a number of projects on which it might form. Opinion in the movement was mainly against it as a distraction from the People's Charter, and there was division but not open schism. The following report of a public meeting at Holloway Head, Birmingham, on 10 August, written by a police spy, throws light on Chartist reasons both for supporting and for opposing the foreign policy movement. Undoubtedly, the opponents had the stronger case, for the movement rested upon some wild allegations, but the arguments they used 'evinced', in Gammage's phrase, 'a narrow spirit.')

'Sir,   August 10th 1840

I was on the platform appropriated for the Speakers and friends a little before twelve O'Clock, while the leaders of the Chartist party were speculating upon the probable result of the meeting, and whether there would be any disturbance in consequence of the opposition of some of their party. Thomson avowed that his object was not so much that he cared about foreign policy, as that by its means they should be able to get up meetings as great as former ones, that they likewise had a chance by its means to get some of the middle classes to their side, which want prevented them at present from proceeding to any ulterior measures, that he did not care whose head they got, but he should be glad to be able to serve out any of the crew who assisted or gave their sanction to the prosecution of any of their friends. In these sentiments most of his immediate friends concurred, while some declared they would have the Charter in Spite of them, and they could do as they liked with all of them. A little before one Mr. C. Attwood arrived, accompanied by Richards, Cardo and Warden, but before the business of the meeting began, and while the reporters were taking their seats, Thomson got up and addressing the people in a very warm manner, pointed out to them the reporter of the Birmingham Advertiser whom he characterized as the greatest villian, Scamp, Vagabond, and everything bad that he could possibly think of, for having reported in that paper that at the Meeting on Wednesday last there were only 150 people, whereas there were upwards of two thousand, and he worked himself up in such a Passion about it that it was with difficulty he could be got down by his friends. Mr. Walson then came forward and moved that Edwin Thomson take the Chair, which he accordingly did, and standing up addressed them as fellow townsmen and fellow slaves, for said he you are slaves and so am I, the brand of slavery is set upon my forehead, and I am deemed unworthy to have any voice in making those laws under which we all suffer. If I was worth so much money it did not matter how I got it; if I plundered for it, like them I should be considered capable of exercising the rights of a free man; it was not the people but the bricks and mortar which was represented. If it was not his conscientious opinion that this movement would forward their Charter more than any other means, it should not have his support. That he prepared to stick to the Charter and to lose his life for it if necessary. That he would never suffer himself or them to be humbugged by any set of Men whatever, and while he had his senses he believed he never should. They had had a Corn-law humbug and a household-Suffrage, and they would not hearken to them because they knew it was only to draw the people from the Charter; but when any man came forward and shewed them a way to get their Charter, they should have his hearty support, hoping they would give every man a fair and unpartial hearing and not be led away by their feelings if any speaker said what was contrary to their ideas, but hear him patiently and then reflect and judge for themselves.

Mr. Warden, late delegate from Bolton then got up, and commenced by attempting to prove by his past conduct, that he must be sincere and right in the way he was now going on; if Mr. Collins had been imprisoned for what the Government chose to call treason and sedition (Collins here said, no not treason), well then sedition only, so had he: if

Collins had suffered in the cause of the people, so had he: if Collins had refused, after suffering incarceration for near nine months, to barter his principles for his liberty, he also, when the promise of release was held out to him, if he would plead guilty, had, with the Gaol staring him in the face, and probably death, in consequence of his then state of health, refused to do so, and there was not an abuse but what he then pointed out to the Court in spite of all they could do to him. He then in the strongest manner pointed out to them the treasonable conduct of the Foreign Secretary, that he was the basest and vilest of Men, that he had sold his Country to Russia, that by his villainous treason he has placed England on the verge of destruction by a War against France and the whole World. He then moved the resolution which was to the effect, "That by the treason of Lord Palmerston, the Country had been sold to Russia, placed on the verge of War with France and left entirely without defence and in the power of Russia, and that the men of Birmingham demanded Justice to be dealt upon the Traitor, according to the laws of the Country." He then spoke at great length and in a very animated manner upon the conduct of both parties in the state, characterizing all their acts as villainous in the extreme, and he did not leave off until obliged to do from exhaustion.

C. Attwood was then introduced by the Chairman as the brother of their respected and good friend T. Attwood. Mr. Attwood said he felt deeply the awful and responsible situation in which he stood, and he should require all the support of the men of Birmingham upon so great an occasion. He was come before them to charge their Foreign Secretary, as a man in his opinion possessing greater talents than any other connected with the Government, in whose hands were placed the destinies of England. He was personally unacquainted with Lord Palmerston, he should have been proud to boast of having such a man of talent in the Country, but he had perverted those talents to his Countries ruin. He had come before the working classes because they were the only classes in the Country who could redeem it from destruction; they were the only class who were exempt from the guilt in which the other classes of the Community were involved, for they had had nothing to do in it, and it was they only who could redeem it. There had never been but one Minister who had equal talents and equal duplicity with Lord Palmerston, and that was Prince Talleyrand, but whereas Talleyrand sold himself for his Country, Palmerston sold his Country for himself. He then held up in his hand a quantity of papers which he said he could not enter into the details of then, as it would take days, weeks, or he might say months to explain them. (I saw the titles; they were the printed reports of the question relative to the boundary between Maine and England, presented by the Queen to the Parliament, printed by Harrison). He placed them on the front of the Hustings and placed his foot upon them, saying thus, I place my foot upon the vile Documents; then entered into a very lengthy statement of the proceedings of Government with respect to Foreign nations:—that one time while treating with the five great powers upon some question, in one room four of them privately, and in the next room, drew up another treaty and actually signed it, leaving out France who knew nothing of the matter. That the foreign Secretary by every possible means had seconded the ambitious views of Russia for the sake of Russian Gold. They had upon occasions left their Ambassador without power to act, by artfully sending him two dispatches of the same date, so that he could not know how to act before writing to his Country for fresh instructions, which would take at least six months to reach him. That they had set aside treaties which they had made, at the command of Russia, had kept upon the question of America boundary, and given the United States a pretext for increasing her Army and Navy to a great extent. That we were ourselves left entirely destitute and feeble, as there are only three ships of the line in England of 100 Men each only, and only mounting Guns in her lower Decks, and one Broadside from a French Frigate would send them to the bottom. That being in this defenceless state, Russia was ready to step in to our assistance against France, and when they had got here would they ever go away again? Certainly not. He then eulogized the Character of the French nation, said they were a brave and generous people, that they were ready to sympathize with the English, that M. Thiers was the declared and decided friend of England, and for that reason the English Government hated him.

Mr. Attwood went on to say that with so small an armament as ours, the French by a short sail could come upon us and over run our Towns, penetrating over to Birmingham—but at the same time France, that brave, generous & patriotic Nation was favourable to the English people. That they look upon them as brethren knit together by one common interest, and if the people of England did their duty and sent forth a strong manifestation of attachment to France, they were ready to receive them with open arms. He seconded the resolution and sat down. I should have stated that Warden in his speech produced and read part of a French newspaper, in which it showed that the French and English ought to be united as one nation and that the people of England did not wish to go to war, or something to that effect. John Collins came forward and said he had an amendment to propose, the substance of which was that while the meeting concurred in all that had been said and a great deal more, yet that no question should divert the attention of the people from the Charter. He said that by a very curious circumstance he was called upon that day to address them under a foreign flag (alluding to the Circassian flag which was placed at the centre of the hustings); he did not understand it. Mr. Attwood had been making a long statement, but he had told them nothing new; he had said that the acts of the Foreign Minister had been villainous in the extreme, but so had been the acts of all the Ministers. They were prepared to hear all that had been said & a great deal more; at the same time he was very much obliged to the Gentleman for bringing forward so much information, as the more they knew their wrongs the more would they be determined in endeavouring to get them redressed. Mr. Warden had said that because he had suffered in the cause of freedom, therefore he must be right; but he denied that, for Roman Catholics had died for their Religion, and Protestants had died for theirs, but that did not prove either of them were right, it only proved their sincerity. Again they had been told the enemy would come upon them, and steal their wives and their cattle. What was that to them? They would not take his sheep or any thing else for he had not got any, and as to their wives, he had seen women breaking stones on the Highway, and doing work like horses. Would there be any thing to fear there? What did it signify to the working classes, if they were to continue to be Slaves, who were to be their masters? He cared not whether the Russians or the French, or any other nation came and conquered them, they could be no worse off than they were now. Let these gentlemen come forward and offer them something whereby they might get their Charter sooner, and he would be with them heart and soul. During the time Collins was speaking, Attwood was giving instruction to Cardo how to reply to his objections, and at length he spoke in so loud a tone and so much of it, that Collins turned round to him and begged he would not interrupt him so much. He said he had come forward and called upon them to impeach Lord Palmerston, but how were they to do it? If they would not give them their just rights, he could not see how they could consent any more to give them Lord Palmerston's head, which was no use to them now it was on, and it would be of still less value off. He could not see how they were more likely to get one than the other. Attwood answered, by Common Law. Common Law! They were as likely to get Common law upon a Lord, as

Common Justice for themselves. Mr. Attwood said, if Lord Palmerston was to cut his Vallet's throat, they could then hang him by Common law, but he believed otherwise. If the Vallet was to cut Lord Palmerston's throat, then it would be a different thing, they would soon hang him. Attwood said he wished he would cut his throat; they should then get rid of him easily. Let them all stick to the Charter, and once get that, and they would then have it all their own way.

Mr. Warden again got up and, laying hold of the Circassian flag, said Mr. Collins had derided that Banner, that they had nothing to do with Foreigners, but he would say in the words of T. Payne "Where liberty is there is my Country". He then went on in a eulogistic strain upon the bravery of the Circassian people, how they had nobly fought for their freedom, and had gained it at the expence of their blood, holding them up as an example that Englishmen ought to follow. He then said he would withdraw his original motion and second the amendment of Collins—(Empson immediately lays hold of Collins and says, "there's a trick in this, they must not be allowed to do that")—with this proviso, that he should be at liberty to bring forward the original motion again. This declaration set Collins's party in a ferment, and he jumped up and said he protested against that proceeding, as they only wanted to play a trick upon them. Warden then withdrew his support of the amendment; then he said Mr Collins has told you he has nothing to lose by the enemies coming, they could not take any thing from him, but he would ask, what they would be likely to get under a Despot like the Emperor of Russia with the bayonets of his Soldiers pointed to their breasts. Empson then spoke & said he very much doubted the sincerity of these men who had come forward; he believed they were sent to entrap them. It was all very fine to talk about cutting off Lord Palmerston's head, but in his opinion it was high Treason to say, and they only wanted to draw the working men into saying so. They all knew of the secret service money & what it was used for. Where did the money come from to pay for all these things (clapping his hands upon the flagstaff and the hustings)? Why from the Carlton Club to be sure! Who was it that paid Cardo, Richards, Thomason, & Warden to go about the Country? Here the Chairman interrupted & said he would not sit there & hear such personalities used towards any one. He very well knew who was meant by it, it was himself. He then began again about the villainous lies which had been told in the Birmingham Journal about Mr. Dee's wine etc. It was with much difficulty that Thompson's friends could get him down, while cries of "Chair" & "question" was called on all sides. Empson then resumed by saying, that Collins was well known to them all, that he himself was known to many of them, and they ought to be listened to and not the strangers in the Town who had only come to make divisions among them, and get them in the power of the law. They would have the Charter & nothing else, and when they had got that, they should have all the power in their own hands, and could do as they liked with it. Thomason was the next speaker but what he said was merely a repetition of what had already been said. He advocated this present movement only as a quick means of getting the Charter. Mr. Hill then got up and took the same side as Empson, and said if these men would only point out to him the means of getting the Charter, he would go with them and spill every drop of his blood for it. Cardo, then rose and declared himself to be as much for the Charter as ever he was, but he was not prepared to say that because he could not get it one way he would not try another. The movement was one which would get them the Charter in much less time than by any other means, and as such he advocated it. Several others wished to get up and address the meeting, but it was very evident that to keep it open any longer would be productive of evil consequences; they were dissuaded from it. One person in the Crowd called out for liberty to speak, and on the intercession of Collins he was allowed, and coming on the platform, he began to speak, but as he was evidently either mad or drunk, the Chairman pulled him down and the meeting closed by passing Collins' amendment, giving a vote of thanks to the Chairman, and three cheers for the incarcerated Chartists. It is the intention, I understand from Thomason, to distribute Tracts etc. among the people upon the Foreign Policy question, & to use every exertion to agitate upon it, with a view on the part of the Chartists to get the Charter through its means, although I do not believe from what I hear among themselves that Attwood is at bottom favourable to the Charter.

most respectfully etc.,

(sd.) James Barnett'

(Report of P. C. James Barnett to the Birmingham Police Commissioner, 10 August 1840. H.O. 40/56)

2. *The Fraternal Democrats*

(The Society of Fraternal Democrats was the principal organ of the class-conscious internationalism of the Chartist Left. Emerging from a growing interest of working-class radicals in foreign affairs in the mid-eighteen forties, it was founded at a public supper at the Chartist City

Hall on 22 September 1845 to celebrate the anniversary of the establishment of the first French Republic in 1792. The society rested upon a conjunction of Chartists like Harney and Ernest Jones with exiled continental revolutionaries living in London, notably the pre-Marxist German Socialists, Schapper, Bauer and Moll, expelled from France for participating in the Blanquist rising of 1839. Important as an educative influence for proletarian internationalism later in the century, the Fraternal Democrats exerted limited influence on Chartism as a whole, which, except during the excitement raised by the 1848 revolutions, remained remarkably insular. The exiles and the Chartists differed in methods of proceeding, the Germans clinging surreptitiously to the passwords and rituals of the continental secret societies like the League of the Just, while the Chartists ran the Fraternal Democrats on open, propagandist lines.[1] The principles of the Society were rehearsed as follows at its first anniversary meeting in September 1846.)

'THE FRATERNAL DEMOCRATS TO THE DEMOCRATS OF ALL NATIONS.
"All men are brethren"

Fellow Men,

… Our principles are expressed in the declaratory motto of our society—"All men are brethren".

In accordance with this declaration, we denounce all political hereditary inequalities and distinctions of "caste;" consequently, we regard kings, aristocracies, and classes monopolising political privileges in virtue of their possession of property, as usurpers and violators of the principle of human brotherhood. Governments elected by, and responsible to, the entire people, is our political creed.

We believe the earth with all its natural productions to be the common property of all; we, therefore, denounce all infractions of this evidently just and natural law as robbery and usurpation. We believe that the present state of society which permits idlers and schemers to monopolise the fruits of the earth and the productions of industry, and compels the working classes to labour for inadequate rewards, and even condemns them to social slavery, destitution and degradation, to be essentially unjust. The principle of universal brotherhood commands that labour and rewards should be equal. Such is our social creed.

We condemn the "national" hatreds which have hitherto divided mankind, as both foolish and wicked; foolish, because no one can decide for himself the country he will be born in; and wicked, as proved by the

[1] See especially Weisser, *op.cit.*, notably Chap. IV.

feuds and bloody wars which have desolated the earth, in consequence of these national vanities. Convinced, too, that national prejudices have been, in all ages, taken advantage of by the people's oppressors, to set them tearing the throats of each other, when they should have been working together for their common good, this Society repudiates the term "Foreigner," no matter by, or to whom, applied. We recognise our fellow-men, without regard to "country," as members of one family, the human race; and citizens of one commonwealth—the world. Finally, we recognise the great moral law, "Do unto thy brother, as thou wouldst thy brother should do unto thee," as the great safeguard of public and private happiness. Such is our moral creed.

Our one aim is the triumph of the principles above enunciated. In pursuit of that object we seek mutual enlightenment, and labour to propagate the principle of general and fraternal co-operation. Once for all we explicitly state, that we repudiate all idea of forming any "party" in addition to the parties already existing in England. We desire not to rival, but to aid all men who are honestly combined to work out the emancipation of the people; and with this object in view, we shall gladly hail the adhesion of all convinced of the justice of our principles, and the purity of our motive. Whether few or many, we shall continue to act in accordance with the duties we believe we owe to our fellow-men, leaving them to judge of us by our actions ...

Signed by the Secretaries:

G. JULIAN HARNEY,	native of Great Britain;
CARL SCHAPPER,	native of Germany;
J. A. MICHELOT,	native of France;
PETER HOLM,	native of Scandinavia;
J. SCHABELITZ,	native of Switzerland;
LOUIS OBORSKI,	native of Poland;
N. NEMETH,	native of Hungary;

September 21st, 1846.'
(*The Northern Star*, 26 September 1846)

3. *The Peoples' International League*[1]

(While the Fraternal Democrats worked closely with the National Charter Association, dissidents from O'Connorism launched their own brand of internationalism in a spirit of class co-operation. William Lovett's Democratic Friends of All Nations founded in 1844 was followed in April 1847 by the Peoples' International League. The latter

[1] Commonly called the People's International League.

was a response to events in Poland, where, following an insurrection in Galicia led by the Polish gentry, the Republic of Cracow, hitherto nominally independent, was annexed by Austria with the agreement of Russia and Prussia, given at a conference in Vienna in November 1846. Palmerston submitted a mild protest against this violation of the 1815 peace settlement, but took no further action. The Peoples' International League drew support from independent Chartists like Thomas Cooper, Henry Vincent and W. J. Linton, and from middle-class radicals like Dr. Bowring and the Rev. W. J. Fox, once a writer for the Anti-Corn Law League. It is instructive to compare the limited concern to obtain self-government for subject nationalities expressed in the resolutions of the League with the social revolutionary principles of the Fraternal Democrats. The Democrats resented the 'namby-pamby liberalism' of the League, which held up English freedom as a model to the countries of Europe.[1] Mazzini, the exiled Italian liberal nationalist, exercised the strongest continental influence on the League.)

'WHEN, last year, in defiance not only of justice, but of their own Treaties, the three Absolute Powers of Europe violated the neutrality and destroyed the independence of the Republic of Cracow; when the rest of Europe, beholding that wrong, did nothing to redress it; and the British People, whatever their indignation, scarcely so much as echoed the protest of their Government; then, observing that general abdication of national duty, that carelessness of national honour, and the want of anything like intelligence upon what are called foreign questions, it was felt by some few men that the time was come for an organisation, whose aim should be to rouse the public mind to a recognition of the rights and duties of Nations, and to furnish, from trustworthy sources, the necessary information through which a healthy public opinion might be formed upon all international questions.

In pursuance of this idea, a public meeting was held on Wednesday, the 28th of April last, at the Crown and Anchor Tavern, Strand (Dr. Bowring, M.P., being in the chair), at which meeting the following resolutions were passed :—

'That an Association be now formed, to be called the "Peoples' International League," the objects of which shall be as follows :—

'To enlighten the British Public as to the Political Condition and Relations of Foreign Countries.

'To disseminate the Principles of National Freedom and Progress.

'To embody and manifest an efficient Public Opinion in favour of the

---

[1] Weisser, *op. cit.*, p. 160.

right of every People to Self-government and the maintenance of their own Nationality.

'To promote a good understanding between the Peoples of all countries.'

'That the following gentlemen shall be the officers of the League for the ensuing year :—

TRUSTEES

MR. W. H. ASHURST.　　MR. P. A. TAYLOR.
MR. JOS. TOYNBEE.

COUNCIL

MR. W. B. ADAMS.
— W. H. ASHURST.
— GOODWYN BARMBY.
DR. BOWRING, M.P.
MR. Wm. CARPENTER.
— THOMAS COOPER.
— Wm. CUMMING.
— T. S. DUNCOMBE, M.P.
DR. EPPS.
MR. W. J. FOX.
— S. M. HAWKES.
— THORNTON HUNT.
MR. DOUGLAS JERROLD.
— W. J. LINTON.
— R. MOORE.
— J. H. PARRY.
— W. SHAEN.
— J. STANSFELD.
— P. A. TAYLOR.
— P. A. TAYLOR, JUN.
— R. TAYLOR.
— J. TOYNBEE.
— H. VINCENT.
— J. WATSON.

AUDITORS

MR. AUSTIN.　　MR. H. MITCHELL.
MR. SOLLY.

SECRETARY

MR. W. J. LINTON.

'That all persons agreeing with the objects of the League may become members on enrolling their names, and paying an annual subscription of *one shilling or upwards*'.

(Secretary's Report to the first Public Meeting of the Peoples' International League at the Crown and Anchor Tavern, Strand, 15 November 1847. Howell Collection, Bishopsgate Institute)

4. *Chartism's European Role in the Year of Revolutions*
(a) The Grand Design of Karl Marx
(While resident in Brussels in the years 1845–48 Marx and Engels elaborated the philosophy of dialectical materialism, and sought to impose their leadership and their views on the less theoretical German revolutionary Socialist leaders exiled in London. They scored a notable triumph in June 1847, when the members of the old League of the Just, Schapper, Bauer, Moll and others merged their organisations into the Communist League. It was to pursue this success that Marx came to London in November 1847 for the second congress of the Communist League, and was commissioned with Engels to prepare the Communist Manifesto. A second purpose of his visit was to cultivate the Fraternal Democrats. As his speech at a gathering of that body to commemorate the Polish insurrection of 1830 reveals, he recognized that Britain, the most advanced industrial nation in the world, must spearhead a proletarian revolution, and that the Chartists had a special role to play. When he spoke he could not wholly foresee the revolutionary holocaust which was to engulf Europe within a few months of that time, but for internationally-minded Chartists his words must have furnished an added incentive to agitate, as the tempo of events on the continent increased.)

'THE POLISH REVOLUTION.

IMPORTANT PUBLIC MEETING
The anniversary of the Polish Insurrection of 1830 was celebrated on Monday last, the 29th of November, by a public meeting, at the German Society's Hall, Drury-lane.

The meeting had been called by the society of Fraternal Democrats, in conjunction with the Democratic Committee for Poland's Regeneration. The room was crowded with natives of England, Scotland, Ireland, France, Germany, Belgium, and Poland. ...

Dr. MARX, the delegate from Brussels, then came forward, and was greeted with every demonstration of welcome, and delivered an energetic oration in the German language, the substance of which was as follows—He had been sent by the Democrats of Brussels to speak in their name to the Democrats of London, and through them to the Democrats of Britain, to call on them to cause to be holden a congress of nations—a congress of working men, to establish liberty all over the world. (Loud cheers.) The middle classes, the Free Traders, had held a congress, but their fraternity was a one sided one, and the moment they found that such congresses were likely to benefit working men, that

moment their fraternity would cease, and their congresses be dissolved. (Hear, hear.) The Democrats of Belgium felt that the Chartists of England were the real Democrats, and that the moment they carried the six points of their Charter, the road to liberty would be opened to the whole world. "Effect this grand object, then, you working men of England," said the speaker, "and you will be hailed as the saviours of the whole human race." (Tremendous cheering.) ...'
(*The Northern Star*, 4 December 1847)

(b) Chartism and the Containment of Revolution in Europe
(Marx was not alone in perceiving the relevance of Chartism to events on the continent. This was also noted by the defenders of order, as the two following extracts from letters received by Lord John Russell after the celebrated Chartist demonstration in London on 10 April 1848 had reached a peaceful outcome, clearly show. The first was from his sister-in-law, the wife of the British Minister to the Court of the King of Piedmont at Turin. Before the Chartists paraded on Kennington Common, revolution had spread from Vienna to the Austrian possessions in Lombardy and Venetia, and Charles Albert, the Piedmontese king, had made war on Austria on behalf of the rebels. Palmerston sought a solution in terms of an Austrian withdrawal from Northern Italy, but there were apprehensions in British diplomatic circles at the beginning of April that the French republican government might intervene not only in Lombardy but in the possessions of the King of Piedmont himself,[1] thus reviving the conflict, which sprang from the first French Revolution. The second letter, from a leading French economist to a secretary of the Board of Trade, refers to the internal situation in France.)

'It has seemed unnatural to me during the past days of anxiety about you & your difficult task of keeping the country safe, not to write to Fanny, but her time was too near, for me to do so. Your admirable arrangements & their full success meet with an approbation which must be a great gratification to you. And if the effect of the failure of this attempt to create mischief has been great in England it is certainly not less so on the continent. All eyes were turned to London perhaps with apprehension greater than that felt there, and people seem to breathe more freely since they have seen that the good sense & good feeling of the country still keeps it safe. You have given an excellent example to the rest of the world, & in these days when all pretend to understand

---

[1] R. Abercromby to Lord John Russell, 4 April 1848. Russell Papers, P.R.O. 30/22/7b, fs. 215–16.

constitutional government it does not pass un-noticed. What is to be the result on Italy of the struggle in which she is now wisely or unwisely, irretrievably engaged. This country feels *now* how serious a game it is playing, & although it does not see how, I believe it hopes more from England than from any other quarter, though we are disliked & abused pretty generally at present, for not having at once chosen to change past language & approve of war against Austria. War is such a sad thing that I do hope you wise people may have discovered some means by which to endeavour to settle matters in a manner less barbarous than by fighting. But the end of war in Lombardy will not be the end of Italian difficulties I fear, for our "Fratelli" are sadly inclined to forget that brothers ought not to quarrel. Whatever you may all think of our King I hope also that his Kingdom may not be allowed to fall to pieces or be swallowed up if it can be helped. How glad I am that *we* need not fight for any of these questions ...'

(Lady Mary Abercromby, Turin, to Lord John Russell, 19 April 1848. Russell Papers, P.R.O. 30/22/7b, fs. 316–20)

'Paris le 16 Avril 1848

Cher Monsieur et Ami,

Le Gouvernement Anglais et la ville de Londres, par leur attitude ferme et résolue devant les émeutiers, viennent de rendre au monde un grand service. Si le désordre eut triomphé ou qu'il eut balancé les chances, il n'y aurait pas eu de limite a l'anarchie sur le continent et surtout chez nous ...'

[The remainder of the letter is devoted to explaining the delicate political balance in France and in the provisional government established at the February Revolution which overthrew Louis Philippe. The moderate Republicans ('Girondins') remain in control, but are challenged by Socialist extremists, strong in Paris (the 'Mountain'). This gives point to his opening remarks.]

(Michel Chevalier à G. R. Porter, 16 Avril 1848. Russell Papers, P.R.O. 30/22/7b, fs. 306–9)

5. *Chartism and the Irish Crisis*

(Early in 1848 Ireland was again poised on the brink of insurrection. The urge came from the Young Ireland, or Confederate, party, a corps of Protestant or anti-clerical intellectuals led by Smith O'Brien, who had seceded from Daniel O'Connell's Repeal Association in July 1846 from impatience of its Catholic tone and gradualist methods. Their movement

progressed slowly, but in the following year John Mitchell, the most
forceful of their number, influenced by the teachings of the agrarian
revolutionary Finton Lalor, emerged as the advocate of a spontaneous
peasant uprising against the Anglo-Irish landlords. The fall of Louis
Philippe's monarchy late in February 1848 encouraged Young Ireland as
a whole to become militant. Its leaders announced the formation of an
armed National Guard, planned to recruit an Irish Brigade in the United
States, and approached the French provisional government for help. No
formal plans for rebellion had been fixed upon, but Charles Trevelyan,
the assistant secretary of the Treasury, learned from one of his Dublin
contacts, Jonathan Pim, nearly a week before the Chartist Kennington
Common demonstration, that a great majority of Irish Catholics would
join an insurrection if they thought it likely to succeed, but that, if no
tumult occurred, the danger would pass away.[1] In England Chartist and
Confederate discontents coalesced, for the London Irish participated in
the Kennington Common demonstration as a body. It seems probable
that the implications for Ireland figured among the calculations of the
Whig government when they made their heavy preparations to prevent
disorder in the London streets, for Trevelyan, with his strong Hibernian
connections, brought early pressure to bear on the prime minister to
organize the London Shopkeepers and curtail the Chartist procession. He
was also active in frightening the wives of cabinet ministers concerning
the outcome of the London meeting. Lord John Russell and the Viceroy,
Lord Clarendon, were unduly alarmed about the danger of insurrection
in Ireland. The Confederate leaders were deeply divided on methods and
lacked the support of the peasantry, debilitated rather than inflamed by
two years of famine. It was the government's own repressive measures
that pushed the country towards the ineffective rising which eventually
occurred in July.)

'Dublin   10 April
48

My dear Trevelyan

Within the last 24 hours the minds of the respectable portion of the
Inhabitants are beginning to be considerably alarmed. What may have
taken place to have caused it I have not been able to learn but such is the
case; from what is seen in the streets there is nothing to indicate that any
thing particular is stirring or in agitation; all are looking anxiously for
the accounts of the result of this day's proceedings in London; whatever
it may be, it will have its due influence upon the Irish and more
particularly upon the Dublin People.

I have just had a conversation with an intelligent Gentleman who is

[1] J. P. to C. E. Trevelyan, 31 March 1848. Russell Papers, P.R.O. 30/22/7b, fs. 223–25.

just returned from a Tour in the Country. He states that the people are all ready, but will act in accordance with the Dublin movement: such I believe is the real state of affairs.

> sincerely yours,
> Harry D. Jones'

(Col. H. D. Jones to C. E. Trevelyan, 10 April 1848. Russell Papers, P.R.O. 30/22/7b, fs. 270–1)

'The termination of the Chartist Meeting has had an excellent effect here, but I am told O'Brien is coming over, burning with rage at the little impression he made in the House.'
(Sir Randolph Routh, Dublin, to C. E. Trevelyan, 12 April 1848. Russell Papers, P.R.O. 30/22/7b, fs. 284–5)

6. *Chartism and the Colonies*
(a) Obstruction of the British India Society
(The British India Society was formed in 1839 to reform the Indian land revenue system, in which taxes were largely raised by deductions from the rent paid by the peasant for his land. By this arrangement, it was argued, cotton growing in India was discouraged and the common people were reduced to destitution. Philanthropic motives underpinned the campaign. George Thompson, the travelling secretary, had been active formerly in the British and Foreign Anti-Slavery Society, and among his motives was the desire to bring free-grown cotton into competition with the slave-cultivated produce of America. But the Society was also supported for economic reasons by British mercantile and manufacturing interests. In Manchester, where the division between classes was acute, the Chartists saw its endeavours as a diversion from their own.)

'MANCHESTER.
LECTURE.—On Friday evening last, Mr. George Thompson delivered his second and last lecture on the claims, resources, and slavery of British India. He was listened to very attentively, and without the least interruption. At the close, Mr. Joseph Brotherton, M.P., rose and said, he had no doubt but the resolution he had to move would meet the support of the meeting, after the eloquent address they had heard. His friend had shewn them that India was inexhaustible in her resources, but millions of its inhabitants had died of famine, the evils of which he attributed to the misgovernment of the British Legislature. They had heard that night that justice to India would be commercial prosperity to England. He saw

that promoting the prosperity of other countries was advancing our own welfare; he deplored, as much as any man, the condition of his own country; he said [he had] impressed upon the President of the Board of Control the necessity of good roads in India, in order that they might be enabled to bring their produce to the sea coasts; but he need not take up any more of their time; as the lecturer had done justice to the subject, he would conclude by moving the following resolution:—"That the objects of the British India Society are worthy the attention of the benevolent and philanthropic exertions of the British public, and connected with the vital interests of Great Britain." Mr. John Brooks seconded it in a speech of some length, and made some exaggerated statements relative to the working classes of this country getting higher wages than they had for thirty years before. (He was saluted with cries of "It's trash, and we know better;" "Trash;" "Sit thee down.") Not feeling satisfied, he rose again, and said that this was a home question, for, could they only accomplish their object, it would give such an impetus to trade, that it would cause the manufacturers of England to build factories, side by side, from Manchester to London. (Cries of "We have too many rattle-boxes already.") The Chairman was about to put the motion of the meeting, when Mr. Campbell, Chartist, rose and said he had an amendment to move; the Chairman objected, by saying that the meeting was called for a special purpose. All now became confusion, amid cries of "Chair, chair," "Order, order," "Go on," and "Campbell, go on, go on; and let us have fair play." Mr. Linney rose and said all that the Chartists wanted was fair play, and that they were resolved to have. (Hear, hear, and cheers.) Mr. Campbell then said, that the reason he came forward to move an amendment was, not that he wished slavery to continue in India, but because he thought it inconsistent in them to stretch their necks fourteen or fifteen thousand miles across the seas for objects of charity, so long as there were so many white slaves here moving among us. He would put it to every working man whether, as exports had increased, the comforts of the people had not been diminished? Then away with that will-o'-the-wisp called extended commerce ... He should move the following amendment: "That the people, prior to travelling to India, or other countries, to emancipate the people, ought to obtain a thorough reform of the Commons' House of Parliament, and then we would have power to free them, being ourselves freemen." [seconded by Linney] ...

The Chairman was then called to put the amendment, and said they were in doubt respecting the amendment being put. A young man in the body of the hall argued that the amendment was quite in order. After consulting his friends behind, the amendment was put and carried by an overwhelming majority ...'

(*The Northern Star*, 12 December 1840)

(b) Anti-imperialism

(The view of empire presented in the following extract appeared in a series of articles on emigration of working men from Britain, which the Chartist leader Ernest Jones, like Cobbett before him, set out to discourage. Despite his Socialist convictions, which were influenced by Marx and Engels, in his dislike of formal empire he drew close to Cobden and Bright and the other luminaries of the middle-class Manchester School, though his opinions were more unequivocally presented.)

'The entire system of colonial government is an error. Some nations think, if they were to lose their colonies, those colonies being great and flourishing, they would lose some tangible advantage. Nothing of the sort. Every advantage derived from a colony would be derived from a free state—be it commercial or otherwise—and the disadvantages, the expense, risk, anxiety and responsibility attaching to colonial and distant dependencies, would be removed. England would derive more benefit from a free state of Hindostan, a free Republic of Australia, than she does from abject, crouching, or rebelling nations—and she would no longer stand before the world as a sanctimonious murderess, painting the profaned cross with the blood of every nation she is strong enough to massacre. In the course of these papers the author will have occasion to reveal some of that "mystery of iniquity" which cries aloud to heaven from every part of earth, and to tear that mask of hypocrisy aside, that would veil its deep died criminality, under the names of honour, interest, and religion.'

(*Notes To The People*, Vol. I, London, 1851, p. 135)

PART IV

Law and Order

1. *The Chartist Challenge*
(a) The Unrest of the Masses
(During the spring of 1839, while the Chartist Convention prepared its Petition for presentation to Parliament, impatience grew in the factory districts. Spurred by hunger and want of employment and whipped up by fiery orations delivered at repeated Chartist meetings, working men equipped themselves with pikes and to a lesser extent with firearms, drilled openly on village greens and studied the textbook of an Italian revolutionary, Frances Macerone, on the technique of street fighting. Fears of insurrection centred upon the large demonstrations which the Convention called simultaneously at Whitsuntide at focal points in widely separated areas. The purpose of these assemblages was merely to test public opinion on the desirability of implementing at a future date the ulterior measures proposed by the Convention to force through the Charter, but men of property were apprehensive lest the meetings themselves might issue in violence. Major General Sir Charles James Napier, the able commander of the troops in the Northern district, believed that the Chartist leaders intended to keep the peace, but feared the effect of some accidental occurrence which might spark off violence in the excited state of the country, and deployed his force with deterrent effect. His assessment was, no doubt, a sound one, and applied generally to the peak periods of Chartist agitation in 1839 and 1848. How much truth there was in the allusion to Dr. Taylor's intentions is impossible to establish. There is supporting evidence from Alexander Somerville of a Chartist 'Secret Committee of War' during the sittings of the Convention,[1] but Taylor's plans appear to have been somewhat provisional.)

'Our great meeting[2] passed off quietly. There was a very general feeling amongst the *respectables* that we should come to blows; and a

---

[1] See Alfred Plummer, *Bronterre* (London, 1971), pp. 107–8.
[2] The Whitsuntide demonstration on Kersal Moor, Manchester, on 25 May 1839.

fervent hope that the soldiers would *make an example*. Wemyss justly said there was as sanguinary a disposition as could well be among the civilians. I adopted several tests to ascertain numbers, and certainly, including women and children, they were under thirty thousand; this is worth recording as a testimony against the Chartist assertion that there were half a million. Mr. Bingham[1] told me today that the presence of troops had prevented a row; that Doctor Taylor[2] came from Glasgow expressly to lead them; that they consulted and decided we were too strong; moreover that they had and still have five pieces of brass cannon concealed. How far his information is good I cannot say; but the 10th Regiment having been suddenly brought up by railroad from Liverpool certainly upset their calculations of our strength. I also puzzled them by the march of a strong troop of dragoons from an out village the morning of the meeting: they thought it might be the advanced guard of a larger force.'

(General C. J. Napier to Colonel W. Napier, 3 June 1839. W. Napier, *The Life and Opinions of General Sir Charles James Napier, G.C.B.* (London, 1857), Vol. II, p. 41)

(b) Insurrectionary Chartism

(What Mr. E. P. Thompson has identified as 'the illegal tradition' in the labour movement, with its underground plotting and arming, nevertheless continued in Chartism, though subordinate to the movement's main technique of intimidating the government by open demonstration. As in 1839, so in 1848, it was mainly in evidence after the popular agitation had collapsed. In the latter year two insurrections were plotted. One, in London, was timed for 16 or 18 June, and was to encompass the erection of barricades and the firing of public buildings. (See Part IV, 7) Nothing came of this, but in the middle of August planned disturbances occurred in the Manchester area and the police shortly afterwards prevented a rising in the metropolis. At Ashton-under Lyne, on Monday 14 August, a policeman was shot dead while watching columns of armed Chartists march through the streets in the middle of the night. The following deposition by an accomplice provides the background of the conspiracy to seize the town. The witness was evidently not with the party which shot Constable Bright, but belonged to a different section sent to the outskirts to command one of the entrances to Ashton. Formation of the National Guards, described in the extract, was approved by a Chartist delegate meeting for Lancashire and Yorkshire on 28 May.[3] It is made clear that the outbreak was designed to

---

[1] An intermediary used by Napier to communicate with the Manchester Chartists.

[2] Dr. John Taylor, an Ayrshire surgeon and extreme physical-force Chartist.

[3] R. G. Gammage, *History of the Chartist Movement 1837–1854* (London, 1969), p. 332.

coincide with similar activities in other towns and that the Confederate rising in Ireland late in July, though in fact crushed by this time, was a source of encouragement to the Chartist extremists.)

'Lancashire to wit. Deposition of John Latimer sworn before James Lord, Esqr., one of Her Majesty's Justices of the peace in and for the said County, this 8th Day of Septr. 1848 at Ashton under Lyne in the said County. John Latimer says. I was 19 years of age last November, and am a cotton weaver. I have lived in Ashton ever since I can recollect. I have been a member of the Land scheme for some time. About the time when the paper produced by Mr. Newton in reference to a National Guard was published, I went and enrolled myself at the Chartist room as one of the National Guards. This was about 6 weeks before Mc. Douall lectured at Ashton. James Milligan was the Colonel over the whole six divisions of the National Guards. Samuel Sigley was Captain over the 6th division. A Samuel Bardsley was Captain over the 5th division. Edwd. Harrop was Captain over the 4th division. A shoemaker named Roberts, over the 3rd. A man named Samuel Fletcher [Smallshaw] was Captain over the 2nd division. Joseph Taylor was first Captain over the 1st division, and he left, and then Joseph Constantine became Captain over that division. There were four lieutenants under each Captain— each of the Lieutenants had twenty-five men under him. I was a Corporal of the first section of the 6th division. William Winterbottom was the Lieutenant over the Section in which I was Corporal. The first section of the 6th Division consisted of Samuel Bottomley, Edward Hamer, John Hallow, Edward Horsfield, William Mann, John Ashton, Daniel Ashton, Stephen Gillson, John Gillson, John Bolton, James Marsh, James Wrigley, John Bertwhistle, John Kettlewell, Alfred Haughton, a man named Walker, William Winterbottom who was Lieutenant, and myself. The number was this at the last, others making up the number to twenty-five having left us before the outbreak. We met according as Milligan directed us, sometimes every night in the week, and sometimes once a week only. Milligan told Sigley, Sigley told Winterbottom and Winterbottom told me, and then I saw the several men and told them of the meetings. This was the same with each division. Edward Flannagan was a leader over other twenty five and William Broadbent was over twenty five also. I have often seen Broadbent at the rooms. We paid a penny a week & our names were called over from a book. I have often seen Aitkin in the room. He came in frequently, and so were all that I have heard tell of being committed.

There was a room that was called the Guard room; it adjoins Aitkin's house. I have seen pikes sold there. John Bardsley, and also a man who lives in Hurst, sold pikes there. I bought one for William Macklin. He was a National Guard. He was a Corporal in the 6th Division, but I don't know the Section. I gave 2s/2d. to John Bardsley for the pike. The Guard room was on the opposite side of the yard to the large room, & Aitkin kept his coals there. I have often seen Bardsley with pikes. Any one who wanted to buy a pike knew where to get it. I bought one for myself from a man named John Allen, a blacksmith. This was about June. He brought some as a sample & I ordered one and paid 2s/6d for it. I afterwards sold it to Stott who was also a National Guard. We were regularly advised when we went up the street to keep together in regular step. We were also advised to hold ourselves in readiness at a moment's notice. We were advised all to get arms. The object was to be a general strike & to get the Charter by rising. Milligan told me this. It was publicly told that we were all to be ready. Pilling was a National Guard. Eckersley was a National Guard also. Milligan gave it out that he was going to Ireland to see how things were going on there. He told me he did not intend to go to Ireland. He came back on the Wednesday, the 9th of August, and I saw him at William Winterbottom's. I, Winterbottom, Flannagan, Constantine and James Willcox, another of the National Guards, were there. We all went to James Taylor's that night. No one was allowed to be a National Guard unless he was in the Chartist Association, but a person might be in that Association without being a National Guard. Taylor, I believe, was not a Guard. Milligan told us he had been to Manchester to meet their select delegates, who were to determine the time when the rising was to be, and he wanted to borrow some money. This money was to pay delegates' wages, and we borrowed it. It was four pounds. We borrowed 17s from Taylor and £3.3.0 from Aitkin. Milligan said every thing was going on first rate. He said this in the presence of Aitkin. He told Aitkin and others it must come to a close before long, as we must either win or lose. Aitkin said he could like it to be settled. I did not see Milligan again until the Friday night the eleventh. He was then in the room. Sigley was there. There was a very large meeting. Milligan told them how Ireland was getting on, and he told them to keep in readiness, for the day was not far distant when our strength would be tested. It was regularly said in the room that every body must be armed and those who were too poor to get [them] must have collections made. It was also said they could have Staves at Bintliss's in Stamford Street. Milligan shewed them how to

form squares. I was one that was drilled. He shewed all the Officers &
Guards how to form squares. He said the Lieutenant must stand at the
right hand of his men & the Corporal on the left hand in the rear. Some
of them were said to have a Mazarone's book,[1] which I understand to be
a book on military drilling. I left soon on Friday night. Eckersley was
suspected of being a spy, and I was sent to him on the 5th of Augt. to
know whether he had not been at the Police Office on the 4th. He said he
had, for making his wife two black eyes. I reported this to the body the
same night. Flannagan charged him with it publicly in the room & on
the Sunday night he was told never to go again.

On Saturday night, the 12th of August, I was at the room also, but
nothing particular occurred. On Sunday the 13th I and Milligan &
Sterndale [Standrick], who was a National Guard & lives on the Moss
side, James Stott, James Willcox, William Winterbottom, James Ratcliff
& Sigley & Constantine met at Mrs. Bowers house in Dukinfield. Her son
is the Captain over the Dukinfield Division, and we went to see him,
how that division was getting on & whether they were ready or not &
how they were going on about the Cannon at Dukinfield Park, whether
they had them ready or not. We all went out of Mrs. Bowers house to a
Beerhouse next door. We sent first to see if the keeper of the Beerhouse
would let us have a private room. We went, and we were shewn into a
room, where we remained about 3 hours. It was between 4 & 5 o'clock
when we left. Some of Bowers men were there also. They said they were
quite ready & they had been & examined the cannons & cleaned them. It
was arranged that the cannons should be brought on the Moss[l]ey Road
& that my Section should be placed there with pikes & guns to barricade
the passage & prevent any communication with the military. The
cannon were to be placed at the point of the wall & fired upon the
military before they came to the barricade. The men there were to be 25
in number & there were 4 cannons. It was also stated that, when the
rising took place, a barricade was to be made of bales of cotton which
were to be taken out of Pickfords' Yard, & then men with pikes behind
the bales & men with guns were to take possession of the windows of the
District Bank & houses. Sterndale volunteered that he would with 6 men
seize Mr. Jowett the magistrate and keep him, so as to prevent him from
sending for military to Manchester. They also said that every one of the
magistrates was to be seized. It was also arranged that every policeman
was to be seized by one Section of the National Guards. Another Section

[1] Macerone. See Part IV, 1a.

was to come to the Town Hall and lock up all the Officers. The whole of the entrances of the town were to be protected by pickets, & people prevented coming in or going out. If the military came in, they were to be fired at, if they did not deliver up their arms. Milligan said that every town in England would rise at the same time, & that the delegate from London, whose name I do not remember, had stated to him that he had two hundred thousand men under him well organized & armed ready for action. It was said the outbreak would be in the night time & very soon. But the time was not then mentioned. We agreed to meet at Bowers at 2 o'clock the following day to receive Milligan's directions. He was to go to Manchester on the Monday morning to see the Delegates. I went home, & at night met Milligan again at Downs, the Odd fellows Arms, but nothing occurred. Milligan and Sigley told me I was working for nothing, that reckoning I was then at work & this meant that I should get no wages as the Charter would be got. By this I understood that the outbreak would commence before the time of paying wages. In consequence of this, I did not go [to] work on the Monday. I went to Bowers in Dukinfield about ½ past 11 on the Monday forenoon. I & Winterbottom went together. Willcox, Ratcliff, Whitehead, a tailor & a National Guard, Sterndale, Bowers, Constantine & another man, whose name I don't know, were there at 5 o'clock, when Milligan came. He said that that night was the night set for the outbreak & we must get ready. We were all to get our own men up at our houses & divide them as we thought best & then we were to do as was previously arranged. My Section was to go out about 11, some twenty minutes before the others, to take Mossley Road. We separated at Bowers, to meet again at Downs the Odd fellows Arms in Ashton as soon as we could get there. I left Bowers & went to the Odd fellows Arms. I, Milligan, and Sterndale came down part of the way together & then separated to meet at Downs. I, Milligan, Sterndale, Constantine & Winterbottom met at the Odd fellows Arms and then about ½ past 8 o'clock Milligan ordered me and Winterbottom to go and get our men ready. I and Winterbottom then saw some of our Section, and I directed them to see the others, & all to come to our house as soon as they could, not later than ½ past 9. I said they were not to bring their arms at first, but they could send for them after. I went home & the men came and Winterbottom went to get directions from Milligan. About ½ past 9 Winterbottom came back & said I must keep them quiet until dark, and then send them for their arms. I told them to go for their arms, & bring them as quietly as they could. They went away and brought pikes & Guns with them. We had two pistols. There was none of them without arms of some kind. Winterbottom went out again, & Milligan and he returned about 11 o'clock & told us to go to the Moss[l]ey Road & take possession of it. I went out with a gun and a bayonet. I had a belt round my body outside my clothes & the bayonet stuck in it. Winterbottom had a gun. Samuel Bottomley had a gun. John Hallas [Hallow] had a pike. William Mann had a pike. Edward Hamer had a gun. John Ashton had a gun. The eldest of the two Gillsons (John) was there also with a gun. John Bolton had a pike, Alfred Haughton had a pike & a number of others. Winterbottom went first & then the men three deep, & I was last, & we marched Park St., then up Park Parade to the Railway Station, then up Warrington St. into Church St., then into Gray St., into Stamford St., then to the Rectory Corner, and right Moss[l]ey Road to Kenworthy's coal pits, where we were halted by word of command from Winterbottom, and then we stood across the road. It was a little after 11 when we got up to the coal pits. When we got there, there were thirty five in number. We formed two deep with pike men, and then those with Guns behind. We stood there, & in a short time a horseman came up galloping, & when he got within about 40 or 50 yards, he screamed out "Murder",[1] & made a sudden stop, & turned round and galloped back. Shortly after, Mr. Ramsden, the schoolmaster of Hurst, came up with a person whom I think is called Cottam. My officer gave me orders to see who it was & I put my bayonet upon my musket, and advanced to them. I said, "Stand. Who are you?" Cottam said, "Jack is that thee?" I said, "Yes". Ramsden said he was going home. I said he must not pass. Those were my orders, & he attempted to come & I held the Gun to prevent him passing. I told him, if I did not do according to orders, I should have to suffer for it. He said, then he would go back & they did so. I had been told that, if any of us did not obey orders, we should be shot. The next were three persons with truncheons. I advanced to them, & told them to stop. They asked, what for, & I saw one putting his hands to his breast. I demanded what they had from the other two, & they gave us up 3 truncheons & I took them and the three men to Winterbottom, and he said they were his prisoners, & he placed them in the front rank before the pikemen. One of them is Chadwick, a son of Thos. Chadwick the Cotton Spinner, another was a son of Leech of Oldham Road Butcher, & the other I was told was another son of the same person. The

[1] A warning, presumably, of the killing of the policeman, which had just taken place in the town.

one that I know to be Leech's son would not go home. The others would have done. I had heard the bugle blown at the barracks twice, once about half an hour before. I advanced up towards the barracks. I went to meet a Corrier [? courier], who was armed with a Gun & Winterbottom had sent him up as far as he durst go towards the barracks to see when the soldiers came out & then to come and tell us. Before I got to him I stopped, & turned round, & then saw that all my men were gone. I came running down, & saw some horsemen & the police, & I made the best of my way across the fields into the Stalybridge Road. I let of[f] some of the men there, & then I went on down Currier Lane and on Dukinfield Brow, & there I met Sigley & Ratcliff on the Chapel Hill. There was about 50 of them there. Some pikes had been broken. Sigley had a gun, Ratcliff had a pike and a pistol, & I had my Gun. Winterbottom was with us, & we all four went over the fields, and Ratcliff hid his pike in a lough in the fields. We stopped in the fields until Winterbottom went home, and came back and we afterwards went to his brother's Thos. Winterbottom's in Dukinfield, where I remained until the night of the following Thursday. ...

(The concluding portion of this deposition reverts to the preparations for the rising at Ashton on 14 August 1848. It shows that the moulding of bullets had been proceeding in the area for about a month before the event, drilling for about three weeks. The officers of the National Guard had resolved at private meetings that the Constables and other authorities were to be seized, and, if they resisted, killed, but this decision had not been communicated to the private soldiers.)

Sworn at Ashton under lyne the 8th day of Septr. 1848 before me James Lord Esqe. one of Her Majesty's Justices of the Peace for the said Coy of Lancaster.
James Lord'
(Case of the Queen v. John Wilde and others, 11 October 1848. H.O. 48/40, No. 34)

2. *Public Order: Its Weaknesses and Defences*
(Major-General Sir Henry Edward Bunbury was a retired officer who had served on the Duke of York's staff in the Netherlands in the 1790s and had later become under-secretary of state for war. A staunch Whig in politics, he had occupied a seat for the county of Suffolk in the unreformed and reformed parliaments, but had since withdrawn to the countryside. Ardently patriotic he took a prominent part in 1859 in pressing for the establishment of the volunteers, but, like his brother-in-law, General Sir C. J. Napier, he was also deeply interested in the

welfare of the working classes. His letter to the Home Secretary throws useful light both on the state of public feeling in the early stages of Chartism and on the operation of the machinery of public order. His criticisms of the defects of the latter, though severe, were echoed by Napier after he assumed command of the Northern District in April 1839.)

'*Private*   Dolgelley, N.W. Decr. 24: 1838.

Dear Lord John,

I am not in general an alarmist; but I must confess that the present state of the Kingdom gives me much uneasiness. I am fully sensible of the vast power inherent in the classes possessing property (a degree of power unparalleled in the rest of the world, because this property is so widely diffused & so intimately mingled throughout the country): nor does it seem probable that any insurrection of the working classes would succeed ultimately in establishing a democratical government on the ruins of the Constitution. Indeed such a result is much less to be apprehended now than heretofore, since the Reform Act has united the middle classes with the aristocracy by common interests. But I do fear that a wide-spreading insurrection of the working people is far from improbable, and that it may be attended with so much of destruction of property, and such a shock to trade & credit & confidence as would be ruinous to this Commonwealth. An individual cannot of course possess such large means, as H.M. Ministers, of knowing what is actually working through the country, or what are the resources of the disaffected on the one hand, or of the Government on the other; but an individual views the prospects more at his leisure, undisturbed by the hopes or fears or bias of party politicks. Looking at the manufacturing districts, it may be presumed that in certain quarters there will be more immediate dangers of mischief, & in others less; but, speaking generally, *the mass is rotten.* Nor, I am sorry to add, do I think that you can rely safely on many portions of the agricultural population. Here again, disaffection would shew itself but partially; but disaffection there is, tho' it might not at first be active. You have not been in the way, of late years at least, of hearing the occasional talk of labourers about "*the great ones*", and the spreading notion of "everything being produced for the rich by the labour of the poor". Our farmers are selfish, & timid *separately*, because they are afraid of the destruction of their property & believe they have enemies among the labourers;—tho' when drawn together in associations, or as armed yeomanry, they are bold enough.

The shopkeepers of the towns are helpless & unfit to defend themselves (very different in this respect from their brethren in France). Your Gentry, putting their political prejudices out of the question, are likewise sadly helpless: and whether under the present Government, or that of twenty years ago, I have always found them inclined to flock with an esprit moutonnier behind the hurdles which they expect the state to interpose between them & the wolf, rather than make exertions for themselves. These three classes of men are to be relied on only when they have been fore-armed, as well as fore-warned, and when they know that there are troops come-at-able for their protection. But if you give them connection, common duties, & clear objects, you will find among them no lack of affection to the cause, nor much want of spirit in playing their parts. A great many of those on whom the tories have thought to set a brand by styling them "Radicals", would be found amongst the most forward to maintain the course of law & good-order. But at present, we are all *separate*; each man speculating on what may happen, & irritating his nerves & his antipathies by his speculations; no one knowing to whom to turn, or what to do, if there should be any sudden explosion. I have seen & I know how much a few active & determined men can do in repressing disturbances in their first stage; and I have also seen how the helplessness of H.M. Justices of the Peace may allow some two or three hundred men, women & boys to bully & terrify half a county. Just look at the working of the present machinery. If fires & riots grow alarming, the Justices of the Peace wait for the Lord Lieutenant—*he* may be an aged or an inactive man, or he may not be resident in the county: but till the Lord Lieutenant comes forward the Justices do nothing *collectively*: while in their respective neighbourhoods some will be found timid, foolish, or lazy, while others may be doing more harm than good by rashness & want of temper. Half the squires (& nobles too) will be crying out for horse & foot, each wanting a troop or a company for the defence of his particular house; and, truth to say, they have little reason to set any reliance on the rural police such as it now is. In short I think we have need of more regular soldiers,—not to be harrassed by marching to the aid of every nervous squire, or to be frittered away in garrisoning every rich man's well-furnished mansion, but for the purpose of holding central points in districts, thus giving confidence to the gentry & yeomanry in general. A shew of available strength within reach has a great influence too in deterring mischievous scoundrels (& it is almost always with small numbers that they make their beginnings) from committing themselves by an outbreak. And here allow me to say, turning from agricultural to manufacturing districts, that it is of great importance, where soldiers are kept in expectation of having to act against large masses of their fellow-countrymen that they should not remain, long at least, in small detachments,—young soldiers under young officers. To be secure that your soldiers shall be proof against seduction it is necessary to preserve to them a confidence in their own superiority, & to keep firm the bond of professional pride & common feeling inherent in large military bodies. At the same time I know that it is not always prudent to make a display of reinforcements, or to assume a menacing attitude amidst great numbers of ill-disposed & daring men, such as the population about Birmingham for instance. The shew of *threatening* may sometimes exasperate their passions & make them break out into acts of violence from which they would otherwise have refrained. But, as I said before, bad men will be in general more daring, & sound men will be dispirited if there be not respectable bodies of troops within reach. Associations of Volunteers (a proportion of whom might be mounted) organized on the most economical plan, & not put under the leading of hot-headed tories, would be of great service. The mounted men would convey despatches, escort stores etc. etc., and thus save the regular cavalry from being frittered away: the foot would be reserves to support the Police, & at least gain time for the arrival of troops. I am one of those who think the whole principle & machinery of our militia faulty & ill-adapted to our circumstances. When I was in Parliament I had turned my mind to the framing of a scheme which might be an improvement; but at that time every head was full of the Reform Bill, & nothing else obtained attention. The present time is very fit & favourable for reforming our militia system, and I have been glad to hear that you have a plan in preparation. I hope that it will be connected with the organization of an effective Police for the rural districts. The present time is likewise favourable for an increase of our regular forces. Canada, Cabul & Russia afford reasons which ought to satisfy the ultra-economists at home; while the violence of the demagogues & the feverish state of the working classes present sufficient motives to the eyes of foreign powers.

I trouble you with all this, *not as a memoir*, but simply as the private sentiments of a country gentleman & old soldier, somewhat uneasy & apprehensive both as to the designs of the disaffected, and as to the adequacy of our means & the forwardness of our preparation to encounter a *Jacquerie*. Pray forgive me for trespassing on your time by so long a letter, and believe me,

My dear Lord John,
Very faithfully yours
Henry Edwd. Bunbury'

(Sir H. E. Bunbury to Lord John Russell, 24 December 1838. Russell
Papers, P.R.O. 30/22/3C fs. 91–95)

3 Intervention by the Authorities: Riot's Cause or Cure?

(In the early spring of 1839 the leaders of the middle-class-directed
Political Union lost control of Birmingham Chartism, which they had
done so much to launch. Under a new working-class direction the
movement assumed a more threatening tone. Meetings were held daily
in the streets and in the Bull Ring, a confined space hemmed in by shops,
to hear reports of proceedings in the Convention. The magistrates of the
newly-created corporation, which was heavily weighted with Liberals of
the Birmingham Political Union type, at first behaved indulgently
towards these assemblages, but were bullied by a local military
commander and the manager of the Bank of England branch, who were
supported by the government, into stiffening their line. On 8 May they
forbade meetings in the Bull Ring and other inflammatory gatherings.
The ban was observed for a while, but with the return of the General
Convention to Birmingham on 1 July, Chartist meetings were again held
in the Bull Ring. Unable to organize an efficient local police, because the
borough charter was contested, the magistrates borrowed a detachment
of Metropolitan policemen from London and used it to suppress such a
meeting on 4 July. As the following evidence by a witness at the trial of
Chartist prisoners at the Warwick assize clearly shows, the result was to
turn an admittedly obstructive and alarming meeting into a riot. Anger
stemming from this intervention did much to stimulate physical-force
Chartism in the summer of 1839. The incident and others (e.g. the
Llanidloes riot of 30 April 1839) tend to support the view of Stevenson
and Quinault[1] that the incidence of violence is closely related to the
actions of the authorities in dealing with the challenges offered to
them—at least in the short run—though it is arguable that long-term
social and economic grievances are intrinsically more important in
creating the climate in which those actions have their maximum effect.)

'... Dr. Booth (examined by Mr. Balguy) on being sworn, said he was
a Magistrate for the Borough of Birmingham, as well as for the county of
Warwick. The Borough had been in a state of extreme excitement,
terror, and alarm, for some time past, produced by the meetings taking
place nightly in the Bull Ring, at Birmingham, which often disturbed the
peace of the town—an assemblage of a great number of persons, from

[1] J. Stevenson & R. Quinault, *Popular Protest and Public Order: Six Studies in British History, 1790–1920* (London, 1974), pp. 26–8.

one to four or five hundred, had met several weeks before the 4th of July. The tradesmen were in such terror that they closed their shops, and business was interrupted; and the tradesmen, as far as they had courage so to do, complained to the Magistrates. A Proclamation was issued at an early period, and the Magistrates did everything in their power to express their repugnance to those meetings. Special Constables were sworn in previous to the 4th of July. The meetings had increased, and that measure had the effect of increasing the alarm of the people of the town. The alarm increased with the complaints of the tradesmen, and the statements made by depositions. The Magistrates found they were obliged to take more vigorous measures than they had hitherto been able to do; and as they had no police or constabulary of their own on which they could rely, their own force being only twenty-three street-keepers, appointed by the Commissioners, and five or six policemen appointed under the direction of the Magistrates; that was all the police force they had. The usual population of the town was about 200,000. They then resolved to take some other steps, and proceeded to the Home Secretary of State, for an able body of police. This was on the day before they expected a large meeting in the Bull Ring, on the Wednesday night; and witness, the Mayor, and Mr. Chance, went to London for the assistance of the police. They left London on the next day, and brought sixty policemen down to Birmingham, who were sworn in as special constables, by Mr. Chance, in the presence of the witness. They found the Bull Ring crowded. It was about eight o'clock in the evening when they left Birmingham to go to town. When they had the police, witness rode into the Bull Ring to ascertain the state of the town; he went on his horse and rode through the Bull Ring. A man was haranguing against Nelson's Monument; it was not an easy matter to get through the crowd. As soon as they saw witness they hooted "Spy", and threw stones at him. He got through them with some difficulty and nerve. He then went back to the police, and communicated to them, and to the Mayor and Mr. Chance, what he had observed. They determined to disperse the crowd immediately. The shops were partially closed, but some of them were not. The Mayor and witness proceeded with the police to the Bull Ring; the Mayor and witness led the way on their horses. They saw six flags, at least, and a man elevated between them was speaking. Witness told them to disperse. Anxious to take the speaker into custody, they directed the attention of the police to him. Witness thought it was not possible to take the man, the crowd were so mingled with each other; those who were near witness could hear what he said. From that moment groaning, hissing, and confusion took place. The lamp near to witness's head was broken with stones; at that moment they seemed to make a declaration of war, and rushed on the police. He saw the police fall while using their staves, as they had nothing else but them; in fact, he saw the police were being overpowered; they were in their London dress. Witness and the mayor immediately rode to the barracks for the military, and returned with them to the Bull Ring, which was still in a state of confusion. On their return witness rode up to Nelson's Monument, and by the aid of the lamp and his spectacles, he read the Riot Act. The mob was then at bay, groaning and hissing, and it was advisable to disperse them. In an hour or two after the Riot Act had been read, the avenues of the Bull-ring were guarded by the military; while the mayor and witness, with the main body, cleared the streets. They were not cleared in that part of the town until three or four o'clock in the morning. Witness continued up all that time, and then went to the police office, and then home. Witness was not absent for a moment, only while he went for the military. He had the opportunity of seeing how the police conducted themselves; they conducted themselves as other constables would in such circumstances—with as much forbearance as their own would do, or perhaps more.'

(*The Northern Star*, 10 August 1839)

4. *Citizen Policing by the Middle Classes: A Chartist Counter-Offensive in the Courts*

(Alarming and well-founded reports that the Chartists of Southern Lancashire and the West Riding of Yorkshire were meeting to be drilled[1], sometimes by old soldiers, provoked Lord Melbourne's government to issue a Royal Proclamation on 3 May 1839 against the practice of military exercises. It was an unhappy coincidence that four days later the Home Secretary, Lord John Russell, wrote to the Lords Lieutenant and the magistrates of the disturbed counties to encourage the principal inhabitants to form associations for the protection of life and property, and offered to equip such bodies with arms at the governments's expense. The Whigs had been driven to this expedient, from which initially they shrank, by the need to provide for local defence at a time when proposals for establishing a professional police force in the counties had not had time to mature and when the military commander of the Northern district was anxious to free his troops for action in concentrated masses in case of insurrection. But the Chartists

[1] For a vivid description of drilling at Ashton see Dorothy Thompson, *The Early Chartists*, pp. 213–16.

were quick to seize upon the irony of arming men of property while forbidding poorer men to organize for what they could represent as self-defence against the New Poor Law and the impending Rural Police. The thoughtless swaggering of a few individuals of the middle classes supplied those of Barnsley, assisted by the legal talents of William Cobbett's solicitor son, with the opportunity to drive home the lesson that the law for the poor must also apply to the rich. The bid misfired. A token victory in the Barnsley petty sessions, described below, was followed by defeat in July at the quarter sessions at Rotherham, where the Grand Jury found no bill against the accused and the court rejected the application of the prosecution witnesses for costs.[1])

'COURT HOUSE, BARNSLEY

CONVICTION OF FOUR OF LORD JOHN RUSSELL'S "RESPECTABLE" PEACE PRESERVATION PHYSICAL-FORCE MEN.

On Wednesday last, an excitement greater than any we have previously known prevailed in Barnsley, in consequence of a charge brought by the Radicals of that town, against Thomas Gomersall, James Frudd, Clerk at Beckett's Bank, George Frudd, warehouseman, and Abraham Newgass, shopkeeper, for drilling and training, in violation of the 60, Geo III., chap. 1.

About twelve o'clock, Mr. F. O'Connor, who had come specially from London, for the purpose, and Mr. R. B. B. Cobbett, of Manchester, entered the Court, which was crowded to suffocation.

At half-past twelve o'clock, the Rev. — Cooke, Chairman, the Rev. — Watkins, — Martin, G. Wentworth, and J. Thornley, Esqrs., took their seats upon the bench.

Mr. Palfreyman, Solicitor, of Sheffield, appeared for the defendants.

Mr. COBBETT briefly opened the case, by stating that he appeared for the prosecution. The informations were laid by Benjamin Haigh, under the 60, Geo.III, chap. 1, upon whose evidence the summons had been granted. It appeared that his client had proceeded according to the instructions laid down in the Proclamation recently issued by her Majesty, and according to the terms of that Proclamation, it could only have a salutary effect if equally applied to the rich man and to the poor man. The Magistrates of course would proceed with great caution as the statute was a penal one; while at the same time, they would bear in mind

---

[1] *Sheffield and Rotherham Independent*, 13 July 1839; *Sheffield Iris*, 9 and 16 July 1839.

that the unrestricted violation of the statute by men in the class of life to which the defendants belonged, would operate as a powerful example to those in that class against whom the proclamation was issued. The defendants had not the excuse of being led away by the inflammatory harangues of popular orators—they could not plead ignorance in justification of the error, and therefore, if obedience was to be enforced, equal justice must be dealt out to all. He thought that any further preface would be unnecessary, and he would therefore proceed to substantiate the several allegations contained in the summons, by evidence which he believed to be incontrovertible.

Mr. PALFREYMAN requested to know upon which of the charges Mr. Cobbett would proceed—as there were several set forth.

Mr. COBBETT said he would go generally into the evidence, and allow the Court to judge how far he had sustained any or all of the charges. He then called

Boaz Haigh, who deposed as follows:— On the 19th of May, he was standing in the row where he lives, between nine and ten o'clock at night. He then saw four of the defendants, Gomersall, the two Frudds, and Newgass. They were in line, across the road; in company with many others. A person said, "Now Thomas"; and another said "No names". Thomas Gomersall then said "quick march". Gomersall was then on the right, rather before the others. Upon the word being thus given, they marched off towards Barnsley, all a-breast. Benjamin Haigh was with witness, but is no relation to him. Benjamin Haigh followed them. They marched towards Barnsley. They walked in line about 150 yards, when Gomersall said "file off". They then went two and two for a distance of about 100 yards. Gomersall then cried "halt", when they all stopped at once, and he formed them again into line. He then gave the word, "quick march", which they obeyed. Saw Newgass at that time. He was not then in line, but was alongside Gomersall. Overtook them again about 300 yards outside the town. Passed them and afterwards saw them again. Saw their faces passing and meeting close by. It was twilight, and he was near enough to distinguish them. It was a clear night. Followed them to the town, and at the side of the Wesleyan Chapel, Gomersall ordered them again, in a lower tone than before, to file off. They accordingly filed off.

Cross-examined by Mr. PALFREYMAN—Works for Mr. Haxworth. Has known Benjamin Haigh six or seven years. He, too, works for Mr. Haxworth. Has known all the defendants above a year. James Frudd is a banker, Newgass is a shopkeeper, Gomersall is a pattern-weaver. There were not plenty of folks about on that night, but very few. George Parker saw them drilling, and shouted "Hallo, there". They stopped Parker, and said they were physical-force men. Does not know what they meant by physical force. Never attended any public meeting. One said, "Charge, bayonets". He did not see a gun or a bayonet with them. Certainly has had opportunities of attending public meetings, but never availed himself of those opportunities. Saw James Frudd step on the road. Did not say that James Frudd went in. Here a most awful scene of uproar, groaning, and hissing ensued in consequence of the attempt by Mr. Palfreyman to show a variance in the swearing of the witness. The dense mass pressed forward, shouting, groaning, and hissing, while the magistrates, seemingly unconscious of the cause, ordered the court to be cleared. The people vociferating "clear the gallery then, or we'll not stir". ...

(After order had been restored the cross examination of the witness proceeded. This completed, the account continued.)

The Court here asked Mr. Cobbett, if he did not think that the evidence was sufficient without producing more witnesses to induce the Court to commit the prisoners or hold them to bail?

Mr. COBBETT replied, that he thought the evidence quite sufficient, but if his learned friend, Mr. Palfreyman, should attempt to shake the evidence which he had adduced, he would then hold that he was at liberty to produce evidence to prove the admission of the parties.

Mr. PALFREYMAN said—Thank God, the days of Charles I are not to be revived, and much as I respect royalty, yet I have no respect for a royal proclamation, when it attempts to supersede the statute law; and I do hold that under this statute you must prove both the *animus* and the illegality of the meeting. The statute was not framed to meet cases like the present. It was enacted in disturbed times; when, for the preservation of the public peace, vigilance and decision were necessary. Even the evidence which has been adduced in support of the allegations presents a variance and a discrepancy which, unless in the anxiety of the bench to render satisfaction to the poor at the expense of the rich, is wholly irreconcilable, and the bench will recollect that the path of duty may be equally departed from by the false notion that the law should be anomalously stretched for the purpose of making examples of the rich for the intimidation of the poor. As well might informations be tendered against those children whom he saw, with a kind of drill-sergeant at their head, walking in their several schools, on the very day named in the information against the defendants.

The Court would recommend Mr. Palfreyman not to rest his defence on any analogy between the case of the defendants and that of school processions, but to adduce the evidence on which he relied. It was ultimately decided that Mr. Cobbett should proceed with his case.

Peter Hoey was called and examined. Was in Buckley's public house on the 19th of May, between ten and eleven o'clock at night. Saw Gomersall there, and heard him say "We were training." ...

(After the cross-examination of Hoey Mr. Palfreyman called two ineffective witnesses for the defence. The first corroborated the drilling and confirmed an admission by Gomersall that he and his friends were preparing to attend the Chartist Whitsuntide rally at Peep Green on the following Tuesday, 21 May. The account concluded as follows.)

Here the evidence for the defence appeared to be closed, and Mr. COBBETT had replied; when the Court requested Mr. Palfreyman to proceed with any other evidence he might have.

Charles Briggs, W. Ostcliffe, the landlord of Stair Foot, Charles Ward, grocer, of Leeds, Richard Ellison, linen manufacturer, William Hepworth, grocer, P. Buckley, landlord of the Royal Oak, were then severally called, and swore that the whole matter was a joke.

The Majority of the witnesses for the defence, however, having subjected themselves to the same punishment as the defendants, the Magistrates received their evidence with proper caution; and after due deliberation and patient hearing, decided that the defendants, Gomersall, the two Frudds, and Fletcher, should give bail to appear at the Rotherham Sessions, on the 9th of July next. The two Frudds and Fletcher themselves in £100, and two sureties of £50 each, and Gomersall, himself in £20, and two sureties in £10.

The required bail was immediately procured, and the case, after a hearing of five hours, was disposed of.'
(*The Northern Star*, 8 June 1839)

5. *Troops in Aid of the Civil Power*
(When Chartist unrest first came to a head in 1838–9 an efficient professional police did not exist outside London and a few large corporate towns. Acts to establish county forces were passed in 1839 and 1840, but the legislation was permissive, and it was not until 1856 that a statute was passed making it obligatory for all counties to set up a

constabulary. Hitherto the army had acted as 'the police force of industrial England'. In times of emergency it developed flexibility in dealing with an elusive crowd, and was able to anticipate the preventive functions of a police. During the Luddite disturbances of 1812 soldiers were formed into mobile patrols.[1] Nevertheless, district commanders like General Maitland on the latter occasion and Napier in the Chartist period resisted the subdivision of their force as much as they could, and, as Lord Melbourne advised the Lord Lieutenant of Lancashire early in 1831, the use of troops for public-order duties could 'produce only a partial and uncertain tranquillity'.[2] With both the Duke of Wellington and Sir C. J. Napier it was an axiom that on such service the cavalry had an advantage over the infantry, in that they could demoralize rioters without killing them.[3] There were, however, fewer cavalry than infantry in the disturbed Northern district: 1029 against 4050 effectives when Napier took up the command in April 1839.[4] Moreover, cavalrymen were not at their best in the cramped conditions of an industrial town, as the first of the two extracts, describing an incident in the resistance to the New Poor Law at Bradford, shows. The second extract, giving an account of a riot at Preston during the 1842 'Plug Plot', reveals that relatively small detachments of infantry could disperse large assemblages, but were sometimes helpless to prevent mischief before opening fire on the crowd.)

(a) 'COPY OF A REPORT from A. POWER, Esq., dated 21st Nov. 1837.

Gentlemen,   *Skipton, 21st November, 1837.*
SINCE forwarding my Report of last evening I have seen Mr. Wagstaff, the clerk of Bradford Union, and have learned from him further particulars of yesterday's proceedings.

The guardians met at the usual time and place for holding their weekly meetings, and proceeded in the election of their relieving officers. The warrants also upon the overseers of the several townships were prepared and signed, and other business transacted, which occupied the Board from ten o'clock until two.

It appears that, during this time, a very considerable crowd, amounting to many thousands, were collected in front and about the

[1] L. Radzinowicz, *A History of English Criminal Law*, Vol. IV, (London, 1968), p. 123.
[2] L. C. Sanders ed., *Lord Melbourne's Papers* (London, 1889), pp. 121–4.
[3] G. Harries-Jenkins, *The Army in Victorian Society* (London, 1977), p. 201; W. Napier, *The Life and Opinions of General Sir Charles James Napier, G.C.B.* (London, 1857), Vol. II, p. 23.
[4] Return enclosed in Lord Hill's letter to Lord John Russell, 1 May 1839. H.O. 40/53.

court-house, where the troop of cavalry were drawn up in line, and the civil force were stationed to guard the entrance to the court-house.

For some time the mob kept aloof, but, a party of them having at length found their way through the special constables to the door of the court-house, both the military and the building were immediately assailed with stones; and at this time (about 12 o'clock) Mr. Paley, the magistrate, read the Riot Act.

From this time until the close of the meeting the cavalry appear to have vainly attempted the dispersion of the crowd, acting with the greatest possible forbearance, and using their sabres only, so far as I can learn.

The magistrates and guardians appear to have left the court-house without any serious molestation; but Mr. Wagstaff, the clerk, was detained in the building and beset by the mob for some hours, who, on the military retiring, demolished the windows on every side, but did not, as appeared probable, proceed to force the doors. About five o'clock Mr. Wagstaff was rescued from his perilous situation by a detachment of the cavalry, attended by the two magistrates, Mr. Paley and Mr. Thompson. On returning through the streets to the Talbot Inn, the crowd closed upon the party in such a manner as to make it necessary to charge them, when several shots were fired, and some persons cut down.

Mr. Wagstaff was at length brought in safety to the Talbot Inn, which he found it impossible to leave until a late hour, when he left Bradford for Keighley, and came forward to me at Skipton in the morning.

All the information which I have at present gained, in addition to that contained in my last Report, is derived chiefly from Mr. Wagstaff, who left the town last night under the circumstances above described.

Many persons have been seriously hurt, both by sabre and gun-shot wounds, but it does not appear that any death has yet occurred.

Three of the rioters have been committed to York for trial. I learn this at a late hour this evening, and also that the town has been quiet during the day.

I have not yet been able to obtain a copy of the minutes of the meeting of the guardians, but will forward one as soon as possible, and report further to-morrow.

In the course of yesterday a detachment of horse and another of infantry were sent for from Burnley, which now remain, as I am told, at Keighley, about ten miles from Bradford.

I am, &c.

(Signed)   A. POWER'

To the Poor Law Commissioners
   for England and Wales.

   (*Papers relative to the Proceedings on Opening the Bradford Union
   (Yorkshire); Fourth Annual Report of the Poor Law Commissioners for
   England & Wales,* 1838, Appendix A, No. 8.)

(b)   'DREADFUL RIOT AT PRESTON.—RIOTERS SHOT
                    (FROM OUR OWN REPORTER)
                              PRESTON, SATURDAY EVENING.
     A meeting of operatives was held in Chadwick's orchard last night,
about 9 o'clock; and, though the numbers in attendance were
considerable, the crowd was not anything like what might have been
anticipated. A detachment of the 72d were lodged in the assembly room
of the Bull Inn, and were under arms all night. It was scarcely
anticipated that any measures would have been taken by the mob to
prevent the factories being started this morning at the usual time.
However, on one of the bells being rung at a little before 6 o'clock, the
mob which had assembled a short time previously in Chadwick's
orchard marched towards the North road (the direction in which the bell
had rung), and the first factory they came to was Messrs. Catteral and
Co's, whose hands they turned out, and then proceeded to Mr. F.
Sleddon's, where preparations had been made for resisting the mob. A
stout resistance was made, Mr. Sleddon himself being on the spot; but
they were overpowered by the immense numbers, after some hard
blows had been dealt out. Mr. Sleddon was slightly hurt in the affray,
and a large number of squares in the factory windows were smashed.
The mob then went to the factories at the west end of the town, and such
as were at work were compelled to relinquish it. At Mr. Dawson's
factory a few squares of glass were broken. By this time the mob had
increased most wonderfully, and included a very large proportion of
women and children; but its general appearance had a more threatening
aspect than at any time during yesterday. When these proceedings were
going on, the mayor and magistrates assembled at the Bull Inn, where
the town-clerk joined them, and it was determined to proceed to meet
the rioters. This was at 3 o'clock, and the public functionaries,
accompanied by the detachment of the 72d[1], went down Fishergate, and

---

[1] About 30 of the 72nd Highlanders were stationed temporarily in the town; the crowd
numbered several hundreds; seven of the rioters were seriously injured and four or five
died. A. G. Rose, 'The Plug Riots of 1842 in Lancashire and Cheshire'. *Transactions of
the Lancashire and Cheshire Antiquarian Society*, Vol. LXVII, 1957, pp. 75–112.

met the mob near Lune-street. The rioters opened two divisions for the purpose of the military passing through; but the orders were, to let no one pass. The mob then proceeded down Lune-street, followed by the military, and when near the Corn-exchange halted. The Riot Act was then read, and Chief-constable Woodford, and Mr. Banister, superintendent of police, endeavoured to persuade the mob to retire, for fear of consequences; and while so engaged, one of the rioters aimed a stone so surely at Captain Woodford that it felled him to the ground, and while there had the brutality to kick him. Immense bodies of stones were now thrown at the police and soldiers, many of the former being much hurt, and part of the mob having gone up Fox-street they then had the advantage of stoning the military from both sides. Under these circumstances, orders were given to fire; the military immediately obeyed, and several of the mob fell. This did not appear to have much effect, for one fellow named Lancaster, who I believe came from Blackburn, came out in front of the mob, and when in the act of lifting his hand to throw a stone, was singled out by one of the 72d, who fired, and he fell. This appeared to put a damper on the proceedings of the mob, and they began to separate, the mayor, military, and magistrates coming up the street. It is scarcely known how many have been wounded, but it is supposed from 12 to 15, some of them mortally. Five have been taken to the House of Recovery, and in the course of the morning one of the five had his leg amputated above the knee, the leg being completely splintered by the ball. A lad was shot through the wrist, the ball grazing his side. It is believed his hand must be amputated. One man was shot in the back, where the ball still remains in the bone, and it cannot be extracted. Two are shot through the chest, and one is in an exceedingly dangerous state. There is also one man shot through the bowels, which protrude in a shocking manner, and he is in a most precarious state. The medical gentleman who has been engaged to attend the sufferers states that he thinks four of the wounded will not recover. As may be expected very considerable excitement prevails. Large posting bills have been stuck up to announce that the Riot Act has been read, and that people are forbidden to be seen about the streets in groups. A proclamation has also been issued and indeed the authorities are using every exertion to prevent any more assemblages. ...

The people are assembling in different parts of the town threatening to revenge the proceedings of the morning. 150 of the 60th Rifles have arrived from Manchester, and should any further disturbance take place, I will despatch the particulars by the first train for London.

The proclamation issued by the mayor states that the people attempted to overcome the military force, and, having proceeded to the destruction of property, the military by lawful command fired upon the rioters. The mayor declares that he will use every authority with which he is invested for the preservation of the public peace.'
(*The Times*, 15 August 1842)

6. *The Metropolitan Police and the Containment of Disorder in the Capital*

(Outstandingly the largest of the English conurbations, London, with its welter of parishes clustered round the ancient City, had had long experience of disorder. The Gordon riots of 1780 had been only the most destructive of a long series of disturbances stretching through the eighteenth century and into the opening decades of the nineteenth. In 1829, however, Home Secretary Peel carried a bill establishing a police force of some 3,300 men of all ranks to operate in the metropolitan parishes exclusive of the proud and independent City of London. Historians have rightly emphasized the success of this body in containing the violent impulses of the London crowd with minimal injury to demonstrators and without recourse to military aid. But the immediacy of the victory has too often been overstressed. It is clear from the two following examples that when Chartism began to build up support in London from 1841 onwards, the police often had difficulties in controlling crowds owing to the traditionally volatile character of the latter. Sometimes they made serious mistakes, as when on 6 March 1848 they allowed a sliver of about 200 people to break away from a large meeting in Trafalgar Square and tour the West End smashing street lamps and windows. An error similar in kind but more serious in its consequences on 8 February 1886 ('Bloody Monday') forced the resignation of a Police Commissioner. Probably the infrequency of serious disturbances in London after 1848 hindered the transmission of experience from one generation of police officers to another. Nevertheless, the extracts also show the peculiar flexibility of the Metropolitan force, manifest on most occasions, which enabled its members to act singly or in line, as the occasion demanded, to prevent or forestall a riot. Though there was initially much opposition to the principle of a professional police force from men of all ranks, on the grounds that a police was foreign and unconstitutional, as well as expensive to maintain, the authorities soon came to recognize in it a solution to the problem of maintaining order. Thus the Chartist disturbances of 1839 precipitated the institution of forces in the English counties[1] and in the towns of Manchester, Birmingham and Bolton, when otherwise police reform would have been held up by insuperable difficulties.)

[1] E. C. Midwinter, 'Law and Order in Early Victorian Lancashire' (*University of York, Borthwick Papers* No. 34) denies the unique importance of Chartism in forcing through

(a) (The semi-political strikes in the North of England in August 1842 produced repercussions in the capital.)

'ATTEMPTED CHARTIST MEETING ON CLERKENWELL GREEN

Last night, shortly after 8 o'clock, a body of Chartists, to the number of about 200, taking advantage of the absence of a large body of police at Kennington-common, Paddington, and other parts of the metropolis, began to assemble, notwithstanding the presence of Inspector Penny and several of the police of the G. division, on Clerkenwell-green, for the purpose of holding an open-air meeting. The procession was headed by a van, which had already taken up its position on the green, when Inspector Penny informed those therein that no meeting would be permitted to be held. In defiance, however, the chair was taken, and the chairman commenced addressing the meeting, which gradually began to augment in numbers. Information was immediately despatched to the station-house of the G division, in Bagnigge-wells-road, where upwards of 100 men were in reserve, who in a few minutes made their appearance at the entrance of the green, under the orders of Superintendent Maisey and Inspector Barton. Their appearance became the signal for general confusion. The speaker and those in the van vanished in an instant, as did also the van, which had the horse harnessed to it. The people, however, were more reluctant to do so, but forming themselves into small groups, continued to groan at, and harass the police, by assembling at various parts. Shortly before 9 o'clock, a man named King commenced addressing a mob from the step of his own door, situate on the green, and on his refusal to go into his house and desist, he was taken into custody by Inspector Penny. The mass of people, amongst whom were a large number of thieves and pickpockets, began to increase every minute, and at this period, in various parts of the green, there could not have been less than from 1,500 to 2,000 persons. The police were assailed with the most frightful yelling, and as they were taking their prisoner to the station-house several stones and other missiles were thrown. At this moment loud shouts were raised at the Hicks's-hall end of the green, and on inspector Barton, who had a large body of his men drawn up in front of the Session-house, arriving at the spot, he found several men in a waggon, which on examination he

---

the Rural Police Act of 1839, but his argument overlooks the fact that the bill was rushed through at the end of the parliamentary session, evidently as an emergency measure. See my *Public Order in the Age of the Chartists* (Manchester, 1959), p. 128, n.4.

found to be half full of rotten turnips, which it was stated had been brought for the purpose of pelting the police. Inspector Barton assured the driver and those who were in the van, if they made the slightest attempt to enter the green, he would direct the men to take the whole of them into custody, on which it was withdrawn. The mob continued to augment, and were evidently determined on harassing the police, who seemed perfectly worn out with incessant duty, by their continuing up to a late hour last night to move about in small detached parties. The alarm of most of the housekeepers on the green was so great that they closed their shops at an early hour.'
(*The Times*, 23 August 1842)

(b) (Though the Chartists had failed to intimidate the government by their much-discussed demonstration on 10 April 1848, the agitation was kept going in London and the provinces by some Chartist leaders acting in conjunction with the Irish Confederates.)

'THE CHARTISTS AND REPEALERS

Yesterday evening Clerkenwell-green presented a scene of very considerable excitement, in consequence of the announcement made by Mr. Williams and the other leaders of the procession on Monday night, that a great meeting would be held there for ulterior purposes, which were not distinctly specified, but which it was known, if carried into effect, would seriously compromise the public peace. The authorities, having had their attention directed to the subject, adopted the most effectual measures to suppress any disturbances. The mysterious manner in which this movement on the part of the disaffected has been conducted rendered it uncertain whether the meeting at Clerkenwell would take place as announced, or whether other arrangements might not be made for carrying out the objects in view. It was necessary, therefore, while a sufficient force was concentrated on the district alluded to, other parts of the metropolis tainted with Chartism should not be left exposed. The police were accordingly disposed in such a manner that while assembled in great force at all the inner stations, 4,000 or 5,000 men could in a very short space of time be marched upon any given point. Three squadrons of cavalry and a strong body of mounted police occupied positions in Clerkenwell and Finsbury, within reach of any commotion that might arise. The following orders were also sent to the various superintendents of the metropolitan divisions:—

"Metropolitan Police Office, Tuesday, May 30, 1848. "It appears to be the plan of the chartist leaders to conceal, as long as possible, the places at which they intend to hold their meetings, and to endeavour, by concerted plans, known only to themselves, to assemble in large numbers at some given point, and to pass from different places, and to move about with a view to some ulterior objects.

"The attention of the superintendents is directed to the notice herewith sent, and they will understand that they are not to interfere with any meeting unless they attempt to move off in a large body, or to walk in procession, in which case they are to have immediate notice that such movement is illegal, and will be prevented.

"All persons resisting the police, or showing or being furnished with arms, on his resisting the police, should, if possible, be taken into custody.

"The superintendents are to report immediately when any assembly takes place, both to the chief office and to the nearest division, and they are to support each other with their whole force, if necessary. And it is further recommended that the earliest notice of such meeting should be sent also to the commissioners of the city police.

"CALLING OUT SPECIAL CONSTABLES—A certain number of circulars will be sent to the various superintendents for them to fill up and to address (as the blanks indicate) to the leaders of the special constables when they receive orders to collect the police, or to move from their respective divisions.

C. ROWAN.

"MOUNTED POLICE.—The following are to assemble at headquarters immediately—H. 8 men, I.12, P.3, N.2, S.5, V.5, R.1, with Superintendents Mallalieu, Bicknell, and Williamson. The mounted force to be under the direction of Superintendent Williamson.

R. MAYNE AND W. HAY."

In addition to the caution issued by the Commissioners of Police on Tuesday, and which was inserted in our impression of yesterday, the following notice was placarded in different parts of the metropolis last evening:—

"NOTICE—Whereas large numbers of persons assembled yesterday evening, the 30th instant, and continued so assembled part of the night in Clerkenwell-green and in the neighbourhood, and committed acts of violence, injury to property, rioting, and breaches of the peace, and the streets and thoroughfares were thronged and obstructed, whereby the peaceable inhabitants of the neighbourhood were interrupted in their lawful business and alarmed, and the public peace was disturbed; notice is hereby given, that such assemblages are illegal, and will not be allowed; and all well-disposed persons are hereby cautioned to abstain from attending, being present at, joining, or taking any part in such assemblages: and notice is further given, that all necessary measures will be adopted to prevent such assemblages at unseasonable hours taking place in any street or thoroughfare in or near the metropolis, and effectually to protect the public peace, and to suppress any attempt at the disturbance thereof.

C. ROWAN,
R. MAYNE.
Commissioners of Police of the Metropolis.
Metropolitan Police-office, Whitehall-place,
Wednesday, May 31, 1848."

These salutary precautions having been adopted, it will excite no surprise that the threatened meeting on Clerkenwell-green did not take place, or rather, we should say, that none of those who summoned the meeting there appeared, and that the promised demonstration of physical force was a most signal failure. A different result appears to have been anticipated in the neighbourhood, for as early as 6 o'clock, though it rained heavily at the time, groups of people were assembled at the street corners leading into the Green, watching for the arrival of Williams, Fussell, Daly, Sharpe, and the other would-be heroes who had threatened, *vi et armis*, to overthrow the Government and sack the Home-office. As the time wore on, the rain ceased, and the numbers assembled on the Green increased considerably. The low population of the neighbourhood, attracted to the spot partly by curiosity and partly to have the excitement of a row with the police, loitered along the pavement, and blocked up the entrance to the Green. The majority of them were ragged boys from Field-lane, and the other densely-peopled streets in that locality. There was a sprinkling, too, of women among the crowd, their shrill voices, and not very choice phraseology, indicating their presence, when the intervening mob prevented their being seen. Not the slightest trace of arms, or of a tendency to employ physical force, was visible, and the assemblage presented the usual unmeaning features of a common crowd. A reporter who produced his pencil and note-book in a rather conspicuous manner was, it is true, surrounded and pushed about, but, as he had the good fortune to be rather tall, an attempt to bonnet him failed. Things were in this state till about half-past 7 o'clock, and there were about three thousand people assembled on the Green, when the sound of horses' feet and the jingling of military accoutrements were heard, and a troop of 60 Life Guardsmen rode at a slow pace through the crowd, which cheered them vociferously as they passed. This sudden apparition had a visible effect upon the assemblage, which began perceptibly to diminish. Still many remained, in the hope that

Williams and his friends would appear, and that the meeting and procession would take place as promised. Fussell was seen hanging on the outskirts of the crowd about 7 o'clock, and nearly at the same time we caught a glimpse of the renowned Cuffay reconnoitering the mob from the pavement. Whether the formidable look of the Guardsmen, on their black chargers, and the glitter of their cuirasses, had struck terror into Williams and his coadjutors, it is impossible to say, but the position which they ought to have filled was supplied by a poet. About 8 o'clock a singular-looking being with long hair, a profusion of beard, and that "air distraught" which is generally supposed to mark a child of the Muses, appeared among the crowd with a bundle of papers in his hand. As he passed along he hawked for the small sum of 1d. a new Chartist song of his own composition. The youths of Field-lane seemed struck with his appearance, and pressed upon the poet's person more familiarly than he approved, particularly as they showed no inclination to purchase his goods. Having tried unsuccessfully to avoid them, he was at last driven for shelter to a lamp-post, which is upon a raised foundation, [and] stands in the centre of the Green. Finding himself unexpectedly in this position, the man of song determined to improve the opportunity by addressing the mob. Accordingly he raised himself to a sufficient elevation by clinging to the lamp-post and amidst perfect silence proceeded to speak. He said that he was not one of those who had the *cacoethes loquendi*, but he had risen to state that he thought the meeting had behaved themselves unbecomingly in hissing two policemen who had just passed by. He considered the police, as a whole, absolutely necessary for the preservation of society, and it was only when they went beyond their duty, as on Monday last, in Whitecross-street, that they deserved to be censured. He was a witness of their brutality on that occasion, and, though he might have secured his own safety by taking refuge in a public-house, yet there was a spirit within him which would not permit him to do so. He had got a blow on the head in consequence, but he hoped they would acknowledge that it had not muddled his brain. Being a Chartist, and holding the principle of equality, he considered that every one ought to provide himself with a good baton, to be used, not offensively, but defensively, if unjustly attacked by the police. As it was necessary for a man to practise what he taught, he had provided himself with a staff, and he advised them to do likewise. (Cheers.) Being a teetotaller and a vegetarian (cries of "Oh, oh!"), he was often attacked by the brewers in the district where he lived (laughter); and the Lord Mayor had refused him justice when he complained, because on principle he had refused to take the oath on the Christian Bible. He was therefore obliged to take the law into his own hands. The poet orator, whose name we understand is Duncan, concluded his speech, which was listened to very attentively, by reciting his new song in praise of equality, and which is entitled "The Smock Frock and the Fustian Coat." This he did, with an amount of theatrical gesture, and of "fine frenzy" in his eye, which to the mob appeared marvellously fine. Before leaving the elevated position from which he spoke, he had the good sense to advise the meeting to disperse quietly, and to declare that it was dissolved. On the poet's departure, confusion and uproar began to manifest themselves. Sections of the crowd began to make those desperate rushes, now in one direction and now in another, which generally precede a riot. It was at this critical moment that a strong body of police appeared on the ground. Entering the Green from the east they formed in line across the open space where the people were gathered, and swept them at once, and without opposition, into the narrow streets and alleys which open from Clerkenwell-green on the west. The movement was executed with military precision, and more than 2,000 men who had a moment before been assembled on the spot disappeared with a rapidity which was almost miraculous. Some hard blows were dealt with the truncheons in clearing the green, and at St. Bartholomew's Hospital seven or eight cases of broken heads were brought in, but none of the injuries thus received are serious. Strong parties of police were placed at all the entrances to the Green, and sections were sent to clear the different streets in the vicinity. About 40 of the horse police patrolled the neighbourhood, and in an incredibly short time, by the judicious arrangements of Captain Hay, the tranquillity of the district was perfectly restored.'

(*The Times*, 1 June 1848)

7 Secret Intelligence

(Though successive Home Secretaries intervened to restrict the practice, magistrates and police officers still resorted to the use of spies when uncovering Chartist conspiracies. The Metropolitan Force was not less forward than the rest, and the spies often acted as *agents provocateurs*. George Davis, who ran a second-hand shop in Greenwich, joined the Chartists in order to betray them, and was sufficiently prominent to represent his locality in the Metropolitan Delegate Council. Between the gathering described below and 16 August, when the police rounded up the London physical-force leaders, he attended a series of meetings at the 'George' in the Old Bailey, and within two hours of each reported what had transpired to Inspector Mark of the Greenwich division. The inspector and his superintendent insisted on his continuing as a spy, promising to compensate him for the loss of business. When he was produced as a witness at the trial of William Cuffay and others, he confessed to having asked large numbers of people to attend Chartist meetings in Greenwich (for the sake of the landlord!) and to having carried loaded pistols (for his own protection!). He had sold guns to the Chartists and used violent language against the Queen.[1] After the trial he was removed from Greenwich for his own safety and given £150 compensation. He settled in Southampton, where he lost his wife in the cholera epidemic of the following year, and was left with three small children to bring up. He appealed twice to the Home Office for further assistance, but without result. In March 1850 John Knowles, a neighbouring Methodist minister, wrote to the mayor of Southampton asking him to intercede with the government on his behalf. The mayor, Richard Andrews, an advanced radical, simply forwarded the letter to the Home Office with the comment, 'I feel but little sympathy for spies in any matter'.[2]

'R. Division   Greenwich Station, 14 June 1848

A meeting of the Chartist Delegate Committee took place this morning at 10 o'c at the Literary Institution, St. John Street, FitzRoy Square, fourteen of the delegates present. McDouall in the chair. Bassett in the Vice Chair. A map of London was produced, and different plans of attack formed. One was to construct barricades near the New Church in the Strand (Temple Bar would form a serviceable one), up Ludgate Hill; one at the end of Cheapside across to Newgate Street, to extend down St. Martins le Grand as far as the Barbican, and then down Aldersgate Street across to Clerkenwell, across Saffron Hill up the back streets to Hatton Garden (where plenty of old materials might be found of houses that have been pulled down), then as far as St. Giles church, from thence to Drury Lane, Russell St., Covent Garden and so back to the Strand. The churches, theatres and other public buildings to be set fire to & pawnbrokers, gunsmiths etc. to be plundered of their arms. Barricades might be carried across Waterloo Bridge to the Kent Road, the Police Station there attacked, and the march of the artillery towards town intercepted, and their guns spiked and ammunition seized.

One of the Delegates (name unknown[3]) said the oil of vitriol was very cheap; and by getting some of this and putting it into small phials, and

---

[1] *Northern Star*, 30 September & 7 October 1848; Mather, *Public Order etc.*, p. 211.

[2] See correspondence in H.O. 40/59.

[3] Later named by Davis as George Bridge Mullins, a surgeon. Inspector Mark's Memorandum of Conversation with Davis, June 1848, H.O. 45/2410.

throwing it among the police and military, it would cause much mischief and confusion.

About 1½ p.m. a quarrel ensued between two of the members named Child & Pitt and the others, and they quitted the room saying they would have nothing more to do with it. McDouall then adjourned the Meeting until 8 o'c in the evening at the "Lord Denman" Beer Shop, Suffolk Street, Blackfriars Road, when they would then take into consideration the sending of two Delegates to Manchester & other parts to warn them of the intended outbreak (which ought to take place on friday or sunday night at farthest).

We were assembled at the "Lord Denman" Beer House about ½ past 8 p.m. (seven present) when a Delegate from the South London District brought a message from Mr. Mc.Douall stating that he had had an interview with Mr. McCrae—and that he was deputed by him to inform the Delegates that they were dissolved by order of the Executive. Upon being questioned, the messenger said he had asked McDouall why they were dissolved, and he said, something had transpired since the morning that had caused this. He also denied all knowledge of his former plans, or even that the Delegates had been assembled for any specific purpose. This announcement caused great consternation, and the meeting immediately broke up. The Delegates present express'd their intention of going to their different localities and telling the members how they had been treated by Mr. McDouall—and advise them to have nothing more to do with the Chartist cause.

(Signed) George Davis.

Taken down by me, R. Mark Inspector'

(From H.O. 45/2410)

8. *Public Order and Popular Liberties*
Section I—The Right to Meet

(In an overall view the Chartists enjoyed a large liberty to meet publicly, but it was not unrestricted. Some statutory limitations were inherited from a more conservative age. Thus the Seditious Meetings and Assemblies Act of 1817 required the promoters of a gathering of more than fifty people to procure a requisition of seven householders to the local authorities. This was not a serious impediment, as the requisitionists could call the meeting themselves if the magistrates refused to do so. It survived merely as an easy way of gaining official countenance for popular assemblies. The act was no longer enforced by governments, except for a special clause applied against meetings in Trafalgar Square in 1848. Chartists were also likely to be interrupted for obstructing the highway if they met in streets and market places, but they were often suffered to do this for lengthy periods. Under both Whig and Tory control the Home Office looked mainly not to statute but to common law for guidance in dealing with political meetings. The principle which it found there was, nevertheless, imprecise, and whether it was to operate in a liberal or in an oppressive way depended heavily on the construction placed upon it by successive Home Secretaries in their correspondence with the magistrates. Governments operated in an area of legal uncertainty, and their prescriptions varied both with the severity of the challenge confronting them in the country and with their own inner political complexion.)

(a) The Common Law Principle:

(On 7 May 1839 the Home Secretary issued a circular letter to the magistrates of 43 towns disturbed by Chartist unrest, calling upon them to put down and suppress 'unlawful Meetings of large Numbers of Persons, some of them being armed with offensive Weapons.' This caused the Nottinghamshire magistrates, who wanted authority to eliminate unarmed and partly armed assemblages, to approach the Home Secretary through their county Member, Colonel Lancelot Rolleston, for advice. The Home Office reply, which was published as a parliamentary paper, ran as follows.)

'Sir   Whitehall, 3rd June 1839
    I have the honour to acknowledge the receipt of yr letter of the 29th ultimo, in which you request, in consequence of communications which you have had with the Magistrates of the county of Nottingham, to receive from me information relative to my circular letter of the 7th ultimo.
    With reference to the second paragraph of my letter, you wish to be informed, whether it is to be understood, supposing *some of the persons* attending a numerous meeting are armed with offensive weapons, that this circumstance will give a character of illegality to the meeting generally. The meaning of the paragraph, I think, will fully appear on reference to the Proclamation, to which I have therein referred. The unlawful meetings described in the Proclamation, are meetings attended by large numbers of persons, which by exciting to breaches of the peace, and by their riotous proceedings, have caused great alarm (some of the persons attending being armed with offensive weapons). As undoubtedly meetings may be unlawful, though no persons present should be armed; so, on the other hand, the presence of *some persons* armed might not be of itself, and singly, enough to make the *general meeting* unlawful, if in other respects the meeting were lawful; for it is possible the attendance

of such persons might be entirely unconnected with the general purposes and objects of the meeting.

Upon the next paragraph of my circular letter, in which general reference is made to the various kinds of unlawful meetings, you inform me the Magistrates are very desirous to receive from me a more explicit opinion as to the circumstances which will give to meetings the character of illegality, and will therefore justify the Magistrates in acting, or rather will require them, in obedience to the law, to act for the maintenance of the public peace. Upon this subject, perhaps, I ought to refer the Magistrates generally to books of authority which treat of unlawful meetings (such books as Mr. Russell on Criminal Law, Burn's Justice, etc.). On consulting these books, and the authorities therein referred to, it appears to me the result is this; namely, that all assemblies, not held by lawful authority, attended by great numbers of people, with such circumstances of terror as are calculated to excite alarm and to endanger the public peace, are prohibited by the common law, and are unlawful, even though they proceed to no act of destruction or injury of persons or property.

This was the opinion of the Judges on the Special Commission in 1831: it is therefore of great authority, and may safely be relied on by the Magistrates.[1]

> I have the honour etc. etc. etc.
> (Signed) J. RUSSELL

Colonel Rolleston, M.P. etc. etc. etc.'

(*Copy of a letter from Her Majesty's Principal Secretary of State for the Home Department to Col. Rolleston M.P., dated Whitehall, 3 June 1839, on the subject of Unlawful Meetings. Return to an address etc. dated July 19th 1839*; Parliamentary Papers, 1839 (448) XXXVIII)

(b) The Cautious Approach:

(When Chartism began, the Home Secretary Lord John Russell treated it with a high Whiggish tolerance. He issued instructions that the large meetings on Kersal Moor, Peep Green and elsewhere in September–October 1838, to elect delegates to the General Convention,

---

[1] The pronouncement is in line with a speech in the House of Commons by W. C. Plunket, later Lord Chancellor of Ireland, in 1819, and with the summing up by Baron Alderson at the trial of Henry Vincent at the Monmouth Summer Assize, 1839. Judge Alderson did emphasize, however, that the attendant circumstances of the meeting must be found dangerous by 'rational and firm men'—a qualification important for civil liberty. See report of the proceedings at the trial. H.O. 40/45.

should be allowed to proceed without interruption.[1] Before the year was out, however, the change to the eerie torchlight meetings at night time and Stephens' persistent advocacy of arming, which showed signs of being followed by the people, drove the government to stiffen its attitude. On 12 December a Royal Proclamation condemned the torchlight meetings and called upon the magistrates 'to prevent all such illegal assemblies' in future.[2] The follow-up advice, given by the Under-Secretary to the magistrates of Stockport, shows that, although the government had indeed intended to put an end to a particular kind of demonstration expressly intended to intimidate the propertied inhabitants of the manufacturing districts, it relied principally on the moral effect of the Proclamation to achieve this, and was not yet prepared to encourage the local authorities to disperse Chartist meetings. This policy stemmed not merely from a humane intention to avoid bloodshed, but also from a cautious desire to keep within the law. Lord Melbourne had been doubtful whether the torchlight meetings were illegal,[3] and his government preferred to leave the decision to the courts. Unfortunately this restraint later gave way before the growing alarm about Chartist military preparations. By the beginning of May 1839 the Home Office was advising magistrates to put down and disperse large armed meetings.[4])

'I am directed by Lord John Russell to acknowledge the receipt of your letter of the 15th instant, and to inform you, with reference to that part of your letter in which you state the construction, put by you on the Proclamation lately issued—namely "that in addition to the torchlight, it is necessary, to make the meeting illegal, that the people attending should behave in a tumultuous manner"—the Proclamation was not intended to intimate to the magistrates, that a night meeting, to be illegal, must be conducted in a tumultuous manner: nor does that appear to be the true construction of the Proclamation: for, unquestionably, night meetings may be illegal, in many cases, though unattended by tumult, or tumultuous behaviour. But night meetings in a room cannot be considered illegal unless some circumstance occurs at such meetings to render them so.

Upon the question, whether, in case a meeting becomes illegal, the magistrates are to disperse it, Lord John Russell directs me to inform

[1] Lord John Russell to the Earl of Harewood, 18 September 1838. H.O. 52/38.
[2] *The Manchester Guardian*, 19 December 1838.
[3] F. C. Mather, 'The Government and the Chartists'. A. Briggs ed., *Chartist Studies* (London, 1959), pp. 372–405.
[4] S. M. Phillipps to the Trowbridge magistrates and the mayor of Monmouth, 3 May 1839. H.O. 41/13.

you, that if no actual breach of the Peace should take place, and no overt act of violence, he would advise the Magistrates not to attempt to disperse the Meeting, but to proceed afterwards against the parties principally concerned. Even if there should be an actual breach of the peace, Lord John Russell cannot undertake, without knowing the particular circumstances under which the magistrates are called upon to act, to advise the magistrates to attempt to disperse the meeting by force. In some very strong and dangerous cases, such a measure might be absolutely necessary: in other cases, it might be unnecessary and imprudent, and not justified by the occasion. In ordinary cases, Lord John Russell is inclined to think, it might be most prudent and most safe, not to adopt that course, but to proceed against the offenders afterwards, upon depositions, in the regular way.

Upon the next question, "whether, if a speaker at such a meeting use inflammatory language, advise the people to arm etc., the magistrates are to cause him to be immediately apprehended and dealt with as a disturber of the peace," Lord John Russell is of opinion that the most effectual and prudent course, as well with a view to the preservation of the peace, as also for the punishment of offenders, will be, not to apprehend immediately the person using such language, but to procure the best information that can be obtained of the language addressed to the people at such an illegal meeting, and to proceed against him afterwards. By adopting this course, Lord John Russell feels satisfied, that, although it appear less immediate and less summary than an arrest at the moment, the magistrates will be less exposed to the risk of failure, and that the ends of justice will be more completely, and in the end, more speedily attained, by the punishment of offenders.

Lord John Russell directs me to assure you, that the opinion of the magistrates respecting itinerant demagogues will have its due weight with him; but that the means adopted must not be more summary and immediate than the law allows. I am to add that it will be of the greatest importance on all occasions of such meetings, that the most accurate information should be obtained as to the language used by the Speakers, as to the incidents and circumstances of the meeting.'
(S. M. Phillipps to the Mayor and Magistrates of Stockport, 18 December 1838. H.O. 41/13)

(c) Prevention and Dispersal
(Strictly interpreted, the Common Law placed difficulties in the way of

preventing gatherings from assembling, as the tendency of a meeting could not be assessed in advance, and gave some protection to peaceful assemblies against interruption. In times of acute pressure, however, governments so construed it as to permit a total clampdown on Chartist and other outdoor meetings. During the excitement following the incendiary Bull Ring riots of 15 July 1839 the mayor of Birmingham was instructed that, although as a general rule a meeting's propensity to creat terror and alarm must be judged by 'its general appearance and accompanying circumstances', nevertheless in the present emergency in the town the magistrates would 'be supported by the Government in taking measures for the prevention and dispersion of any meetings which may cause terror and alarm to the peaceable inhabitants'.[1] During the 'Plug Plot' disturbances of 1842 the magistrates of many towns and districts, once they had recovered from their early inertia, banned all public meetings within their jurisdiction while the unrest continued. The Conservative Under-Secretary at the Home Office, Manners Sutton, lent his sanction to such proceedings when approached by the Lord Lieutenant of Worcestershire about meetings at Dudley, where O'Neill and other Chartist orators used violent language to encourage the colliers to strike. It was admitted that the neighbourhood was quiet at the moment, though not expected to continue so.[2])

'I have the honor to ackge the rect. of yr. Lordship's letter and the enclosure: I am fully aware of the dangerous and illegal tendency of Mr. O'Neil's conduct and language, and I fully concur with your Lordship in considering that his apprehension would be of the greatest importance, and have the most beneficial result. Upon consideration however I am of opinion that the deposition forwarded to me by your Lordship would hardly of itself justify this step. I have however full confidence that your Lordship will not allow the law to be violated with impunity, and at the moment it is of more peculiar importance to assist its authority in the case of a Ringleader. With regard to your Lordship's question as to the power of the magistrates to suppress the large meetings which have taken place in Worcestershire: I have the honor to inform your Lordship that all meetings in large numbers in present circumstances have a manifest tendency to create terror and to endanger the public peace, that as such they are illegal, and upon notice given that they will not be allowed to be held, they ought to be dispersed.'
(H. Manners Sutton to Lord Lyttleton, Hagley, Stourbridge, 19 August 1842. H.O. 41/17)

[1] H.O. to mayor of Birmingham, 24 July 1839—two letters. H.O. 41/14.
[2] Lord Lyttleton to H.O., 18 August 1842. H.O. 45/263.

(d) Some Relevant Distinctions :

(Usually, however, governments, especially Whig governments, adopted a discriminating approach to Chartist meetings. In 1848 a distinction was drawn between mass demonstrations in towns, such as that on 23 May to welcome McDouall to Bradford, when sections bearing tricolour flags with pike heads and sporting inflammatory slogans marched to a meeting of 10–12,000 people[1] and similarly large gatherings like the semi-religious camp meetings on the surrounding moors. In general, policy was designed to counter intimidation, a weapon on which some of the leading Chartists, including O'Connor, at first mainly relied to achieve their political objective, rather than to check freedom of public discussion.)

'I am directed to acknge the rect of yr letter of the 14th inst. & to inform you that the magistrates must exercise their own discretion as to the course to be pursued with reference to meetings held in the neighbourhood of Bradford, regard being had to the character of the meetings & the circumstances under which they are held. Large meetings such as those which have recently been held or attempted to be held in London & in some other large towns have assumed a clearly illegal character from the numbers of persons invited to attend them & the danger to the public peace & security which in some cases has actually occurred & which there was reasonable ground generally for apprehending. Such danger would probably be much diminished in the case of a meeting held at a considerable distance from a town & although the circumstances under which the meetings referred to in your letter may perhaps justify their being stopped, Sir G. Grey wd suggest to the magistrates whether if they are prevented in the immediate neighbourhood of the town, it wld not be more expedient with regard to those at some distance & when no breach of the peace occurs to abstain from any direct interference, but to procure accurate information of the language used by the speakers & to take proceedings agnst any parties when speeches are of a treasonable or seditious character.'

(Draft of reply by Under-Secretary at the Home Office to a letter from the Mayor and Magistrates of Bradford dated 14 June 1848. H.O. 45/2410 AC.)

Section II—Freedom of Association

(Freedom to associate for political purposes was not in serious jeopardy

---

[1] Mayor and magistrates of Bradford to H.O., 24 May 1848. H.O. 45/2410 AC.

during the Chartist period, but was circumscribed by the provisions of two statutes passed in earlier times. One, the 1799 Law against the Corresponding Societies (39 George III c.79) banned all associations prescribing for their members oaths or declarations not required by law or consisting of separate divisions, each with its own officers. The other, the Seditious Meetings and Assemblies Act of 1817 (57 George III c.19) prohibited those which elected delegates to confer with other clubs. The government has been credited with liberality by historians[1] for not using these laws against the Chartists. It did not deliberately employ them to put down peaceful associations, and by and large the statutes cannot be said to have imposed any considerable restraints on Chartist organization, though it was deemed prudent to revise the constitution of the National Charter Association in order to remove some illegal features in 1841. But the laws were not entirely a dead letter. They were held in reserve by governments to be applied, if necessary, in restraint of suspected conspiracies. On 30 April 1839 Lord John Russell referred the magistrates of the Wiltshire clothing district to the 1817 act, when he was informed that the Chartists of the region had formed an association of branches with separate officers or delegates and that an armed demonstration at Devizes had been organized at branch meetings.[2] Early in June 1848, as the document shows, the government considered legal proceedings against the National Charter Association on the basis of its new and imprudently drafted constitution. That also was a time of mounting disorder in the country, when Ernest Jones, a member of the N.C.A. Executive, spoke unguardedly of links with insurrectionists in Ireland. If, on these occasions, prosecutions were not brought under the above-mentioned acts, this was probably the result less of the government's scruples than of the success of other methods of handling the emergency.)

'*Case*

Touching the Organisation of a "National Charter Association"
The following is Copy of a letter from   Mr. Waddington
Whitehall
5th June 1848.

Sir

I am directed by Secretary Sir George Grey to transmit to you the enclosed papers relative to the organization of a "National Charter Association",—and to request that you will lay the same before the Attorney and Solicitor General, and move them to favor Sir George Grey with their *early* opinion.

---

[1] M. Hovell, *The Chartist Movement* (Manchester, 1966), p. 198; L. Radzinowicz, *A History of English Criminal Law*, Vol. IV (London, 1968), p. 247.
[2] Lord John Russell to W. Ludlow Bruges M.P., 30 April 1839. H.O. 41/13.

1st. Whether the "National Charter Association", if organized on the proposed Plan, is illegal:

2d. If it be illegal, what is the proper course to be pursued against parties who are Members of it.

(Signed) H. Waddington

Geo. Maule, Esq.'

'The papers inclosed in the above letter are hereunto annexed.[1]

The Attorney and Solicitor General are requested

To advise upon the questions put in Mr. Waddington's letter.

1. We are of opinion that the National Charter Association if organized on the proposed plan is an unlawful combination & Confederacy within the statutes 39 G 3, c 79 s 2 and 57 G 3, c 19 s 24, and

2. that any person being a member of that association or directly or indirectly maintaining correspondence therewith or aiding or abetting or supporting it, may be proceeded agst by indictment or before justices in a summary way as prescribed in the stat. 39 G 3, c 79 s 8.

John Jervis
John Romilly

Temple, 13 June, 48.'[2]

(Case Submitted to the Attorney and Solicitor General by the Treasury Solicitor, George Maule, at the instigation of the Home Secretary, Sir George Grey. H.O. 48/40, No. 16)

Section III—Freedom of the Press
(Restrictions on the printed word constituted a more serious restraint on working-class opinion than those on meetings and associations. The most damaging stemmed from the operation of the Stamp Act of 1836, which, though it reduced the stamp duty on newspapers from four pence to one penny per copy, intensified the difficulties of publishing cheaply by evading the stamp duty altogether. The authorities were empowered to issue warrants to search for unstamped journals and to

---

[1] These are two printed papers—one relating to the Chartist National Assembly, which had revised the constitution of the N.C.A., the other a copy of the new constitution.

[2] The case is minuted in the Home Secretary's handwriting.

'I will see the Commrs. of Police upon this

G.G.'

seize presses. The case of the *Western Vindicator*, an unstamped paper edited by Henry Vincent, which circulated widely in the West of England and South Wales, illustrates the pressure which could be exerted upon these once numerous organs of the 'pauper press'. In the excitement following the Newport rising, worried West country notables hustled the Home Secretary, Lord Normanby, into deciding to prosecute the publishers of the journal for sedition. Further reports from the Lord Lieutenant of Monmouthshire that the *Vindicator* was still being read to workmen in the beerhouses of the disturbed districts of his county caused the Home Office to instruct the Clerk to the Newport magistrates, Thomas Jones Phillips, to transmit to him copies, which were being sold in shops or by hawkers, so that a prosecution, presumably for selling unstamped newspapers, might be considered. The zealous Clerk first caused eight copies to be bought, and then organized a police raid at midnight on the shop of Elizabeth Edwards, the widow of an imprisoned baker, seizing her stock of *Vindicators*, which he forwarded to the Home Office. A further confiscation was made on the same premises a few days later. Both were carried out in an entirely irregular manner, no warrant having been issued as the law required. The Home Office drew attention to the error, but other seizures were effected by the mayor of Cardiff, and the *Western Vindicator* was driven out of circulation.[1]

'FAREWELL!

Let not our Readers think we are going to leave them entirely. No! We part but for a short period. Robbed and plundered as we have been, by fellows self-appointed to the task, we find ourselves unable to proceed. Look on this picture!

CENSORS OF THE PRESS!!!
CARDIFF—A MAYOR!
NEWPORT—THE POLICE!!
MONMOUTH—A SOLDIER!!!

We shall be fully occupied for a week or two, settling the above gentry; after which we shall make our re-appearance. Rally, Chartists! a great principle is involved. THE LIBERTY OF THE PRESS is gone!

By his own Appointment!!!
THE RIGHT WORSHIPFUL THE MAYOR OF CARDIFF
CENSOR OF THE PRESS!!!

---

[1] See correspondence in H.O. 40/45; also D. Williams, *John Frost: A Study in Chartism* (Cardiff, 1939), pp. 257–8.

THE LIBERTY OF THE PRESS is departed from England: the Mayor of Cardiff has turned ROBBER; and appointed himself *the arbiter of what shall and what shall not be published*! A parcel of *Vindicators* directed to our agent in Cardiff, was seized by order of the Mayor; and forwarded by him to the Secretary of State, calling his attention to the alarming nature of the contents of the paper! Mark! Not to its infringing law by being an unstamped newspaper (which it is not[1]); but because he, the said Mayor, does not like its politics! Farewell the Liberty of the Press; if this act pass with impunity! A pretty state of things, truly. A Mayor wishes to have the opinion of the Secretary of State in reference to the character of a periodical; and obtains the same by stealing them! We know there is little justice for a Chartist, but we will try if there be any virtue left in the law! If the law protect us not—then farewell every *moral hope*! Chartists look to it! *You must not MEET! You must not WRITE!* A censor of the press in our country! An officious dignitary, deciding *what shall and what shall not be published*!!!

We thank the *Sun* for his remarks upon this case; will the Tory press be safe, we ask them? We expect their aid, to save the Press from being reduced to a worse condition than ever it was in France!

We wait the reply of this Corporation worthy to the annexed letter:—

Western Vindicator Office, Bath

Sir—Having been informed that you have presumed to appropriate to your own use, a parcel containing *Western Vindicators*, my property—I have sent you the invoice. I shall have no objection to open an account with you; but think you have a strange way of doing business. This act of yours has deprived my readers in Cardiff of their papers. If you had wanted them, you should have purchased them of my agent, or written to me. I am rather doubtful of the honesty of your intentions, so herewith apprise you—that if the account be not settled within three days from the date hereof, legal proceedings will be taken against you—not for the debt. Oh, no! I shall proceed in a different manner! I should have thought a Mayor would have known enough of law, not to have so far forgotten himself as to commit an act of felony.

I am, Sir, yours respectfully,

Francis Hill

14 Northumberland Place,
Market Place, Bath.

---

[1] It sought to evade the stamp regulations by publishing news in the guise of articles. D. Williams, *John Frost, a Study in Chartism* (Cardiff, 1939), pp. 137–8.

December 11, 1839

THE MAYOR OF CARDIFF
TO FRANCIS HILL
Dec.7   To 3 dozen *Western Vindicators*

0–5–0

ANOTHER SEIZURE !!!
BY ORDER OF THE SECRETARY OF STATE
'Now by St. Paul the work goes bravely on'
In Newport an immense number of *Vindicators* have been seized.
Huzzah!
Martial Law or "Majors" & "Minors" !!!

THERE is a posse of soldiers in the town of Monmouth; and amongst them is a Major, who, if we do not comfortably locate him within a prison shortly then there is no justice in England! But this we knew before. Yet we will try it.

This red-coated *gentleman* has established *on his own sole authority*, MARTIAL LAW IN MONMOUTH!!! We do not expect much CIVILITY where the MILITARY are in the ascendant; but we will try the CIVIL Law on this Major.

Will our readers credit it, that a soldier—a redcoat—has *with impunity seized on a poor boy, ransacked his newspapers & periodicals to search for* VINDICATORS; and kept him in custody FORTY MINUTES!!! He was pleased to threaten the boy, that if he ever caught him with VINDICATORS, *HE WOULD HAVE TORN THEM TO PIECES*!!! The magistrates have ordered the arrest of any one who crys the Vindicator! Even this may be tolerated; but when the soldier—whose only occupation in England appears to be the keeping the people in subjection, take the law into their own hands; then, indeed, has liberty become a mockery, and the power of the strongest is the only acknowledged authority. Be it so. We shall become strong when our time comes.'

(Extract from *The Western Vindicator*, 14 December 1839, in H.O. 40/45)

PART V

Chartism and Social Class

Section 1. Some Chartist Social Types
The following are not presented as full short biographies, merely as passages indicative of the experiences which led their subjects into Chartism.

(a) The Professional Man:

(Although the professions were still taking shape during the first half of the nineteenth century and sharp distinctions of status existed among those who were coming to be recognized as professional, professional men or men with professional training figured prominently in the Chartist leadership and by reason of their formal education left a disproportionate imprint on the movement's ideas. Long established gentlemanly professions such as the English bar or the Established clergy provided few recruits. Neither Ernest Jones nor Bronterre O'Brien, who never completed his qualification, were typical practitioners of the former before they became Chartists. Lower professions—schoolmasters, Dissenting ministers, surgeons and doctors—were more liberally represented, and their Chartism was often closely related to their personal frustrations and the social needs of the workers to whom they ministered. Chartist surgeons included Peter Murray McDouall, Dr. John Taylor, Dr. William Price of Pontypridd, George Bridge Mullins, one of the London conspirators of 1848, and Matthew Fletcher, of whom a pen portrait follows. W. S. Villiers Sankey, the Chartist poet, was a medical theorist and graduate of Cambridge and Dublin.)

'MATTHEW FLETCHER

In the delegate for Bury is to be found one of the few, but gratifying, instances in which the force of sympathy has induced men to come out from the narrow and privileged circle in which their fortunes have been cast, to espouse the cause and promote the interests of the less favoured and more suffering classes of their fellow-men.

Mr. Fletcher was born at Bury, in Lancashire, in the year 1796. He received his elementary and classical education under the direction of Mr. Allard, a dissenting clergyman, at the Grammar School of his native town. He was apprenticed to Mr. Goodland, a surgeon, who has acquired considerable distinction in his profession, both as a practitioner and as an author. Mr. Fletcher completed his studies at Bartholomew's Hospital, and was admitted as a member of the London College of Surgeons, in 1817. After having resided for a few months at Bolton, where he saw but slight hopes of professional success, he commenced his career in his native town, and in a few years acquired an extensive and valuable practice.

Mr. Fletcher was educated in high Tory principles, and the remarks of two of the most distinguished writers of that party, Hume and Bolingbroke, on the consequences of the funding system, first led him into the train of observation and inquiry which caused him to adopt the political creed, he has ever since, "through evil report and good", maintained. Among the social evils which our corrupt system of government had produced, the abuses of the Factory System particularly attracted his attention ; and in his intercourse with the mill-owners, he was not sparing in animadversions on the dishonesty and cruelty of their conduct towards their workpeople. This was a course not likely to promote the interests of a young professional man, and he was soon stigmatized as "a Radical", which, in the circle he moved in, was considered a more serious moral stain than a charge of pecuniary dishonesty would have been.

While Mr. Fletcher maintained that the representation of the working classes in the House of Commons was the only means of obtaining a redress of their grievances, he constantly insisted on the importance of forcing their grievances on the attention of all classes, as the most irresistible argument for the restoration of the constitutional rights of the people.

At the close of the year 1829, Mr. Fletcher, in an introductory lecture to a course of mechanics, argued that a decided and constantly increasing reduction of the hours of labour, was the only thing calculated to prevent the social and political evils which the factory system was entailing on a great portion of the people of England. He afterwards handed over to Mr. W. R. Greg, the results of his observations on the condition of the factory workers, which formed the

CHARTISM AND SOCIAL CLASS

greater part of the materials for Mr. Greg's pamphlet on the factory question—a pamphlet which Mr. Oastler has denominated his "great gun". After Mr. Greg found it convenient to retract his opinions on this subject, his brother, Mr. R. Hyde Greg, in an elaborate reply to the arguments of different authors, on the evils of the factory system, threw back the responsibility of the facts and arguments in Mr. W. Greg's pamphlet on Mr. Fletcher; but he did not attempt to deny them. When the factory system assumed the character of a political question, Mr. Fletcher joined in the agitation set on foot by Mr. Sadler and Mr. Oastler; and took a prominent part in it during the whole of its progress.

When the Reform Bill became the great national question, Mr. Fletcher, though he had suffered bitter and almost ruinous persecution from the Whigs of his own district, on account of the part he had taken in some parochial disputes, zealously joined in the agitation of that measure. But while he supported it, as calculated, by breaking in on the corrupt system, and teaching the people their power, to lead to further and more efficient reforms, he warned the men of Bury to beware, lest in putting down the old aristocracy, they should throw themselves into the power of the worst of all forms of government, a commercial oligarchy. When the bill had passed, Mr. Fletcher seeing that from the influence of the Earl of Derby, the lord of the manor, and some powerful local influences, Bury was in danger of becoming a close Whig borough, brought forward a candidate on the principle of Universal Suffrage, and during a period of six months, he kept up a fierce paper war with the united Whig and Tory parties. At the election, the Radicals polled just half the number of the united factions. From that time a powerful radical party has existed in Bury.

When an attempt was made in 1837, to carry the New Poor Law into effect in Lancashire and Yorkshire, Mr. F. having heard of the intended visit of Mr. Power, the commissioner to Bury, called, in a few hours, a large meeting of the inhabitants, and elicited from Mr. Power certain admissions, which have since been used as powerful weapons in the hands of the anti-Poor-law agitators. The report of their meeting ran like the "fiery cross" through Lancashire and Yorkshire, and Mr. Power, who had previously succeeded in deluding the people of several towns, was met at every step with the fiercest opposition. Mr. Fletcher declared his determination to resist, by every means, that unconstitutional act of Parliament, and the feeling was responded to by the people. Up to the present moment, the commissioners have not dared to attempt the enforcement of "the bill" on the people of Bury.

Mr. Fletcher has taken an active part in the Chartist agitation, and was unanimously elected the representative for his native town, in the General Convention. He is understood to have been one of the persons against whom warrants were issued, at the time of Mr. Stephens' arrest. ...'

(Portraits of Delegates, No. V. *The Charter*, 31 March 1839)

(b) The Self-Improving Tradesman:

(Though not among the most aristocratic trades, building workers were relatively well-to-do skilled artisans. Not all of them prospered, however, especially in the lean years following the collapse of the Operative Builders Union in 1834. The slaters were the least fortunate, losing both their national and their local trade-union organization in the reverses of that year, so that their work was pirated by jobbing plasterers or bricklayers.[1] The nominal weekly summer wage of a craftsman who had served his time to the trade was about 18/- to 24/- per week in the 1830s in the provinces, but labourers could claim no more than two-thirds of that sum,[2] and, as work was not easy to obtain, the average weekly take-home pay was much less. A return made by local working men's associations to a questionnaire circulated by the Chartist Convention in 1839 put it at 10/- to 18½/-.[3] Despite these handicaps, Robert Knox, whose trade this was, followed the paths of self-education characteristic of skilled craftsmen, and thus found his way to Chartism. He represented County Durham in the 1839 Convention.)

'ROBERT KNOX

In the accompanying sketch, our artist has admirably succeeded in portraying the delegate for the county of Durham. Mr. Knox, who is now in his twenty-fourth year, is a native of Dunse in the County of Berwick. He is by trade a slater, and belongs in all senses of the word to the working class. At the early age of eleven, he was obliged to submit to the toil of a labourer, and he has ever since continued to work at his trade. About two years since, he went to Sunderland to obtain employment, and the intelligence of his mind and the integrity of his character, soon procured for him the confidence of those with whom he associated. A congeniality of disposition and a similarity of pursuit

[1] R. W. Postgate, *The Builders' History* (London, 1923), pp. 115–16.

[2] A. L. Bowley, 'The Statistics of Wages in the U.K. during the Last Hundred Years, Pt. VI. Wages in the Building Trades. English Towns'. *Journal of the Royal Statistical Society*, Vol. LXIII, 1900, pp. 297–314.

[3] D. J. Rowe, 'The Chartist Convention and the Regions', *Econ.H.R.*, 2 Series, Vol. XXII, No. 1, 1969, pp. 58–74.

introduced him amongst the members of the mechanics' institute there, and he, for the first time, we believe, became deeply interested in political questions. The members of the mechanics' institute at Sunderland are the leaders of the Chartist Movement there; and through his intercourse with them, Mr. Knox soon had his sympathies awakened on behalf of the large mass of his fellow men, whom he found condemned to unremitting toil and hopeless poverty; and his determination was at once formed to labour for their emancipation. In the month of December last, he attended several public meetings at Hetton-le-Hole, and other places in the neighbourhood, and on New Year's Day, he was elected at a large public meeting at Sunderland, to represent the county of Durham, in the General Convention. In person Mr. Knox is about five feet ten in height, and is of a comparatively slender frame; his limbs, however, appear to be well knit together, and he evinces a capability of enduring a considerable amount of hardship and fatigue. His physiognomy evinces much sternness of purpose and abstraction of thought. He would strike the practised physionomist as being one of the Cassius class, whom Shakespeare represents as thinking much, and being to tyrants, therefore, always dangerous. There is an air of melancholy in the expression of his face, which would induce a belief that he is a man of sorrows; but even a slight acquaintance with him is sufficient to prove that he possesses a heart full of kindness, and that, with a large capacity for sympathy, he is fitted to enjoy pleasure and communicate it liberally to others. We have never heard Mr. Knox deliver what may be termed a speech, and we incline to think that public speaking is not his forte. When he does take part in any discussion, he delivers himself in the fewest possible words. He appears to delight rather in abstract speculations, and in discussing ultimate principles, than to deal with the every-day occurrences of life. He possesses much acuteness and penetration of mind, and has the enviable faculty of readily divesting a subject of all extraneous and irrelevant matter. The position which Mr. Knox occupies in society has afforded him but small means of acquiring knowledge, but it is evident that he has an extensive acquaintance with the literature and history of his country. He is a zealous supporter of temperance societies, and was, for some time, secretary to the temperance society in his native town. ...'
(Portraits of Delegates, No. IV, *The Charter*, 24 March 1839)

(c) Downgraded Artisan:
(Tailors supplied Chartism with a large proportion of its second-rank

leaders. This was partly because of their numbers. In London Mayhew placed them fourth in order on the list of employed persons. It was also due, however, to their trade history, illustrated by the career of William Cuffay, the London physical-force Chartist. Down to the trade-union débacle of 1834 the London tailors had successfully maintained their artisan status with some assistance from an Act of 1768, 8 George III, c. XVII, which regulated hours of labour to 12 per day, with the intention of concentrating production on the master tailors' premises. From that time forward until mid-century the statute was increasingly infringed, piece work was substituted for time rates, and work was taken out of the employer's shop by sub-contractors ('sweaters'), who undercut accepted prices by engaging female and other cheap labour. Though some fortunate workmen still found continuous employment in 'honourable' shops for earnings ranging up to 30/- per week, many more were reduced, outside the brisk season, to casual labour on 'sank work', making soldiers', police or mail clothing at 4/- a week.[1] Cuffay was evidently among the less favoured.)

'MR. WILLIAM CUFFAY

WILLIAM CUFFAY, loved by his own order, who knew him and appreciated his virtues, ridiculed and denounced by a press that knew him not, and had no sympathy with his class, and banished by a government that feared him, has achieved a celebrity that fully entitles him to a place in our Portrait Gallery. He was born in the year 1788, on board a merchant ship, homeward bound from the Island of St. Kitts, and is consequently sixty-two years old. Cradled on the vast Atlantic, he became by birth a citizen of the world, a character that, in after life, he well maintained. His father was a slave, born in the Island of St. Kitts; his grandfather was an African dragged from his native valleys in the prime of his manhood. On arriving in England, himself and his parents became free, and during his services in the cause of Democracy, he, the stern man, has often shed genuine tears of gratitude for this boon, and declared that the sacrifice of his life and his liberty if needed, was due to the complete emancipation of that nation which had inscribed his name upon the list of free men, and this burst of generous feeling has been, as events have proved, no idle boast, nor has it fallen without producing its effect upon the hearts of his fellow toilers.

Soon after his arrival in England his father procured a berth as cook

[1] E. P. Thompson and E. Yeo, *The Unknown Mayhew: Selections from the Morning Chronicle 1849–50* (London, 1971), pp. 181–227.

on board a man-of-war, and Cuffay spent the years of his childhood with his mother at Chatham: though of a very delicate constitution, he took great delight in all manly exercises. As he advanced toward manhood, he entered the ranks of the proletarians as a journeyman tailor, and was reckoned a superior workman. He was thrice married, but has left no issue: his only child, a boy, died in its youth. Scrupulously neat in his person, he carried a love of order and regularity even to excess in all his transactions, whether social or political, this characteristic procured him much esteem and adapted him to fill offices which men of greater talents sought for in vain; during his whole career, he occupied an active post in the ranks of his own trade and was never found wanting in any of the requisites essential to the maintenance of a character for sterling and unflinching integrity. In a letter written by one who has known him upwards of forty years, he says, "Cuffay was a good spirit in a little deformed case: I have known some thousands in the trade, and I never knew a man I would sooner confide in: and I believe this to be the feeling of thousands in the business to this day. It was always his great delight to take young men by the hand and instruct them, not only in the trade, but mentally." He disapproved of the Trades' Union movement in 1834, and was nearly the last of his society in joining the lodge; but ultimately he gave way, and struck with the general body, remaining out until the last, thereby losing a shop where he had worked for many years; since which time he has had but very partial employ. He early saw through the deception of the Reform Bill, and from 1839, when the struggle for the Charter commenced, until his banishment, dedicated his whole energies as a worker to the task of enfranchising the millions; in 1840 he was elected as a delegate from Westminster to the Metropolitan Delegate Council, an office which he ably discharged during the long and energetic existence of that body in 1842, when the Chartist Executive, with the exception of Morgan Williams, were arrested; he was elected by acclamation, together with Thomas Martin Wheeler, John George Drew, and James Knight, to supply that vacancy. In 1845 he was appointed one of the auditors of the National Land Company, which office he held until his arrest: he was a member of nearly every Convention which was called into existence during these exciting times, and fulfilled his duties with honour to himself and satisfaction to his constituents. Elected as one of the delegates for Westminster to the National Convention and Assembly of 1848, he allowed his enthusiasm to overcome his usual cool judgment, and was singled out by the press for ridicule and vituperation: he bore it unflinchingly, he even seemed to glory in it. As early as 1842 he had been especially singled out by the *Times* as a leader of the opposition in London to the Anti-Corn League, which facetiously denominated the Chartists as the "Black man and his Party". Entrapped by the infernal spy-system into an almost involuntary attendance at the so-called insurrectionary meetings in the autumn of 1848, he fell a victim, but he shrunk not: flight was open to him, but he refused to avail himself of it, and during his confinement, both prior and after his sentence, his spirits maintained their usual equilibrium.

Notwithstanding the Government punishment of transportation for twenty-one years, it has been intimated that on reaching his destination he will receive a ticket of leave giving him his freedom in the colony. We trust this is a fact; but whatever may be his after fate, whilst integrity in the midst of poverty, whilst honour in the midst of temptation are admired and venerated, so long will the name of William Cuffay, a scion of Afric's oppressed race, be preserved from oblivion.'
(*Reynolds Political Instructor*, No. 23, Vol. 1, 13 April 1850)

(d) The Outworker Turned Poor Factory Operative:

(It is wrong to think of factory workers as a homogeneous group, well paid except during trade depressions, and totally distinct from indigent handloom weavers. Factory inspector Leonard Horner remarked in 1842 that 'with the exception of the mule-spinners, dressers, overlookers, mechanics, and a few others, all of whom constitute but a small proportion of the whole, the majority of workers in a cotton mill receive very moderate wages'.[1] In a sample drawn from Manchester and the surrounding towns about one-sixth of the factory operatives were paid wages ranging from 22s 8½d to 29s 3d per week in 1833. The favoured proportion must have been much higher among heads of households, for the employees in the lowly paid occupations were mainly women and children. Nevertheless, a significant number of adult males competed with women workers for jobs as tenters, warpers and power-loom weavers at 7s 5½d, 12s 3d and 10s 9¾d respectively in the earlier eighteen-thirties.[2] In times of economic collapse, as in 1841–42, when wages were slashed, operatives of this kind were almost as liable as the more permanently depressed outworkers to be driven by despair to acts of collective violence. The defence submitted by Richard Pilling, an ex-handloom weaver, who like many of his type had turned to the power loom, at his trial at the Lancaster assize in March 1843 for the part he had played in the semi-Chartist 'Plug Plot' of the preceding

---

[1] Quoted from D. Bythell, *The Handloom Weavers* (Cambridge, 1969), p. 135.
[2] F. Collier, *The Family Economy of the Working Classes in the Cotton Industry 1784–1833* (Manchester, 1964), p. 69.

August, brings this out. It illustrates the importance of family earnings rather than the incomes of individuals as determinants of the standard of living. Pilling's speech moved the court to tears, and sentence was never passed on him and his co-defendants.)

'Gentlemen, I am somewhere about forty-three years of age. I was asked last night if I were not sixty. But if I had as good usage as others, instead of looking like a man of sixty, I should look something like a man of thirty-six. I have gone to be a hand-loom weaver, when I was about ten years of age—in 1810. The first week I ever worked in my life I earned 16s. a week by the hand-loom. I followed that occupation till 1840. Then I was the father of a family—a wife and three children. In 1840 I could only earn—indeed the last week I worked, and I worked hard, I could only earn 6s. 6d.; but I should do that or become a pauper. I should go to the factory, which I detested to the bottom of my heart, and work for 6s. 6d. a week, or become a pauper. But although I detested the factory system, yet, sooner than become a pauper on the parish, I submitted. I was not long in the factory until I saw the evil workings of the accursed system—it is a system, which, above all systems, will bring this country to ruin if it is not altered. I have read some of the speeches by the late *Mr. Sadler* and I have read many letters of that noble king of Yorkshire—*Richard Oastler*—I have read many of his letters, and very shortly I became an advocate of the Ten Hours' Bill. I continued to advocate the Ten Hours' Bill up to the present day, and as long as I have a day to live, so long will I advocate the Ten Hours' Bill. After working in the factory seven years, a reduction began to creep in, one way or the other. I was a resident at Stockport. A reduction crept in on one side and another. There were some masters always who wanted to give less wages than others. Seeing this to be an evil, and knowing it to be injurious to the master, the owner of cottage property, and the publican—knowing that all depended on the wages of the working man, I became an opponent to the reduction of wages to the bottom of my soul; and, as long as I live, I shall continue to keep up the wages of labour to the utmost of my power. For taking that part in Stockport, and being the means of preventing many reductions, the masters combined all as one man against me, and neither me nor my children could get a day's employment. In 1840 there was a great turn-out in Stockport, in which turn-out I took a conspicuous part. We were out eight weeks. We were up every morning from five to six o'clock. Upwards of six thousand power-loom weavers were engaged in that turn-out. We had our processions. We went to Ashton, Hyde and Dukinfield in procession. We had our processions in Manchester, and all over the country, and we were not interfered with. No-one meddled with us—no one insulted us. We were never told, at this time, that we were doing that which was wrong. Considering, from the Act of Parliament that was passed when the combination laws were repealed in 1825, that I had a right to do so, I did believe as an Englishman and factory operative that, in consequence of that Act, I had a right to do all that ever lay in my power to keep up wages.

In 1840 the master manufacturers, to the number of about forty, had a meeting, and they conspired together—if there is conspiracy on the one side there is conspiracy on the other—and they gave us notice for a reduction of 1d. a cut. Some people think 1d. is a small reduction, but it amounts to five weeks' wages in the course of the year. It is 2s. 6d. a week. Thus by that reduction they were robbing every operative of five weeks' wages. I knew that Stockport would be injured in consequence of that reduction. I knew the result would be that the master-manufacturers themselves would be injured by it. My prophecy is fulfilled. One half of them is broken, and the other half is insolvent. When they gave notice of that reduction, they said: "Blackburn, Preston, and all the manufacturing districts, are paying less than us, and we shall all break unless we come down to the Blackburn prices." What was the result? Hyde, Ashton, Stalybridge, Bolton, Wigan, Warrington, Preston, Blackburn, reduced. In another year all the towns in the manufacturing districts reduced again. Not content with that reduction, about twelve months after, they took off another 1d. a cut, besides taking 2s. off the throstle spinners who had only 9s. a week, and 1s. 6d. off the card spinners, who had only 8s. a week, and so on. When they took the other 1d. a cut off, I pulled all the hands out, and we went round again to all the manufacturing districts, and brought things to a level again. The manufacturers of Stockport met again, and said, "We cannot compete with Blackburn and Preston, and we must reduce again",—and this is the way they will go on until at length they reduce so low that we shall all become paupers.

Gentlemen, I went to Ashton. Myself and my two sons were then working at the mills for 1s. 0½d. a cut. Our work was thirty cuts a week—which makes 1l. 11s. 3d. When Stockport reduced, my employer took off 1d. a cut; then he took off ½d. a cut. I am not blaming him; he was only following others. If one master reduces, the others must reduce also. They all have to meet in one market, and if one man at a certain price has 1d. profit, and the other only ¼d., he who has only the

½d. will break. I was in very poor circumstances then, having a wife and seven children to support; and only three of us earning wages, as I told you. My wages then (two years and a half ago) was 1l. 11s. 3d. He then took 1d. off for every cut. I had to pay 3s. for rent, 1s. 6d. for fire, 6d. for soap, and 2s. for clothing, leaving, after reckoning all up, about 1l. a week for provisions. When he took this 1d. off it caused a reduction in my wages of 2s. 6d. Shortly after he took off ½d. a cut, which was a reduction of 1s. 3d. a week more. Fifteen months since, they took another 1d. off; then they took a ½d. a cut off, and at the mill we worked at we turned out against the ½d. Three men who were out on that strike were turned off, when the hands returned to their work. I am not ashamed to state that I did all I could along with other individuals to prevent the reduction. We accomplished that ...

My Lord, and gentlemen of the jury, it was then a hard case for me to support myself and family. My eldest son but one, who was sixteen years of age, had fallen into a consumption last Easter and left his work. We were then reduced to 9½d. a cut, which brought our earnings down to something like 16s. a week. That is all I had to live on, with my nine in family, 3s. a week going out of that for rent, and a sick son lying helpless before me. I have gone home and seen that son—(here Pilling was unable to proceed for some time)—I have seen that son lying on a sick bed and dying pillow, and having nothing to eat but potatoes and salt. Now, gentlemen of the jury, just put yourselves in this situation, and ask yourselves whether seeing a sick son that had worked twelve hours a day for six years in a factory—a good and industrious lad—I ask you, gentlemen, how you would feel if you saw your son lying on a sick bed and dying pillow, with neither medical aid nor any of the common necessaries of life? Yea, I recollect some one going to a gentleman's house in Ashton to ask for a bottle of wine for him, and it was said, "Oh, he is a Chartist, he must have none." Oh, such usage from the rich will never convice the Chartists that they are wrong. Gentlemen, my son died before the commencement of the strike, and such was the feeling of the people of Ashton towards my family that they collected 4l. towards his burial. Gentlemen of the jury, it was under these circumstances that I happened to call at Stockport, excited I will admit by the loss of my son, together with a reduction of twenty-five per cent; for I will acknowledge and confess before you, gentlemen of the jury, that before I would have lived to submit to another reduction of twenty-five per cent, I would have terminated my own existence. That was my intention. Let us now come to the facts of the case. ...'

[Here follows an account of the origins of the Plug Plot disturbances of
August 1842.]
(Trial of Feargus O'Connor and Others, 1843. J.E.P. Wallis, ed., *Report
of State Trials*, N.S., Vol. IV, 1839–43 (London, 1892).

(e) The Soldier:
(Samuel Holberry died in York gaol on 21 June 1842, while serving a
four-years' sentence for conspiracy resulting from an abortive Chartist
rising at Sheffield in January 1840. Arms and combustibles had been
found at his house. Holberry's bucolic background was an unlikely seed-
plot of Chartism, and the view expressed in the extract that he developed
his political opinions in reaction against the soul-destroying routine of
the British army in the years between Waterloo and the outbreak of the
Crimean War seems credible.)

'BIOGRAPHICAL SKETCH OF THE LATE SAMUEL HOLBERRY

(Communicated by a friend at Sheffield)
... Samuel Holberry was born November 18th, 1814, at Gamston, a
small village in Nottinghamshire, and situate three miles to the south of
East Retford. His parents, John and Martha Holberry, are natives of the
same county, as have been the progenitors for periods extending as far
back as their respective "lineages" can be traced. John (the father of
Samuel) has pursued throughout life the occupation of a farm-labourer,
and has lived for forty-eight years in a cottage under the Duke of
Newcastle. Samuel was the youngest of a family of nine children. At the
time we write (1843) four sisters and two brothers are residing in the
neighbourhood of Gamston; one sister died many years ago at the age of
eighteen, and one brother, a soldier, is supposed to be in America, but
has not been heard of for some years. Samuel acquired the first
rudiments of education at the church school of his native village, and
subsequently attended a day school under the superintendence of a Mr.
Blincorn. ... We believe ... that when a comparative child he worked for
a short time at a cotton factory at Gamston, and that his boyhood and
youth were passed as a farmer's servant. His last situation in this latter
capacity, was with Mr. Solomon Waterhouse, of Clayworth, about five
miles north of Retford. But the monotony of a farm labourer's existence
had no attractions for the subject of this sketch; of an ardent

temperament, he was anxious to "see the world", and push his fortune amid scenes more distant and exciting than those of his native home. In fact, a *soldier*'s life was the one which charmed young Holberry; nor can this be wondered at, seeing that he had an elder brother in the army, and that three of his maternal, and two or three of his paternal uncles had also worn the scarlet uniform. Accordingly, when little more than seventeen years of age, Samuel enlisted in the 33rd regiment of foot; his discharge states that he was enlisted at Doncaster, on the 24th of March, 1832, at the age of eighteen years; the reason of this is, that he had previously been refused admission into the army on account of his youth, and now stated himself to be older by a year than he really was to overcome that objection. From Doncaster he was immediately marched to Gosport. ... It is known, however, that he was never out of the United Kingdom: he was in Ireland a short time, and was also stationed at Woolwich, and, for a longer period, at Northampton. During his military sojourn in the latter town, he attended an evening school, and availed himself generally of the too few opportunities allowed by his then position, to acquire really useful knowledge. As his mind improved, he began to see through the false glare of military "glory" which had so much enchanted him when a boy; and this, aided by the slavish discipline to which he was as a matter of course subjected, speedily inspired him with a disgust for the "life of a soldier". He accordingly now acceded to the before frequently expressed solicitations of his parents, to quit the army. His discharge was purchased, and he pronounced his farewell to the "ranks of glory" after a service of three years and twenty-five days. His discharge bears honourable testimony to his character; and though the praise of military officers is not of any great importance in Chartist eyes, yet it must be admitted that even such testimony is evidence in support of the morality and probity of the subject of this memoir. ...

After rusticating in his native village—and enjoying the hearty congratulations of his affectionate parents and other relatives for a few weeks—he proceeded to Sheffield, and obtained employment at Mr. How's cooperage, where he remained about twelve months. He was then engaged by Messrs. Baines and Co., distillers, with whom he remained about eighteen months. Some differences in the firm itself having induced them to discharge Holberry and some other of their workmen, he visited London, where he procured employment at a distillery in Upper Thames Street. After sojourning in the great metropolis for about ten months, Holberry returned to Sheffield at the request of his former employers, in whose service he was retained until within three months of his arrest, when certain arrangements between Mr. Baines and his partner resulted in again depriving Holberry of his means of subsistence; over and over again has Mr. Baines expressed regret that he ever parted with so valuable a servant. We may add that poor Holberry filled a situation of great trust and confidence.

As some proof of his frugality and sterling honour, it may be stated that in less than three years after his discharge from the army, he paid back in full the sum of twenty pounds to his parents, advanced by them to purchase his discharge. What better evidence than this simple fact can be required to prove the existence of an independent spirit and virtuous heart, in one filling but an humble situation in society, and as a matter of course, but indifferently remunerated for his labour?

Some few months after leaving the army, and settling in Sheffield, Holberry made the acquaintance of his future wife, Mary Cooper, to whom he was united on the 22nd of October, 1838. ...

In all probability Holberry first acquired a taste for politics during the period that he was in the army, as Mrs. Holberry states that he had adopted the principles of Radicalism before she became acquainted with him. Towards the end of 1838, he became a member of the "Sheffield Working Men's Association", at that time assembling in George-Street, but shortly afterwards removed to Figtree Lane; and in which body Holberry speedily became remarkable for his indomitable zeal ...'
(*The English Chartist Circular*, Vol. 2, No. 118)

Section 2. Chartist Attitudes to Other Social Classes
(a) Two Appeals to the Capitalists to Unite with the Working Classes Against the Aristocracy:
(The *Chartist* was first published on 2 February 1839 as a rival to the recently launched organ of the London Working Men's Association, the *Charter*. Its viewpoint was that of the moderate not the doctrinaire wing of moral-force Chartism,[1] and in its acceptance of popular sovereignty and the legitimacy of pressurizing parliament, as well as in its professions of concern for 'the wants and privations' of working men, it was not untypical of the Chartist movement as a whole. The following editorial comment stemmed from the rejection by the House of Commons, by a majority of 189, of C. P. Villiers' motion that the case against the Corn Laws should be heard at the Bar of the House. The division took place on 19 February 1839.)

[1] Dorothy Thompson, 'La Presse Ouvrière Anglaise 1836–1848'. J. Godechot ed., *La Presse Ouvrière 1819–1850* (Paris, 1966), pp. 17–42.

'... Never, never will the bread tax be taken off so long as the House of Commons continues to be a parlour full of country squires, and that obsolete feudalism, the House of Lords, is suffered to control the will of the nation. For the repeal of the Corn Laws not a working man throughout England or Scotland will move a muscle—for THE PEOPLE'S CHARTER there are at least two millions ready to hazard their lives. Are you, then, galloping on to ruin, Ye Master Manufacturers? Are you goaded down the steep by the tyrant agriculturists? Hoist, then, the banner of the People's Charter! Cease to cry to the landlords for corn. Seize the sickle of Universal Suffrage, that will cut it bravely. Our cause is, in reality, the same; if you mean fairly, our interests ought to be identical. Without your capital our labour is less available; without our labour your capital is useless. We are united by a bond of interest; but these lazy drones, these vermin-breeding squires, *they* are of use to no-one—they are a dead weight upon the kingdom— an incubus upon the industry of the earth. If they were every one of them swept away to-morrow, the nation would know it only by feeling herself lightened of a heavy weight. Why, then, should we by being divided, suffer them to rule us both—to starve us and to ruin you?

Soon—very soon—will you see how vainly and foolishly you look towards St. Stephen's for redress. Very soon will you become convinced that thence nothing is to be hoped for—nothing to be obtained. Raise, then, the cry of "Universal Suffrage and the Ballot!" Let the Manchester Corn Exchange echo to the sound, and let every one of those merchants be as loud in re-echoing this gathering cry as he was in wasting his voice upon the Corn Laws. Soon shall you see the difference. Soon shall you have dense masses of men swarming round you, and ever increasing and ever conjoining, until one vast sea of human heads shall darken the horison all around, and millions stand ready to echo the cry, and follow where you may lead.

The people of England have never refused its due influence to property; they have usually paid it more than it should justly have. Universal Suffrage, with the help of God, they *will* have. With your assistance, Ye Capitalists, they may get it more speedily perhaps, certainly more quietly; but have it they will, whether you are with them or against them.'

(*The Chartist*, 23 February 1839)

(The Rev. William Hill, a Swedenborgian minister from Hull, who was brought up a hand-loom weaver, was editor of the popular *Northern Star* from its foundation until 1843. After his attacks on the N.C.A. Executive had led to his dismissal by O'Connor, he brought out his own journal *The Lifeboat*. In the following article from that paper the under-consumption analysis of distress, which was a familiar feature of labour economics, was used to affirm the identity of interest of middle and working classes against the aristocracy. As in the previous extract, however, the middle classes were being asked to collaborate on working-class terms. There was no offer to support the Anti-Corn Law League.)

'ORIGIN AND DUTIES OF THE MIDDLE CLASSES

The history of the entire feudal system shows that its tendency has always been to reduce all society to two distinct classes—Baronial Lords or Chiefs, and their serfs or followers. This arises naturally and necessarily out of the doctrine that might consitutes right—the doctrine of marauding banditti of all descriptions. Such was, for a long period after the conquest, the state of society in this country. The robber chief, WILLIAM, whose hordes ravaged the whole land under his direction, took possession of all the soil, and calling it his own, parcelled it out among his followers; and these held it absolute of all other controul.[1] The great body of the people were called serfs or villeins; and they were *slaves*, not merely in the proper but in the conventional meaning of that term. They had no right of property even in their own labour—no power to move from place to place without permission; and held even their "goods and chattels" by favour of the "lord".

We do not find before the year 1207, any recognition of a class of free labourers who were at liberty to barter their services to the best bidder.

This step, once obtained, the "rise" in the social scale which it indicated gave a new tone to the whole character of those who had attained it. They were now "free". The shackles of absolute bondage had fallen off. Their limbs were their own; their energies were their own. The spirit which had for ages lain dormant aroused itself; they shook off the lethargy which had benumbed their faculties, and sprang like uncaged eagles from their forced bed of lowliness. They went forth into the wilds of the uncultivated country; they demanded and obtained a sufficiency of land whereon to live and to labour for their sustenance; and thus were enabled to command the necessaries and such of the comforts of life as were then commonly known and enjoyed. This was

---

[1] For the history of this ancient radical 'myth' see Christopher Hill, *Puritanism and Revolution* (London, 1969), Chap. III, 'The Norman Yoke'.

the beginning of the middle class—the half-way men between the tyrants and the slaves—the farmer class of villagers who occupied the land on terms of rent.

But, though the land supplied in return for their labour many of the necessaries of existence, they yet needed others which were not easily obtained without further arrangements and to remedy the inconvenience of many wants, certain individuals possessing some knowledge of the different articles of commerce then in demand, stepped forth from the ranks of mere industrial production, and opened public shops and stores for buying, selling, and distributing the produce of their fellows, depending for their own subsistence on the profits they acquired by their interchanges. Thus was formed and brought into being that "middle class" which has since reared itself into so much importance, and now threatens to overthrow the power of "the ancient aristocracy", and rear upon its ruins a "plutocracy" more hideous and hateful in its modes of oppression than even its feudal predecessor.

From the labouring classes this rival and bastard "aristocracy of money" sprung in the first instance, and on them and their power of consumption do they still depend.

Up to the invention of the steam engine, they were equally dependent on the labourer to produce as to consume their merchandise. But machinery has wrought a great change in this respect. They are now able to dispense with much of the labour which they formerly required, by the substitution of inanimate productive power. But though the machines—which can be had for money—can *make* the several fabrics of manufactured merchandise, they cannot *buy* them, nor wear, nor use them; and hence the dependence of the middle on the labouring classes is clearly just as great as it ever was.

The cursed feudal system, in its very nature, concentrates all the original wealth of the country—its lands and minerals—in a few hands; and though these possess all, they can only consume a comparatively small portion; and hence the great body of the people, who are poor, and who depend on labour for subsistence, are the chief consumers, and in proportion to their power of purchasing must be the profit and prosperity of those who have to sell. ...

Various causes, which we will not now stop to enumerate, have operated through a long series of years to the detriment, and indeed almost to the destruction of the consuming power of the working classes. They have been sinking lower and lower, till a large proportion of them have reached absolute destitution. Their powers of purchase and consumption are consequently narrowed to so great a degree that the immense stocks of manufactured fabrics which the improved machinery of modern times accumulates, can find no purchasers, but lie piled up in the middle-class men's warehouses and only "change hands" by being shifted out of the ware-room of the manufacturer to that of some "slaughter-house" merchant who buys them at less than the cost of production—sometimes at less than half that cost—to "lay up" till the demand may come, or to sell *cheap*; by which he causes the next lot made to be in like manner unsaleable. Hence the profits of manufacturers have become so reduced that it is only under fortunate circumstances and with large concerns that a living can be had at all. Hence our manufacturers and merchants have lately and for years been following each other into the gulf of bankruptcy with a rapidity of succession truly frightful. ...

In such a state of things as this it seems almost incredible that any class of men thus situated should not see the point where their interest and their duty meet, in the protection and elevation of the labouring classes; in the enabling of them to make a market for the increased stock of produce which is continually being made, and thus to keep up the healthful circulation of the nation's wealth, which, like the blood of the body, social and politic, if it stagnate, must produce disease and ultimately death. If the middle classes purpose to escape destruction, they must lay aside their narrowness of party and caste view of things, and take in an enlarged field of observation; they must consider the best means of giving to the mass of the whole people a consuming power equal to the existing means of supply; and if the means of so doing should even involve the recasting of society in a new mould—if they should make necessary the subversion of old usages and institutions, worn out by time and become unsuitable to the circumstances of society, they must at once, and like men of sense and discrimination, apply the knife to the gangrene, and cut away the decayed flesh, that the free action of the blood be not impeded. But instead of this, we see them stickling for their individual pre-eminence, and afraid of losing their class distinction; and seeking, therefore, the restoring of their lost prosperity by the opening out of new connections and extended foreign relationships, by which they vainly hope to find a market for their produce equal to the national necessities. Here is the grand secret of the mistakes into which for want of more extensive views, a large portion of the middle classes have been led by the grovelling and interested exertions of a very small portion of those whose utter heartlessness and

selfishness sees an opportunity of converting general distress into the means of present and transitory individual aggrandisement. This is the whole secret of the anti corn-law Movement.'
(*The Lifeboat: A Weekly Political Pamphlet*, edited by *William Hill*, No. 6, Vol. I, 6 January 1844.)

(b) The Case Against the Middle Classes:
(From the outset, however, the view that the real enemies of the people were the capitalists was heavily represented in Chartism. It was especially strong in the North of England, where the economic rift between masters and men was most pronounced. During 1839 Chartist dislike of the middle classes broadened and deepened. This was due partly to the rivalry of the Anti-Corn Law League, founded in March, but also to the activity of the reformed corporations, and of middle-class volunteers and special constables, against Chartist agitators. Class hatred now extended beyond outstandingly unpopular economic groups, like the 'cotton tyrants' previously denounced by Rayner Stephens, to the class as a whole, and even the moral-force Chartists shared it. In an article, to which the middle-class *Bolton Free Press* took exception, the *Charter* added to its criticism of the aristocracy for creating the Corn Law, an indictment of the middle classes for establishing the New Poor Law. It was to the latter that the *Free Press* objected, and the following was the *Charter*'s reply. The break with old-style Radical social criticism, cast in political and anti-aristocratic terms, was not complete. The charge against the middlemen was one of guilt by association with an aristocratic party, the Whigs, and the middle classes were denounced for their political role in influencing parliament rather than for their economic function as employers of labour. Dr. Iowerth Prothero has noted the tendency in early Chartism to see political relationships as primary.[1])

'MIDDLE-CLASS LIBERALISM

... The *Bolton Free Press* does us but justice, in intimating that THE CHARTER has not hitherto held up the middle classes to 'public odium', nor 'pandered to the prejudices of the working men', by an unmeasured vituperation of those above them in the scale of society. We could not close our eyes to the sordid selfishness by which the middle class is characterised, but we did hope that the crushing despotism of the aristocracy, of which they as well as the working men are the victims, would, in due time, awaken them to a sense of their own real interests, and induce them to join the working men against the common enemy of

[1] 'Essays in Review—Chartism Early and Late', *Labour History Society Bulletin*, No. 24, Spring 1972, pp. 51–5.

both. Recent events have satisfied us that this hope was fallacious. For however hostile may be the interests of the aristocracy to the interests of the rest of society, the most bitter and virulent enemies of the labouring class are found amongst the middle classes. 'Unmerited obloquy!' Let the inmates of the county gaols—the Lovetts and the Collinses—answer that accusation. By whom have the peaceable meetings of the working men been dispersed by brute force? And at whose instigation have the hundreds of victims who now occupy felons' dungeons in almost all parts of the kingdom been persecuted with a degree of virulence unknown even in the worst days of Tory domination? The answer is, the middle classes—the 'respectable' tradesmen—the 'shopocracy'. It is by these that the government has been incited to make war upon the Chartists; these are the men who, even upon the threshold of the jury-box, have avowed their desire to see 'all the Chartists hung', and in cases where the government were satisfied with trying men for sedition, these persons have expressed an anxiety to find them guilty of treason! There are no doubt many sincere friends of the people among the middle classes; but speaking of them as a class, they cannot be justly spoken of as other than fiercely hostile to the rights of the people. ...

The *Bolton Free Press* objects to our reference to the Poor Law, as 'a specimen of middle class legislation', because, as he avers, 'the middle classes have not power enough in themselves to carry any measure'. But, admitting this to be true, they are not less guilty of the injustice and cruelty involved in that law, than if it had been their own spontaneous and deliberate act, seeing that they give power to the aristocracy, whose measure the Poor Law is said to be, by their resistance to radical reform. ...

But we will not do injustice even to the aristocracy, by exposing them to more hatred than they deserve. Undoubtedly they and their representatives did give, for the most part, their support to the New Poor Law Bill. But let it not be forgotten, that the measure emanated from a government which professed to represent the middle class—from a government, the most eloquent and popular member of which, in a memorable speech in support of the Reform Bill, argued the claims of the bill as one on behalf of the middle classes—'of the thousands and tens of thousands of the middle orders of the state; the most numerous, and by far the most wealthy class in the country; the depositaries of sober, rational, intelligent, and honest English feeling', a section of the people, to whom it was 'necessary for the government to apply for support, not for the purpose of saving this or that administration, but because no thinking man could ever dream of the possibility of carrying on any government in spite of those middle classes'. Such was the object and such the necessity of the Reform Bill, according to Lord Brougham; and however far it has fallen short of its object, it has undoubtedly placed great power into the hands of the middle classes, which, if honestly and generously exercised, would have averted many of the calamities under which the country has suffered and is still fated to suffer. The aristocracy, as we have said, did undoubtedly support the Poor Law— projected and matured by the avowedly middle class government,—but so also did the immediate and delegated representatives of the middle classes. Anyone not cognizant of the fact, would infer from the language of our contemporary, that the middle class representatives in parliament, although 'not powerful enough of themselves to carry any measure', had opposed, as strenuously as they could do, the passing of the New Poor Law. But nothing could be further from the truth. The division upon the second reading of the bill gave a minority of—how many do our readers suppose?—a minority of TWENTY-TWO! And in this minority there were no more than thirteen English members, of whom three were returned by places in which the landed interest predominated—leaving ten to represent the middle class, whose generous sympathies are paraded by the *Bolton Free Press*! The division on the third reading, however, may furnish a more accurate index of the feeling of the representatives of the middle classes towards the measure and those whom it was intended to affect. What, then, was the minority upon that motion? It amounted to fifty-two, of whom eighteen were representatives of the landed aristocracy, reducing the middle class representatives, who opposed its passing to thirty-four; the large majority of them voting upon the other side, and amongst the rest, the representatives of the City of London, Finsbury, the Tower Hamlets, Westminster, Lambeth, Northampton, Greenwich, Huddersfield, Bolton, Halifax, Macclesfield, Sheffield, Lincoln, Coventry, Derby, Glasgow, Blackburn, Rochdale, Preston, Walsall, Kidderminster, Edinburgh, Leeds, Manchester, Paisley, Dundee, Bury, Wolverhampton, and other places, where the members are undoubtedly returned by the middle classes, and may be fairly presumed to represent their feelings.

Let us hear no more, then, about the New Poor Law being a measure that was carried by the aristocracy, and that only because the middle class legislators were not powerful enough to resist it. It may be true enough that they had not sufficient strength to oppose it with success, but, like 'the reforming ministry' of Lord Melbourne, they seem desirous of sharing the odium of all anti-popular measures with the Tories; and they join them, therefore, in carrying such measures through the legislature.

And thus it has been, and continues to be, upon every other question in which popular interests are bound up. Repeal of the Corn Laws—Extension of the Suffrage—Vote by Ballot—Repeal of the Rate-paying clauses in the Reform Bill—inquiry into the alleged grievances and sufferings of the people—reduction of the pension list—and fifty other measures intended to affect beneficially the interests of the masses, have been opposed and rejected, not by the representatives of the aristocracy alone, but by the representatives of the middle classes; and if an excess of hostility has been exhibited on either hand, it has been almost exclusively exhibited by those whom the *Bolton Free Press* charges us with having calumniated, because we spoke of them as being opposed to popular measures.

One very striking illustration of the indifference of the middle classes to such measures as involve popular interests—and we need not remind our contemporary that 'he who permits oppression, shares the crime'—is furnished by the *Bolton Free Press*, in the very same paper in which THE CHARTER is condemned for questioning their sympathy with the working men. The Corn Laws—so ably and perseveringly assailed by our contemporary, have found an eloquent and powerful antagonist in Mr. Paulton, who, upon his return to Bolton, after an extensive tour of 'agitation' against those laws, was to receive the honour of a public dinner. And how many joined in this demonstration of respect, and of a desire to obtain a repeal of the 'starvation laws'? The registered electors of Bolton exceed 1,000; and it might fairly have been presumed, that if the middle classes there really sympathised with the distresses of the people, and regarded the Corn Laws as a minor source of those distresses, at least one third of the electors would have been present at the Paulton dinner. But was it so? By no means. The *Bolton Free Press* says, nearly *a hundred* sat down to table! Alas! the fact is too apparent every where to be any longer concealed, that the working men must 'work out their own political salvation, without the assistance of either "shopocrat" or "aristocrat".'

(*The Charter*, 17 November 1839)

(c) The Class Struggle in Verse:

(In later Chartism a more elaborately intellectualized understanding of the class struggle, based on a reading of historical development, made its appearance. This was especially strong among Chartist-internationalists of the Fraternal Democrat mould, in touch with Engels and with Marx. A poem by Ernest Jones published in 1846, shortly after he joined the Chartist movement, gives recognition to a *bourgeois* revolution preceding the proletarian revolution. The thought was further crystallized by Julian Harney, speaking in London on 21 February 1848 at the commemoration of the Cracow insurrection: 'Now, that the claws of kings are clipped, and aristocrats have had their teeth drawn, the people find in the *bourgeoisie* their most deadly enemy.'[1] His speech, like Jones' verse, assured working men that their own deliverance was at hand and urged them to act independently, but it was more explicitly anti-*bourgeois* than the poem.)

'LABOUR'S HISTORY

Beneath the leaf-screened vault of heaven
Lay a child in careless sleep,
Amid the fair land, God had given
As his own to till and reap.

From afar three Outlaws came;
Each seemed to each of kindred guise,
For each one thought—felt—hoped the same:
Upon the fall of man to rise!

The first one wore a golden crown:
The second raised a mystic sign,
And darkened, with a priestly frown,
The faith that might have been—divine!

The third flashed forth his flaming blade,
And reeked of blood and sulphury strife;
He gloried in his horrid tra-d—
A hireling, taking human life!

They bound the child in slumber's hour,
With chains of force, and fraud, and craft,—
And, round the victim of their power,
*King,—Priest,—*and *Soldier* stood and laughed.

Then centuries raised from time's dark womb
A bloated form, in cunning bold:

[1] *Northern Star*, 26 February 1848.

The gold-king of the mine and loom,
Who tramples all that bows to gold.

On feudal power denouncing hate,
He challenged it the strife to bide,—
For money bought the church and state,
And money deadened martial pride.

Before their battle they arrayed
Each sought the slave and promised fair—
And those, who conquered through his aid,
Tightened his chains and—left him there!

But now the child has grown a man,
Thinking, reasoning, strong and bold,—
And they, who that false game began,
Are withered, feeble, failing, old!

And, lo! those chains of Priests and kings
As grows the frame, expanding under,
Those cankered, miserable things!
Burst like rotten threads asunder.

Rise then, strong self-liberator!
Hurl to earth the weak oppressor!
Scorn the aid of faction's traitor!
Be thyself thy wrong's redressor!

Kings have cheated—Priests have lied—
Break the sword on Slavery's knee,
And become, in manhood's pride,
That, which God intended—FREE!'

(*Chartist Poems by Ernest Jones* (London, 1846). Miscellaneous Volume Re Ernest Jones. Manchester Central Reference Library: Department of Manuscripts.)

(d) The Middle Class Distinguished From the Money Lords:
(For six years from 1851 Ernest Jones led the Chartist remnant along a doctrinaire course of refusing to collaborate with middle-class reformers. This rested largely upon his belief that the economic interests of capital and labour were irreconcilable. He nevertheless recognized that farmers and shopkeepers, though middle-class, had much in common with working men and might unite with them if they accepted the latter's

terms. The article from which the following is extracted begins with an indictment of competitive trading overseas, which has led to the crippling of food production at home and the cutting of workmen's wages, and will soon result in the curtailment of food imports from abroad, because gold, artificial products and the raw materials of industry are needed instead. Jones' case is that the 'middle class', which contributed these evils, is now beginning to suffer from them. He proceeds :)

'THE DECLINE OF THE MIDDLE CLASS,
A LETTER
TO THOSE WHOM IT MAY CONCERN

... Let me define whom it is that I address, for the term middle-class is much misunderstood and misapplied. By middle-class I understand those who are equally removed from the great employer, and the poor employed—it is not the millowner and mineowner, the banker and landlord, the great capitalist of physic, law, or religion,—but it is the farmer, and the retail shopkeeper, who are comprised under the denomination—and these, I say, are becoming the sufferers under the system. First it crushes the working-man, but IT DOES NOT STOP THERE—it seizes the order next above, and to that order I now wish to speak a word of warning.

In all countries the prosperity of the middle class depends on the prosperity of the working classes; for it depends on HOME TRADE, and home trade cannot flourish without high wages, or self-supporting labour, on the part of the toiling population. Shopkeepers, you have to choose between paupers and customers: which are the most profitable to you? Between one large farmer employing four or five beggared serfs— or one hundred independent yeomen, with happy affluent homes on the same amount of land? If you think the latter more profitable, help to break down the landed monopoly, and place the people on the soil! You can do it—you are electors—you have the constitutional power in your hands, if you did but all know how to use it, and had the courage to use it well! Which is best for you—one large manufacturer employing 1,000 half-starved slaves, who are sure, nine-tenths of them, to perish in the workhouse,—or, the manufacturer's purse being reduced to less dimensions, one thousand happy customers showering their copious earnings in your tills? If you prefer the latter, help to break down the monopoly of machinery, and put an end to the competitive labour surplus, partly by drafting that surplus on the land, partly by enabling it to toil for its own benefit, and by thus raising the wages of the hireable portion.

Do you think you would be the losers, if the incomes of royalty, peers, bishops, ministers, ambassadors, landlords, mill-lords, mine-owners, bankers, usurers, and cut-throats were diminished by three-fourths? On the contrary, you would be the gainers, if the wealth thus monopolised were distributed aright. ...

ERNEST JONES

As it is, you are slaves yourselves, while you are enslaving others. Though a fraction of you possess votes, that fraction dare not use them. You are as a class as much disfranchised as we are. It is a fallacy to say the House of Commons is a *middle-class* house. *It is not.* It is a LANDLORD and MONEYLORD HOUSE. The only difference from old times is, that, whereas the former then had it to themselves, they now share it with the latter, and the latter have the largest share of its influence. Having no working-class reserve of customers to fall back upon, the rich have it in their power of exclusive dealing, to ruin you whenever they please. You are therefore obliged to submit to their caprices, to cringe at their carriage doors; you dare not even ask them for the settlement of their accounts. Then arrange yourselves for your political and social slavery; enfranchise the people, without whom you are powerless. Help them or they won't help you. Your interests are diametrically opposed to those of the rich; they sacrifice *home trade* for *foreign trade*, and in home trade the foundation of your prosperity is fixed, while the great manufacturers interest is to cheapen wages, and thus to destroy a home-trade, of which his foreign commerce makes him independent.

Are you afraid of enfranchising the people? Is it not the boast of the great class papers, that the working classes are conservatives? That for two "men of action" there are ten "men of order"? *If that be true, why fear to enfranchise them? If it be NOT, then tremble to withhold the franchise any longer.*

ERNEST JONES.'

(*Notes to the People*, Vol. I, London, 1851, pp. 151–54)

Section 3. Middle- and Upper-Class Views of Chartism and the Charter
(a) Middle-Class Opinion Assessed from Within:
(In Bolton relations between the Chartists and the middle-class radicals

were at first particularly friendly, and the former had chosen Joseph Wood, one of the latter, to represent them in the General Convention. During the winter of 1838–39, Poor-Law and Corn-Law questions, the incorporation of the borough, and the heightened physical-force tone of Lancashire Chartism began to drive a wedge into the alliance. The Reform Association's dinner to Joseph Wood early in February was designed to restore amity. Thomas Thomasson, who responded to the toast, was a Unitarian manufacturer of the town. Though not himself a Chartist, he had seconded a motion in the previous September that the Reform Association approve the principles of the People's Charter. His assessment of the opinions and motives of others of his order may well have been influenced by his own advanced views, but it is not without persuasiveness.)

'... "May the Middle and Working Classes learn that their true interests are identical."

Mr. Thomasson, in rising to respond to this toast, said he happened to be one of those who think that the interests of the middle and working classes are identical, but at the same time he firmly believed that neither of the two classes were, generally speaking, of that opinion. On both sides there existed much jealousy and ill feeling. The middle class seemed to think that the extension of the suffrage to the working class would not be attended with benefit. This belief on the part of the middle class arose from their being subject to the common feelings of human nature. They possessed at present irresponsible power, and they could not be persuaded that the interests of the community were worse managed than if all had a share in the representation. Although belonging to the middle class, his own opinion was that universal suffrage would be for the benefit of all classes of the community (cheers). Possessing as he did several social advantages of a superior kind—a certain amount of wealth and what was commonly reckoned a liberal education—he should feel ashamed of himself were he to say that he was unable to do without exclusive political power in addition to these advantages. In a commercial nation like this wealth would always command protection (hear, hear). Were he inclined to go on the exclusive principle at all, he would be inclined to exclude the wealthy rather than the poor from any share in the representation; because where wealth was worshipped, so much as it is in this country, there could never be any danger of its exclusion from a due share of political power (cheers). With regard to the jealousy which the working classes had of those above them in the social scale, he felt no surprise at it. Believing as he did, that much of the misery which exists among the people is owing to mis-government, and believing also that the middle and higher classes are responsible for the errors of government, it was natural that those who were exposed to suffering should feel angry at those who might thus in some measure be reckoned the cause of those sufferings. He had always borne testimony to the patience of the working classes. They had endured for many years the most extreme privations with hardly a murmur. It was said by those who opposed the extension of the franchise, that the working classes wanted to get power only that they might make a general scramble. For his part, he believed that the wealthy classes would be less in danger; property would be more secure with universal suffrage than it was under the present system. He was quite aware that among the workingmen there were some who held delusive notions about the advantages that would flow from the extension of the franchise. There were some who imagined that if the People's Charter were obtained they would not require to labour very much: but it would be wrong to withhold the suffrage from all because a few held erroneous notions. There were some who imagined that machinery was an evil to society, or, at least, to the workingmen. Now, he was quite prepared to grant that, as things were ordered at present, it had not produced those benefits to the working classes of this country which it might have done. But surely this evil was not essential to the use of machinery. Surely it was not an evil in itself, that, in spinning, the productive power should, by successive inventions, have been increased thirteen hundred times (hear, hear). The evil was that a small class had interfered to prevent the benefit from being properly distributed (cheers). The toast which had been given was, "May the middle and working classes learn that their true interests are identical". Now, if it was for the interest of the two classes to unite, there must also be great care taken not to throw away any advantage, or to quarrel with any ally, either on the one side or on the other. A previous speaker had called Mr. O'Connell a political scoundrel. He was not going to justify the course pursued by Mr. O'Connell, but he might remind them that Ireland was much indebted to the labours of that individual. Then, with regard to Mr. O'Connor, he would bear testimony to the untiring energy which he had given to the cause of universal suffrage; but he (Mr. Thomasson) would not therefore assent to all Mr. O'Connor's views. He differed very widely from him on the Corn Laws, as well as other questions. Mr Oastler again, although a Tory, had called attention to those who work in factories, and, no doubt, had thereby done much good. Still he was opposed to any extension of the suffrage, and, therefore, he was in general opposed to the Radical

Movement. Mr. Stephens was one who had been very active in opposing the Poor-Law Amendment Act. This was a very ticklish subject (hear, hear). But, differing as he did from many of the views held by Mr. Stephens, he could not but admit, that, in all probability, many of the harsher features of the bill had been much softened in their operation by the opposition which Mr. Stephens had been so instrumental in creating (cheers). ...'

(*The Bolton Free Press*, 9 February 1839)

(b) An Aristocratic View:

(The following is extracted from Lord John Russell's speech on the Petition presented by the National Charter Association on 3 May 1842. Allegedly bearing 3,317,752 signatures the Petition attacked the National Debt, the New Poor Law and working conditions, as well as asking for the six points of the Charter. After expressing his sympathy with the people in their sufferings while repudiating the social doctrines embedded in the document, Russell came to the crux of his case against acceptance. His argument was at once utilitarian and conservative.)

'... I am aware, that it is a doctrine frequently urged, and I perceive dwelt upon in this petition, that every male of a certain age has a right, absolute and inalienable, to select a representative to take his place among the Members in the Commons House of Parliament. Now, Sir, I never could understand that indefeasible and inalienable right. It appears to me, that that question, like every other in the practical application of politics, is to be settled by the institutions and the laws of the country of which the person is a native. I see no more right that a person twenty-one years of age has to elect a Member of Parliament, than he has to be a juryman. I conceive that you may just as well say that every adult male has a right to sit upon a jury to decide the most complicated and difficult questions of property, or that every man has a right to exercise the judicial functions, as the people did in some of the republics of antiquity. These things, as it appears to me, are not matters of right; but if it be for the good of the people at large, if it be conducive to the right Government of the state, if it tend to the maintenance of the freedom and welfare of the people, that a certain number, defined and limited by a reference to a fixed standard of property, should have the right of electing Members of Parliament, and if it be disadvantageous to the community at large that the right of suffrage should be universal, then I say, that on such a subject, the consideration of the public good should prevail, that legislation must act upon it as on every other, and that no inalienable right can be quoted against that which the good of the whole demands. The hon. Gentleman who spoke last said, that my right hon. Friend, the Member for Edinburgh (Mr. Macaulay) had given a terrific representation of the people of England—had described them as sanguinary and as anxious to destroy, to commit massacre and to plunder. Now, Sir, my right hon. Friend made no such representation. For my own part, I think it is very likely that at many elections, even if universal suffrage were in operation, you would find that respect for property, respect for old habits, and general regard for the constitution of the country, would produce results not very different from those which are produced when property is one of the qualifications required for the franchise. But although that might be generally the case, I do not think that in the present state of popular education—I will not say whether a standard of education sufficiently high can ever be obtained among the labouring classes—but in the present condition of the people at large, I do not think you could be sure that there might not be, in a state of popular ferment on the occasion of some general election, Members returned to this House whose votes would be favourable to the destruction of our institutions, and would shake the security of property. Sir, this constitution is, I think, too precious, and the arrangements of society are at the same time too intricate, to allow you to put them to such a hazard. I can well believe, that in the United States of America— the only country which I should at all compare with this for the enjoyment of liberty and the full fruits of civilization—I can well believe, that in that country, where there is no monarchy, where every office is elective, where there is no established church, where there are no great masses of property, universal suffrage may be exercised without injury to order, and without danger to the general security of society. But in this country, where there are so many institutions, which, while I believe them to be of the utmost value in holding society together, are at the same time the possessors of great property—I speak of such institutions as the aristocracy and the church—and which might, therefore, be held out as prizes to a people in distress, I do not think it would be safe at one moment to destroy the existing system of representation, and to establish universal suffrage in its place. ...'

(*Hansard Parliamentary Debates*, 3 Ser., Vol. LXIII, 1842, pp. 73–5)

PART VI

Chartism and Contemporary Political Movements and Parties

(The British political scene at the time of the Chartist movement was characterized by relatively clear-cut party divisions within the House of Commons and by the lively exertions of highly organized pressure groups in the country. As D. E. D. Beales has emphasized[1], the informal alliance of Whig-Liberals and Irish M.P.s in 1835 inaugurated a decade in which a virtual two party system existed until Peel's great reversal on Corn Law repeal shattered the party of the right. A closer examination reveals that on the left parliamentary Radicals often acted independently of the Whigs, while the Conservative benches during Peel's second ministry (1841–45) were filled with gangs of caballing rebels. Even so the loose components tended to gravitate towards the two opposite poles—'Liberal' and 'Conservative'—and 'independence' in M.P.s was largely a thing of the past. The external pressure groups were much more detached, but even they had preponderating allegiances—the Ten Hours movement to the Tories, the Anti-Corn Law League and the various middle-class suffrage agitations to the Whigs. Chartism's political objectives gave it natural affinities with the latter alignment, but the extremism of its programme judged by contemporary standards and the radical social undertones of the movement ensured that it emerged in rebellion against its background. How its leaders handled the strategy of dealing with the other political entities of the age—whether by remaining independent, or by consistent commitment to one side, or by sheer opportunism—and how the others responded, forms the subject of the extracts in the ensuing section.)

1. *Early Support for the Charter from Middle Class Radicals*
(In Bolton, as in Birmingham, Chartism grew out of a context of joint middle- and working-class radical activity. The Bolton Reform Association, founded in August 1837, had a committee of electors and non-electors, and was led by prominent cotton manufacturers, such as Henry Ashworth of Turton and Thomas Cullen. William Naisby was a

---

[1] *The Political Parties of Nineteenth-Century Britain* (Historical Association Appreciations in History Series No. 2, London, 1971), p. 12

draper and the Unitarian, C. J. Darbishire, was to be mayor of the newly incorporated borough. Some of these notables preferred piecemeal reform, and a Bolton petition was presented to Parliament for household suffrage, the secret ballot and shorter parliaments. When, however, in September 1838, the movement for the People's Charter began to gather support in the town round a separate Working Men's Association, the middle-class radicals decided to support it, as the best means of retaining the allegiance of the working men. The meeting described below was followed, about a week later, by one at which Thomas Thomasson, the Unitarian manufacturer, seconded a resolution approving of the People's Charter. As the year drew to its close, the allies pulled apart over the question of torchlight meetings, and at the beginning of 1839 the middle-class reformers established an Anti-Corn Law Association.[1]

Bolton was not the only town where, during the Reform Bill struggle, middle-class radicals had raised the hope that they might afterwards assist working men to obtain a more democratic franchise. Those of Manchester struck a bargain during the 'May days', later to concede universal manhood suffrage, if the working-class leaders would support the Reform Bill. The middle classes withdrew from the compact as soon as the crisis was over.[2] These incidents lend substance to the Chartist feeling of betrayal.)

'PUBLIC MEETING IN FAVOUR OF THE PEOPLE'S CHARTER

On Monday evening a public meeting was held at the theatre to consider the propriety of supporting the "People's Charter". By half past seven o'clock, the hour appointed, pit, boxes, and gallery were crowded to excess and many hundreds went away without being able to gain admission.

Mr. John Parsons moved that Mr. William Naisby should take the chair. This motion having been duly seconded, a person in the pit said he thought it would be as well that a working man should be called on to preside; he would therefore propose Mr. John Baron as chairman. It was observed that Mr. Naisby was as much a working man as Mr. Baron, although in a different line. Mr. Naisby was then called to the chair by the unanimous voice of the meeting.

The Chairman said he would most gladly have given place to any working man on the present occasion. However as the meeting had chosen to call on him to preside, he would do his best to fulfil the duties

---

[1] For the above information I am indebted to a Southampton undergraduate dissertation on 'The Early History of Chartism in Bolton 1838–1840' done under my supervision by Sheelagh A. Roberts.

[2] Absalom Watkin, *Extracts from His Journal, 1814–56*, (London, 1920), pp. 159–63.

of the office. Having read the requisition to the boroughreeve and constables, requesting them to call the meeting, he mentioned that it had been refused, and in consequence the requisitionists had called it themselves. ... Most people were now tired of asking the boroughreeve and constables to call public meetings, as it only subjected those who waited upon them for that purpose to insult. ... He was glad to say that in this town the authorities would not be allowed to insult the people much longer. The charter of incorporation which was now granted, would enable the people to choose men who would not dare to insult them (cheers). When the people's charter was obtained, which he trusted would not be long, the House of Commons would no longer insult the people or despise their petitions. The present movement in favour of reform had come from the workingmen, and it was right that it should do so. He considered that the working classes had as much interest in procuring reform as the middle classes had ...

[Three resolutions were moved jointly by middle- and working-class speakers and carried. The first approved of the principles of the People's Charter, the second adopted the National Petition, the third appointed a committee.]

Mr. Joseph Lomax, weaver, moved the fourth resolution. He replied to the objection that the working classes were not intelligent, by referring to the agitation carried on by them in 1819, and succeeding years. The government was at that time so afraid of the increasing intelligence and strength of the workingmen, that they raised up a brick and mortar qualification to prevent the enfranchisement of the working classes. When the Reform Bill was before the country, the people assisted the £10 householders in procuring that measure, on the express condition that when it was obtained the reform electors would assist in extending the suffrage to the non-electors. The men of Bolton had then met in that very theatre for the purpose of passing resolutions in favour of the Reform Bill. The middle class Reformers said at that time that if the people would assist in getting the £10 franchise, those whom it would enfranchise would do all in their power to promote universal suffrage at a future period (cheers). The time had now arrived for the middle classes to assist the non-electors in obtaining their rights, and he would therefore call on them to redeem their pledge (cheers). There were two ways of assisting the people—by signing the National Petition, and by subscribing to defray the necessary expenses connected with public meetings. He concluded by moving—"That this meeting recommends the committee of the Workingman's Association to solicit subscriptions from the public for the purpose of defraying the incidental expenses of petitioning, and walking in procession to Kersal Moor[1] on Monday next" ... [seconded Warden]

C. J. Darbishire, Esq., in allusion to what had fallen from the mover of the last resolution about the promise given to the non-electors of this town, said, he was one of those who made that promise, and he was exceedingly happy to have the present opportunity of redeeming that pledge (cheers). At the meeting referred to, a number of the more wealthy Reformers were very much afraid that the *Belgians* would come down in large numbers and oppose the resolution in favour of the Reform Bill. A promise was therefore made that, if the people would assist in carrying the Reform Bill, those to whom it gave the franchise would return the obligation by assisting to extend the suffrage. He was of opinion that every man who was able to give an honest and intelligent vote ought to possess the franchise; and he felt convinced that among the great body of the working-classes there was a sufficient amount of honesty and intelligence to exercise the suffrage in a proper manner.

The resolution was put from the chair and carried unanimously.'
(*The Bolton Free Press*, 22 September 1838)

2. *The Chartists and the Anti-Corn Law League at War*
(Between Chartism and the Anti-Corn Law League a persistent battle raged, especially in the years 1839–42. This was partly because the two movements competed for attention at the same time and partly because the subsistence theory of wages, propagated by Ricardo, caused the Chartists to believe that reduced corn prices, resulting from repeal of the Corn Laws, would cause wages to fall. They, therefore, interrupted Anti-Corn Law meetings, moving amendments in favour of their own question. The following extracts from the diary of Edward Watkin, organiser of the Mancheser Operative Anti-Corn Law Association, show how Watkin used the hostility to Chartism of the O'Connellite Irish of Manchester to turn the tables on the Chartists. Though action of this kind may have rendered it easier for the Leaguers to hold their meetings, it did nothing to remove working-class hostility towards the League.

Dr. William Willcocks Sleigh was not a Chartist but an itinerant lecturer for the agricultural Protectionists, to which group the barrister Charles Wilkins also belonged.)

'I will now refer to my diary for details of a remarkable event in the history of free discussion in Manchester.

[1] A regional Chartist demonstration, addressed by Stephens and O'Connor, was held on Kersal Moor on 24 September.

Here are extracts:

"May 9, 1841

We—the Operative Anti-Corn Law-ites of Manchester—have managed to unite the repealers of the Union against the Chartists. Last Wednesday evening the latter called a meeting to pass a vote of censure upon O'Connell. We sent all our men, and also the repealers, and entirely upset them. The malcontents left in an unusual hurry." ...

"May 23

On Monday evening last the Chartists held a meeting in Carpenters' Hall for the purpose of continuing McDowall as a member of the Convention* a fortnight longer, and also—but this did not appear in the bills—for that of passing an address to the Chartists of Newry.

Our associates and the Irish and other repealers of the Union and the Corn Laws mustered in full strength, and we had as pretty a row as I ever witnessed. The Chartists were driven out of the hall four times. We regularly thrashed them and passed our own resolutions.

On Tuesday we mustered all up for the meeting in the town hall, where we gained another complete victory.

On Friday a public meeting took place in the town hall, Salford, which we attended, and were *victorious* also.

On Thursday night there was a tea party in the Corn Exchange, which went off admirably. I was there, but had to leave for near an hour to attend a committee meeting of the O.A.C.L.A. We resolved upon a committee to make arrangements for the public meeting to be held in the race week.

On Saturday morning we waited upon the League and got all our requests as to the public meeting granted. We are to have plenty of flags, &c., &c."

"May 30, 1841.

Last Monday evening I went into No. 1 District, where we formed an association.

On Tuesday evening I went into No. 3, where we had a spirited meeting.

On Wednesday evening down into Salford, and then up to Kennedy's, in Cable Street (Manchester).

On Friday evening at the Carpenters' Hall—a meeting of

---

* Watkin's footnote omitted.

Requisitionists—near 2,000 there. I spoke, and we agreed that we should hold a meeting in the open air next Wednesday morning at 11.

During the week I have been uncommonly busy as a member of the meeting and procession committee. The procession we hope to be a great affair.

Our requisition of the working classes to the mayor was signed by 5,690—it was completed on Wednesday afternoon, 27th May, and five of us went over with it. The mayor opened his eyes when he saw it, but, after humming and hawing, he declined to give an answer until Friday. On Friday morning we received his reply—politely declining to call the meeting.

The Chartists threaten to give O'Connell, who is coming to Manchester on Tuesday morning, a 'welcome'. I hope they will not attempt it, as, if they do, blood will be shed. *Nous verrons.* They also talk of opposing us on Wednesday next."

"Saturday, June 5

On Monday evening last I went into Salford, and spoke to the Salford repealers on the necessity of backing our movement on the following Wednesday. I afterwards went to Kennedy's, in Cable Street (Manchester), on the same errand.

On Tuesday morning I went to the Mosley Arms to see O'Connell, and afterwards went to a meeting which he addressed in the fields* behind Carpenters' Hall. In the evening I went to a dinner, in the hall, in honour of the 'Liberator'.

On Wednesday morning I was up before six, and went immediately to Newall's Buildings. I found Howie sending off the flags to the various districts. I went thence to Stevenson Square, where the hustings for the meeting were part erected. A few of the Chartists were there even at that early hour, and cheek by jowl with the hustings was a machine for the accommodation of the Chartist orators. I went from the square to Kennedy's, in Cable Street, and thence to Timothy Mulhearn's. At this man's house I found about a score of 'boys' all ready for 'work'. These men were ostensibly 'flag-bearers', but by their being ornamented with good blackthorn sticks it was clear they understood the real meaning of their office—viz., that of A.-C.L.** police.

I took these men with me to the square, and we rather astonished the

* Watkin's footnote omitted.
** Watkin's footnote omitted.

Chartists, who had increased somewhat in numbers by this time, with our appearance.

I got my horse, and we went back to Kennedy's, where our band assembled. After some preliminary preparations we marched up Oldham Road, down Livesey Street and George's Road*, to the 'Queen Anne', in Long Millgate. Here we took in tow the procession forming there, and went all together to Stevenson Square. We got there at a quarter to ten. The place was nearly filled with people. The Ardwick, Hulme, Salford No. 1, Newton and Failsworth, and Ratcliffe detachments had arrived, and were either in the square or in Lever Street and Hilton Street. We found it would be impossible to form the procession as we had intended, and we resolved to hold our meeting first. I rode about and got as many of our friends as possible to get in front of the hustings. I also got the principal part of the flags either reared against the walls of the church** on one side, or Robertson's mill on the other, or else furled and tied to the pillars of the hustings. By this time Dr. Sleigh and his son, with Charles Wilkins† were come, and all the Chartist leaders were arrived. The police had taken possession of the Chartist hustings, much to the mortification of the 'Convention', all the members of which, we were told, were on the ground.

At half-past ten I went on the hustings. Almost immediately after a body of Chartists from the country, carrying two banners, one of which had inscribed on it, 'No new poor law', and the other, 'Down with the Whigs', made their appearance, and began to advance to the front, pushing our friends to the right and left. This was submitted to pretty quietly, but at last from the violent conduct of the parties, and from the view of the hustings being partly hidden by the flags, an attempt was made to pull them down. This was immediately resisted, and the Chartists showed their preparation for a row by drawing forth short staves, with which they began to lay about them. Our Irish friends, made desperate by seeing this, and particularly by the brutal conduct of a fellow who nearly killed a poor man with a blow from an iron bar, rushed at the flags, tore them down, broke the shafts in pieces, and laid about them to such good effect as to drive the Chartists out of the square,

* Watkin's footnote omitted.
** Watkin's footnote omitted.
† Dr. Sleigh was a noted Irish barrister and Orangeman of the period. Charles Wilkins was the still more noted actor-barrister, Whig-Tory agent and eventual Serjeant-at-Law. [Watkin's footnote]

leaving a kind of lane about four yards wide, next the church, and reaching down as far as Lever Street. At this moment a kind of desire manifested itself on the part of the men immediately in front of the hustings to join the affray. Seeing this, I jumped on the hustings rail, and pulling off my hat, said—'Englishmen and Irishmen—many of you know me—you know that I am a repealer of the Union, and also a repealer of the Corn Laws. As your friend, and the unflinching supporter of the rights of the labouring millions, I call upon you to keep the peace. As you wish to see carried out the measures you are here to support, and as you value freedom for your country, remain perfectly quiet, and do not be provoked to leave your places by the conduct of men who, I believe, are hired to come here and disturb the meeting. Will you keep the peace? There.' 'Yes; yes', resounded from all parts. 'Well, then', I continued, 'all of you who are determined to do so, hold up your hands.' At least three thousand hands were immediately held up. I then called for three cheers, which were given, and I then retired. On leaving the front of the hustings, I was thanked by John Brooks, Sir Thos. Potter, and others, for having, to use their words, 'preserved the meeting'. At precisely eleven, I rose and proposed Cobden as chairman. McGowan seconded him, and he was carried by ten to one. The Chartists, who had returned in part, voted against us, and made a slight noise, which was drowned in the cheers of the rest of the meeting.

Cobden briefly opened the proceedings, and then called upon Warren to move the first resolution. Warren not being on the hustings, I was compelled to step forward and do it myself. As the spooney had the copy of the protest we intended to submit in his pocket, and as I had no copy, I was obliged to move a resolution which we never intended to put— 'That in the opinion of this meeting, the Corn Laws are unchristian, impolitic, and unjust'. J. Daly seconded it. In moving it, I took care to pitch into Wilkins, about his political harlequinism, thus in some measure preparing him for a warm reception from the meeting. When the motion had been duly moved and seconded, Dr. Sleigh, Bairstow, Connor, and others, wanted to speak. After some little interruption, Dr. Sleigh was allowed to speak. He was heard with great patience so long as he stuck to professions of regard for the working classes, but as soon as he told them the Corn Laws benefited them, his voice was drowned in uproar, and he was not allowed to go on. At last he sat down, and the motion was put and carried, with twenty or thirty dissentients, out of a meeting of perhaps thirty thousand. Warren, who had just arrived, moved the protest. Finnigan seconded it, and it passed, with five dissentients. McGowan* and Ridings then moved and seconded the adjournment of the meeting until the effect of the protest on the votes of the Houses was seen. This was carried unanimously. The Rev. Daniel Hearne then moved Cobden out of the chair, and a vote of thanks was given to C., who ably responded. We then formed in procession, and marched to the New Cross, down Oldham Street, Market Street, over Victoria Bridge, Chapel Street, over New Bailey Bridge, up Bridge Street, King Street, Mosley Street, down Oxford Road, Rusholme Road, round Ardwick Green, down London Road, Piccadilly, Market Street, into St. Ann's Square—where we paused, and after sundry cheers for total repeal, the Queen, &c., &c., we separated. Thus ended one of the finest days' work Manchester ever saw."

This is the true story of how physical force was knocked on the head in the interests of a free platform and the peace of the country.

One incident I cannot forget. When my part was performed, I left the platform to see that all was prepared in the event of another attack of the enemy. The wounded of the attacking party were being taken to the infirmary close by. One big, shock-headed, dirty fellow—I really believe it was the fellow who used the iron bar when the meeting was attacked by the Chartists—was being carried away. His head was certainly well broken, and he kept muttering, "Oh!—these 'moral force Whigs!'— these 'moral force Whigs'."

The epithet "moral force Whig" went out of fashion. We were young and zealous then.'

(From E. W. Watkin, *Alderman Cobden of Manchester* (London etc., 1891), pp. 68–9, 71–8)

3. *The Electoral Alliances of Chartists and Tories in 1841 : Some Undertones*

(The Nottingham by-election of April 1841, when Thomas Cooper and other Chartists assisted the Conservative John Walter in his successful campaign, furnished a precedent for the O'Connor-backed strategy sponsored by the greater part of the movement at the general election in July—that of supporting Tory candidates against Whigs at the polls. R. G. Gammage's *History of the Chartist Movement 1837–1854* ascribed the adoption of the policy to the strength of 'the feeling against the Whigs'[1], but the following report of an illiterate informer (Wright) to the

* When Dr. Sleigh, in the height of tumult, exclaimed, 'Irishmen, hear me, I am an Irishman!" McGowan retorted, "So was Castle-r-a-a-y!" with prodigious effect. [Watkin's footnote]
[1] *op. cit.*, p. 193.

Superintendent of Police at Derby suggests that the motive was opportunistic—to demonstrate Chartist electoral strength. The report concerns a meeting of Chartists at the Northern Star public house in June 1841. It would be wrong to infer from the alignment that Chartism preferred Toryism to Whiggery. In advocating it, even O'Connor urged that the end product might be to make the Whigs more amenable in future to Chartist pressure[1], and there were others, like O'Brien, who felt strongly that the Chartists should hold aloof from both parties.)

'Dear Sir,

According to your Request I went to Turner's at the Northern Star and there was only three in the Kitchen. In about ten minnits they went. I looked at the newspaper a minnit or two and in comes Turner. Mr. Wright, how do you do, you are all alone. Yes sir, but you have company up stares I here. Yes they are the Chartists, will you walke up. Yes I have no objection. I went up and there was a Room full. I got into Conversation with a strainger or two and staid until their buisness was nerely settled. There was Mr. Biarstow[2], Mr. Skevington[3], Mr. Roe and several others of the heads of the Chartists at the head of the Table. The Reason of Mr. Biarstow not speaking, he had been at Loughborough and arived two late in Derby to speak but will speak to night Monday. One part of them is for going on the Tory side,and the other on the wigg side, which thay could not Decide then and it was defered until tomorow Monday. Mr. Biarstow entered into his Electioneering buisness at Nottingham with Walters, and said thay only did it to show that thay could either send Tory or wigg but Mr. Walter would not come in again, and thay found with the Chartists and Torys joining thay had a majority of 4 over the wiggs. A great many was for acting on that principal here, which a vote of censure was passed on a few that had and would go on the wigg side. A Councill was chosen and today Monday it was to be decided by vote wether thay should go on the Tory or wigg side here. I find that where thay can put up a Chartist thay will then go with the wiggs; if not a Chartist then join the Torys. This is the plan thay mean to adopt, but I will indeavour to get more information tonight for you and all through the buisness you may Depend on me'

(Ms. Volume, 'The Chartist Movement in Derby, 1841: Original Correspondence.' Derby Public Library)

[1] Alfred Plummer, *Bronterre*, p. 159.
[2] Jonathan Bairstow, a leading Chartist lecturer, especially active in the East Midlands.
[3] John Skevington, the leader of the Loughborough Chartists.

4. *The Birth of the Complete Suffrage Movement*

(The Complete Suffrage movement was one of several initiatives taken by middle-class reformers in the early 1840s to conciliate the Chartists, who had opposed bitterly the Anti-Corn Law League. Though motives of expediency, notably the desire to strengthen the League's position, were present in varying degrees in all of these, Complete Suffrage was the most altruistic. Launched in November 1841 at a separate meeting following an Anti-Corn Law convention in Manchester, by Joseph Sturge the Quaker, it appealed to a minority of democrats among the middle classes, chiefly, as the extract shows, to the socially concerned radical Dissenters and Quakers, who also wished to abate the political privileges of the Established Church. Henry Solly was a Unitarian minister from Yeovil. The early promise of agreement with the Chartists shown at the first Birmingham conference in April 1842 was belied later in the year. During the summer the O'Connorite Chartists followed the example of the New Movers, and made overtures of friendship towards Complete Suffrage, but the experiences of the strikes in the manufacturing districts in August reawakened the mutual animosity of O'Connor's followers and the Anti-Corn Law League, with unfortunate consequences for the Complete Suffrage movement. A second joint conference of the Chartists and the Complete Suffragists had been arranged for December to agree on a document in which the previously concerted demands might be embodied. O'Connor now attempted to wreck this by swamping it with his own supporters. The middle-class leaders responded by preparing a document of their own, the Bill of Rights, which they proposed to substitute for the People's Charter. The outcome of this manoeuvre was to sever the Complete Suffragists at the Birmingham conference from both the O'Connorites and the New Move Chartists. The extract describes the earlier conference, in April.)

'BIRMINGHAM COMPLETE SUFFRAGE CONFERENCE

Early in the year 1842, Mr. Bainbridge showed me a copy of a new weekly newspaper, called *The Nonconformist*, edited by a Mr. Edward Miall, which was primarily established for the advocacy of the independence of the Christian Church of all State endowments and State control, but which was also warmly sympathising with the sufferings of the working classes, and with their endeavours to obtain a fair representation in Parliament. It was giving prominence to the proposals of Joseph Sturge and Sharman Crawford, M.P., for the formation of a "Complete Suffrage" League, the objects of which closely resembled those of the National Chartist [sic] Association. The three gentlemen now named, and their supporters, felt deeply both the serious condition of the Industrial classes, and the immense importance of showing them that they had earnest and devoted friends among the middle class, who would work heartily and faithfully with them, shoulder to shoulder, for conferring on them the rights and privileges of citizenship. It was with no ordinary satisfaction that Bainbridge and myself, with the best of his mates and colleagues, hailed this new movement. I had been working hard for some months at the pamphlet mentioned above; and which, in my attempt to vindicate the fitness and duty of conferring those rights as set forth in the People's Charter, had swelled to the size of a small volume. It was nearly ready for publication, and not long after was printed and published under the title of "What Says Christianity to the Present Distress?" Hence I was thoroughly prepared to enter into this movement; and, when Joseph Sturge and his friends, a little later, resolved on holding a conference at Birmingham, to which all the Chartist Associations were to be invited to send delegates, I joined with the Yeovil Chartists in labouring to promote it, and sent Mr. Sturge and his friends a copy of my little printed appeal. Bainbridge and his colleagues wanted me to attend the conference as their representative, an invitation which I earnestly desired to accept. But then once again, the pecuniary difficulty came in the way. My printer and publisher in London had not treated me very well—sending me proofs in pages, instead of in slips, and running up the expenses in a way that began to alarm my Chancellor of the Exchequer, who had courageously and sympathetically encouraged me to print the pamphlet, but who had not counted on having to pay about £25 in consequence. But at this juncture, also, the brave friends of the working classes at Bridport again came forward. Mr. Stephens, to whom I had sent a copy of "What says Christianity," etc., wrote to me saying that if I would represent the Bridport friends of Joseph Sturge and Edward Miall, as well as the Yeovil Chartists, they would pay my travelling expenses; and early in April, 1842, I set out joyfully for Birmingham, where I was most cordially welcomed. William Lovett, John Collins, and their adherents, came in considerable force,* though in some "fear and trembling", lest they should be entrapped into any compromises or concessions that might ruin their characters with those who had delegated them, even if the Chartist movement itself were not otherwise injured. But fortunately Feargus O'Connor, and therefore his party, stood aloof, not choosing to accept any offers, or a share in the leadership of any movement, which would commit them to an alliance with middle-class and moderate-

---

* Lovett and Collins, after the Birmingham 'Bull-Ring riots,' had been unjustly imprisoned in Warwick goal (sic), on trumped-up charges, where they wrote a capital pamphlet on 'Chartists and Chartism, Education, Moral Force, etc.'

minded men like Sturge and his friends. Two or three, however, able and earnest men, who had been ranked among the O'Connor party, especially Bronterre O'Brien, a remarkable and generous-hearted man, did come, and, after the first day of the conference, gave cordial and effective help. The only minister of religion, beside myself, who attended it, was the Rev. Thos. Spencer, M.A., Perpetual Curate of Hinton-Charterhouse, near Bath—an exceptionally fine specimen of a clergyman of the Established Church—a large-hearted, benevolent, and far-seeing man, whose son, Mr. Herbert Spencer, may be proud of his father, as the father, somewhere or other, must be of his son. J. Humphrey Parry (an eloquent and sympathetic friendly barrister), with Henry Vincent, Lowery, Philp, as well as many other thorough-going leading moral-force Chartists, came to the conference, and loyally supported Lovett and Collins at its meetings.

But while Messrs. Sturge, Miall, Sharman Crawford, Rev. Thomas Spencer, H. Parry, Albright, and other middle-class supporters of "Complete Suffrage," met the Chartists and conferred with them just as frankly and honestly as Lovett and his friends met themselves, a painful feeling was at first excited among the Chartists when they found that a well-to-do, energetic young Quaker "cotton-lord," had come from Rochdale to take part in the Conference as a friend of Mr. Sturge. For they were full of suspicions (for which there had often been only too much reason), and they thought this particular specimen of the capitalist class showed dangerous symptoms of an overbearing disposition, and a desire to dominate the delegates. They little thought that in less than twenty years that young man would be looked to by the Democracy of the United Kingdom as their bravest and doughtiest champion, or that he would, therefore, be an object for the obloquy and hatred of a large proportion of the ruling classes. It was John Bright who had thus descended upon us, and it is needless to say that John Bright could hardly avoid even then being recognised in any public meeting as a man of mark, possessing an indomitable will, and of reserved, if not haughty, character. Hence the Chartist delegates were as much surprised as gratified to find that not only Mr. Sturge and his immediate coadjutors, but even this sturdy Rochdale capitalist, were willing to meet them and their demands in a friendly and conciliatory spirit. Yet how much depends in such cases on the character of the leaders. With Sturge at the head on the one side and Lovett on the other, it was not wonderful that mutual confidence was speedily established, difficulties were smoothed away, concessions, where necessary, made (chiefly, I admit, by the

Sturge party), and (for the first three days of the Conference), thoroughly amicable agreements at last arrived at. But there was one great danger still a-head. On the fourth and final day the last of the six points of the People's Charter was to be discussed—Annual Parliaments—and to this, I believe, all of Sturge's friends, including myself, naturally had had a strong objection. Our antipathy to it was known to the Chartist delegates, and they were in a state of great excitement and trouble. For on the one hand they felt the greatest reluctance to resist the desire of the friends who had come forward, as they thought, so manfully and generously to co-operate with them in gaining their political rights and freedom, at the cost of so much social obloquy and mis-representation, and on the other, they knew that if they consented to have even this comparatively unimportant point removed from their Charter, and replaced by "triennial Parliaments," the whole of the O'Connor party, the *Northern Star*, and many even of their own constituents, would at once declare that they had betrayed the Chartist cause, and they would return to their homes discredited men, whose political life and labours were thenceforth ruined. While if they refused compliance, and thereby alienated their new and influential friends, they would not only be nullifying the whole labours and results of the Conference, but would probably be depriving themselves of all help from men who, in every other respect, had shown what invaluable assistance they could render to Lovett and the moral-force, educational party among the Chartist working men. It must have been a terribly anxious time for them, that Thursday night and Friday morning. They represented the matter forcibly to Mr. Sturge and the rest of us ; some of them admitting that the difference between Annual and Triennial Parliaments was far too trifling to compensate for the serious evils which insistence on it would cause, but pleading for one more concession to save their political lives and future usefulness, which they had come to the Conference carrying in their hands.

Their gladness and thankfulness, therefore, was proportionately great, when it was announced at the afternoon sitting on the last day of the Conference that the "Complete Suffrage" friends had agreed to waive their objections to placing Annual Parliaments in the programme for future action (though, of course, not pledging themselves to individual advocacy of that point). I was asked to move the resolution which was drafted to give effect to this decision, and to the surprise and delight of the delegates, even John Bright abstained from opposing it, and it was carried triumphantly and unanimously.'

[Henry Solly, *"These Eighty Years" or The Story of an Unfinished Life* (London, 1893), Vol. I, pp. 175–9]

5. *Chartism and Young England*

(Young England was a literary and political movement at once very different from, and also akin to, Chartism. Most Chartists were too practical to share its romantic evocation of the Middle Ages by moonlight and too democratic to be drawn by the idealizing of the monarchy and 'ancient' aristocracy, which induced one of its leaders, George Smythe, to plead for the revival of 'touching' for the King's evil.[1] Nevertheless, a sense that property had its duties as well as its rights prompted the movement to concern itself with the 'condition of England question' and other popular causes. In 1844–45 Thomas Slingsby Duncombe, the Chartist champion in the House of Commons, was supported by Young England M.P.s. in his efforts both to frustrate an oppressive new Master and Servant Bill, which would have facilitated the imprisonment of strikers, and to unmask the security opening of correspondence at the Post Office. At the end of the former year O'Connor was thinking of an alliance with this Tory *partie carrée* against Peel. The speech, from which the following was taken, was, on his own confession, an unprepared 'fling at all subjects'. It had referred to Duncombe's defeat of the Master and Servant Bill in the previous May, but the suggestion regarding Young England stemmed mainly from O'Connor's plan to create a small pro-Chartist party in the Commons.[2]

(a)   '... Lord Ashley, Lord John Manners, Mr. D'Israeli, Mr. Busfield Ferrand, in fact the Young England party, had resolved to make a dead set at all other parties in the House during the coming session. He looked on Young England as coadjutors, to a certain extent. He thought Young England would be inclined to court public opinion—perhaps attend some of their meetings, or call some of their own. In that case he would recommend that some of their best speakers should be selected to meet them, in a friendly spirit, and instruct them. (Hear, hear). ...'

(From a lecture by Feargus O'Connor on 'Trades Unions and Their Effects on Society' delivered at the Investigation Hall, Marylebone, on 17 December 1844. *The Northern Star*, 21 December 1844)

(Opportunist considerations aside, a commentary in *Reynolds Political Instructor* shows how little respect Chartist opinion had for the principles of Young England.)

[1] Robert Blake, *Disraeli* (London, 1969), pp. 168–9.
[2] See above I, 6c.

(b)   'LORD JOHN MANNERS TRIBUTE OF RESPECT
TO AMERICA
FEUDALISM AND REPUBLICANISM.—
PROTECTIONIST POLICY OF AMERICA AND ENGLAND
CONSIDERED.

LORD JOHN MANNERS, one of the leaders of the "Young England"
party, has just been returned to parliament to represent the old and
reputable borough of Colchester. We are neither pleased nor grieved at
his lordship's success. As the balance of parties stand at present, his
return is a subject of no great importance, and, to speak plainly out, as
the parliament is at present constituted, we are not over anxious about
electioneering struggles; and if there was no more important incident
arising from an election than the return of a member to sit in a House of
Commons, governing a people without representing them, we would
not waste a single drop of ink on an event of so trifling a moment. His
lordship, in his hustings' oration, was pleased to eulogise the acts of the
great American Republic. What an anomaly! the admirer of feudalism
eulogising a Republic. No two theories could be more opposed to each
other than feudalism and republicanism. They are opposites, and stand
related to each other as closely as do two ends of a pole. Feudalism is a
systematised despotism which, in theory and practice, contends for the
superiority of classes and ranks, granting the right of life to the lowest in
the scale, but refusing political and propertied rights to all but the
privileged. In temporal feudalism we behold the serf, the squire, the
knight, the count, the duke, rising gradually up to the great Suzerain
head, which head may be called prince, duke, king, or emperor. Such a
system makes plain two results; first, that if the practice be the exact
reflex of the theory, no political power can be possessed by the great
mass of the labouring population, who are invariably treated and
understood to have no right to be treated otherwise, than as villains or
serfs, mere vegetable substances to be eaten up and used without their
own consent by all those who are their superiors.

His lordship may demur, not to our definition of feudalism, but to our
looking upon him as its representative. We have noted his lordship's
career as a politician, have read his speeches in and out of parliament,
and Lord John Manners has said many good things, many admirable
sayings against the present system. But these good sayings have been in
opposition to the present system only, and not in the propagation or
defence of any advanced theory giving to men extended privileges and
political rights. If forced to choose between organised and acknowledged

feudalism, spiritual and temporal, as unalterable, and commercial liberalism, which is only loosened feudalism, feudalism unbound in its responsibilities but strengthened in its exactions, each part claiming liberty of action to ensure for itself more power, and all combining to trample on the weakest (not as vegetables of the earth, but as the flesh of animals that have been slaughtered to be devoured). We would prefer feudalism, but we adhere to neither, and look beyond both, in hopes that the time may come when all may enjoy more liberty and better order; when the better parts of past and present will be absorbed in a future better than both. Whether Lord John Manners, and the few educated gentlemen and noblemen who act with him, confess it or not, we cannot look on them in any other light than the advocates of feudalism, the advocates of principles unfitted for either the present or the future; and the Young Englanders are only useful in complaining of and acknowledging evils they never can hope to remedy. The speeches of Lord Manners and his political colleagues are often fascinating, refined in language, and scholarly in expression, but never startling or grand; containing no assurance of enlightened civilization, and seldom do more than inform us of evils generally admitted by all. Man in all ages has struggled against feudalism, even as he now struggles; and M. Guizot is obliged to confess that "this is perhaps the only tyranny that man, to his eternal honour, never would yield to. Whenever he perceives that his master is but a man, as soon as the will which weighs upon him is but a human individual will like his own, he grows indignant, and submits to the yoke with wrath. ...'

[The remainder of the article is devoted to distinguishing between the true grounds for admiring the United States, viz. the recognition given to the people in her constitution, and those which attracted Lord John Manners, i.e. the supposed affinity of American Protectionism with its English aristocratic counterpart. The author also points to the differences between the two kinds of protection.]

GRACCHUS'

(*Reynolds Political Instructor*, 9 March 1850, pp. 142–3)

6 Peel and "Repeal": A Chartist View

(Notwithstanding his brief dalliance with nostalgic Tory rebels, it was to the rising architects of Victorian England that O'Connor realistically turned in his quest for allies in the parliamentary arena. From August 1844 he started to praise Cobden. Moreover, when, on 27 January 1846, Sir Robert Peel announced in the Commons his package for repealing the Corn Laws over a three-year period, while compensating the landed interest with public loans for the improvement of agriculture and a modification of the settlement laws to stem the flow of paupers from town to countryside, the *Northern Star* delivered an encomium upon the prime minister. The courting of Peel was a pursuit of men more than of measures. It entailed no acceptance of the general principle of free trade. The following extract from the *Star*'s effusive article shows that the motives were essentially opportunistic: a hope that the Chartist Land Scheme might benefit from the reforms—as by a reduction in the market value of the land to be purchased[1]—and a desire to profit from the political divisions which Peel's unsettlement would provoke.)

'ALL—MIGHTY PEEL

... Having perused this NEW CONSTITUTION over and over again, we find it so complete in all its parts as to render any selection of the gems a task of no small difficulty. There are a few, however, which shine and glitter with such peculiar magnificence and splendour, that we cannot abstain from dignifying them with particular notice; and first and most brilliant stands the passage we have selected as the heading of our comment, and here, to distinguish it, we reprint it, that all may feast upon it, in THE HOPE OF FATTENING UPON IT. Peel says—

"THERE IS A DREAD—A NATURAL DREAD—OF COMPETITION ON THE PART OF AGRICULTURISTS. IT IS IMPOSSIBLE, I THINK, FOR ANY MAN TO DENY THAT AGRICULTURAL SCIENCE IS YET IN ITS INFANCY IN THIS COUNTRY. BUT THERE ARE MEANS OF MEETING THIS COMPETITION WHICH IS SO MUCH DREADED, BY THE APPLICATION OF CAPITAL, SKILL, AND INDUSTRY; AND BY THE ADOPTION OF THOSE MEANS I FEEL PERSUADED THAT BOTH THE AGRICULTURISTS AND THE LABOURING MAN WILL BE ABLE TO MEET THE COMPETITION WHICH WILL BE RAISED UP AGAINST THEM. AND, IN ORDER TO FACILITATE THE EFFECT, WE PROPOSE THAT THE STATE SHALL ENCOURAGE AGRICULTURAL INDUSTRY."

Here, then, is the promised fulfillment of our every hope. Here is the realisation of our prison dream, of our dungeon aspiration. Here is the manly confession that the science of agriculture is but IN ITS INFANCY, while, throughout, we recognise those details which are to nurture it to a giant strength. Talk not to us of any other native industry, or protection for it, or of honourable or emulative competition, beyond

---

[1] D. Read & E. Glasgow, *Feargus O'Connor, Irishman and Chartist* (London, 1961), p. 121.

that which is to be found in the cultivation of the soil, for the benefit of him who tills it; the surplus from a nation of happy individuals increasing the national store to an extent that may defy the free competition of the Frenchman who cultivates the banks of the Seine, the Dutchman, or the Belgian, who cultivates the alluvial soil, or the banks of the Scheld, or the foreign slaves who cultivate those rich and productive valleys that haunt the fears of a pampered aristocracy, but will have no dread for the consumer who is his own producer.

The alteration made in the duty upon all articles of food, and its total annihilation upon animal food, dead or alive, upon vegetables of all descriptions—its comparative nothingness upon the important articles of butter and cheese, and though last not least to us just now, the promised reduction in the article of timber, will give an impetus to native industry in the right direction. It will invite the foreigner to furnish those articles of food which require but little labour in the production, while, to contend against foreign competition, it will compel the landlords and the farmers to apply a larger amount of native industry to the cultivation of their lands. ...

Now, had free trade been proposed in Whig style—had it been granted as a boon to the increasing power of the League, and as a sop to the moneyed interests, unaccompanied by those wise, salutary, and statesmanlike adjustments proposed by Sir ROBERT PEEL, not all the power at the disposal of government could have averted the horrors of a revolution. Upon the one hand, the arrogance of the triumphant League, and the vengeance of the coerced aristocracy, both extensively represented in the Lords and Commons, would have caused a hurricane within, while the haphazard use of the triumph by the capitalists would have roused the nation to a state of mad revenge. The fact is, that the people never again will tolerate the ascendancy of Whiggery in this country, while the working of the new State machinery must, as surely as effect follows cause, lead to the no distant acceptation of Chartist principles; when out predictions will be dignified as prophecies.

Now is the time to force popular concessions in the last moments of a dying aristocracy. Now is the time, when their own privileges are threatened with sudden death, to awaken them to a comtemplation of those they have so long withheld from others. Believe us when we say, that the future interest of landlords and cotton-lords will be more antagonistic than those of landlords and labourers; and now, for the first time in the history of this country, the ear of labour must be prepared to hear long suppressed truisms from the lips of a proud but humbled oligarchy. Honour, then, to the man that has made the deaf to hear, and the dumb to speak! If there are some interests that will consider themselves hardly dealt with, let it be borne in mind that England has long struggled against one old and dangerous abuse, and that all must bear an equal share in any reverse that its destruction involves. The nation is recovering from a long and loathsome pestilence, under which it has recently grown worse and worse; the infection is about to be removed, and it is not too much to expect that every member will derive health, strength, and activity from the change; and should we be called into action to struggle against the ranks of monopoly, we have the authority of our chief, and we have permission to state it, that DUNCOMBE, fully, cordially, and entirely, approving of the ministerial propositions, will lead the democratic party in support of them.

Our convictions square with those of our leader; and therefore we have reason to anticipate undivided popular support in aid of them. "United we stand, divided we fall." Let "Onward and we conquer!" "The measure, the whole measure, and no frittering down to Parliamentary necessities, or party expediency!" be our watchwords. Let PEEL deal with the landlords and free-traders, and subsequently they will unsparingly deal with the church lord, the fund lord, the pauper lord, and the fixed salary lord. ... PEEL has earned for himself a glorious immortality, by his bold and manly bearing; and if little JOHN and the Whiglings should attempt to oust him upon a promise of a more speedy settlement of the question, and with adjustment to be applied, and prudent concessions to be offered, when revolution stares us in the face, let the nation rise as one man; and with the voice of thunder and finger of scorn, motion the ghost back to that tomb which it prepared for Chartism, but in which we have enshrined the remains of Whiggery. Greedy of power, and not cognisant of its own weakness, and of the popular detestation in which it is held, the impudent, brazen-faced jade mayhap may try the dodge; and, therefore, we have deemed it necessary to sound the warning note.

It would be impossible to analyse all the charms of this New-year's gift as they deserve; suffice it then, to say, that it is calculated to make us GREAT AT HOME, and therefore great abroad; to convert ancient enmities into new affections; to turn old suspicion into young confidence; and in the end, to lead us to peace through prosperity, to happiness through plenty, and to contentment through PROTECTION. It is a measure which henceforth will change competition from pernicious strife into honourable emulation, conferring benefits upon all,

and injury to none. The science of agriculture is BUT IN ITS INFANCY ; and Peel's all-mighty measure is pre-eminently calculated to nurture it to a giant strength. It is indeed an

ALL-MIGHTY MEASURE!'

(*The Northern Star*, 31 January 1846)

7 *Collaboration between Chartists and Radicals to Amend the Great Reform Act*

(With the absorbing and socially divisive Corn Law question out of the way, interest in suffrage extension returned, and links were established in 1847 between the Chartists and the Left wing of middle-class radicalism to promote it. The National Alliance, sponsored like Complete Suffrage before it, mainly by the political Nonconformists, promised universal manhood suffrage. Curiously, however, it was the campaign to support Thomas Slingsby Duncombe's more limited motion to abolish the rate-paying clauses of the Reform Act that obtained the strongest Chartist adherence. This was largely because of Duncombe's peculiar influence with the National Charter Association, of which he was a member. As the report shows, the movement was backed by prominent mainstream Chartists—O'Connor, Thomas Clark and Edmund Stallwood— as well as by Duncombe's fellow Ultra-radical M.P.s—De Lacy Evans and Wakley—and by advanced middle-class reformers such as Lawrence Heyworth. The motion was defeated in the Commons on 23 February, but the trend towards union for piecemeal reform was not aborted. After the failure of the Chartist National Petition of 1848 Clark and several other Chartist leaders, including a hesitant O'Connor, moved to collaborate with Cobdenite advocates of cheap government in the National Parliamentary and Financial Reform Association, which sought a one year ratepaying householder vote, together with the secret ballot, triennial parliaments and more equal electoral districts.)

'REPEAL OF THE RATE-PAYING CLAUSES OF THE REFORM ACT

GREAT PUBLIC MEETING IN THE METROPOLIS

On Wednesday evening a crowded meeting was held at the Crown and Anchor Tavern, Strand, for the purpose of petitioning the Legislature to repeal "the obnoxious, vexatious, and oppressive clauses of the Reform and Registration Acts", so unjust in principle, unsound in policy, and hostile to the spirit of that reform which national progression demands, and government undertook to concede. There were several friends of the popular cause present; amongst others, Mr. Thomas Wakley, M.P.; Mr. Thomas Duncombe, M.P.; Gen. Sir De Lacy Evans, M.P.; Mr. Charles Cochrane; Mr. Feargus O'Connor; Mr. Laurence Heyworth; Mr. E. Jones; Captain Houghton, R.N.;—De Conway Esq., and the officers of the National Charter Association.

Mr. THOMAS WAKLEY, M.P., was called to the chair amid long and prolonged applause ... He was informed that the present movement had originated with the non-electors, who generously came to the aid of those empowered to register. This proceeding was highly to their credit. Under the provisions of the Reform Act, there were various persons qualified to register; the franchise certainly was not by any means so extensive as they could wish, or as was necessary to insure a pure and patriotic House of Commons, but the privilege conceded to persons holding houses of a certain value was considerably restricted by rendering twelve months' residence or occupation necessary, and in many cases occupation for one year and eleven months was indispensable. It was furthermore provided that all rates and taxes due on the preceding 6th of April, should be paid before the 20th of July, or that such non-payment should disqualify the temporary defaulter from establishing his claim to the franchise. Now, that provision had the effect of depriving not only some of the richest men in the kingdom of their votes, but it disfranchised numbers of the middle classes, and those engaged in laborious and industrial pursuits. The county voters had no such clog imposed on them ... In conclusion, the chairman recommended that the question of abolishing the restrictions should be generally agitated; ...

Mr. STALLWOOD, the secretary, read several letters received in reply to invitations from the committee to attend the demonstration. Lord John Russell simply declined, without assigning any reason; Sir Benjamin Hall, M.P.; Mr. W. Williams, M.P.; Dr. Bowring, M.P.; Mr. George Thompson, Lord Robert Grosvenor, M.P.; Sir William Molesworth, M.P.; Mr. W. S. O'Brien, M.P.; Captain Pechell, M.P.; Mr. C. Lushington, Mr. Sharman Crawford, etc., excused themselves in consequence of previous engagements, but promising to give their cordial support to the movement, and to exert themselves to carry out the object of the promoters. Colonel Thompson enclosed £5 to assist in defraying the expenses of the meeting. The members for East Surrey, Tower Hamlets, and the Borough of Lambeth, had sent no answer to the invitations forwarded to them.

Mr. THOMAS CLARK moved the first resolution.

"That it is the opinion of this meeting, that the Rate and Tax-paying clauses in the Reform and Registration Acts are vexatious, unnecessary, and oppressive, and opposed to the progressive spirit of the age, and that they should be repealed forthwith."

Mr. Clark, who on rising had been greeted with great applause, said that in his opinion those clauses were not only unjust and oppressive, but the Reform Act itself was so. A different spirit, however, characterized the age in which that Act was passed from that which now happily existed, and, thank God, they had lived to hear Lord John Russell declare that finality was at an end. In his opinion, if these oppressive provisions, which they were assembled to protest against, were repealed, the constituencies would be more than doubled. (Applause.) ...

General DE LACY EVANS said that some of the Gentlemen who had written to them that evening, stated that they had 14 years ago voted against the rate paying clauses of the Reform Act. He also had the honour of voting against these clauses thirteen years ago. (Hear, hear.) It was said that these clauses were to have *bona fide* rate payers electors; but his belief was that the real object of the proposers of the Reform Bill in framing those clauses, was to clog the elective franchise by every possible means. He was not one of those who thought that the Reform Bill had done no good. On the contrary, he believed it had effected much good; but still it might be made more useful for the people. ... He should support his hon. friend's motion. (Cheers.) He congratulated them on the modesty of their present movement, and trusted they would succeed in obtaining their object. (Applause.)

Mr. F. O'CONNOR then rose and was received with great cheering. While, he said, he admitted that part of the gallant general's observations in reference to the modesty of the meeting, he denied the assumption, that because they were modest, they were therefore insensible to the injustice and the iniquity of the Reform Act. (Hear, hear.) No, they would never cease until they had completely reformed the Reform Act itself. In coming forward on the present occasion to get rid of the rate paying clauses of the Reform Act, they were only going to assist the more liberal portion of the representatives of the people from the unjust operation of the clauses in question. He called the party of which Lord George Bentinck and Lord Stanley were the head, the Loyal Royal Landcrab aristocracy. (Laughter.) Now this class would take advantage of the ratepaying clauses to turn out the present government; ...

After a few observations from Mr. Hansome, the resolution was put to the meeting and agreed to.

[A motion was then proposed in favour of a petition for the repeal of the ratepaying clauses of the Reform Act]

Mr. ERNEST JONES, who was received with much applause, said he hoped the burst of popular feeling honourable members on that platform had witnessed, would give them a better idea of popular feeling than they could obtain in the house; if this feeling was elicited by the desire to obtain even so trivial an amendment in the vexatious clauses of that most vexatious act, miscalled "Reform"; he left them to judge how intense the feelings of the people must be for that true reform—their Charter. (Loud cheers.) The speaker then proceeded to show the inconsistency of an act based on the property qualification, which deprived of the vote those living in furnished lodgings, an intelligent, wealthy and numerous class, consisting largely of professional men; an inconsistency further proved by the exemption of county voters from the rate-paying clauses ... These clauses turned the property qualification of the Act into a tax-paying qualification. The speaker then illustrated the unconstitutional power they gave to parish officers, and to the revising barrister, of preventing men of democratic principles from exercising their right to the vote. To mend the Reform Act thoroughly was hopeless. It reminded him of an anecdote of the poet Pope, who was a very small deformed man, and had a habit of saying—"God mend me! God mend me!" A beggar, hearing him one day, replied—"God mend you! He had better make a new one altogether." The beggar's advice applied to the Reform Act. The best way of mending that is to make a new one altogether. (Loud cheers.)

Mr. DUFFY supported the motion. The petition was then unanimously adopted.

Mr. DUNCOMBE, M.P., then came forward, and was received with enthusiastic cheering. He commenced his observations by admitting, in reference to an assertion made by the last speaker, that the last year a Parliament had to live was the best for the people, for they had then a chance of getting what they desired. (Hear, hear.) It was acting on this assumption that he was induced to bring forward his motion for a total repeal of the rate-paying clauses of the Reform Act. (Hear.) And here he might state, that if he were successful in getting rid of these clauses, he would not even then be satisfied until he succeeded in altering materially the Reform Act. (Hear.) ...

Mr. DOYLE, in an effective speech, which was loudly cheered, moved the third resolution:

"That a deputation consisting of Joseph Hume, Esq., M.P., Charles Cochrane, Esq., Ernest Jones, Esq., Messrs. Philip M'Grath, C. E. Wagstaff, J. Savage, J. Shaw, George Rogers, J. Sewell, T. M. Wheeler, and Edmund Stallwood, be appointed to wait on Lord John Russell, to impress on Her Majesty's Government the necessity of an immediate repeal of the Rate and Tax-paying clauses in the Reform and Registration Acts."

Mr. GRASSBY seconded the resolution.

Mr. LAWRENCE HEYWORTH, who was loudly cheered, said he had not come there to make a speech; however, he thought this was a step in the right direction. He thought it would be a great good if every man possessed equal political privileges. ... He agreed with some of the speakers who had preceded him, that it would be well to repeal the Reform Act, and that the franchise should be conferred on all. (Loud cheers.) He was sure it was only necessary to call meetings like this to convince all of the great benefits which would be derived from such a course. (Great applause.)

The motion was carried by acclamation ...'

(*The Northern Star*, 20 February 1847)

8. *Ourselves Alone*

(Not all O'Connor's past prestige could carry the National Charter Association with him in this course of winning the Charter by instalments. His powers were failing, his reputation was tarnished by the discrediting of the Land Scheme, and, in a period when the interests of working men were turning from political agitation to trade unions and co-operative enterprises, only the staunchest Chartists remained for long loyal to the cause. To these compromise did not usually appeal. Early in 1850 Harney captured the Executive of the N.C.A. for Chartist-Socialism, thus renewing the breach with the middle classes, and when, two years later, Ernest Jones took over the leadership of Chartism from him, his policy was one of aloofness from campaigns for partial reform of parliament. Jones reaffirmed the traditional Chartist argument that moderate concessions merely increased the numbers of those opposed to complete democracy and weakened the forces of those fighting for it. 'Six million non-electors could sooner wrest their rights from 800,000 electors', he claimed, 'than four millions could from three'.[1] This was a fallacy. The more diverse a governing class, the more likely it was to dissolve into factions which would endeavour to strengthen themselves

[1] J. Saville, *Ernest Jones: Chartist* (London, 1952), pp. 167–71.

by enfranchizing allies outside the political nation. The attitude became increasingly difficult to sustain, when, from the time of the Crimean War, evidence of administrative incompetence, allegedly due to aristocratic patronage, rekindled the reforming spirit of the middle classes, and advanced groups among the latter again offered substantial enlargement of voting rights. A new middle-class initiative was launched under Roebuck's chairmanship in June 1857. This proposed a rate-paying franchise, but Jones stood out for universal suffrage, and at a conference in St. Martins' Hall, London, on 8 February 1858, a committee was established, which formed the Political Reform League, to work for that principle. Most of the leading parliamentary reformers of the age withheld their support from so extreme a cause. But Joseph Sturge, the wealthy Quaker, became president of the new association, P. A. Taylor, a leader of the Manchester School, seconded a resolution at the Guildhall in favour of universal suffrage, and six lesser middle-class reformers served with Chartists and trade-union leaders on the constituent committee. As the following report shows, however, a minority of London Chartists also held out against the middle-class alliance and formed their own organization for the whole Charter.)

'The Chartist Reorganization

The Reorganization of the Chartist Movement by the parties who are now members of the "National Political Union for the Obtainment of the People's Charter", was commenced on Sunday, February 24th of the present year. Some 30 or 40 persons from various parts of London then assembled at No. 81, High Holborn. It was altogether an introductory and initiatory meeting to take into consideration the advisability and likewise the practicability of a reorganisation for *the whole* Charter, and with a view of testing the sentiments of the meeting, and as a basis upon which a committee might have some common ground of union to act upon, an Address and a Plan of Provisional Action, which had been previously drawn up, was submitted for discussion. As the Address and Plan was debated on two or three successive Sunday evenings, and as it clearly sets forth the reasons which induced the Members of the Committee to act separately and independently, we think it the more advisable course to let the Committee speak for itself, just premising that it obtained nearly 100 signatures of the leading Chartists of the Metropolis.

Brother Chartists,—In the present condition of our movement we need offer no excuse for addressing you by other than the usual channels of communication. At a "conference" recently held in London we have witnessed but the logical results of that blighting and destructive policy whose tendency has been to alienate us from each other, to divide and sever our ranks, and ultimately destroy that cause for which thousands of the earnest and thoughtful among us have worked and suffered.

Under the specious promise of a union with the Middle Classes, we have seen our cause degraded and burlesqued. The principal movers in the recently attempted compromise have placed themselves beyond the pale of our political recognition, and it is now to be seen whether there is not sufficient of the old spirit remaining to enable us to gather up the scattered elements of our strength, and in a dignified manner carry our holy cause to a successful issue.

We believe Chartism is not a thing of the past, that it may be revived again in all its vigour, and that the millions who have sanctioned and supported its cause, may be induced to band themselves together once more in furtherance of its great and important objects. We the undersigned are prepared to take the initiative in the good work of reorganizing the movement for the whole Charter, and hereby declare that we are not bound, nor will we be bound, by the acts of the late conference, but that we will use our utmost exertions to continue with dignity and spirit that movement which has been so disgracefully lowered in public estimation. We are anxious that you, our Brother Chartists, who have earnestly struggled for the cause, and are not disposed to see it abandoned, should take a position similar to our own. If you believe that the political enfranchisement of the people cannot be secured without the full accomplishment of the People's Charter, we entreat you in order consistently to give effect to your views to admit of no compromise, to support those who now offer you the hand of union and fellowship, and work with them for the success of that cause you hold so dear. It has been shown clearly in the past, that the working classes must accomplish their freedom without the aid of any other class in society, and that could adventitious aid be secured by the compromise of any of our principles, the full enfranchisement and social happiness of the people, would be retarded rather than promoted.

If properly organised, the army of Labour is sufficiently strong to fight its own battle, without sending a recruiting sergeant to the ranks of men who could grant us the charter to-morrow were they honest. Such confessions of weakness degrade our cause.

Therefore of unions and compromises let us heed not, but let us gather up our strength for the useful mission that is before us. To succeed in our good work, we must ignore the policy of days gone by, we propose to raise our movement above the trammels of personal scurrility and internal commotion. While we offer no opposition to any Reformers, we will unite with none who go for less than our charter. We will exclude none from our ranks, but we will keep our army intact.

In order to obtain unity of action, we propose that the following principles be kept in view, and as far as possible adhered to by the members.

1. That we form no union with any class or body of men whose object is the obtainment of any Political Reform short of the People's Charter.

2. That while we recognise the right of any member, in his individual capacity, to aid any body of Reformers, the Society will not be compromised by the steps taken by any individual member.

3. That no opposition be offered by the Association to any body of Reformers.

4. That we recognise no Address issued by any Newspaper Editor or any other person, unless the same be recognised by the Executive.

Further, we propose to open the campaign at once, and earnestly ask your support to the following

Programme of Provisional Action

1. That a Committee of known Chartists be immediately formed in London.

2. That from this Committee a Provisional Executive be appointed. The Provisional Executive to consist of seven, whose duty it shall be to carry out the objects of this address and further the interests of the Association.

3. That the Provisional Executive shall hold office until the ramification be so extended throughout the country as to render it expedient to elect a more permanent body.

To those who, with us, have deplored the absence of a healthy Chartist Literature, not one word need be said about the necessity of establishing an organ which shall be the reflex of our movement and the exponent of our principles. Suffice it, that the necessity exists, and must and will, we hope, be supplied, and to this end we would strongly advise that immediate steps be taken to raise the necessary funds, and that in order to obviate the possibility of any individual making the paper his own personal property, the Shareholders be protected by the Limited Liability Bill.

Should the foregoing declaration of principles and objects meet your approval, you are earnestly solicited to communicate with us forthwith, in order that vigorous steps may be taken to revive once more in all its glory and strength, that cause which has for its objects the political and social emancipation of our people.

On Sunday, March 12th, a long debate ensued relative to the name by which the Association should be known, when, after several names had been submitted, it was then determined to retain the old name of the "National Charter Association", most of the persons present having been members of it. At a subsequent meeting, however, the motion was rescinded, and the name changed to that which heads this article, it being considered in every respect a better name, and more distinctive of our particular body, to go the country with.

On the same Sunday evening a Provisional Executive was elected by ballot. The election fell upon:

MESSRS. T. M. WHEELER.

WM. TAYLOR.

WM. SLOCOMBE.

J. B. LENO.

JOHN M'GILCHRIST.

JOHN NASH.

HENRY DORMAN.

At a subsequent meeting of the Committee, Messrs. Wm. Taylor and Dorman having resigned,

MESSRS. RICHARD ISHAM

and

WILLIAM STAINSBY

were elected in their stead.'

(*The National Union: A Political and Social Record, and Organ of 'The National Political Union for the Obtainment of the People's Charter,'* No. 1, May 1858)

PART VII

Chartism and the Labour Movement

1. *Trade Union Involvement in Early Chartist Demonstrations*
(The area rally at Kersal Moor, Manchester, on 24 September 1838, was one of a number of such gatherings held about that time in various parts of the country to advertise the incipient Chartist movement and to elect delegates to the forthcoming General Convention. Processions marched to the ground from surrounding towns to form a crowd which probably numbered 50,000 people, though a contemporary journal estimated 300,000. The Manchester contingent was marshalled by the two main Chartist bodies in the town—the Political Union and the Universal Suffrage Association. Among the processionists figured the trades of Manchester, bearing the official insignia of their unions. These ranged from the rising and relatively well-to-do engineers and iron workers to the declining tailors and shoemakers. The Friendly Society of Cotton Spinners also marched to Kersal Moor.[1] Evidence of a similar corporate involvement of trade societies in an early Chartist demonstration comes from Glasgow, while in several of the larger English towns these bodies helped to collect signatures for Chartist petitions and contributions to the National Rent. It is clear that there was much initial goodwill from the unions towards Chartism, springing from approval in principle of the Six Points and a desire to render the administration of the law more favourable to combinations of workmen. But the impulse was mainly local, at which level regional unions of trades, transcending sectional prejudices, had long been attempted in a number of towns and cities. The growing tendency of craft unions like the Old Mechanics to centralize their funds was adverse to such collaboration and, therefore, to expressions of political feeling.)

'The members of the Manchester Union met before eleven o'clock, in Smithfield, for the purpose of proceeding to the ground, and the following is the form of procession taken by them, and by the people of the surrounding districts, the order of the processions from some of

[1] *The Stockport Advertiser*, 28 September 1838 (abridged from *The Manchester Guardian*).

which we have been but partially enabled to learn, many of them having arrived on the ground without the order in which they were marshalled having been announced.

ORDER OF PROCESSION.

Two Trumpeters on horseback

Marshals—Messrs. Nightingale and Richardson.

Emblem of Unity—A bundle of Rods tied together.

Manchester Concert Band.

Large Silk Banner of the Union,

Shewing on one side a figure of Justice, holding in her hand a balance, supported by the British Lion, the emblems of Wisdom, Unity, Peace, and Strength, surmounted by a British Standard, with the motto,— "Peace, Law, Order." Inscription—"Manchester Political Union." Reverse—"Universal Suffrage, Annual Parliaments, and Vote by Ballot."

Vice-President.   President.   Vice-President.

New Poor Law Banner—Repeal of the New Poor Law.

Treasurer.   Secretary.   Treasurer.

Banner.   Banner.   Banner.

The   Red   Rose   of

England,   Harp of Erin,   Thistle of Scotland.

White and gold.   Green and gold.   White and gold.

Members of the Committee four abreast.

Delegates from the country four abreast.

Union Jack.   Union Jack.

White silk Banner of the Universal Suffrage Association.

Labour the source of all wealth—Liberty & Equality.

Members of the Political Union four abreast.

No. 1. District Marshals.

Messrs. Forresters' Brass Band.

Union Banner.

Britannia seated on a rock, trampling on the chains of despotism, holding in her right hand the trident of Neptune, surmounted by a cap of liberty, and in her left hand the "People's Charter," while the British lion rouses to maintain the Charter; the following motto in a semicircle over her head,—"For a nation to be free, 'tis sufficient that she wills it" Reverse—"England expects every man, THIS DAY will do his duty."

White silk ground, gold letters shaded, cap of liberty, scarlet; motto— "The earth is the right of men." Reverse—"He that will not work, neither shall he eat;" 2nd Thessalonians, ch. 3 v. 10.

Massacre on Petersfield, description of.

White ground, black letters, "Universal Suffrage,"

"Vote by Ballot."

Members of the Union.

White banner.—Inscription—

"If we are too ignorant to make taxes, we are too ignorant to pay them. If we are too ignorant to make laws, we are too ignorant to obey them."

Banner—Full length portrait of Henry Hunt, Esq.

Inscription—"The man who never deserted the people." Reverse—"Equality the first law of nature." "First want of man—chief bond of our Association."

Members of the Association, four abreast.

TAILORS.—Banner Arms of the Trade.—Motto, "Peace, union and justice."—Members four abreast.

MECHANICS.—Manchester Borough Band.—Banner Arms of the Trade, inscription, Steam-engine and Machine-makers' Friendly Society.—Motto, "Every man has a right to one vote in the choice of his representative—it belongs to him in his right of existence, and his person is his title-deed."—Members four abreast.

SMITHS AND FARRIERS.—Banner of the Trade—Members four abreast, wearing new white leather aprons, and bearing emblems of the trade.

SMITHS AND WHEELWRIGHTS,—Banner, "Wheelwrights' and Blacksmiths' Society." Reverse, "Loyal free, industrious society on the order of charity."—Members four abreast.

FUSTIAN SHEARERS.—Marshal, John Franklin. Banner, "Universal Suffrage, Annual Parliaments, Vote by Ballot, No Property Qualification, and Payment of Members for their services." Reverse,—"Friendly Society of Fustian-shearers." Members four abreast.

CARPENTERS AND JOINERS.—Marshals, Messrs. Clay and Armstead. Banner of the trade. Members four abreast.

MEN'S BOOT AND SHOEMAKERS.—Banner, bearing the arms and other insignia of the trade. Motto—"United to maintain our rights inviolate; prosperity attend the justness of our cause." Reverse, "The Friendly Institution of Boot and Shoemakers." Members four abreast.

LADIES' SHOEMAKERS—Banner of the trade, with Members four abreast.'

(*The Northern Star*, 29 September 1838)

2. *The 'No Politics Rule' in Trade Societies*

(The unions of the economically stronger trades—engineers, printers, bookbinders, watchmakers, coachbuilders etc.—usually adopted a cautious attitude towards Chartism. Some ruled out politics from discussion at branch meetings. This was connected with their status as friendly societies. Suspected by governments before 1830 of harbouring revolutionary designs, benefit societies generally, with a few exceptions, developed the practice of avoiding entanglement in party politics, and the tradition was followed by the trade unions, which registered as friendly societies, first to avoid prosecution under the Combination Laws and later to obtain protection for their funds. An unsuccessful bid to remove the ban was made at the congress of trade delegates, which assembled in Manchester at the height of the semi-Chartist 'Plug-Plot' strikes of August 1842.)

'Mr. Stott, delegate from the bookbinders, came forward and moved the following resolution:—

"That this meeting do strongly recommend that all trade societies do from henceforth make political enquiry and discussion lawful and necessary in their various lodge's meetings, and society rooms; and that they embody in their rules a law for the adoption of this great principle."

Mr. Higginbottom seconded the resolution.

Mr. Morrison could not see the necessity of passing a resolution of that description, nor did he think it was at all applicable to the subject for which they had assembled ...

Mr. M'Cartney agreed to the resolution, inasmuch as it would show that they, as delegates of the working classes, were aware of one of the main causes of political ignorance and mental slavery,—which causes were that the discussion of politics had been excluded from all sick and benefit societies. He then said there were men in from no fewer than twenty places at a great distance, who had been delegated for the express purpose of ascertaining the decision of that meeting, so that they, in their localities, might know what steps to take.

Mr. Duffy agreed with the resolution, though he must confess it was from the business of the meeting.

Several other delegates saw the utility of such a resolution being passed, but thought it would be more in place as the last, instead of the first.

The resolution was withdrawn, with an understanding that it would be brought forward at another stage of the proceedings.'
(*The Northern Star*, 20 August, 1842)

3. *The Trade Unions and the 'Sacred Month'*

(The notion of a general strike is older, much older, than the trade-union movement. Drawing inspiration from the secession of the plebs to the Aventine Hill in Roman times, it figured in the European radical tradition as a weapon of the whole people against oppressive minorities controlling governments. French Revolutionary writers, notably Volney, propagated the idea, and it was given its first outstanding English expression by William Benbow, a veteran radical of the Peterloo era, in a pamphlet published in 1832, advocating a month's cessation of labour and the calling of a national congress to reform society.[1] In 1839 the Chartist leaders proposed the general strike or 'sacred month' as an ulterior measure to gain the Charter, but they hesitated to launch it. On 17 July a thin meeting of the Convention resolved to begin it on 12 August. Seven days later the decision was reversed, and a Council was next appointed to discover a line of action which the rank and file of the movement would support. After taking soundings, the Council recommended the holding of a demonstration in *lieu* of the strike. The Convention's retreat from the 'sacred month' policy was mainly due to the belated intervention of the moderate physical-force leaders, Bronterre O'Brien and Feargus O'Connor, who had never placed much faith in it, even though they had previously supported strike action in the hope of intimidating the authorities. The Council's resolution shows, however, the extent to which the cautious attitude of the trade unions was accounted a limiting factor on Chartist physical-force strategy.)

'COUNCIL OF THE GENERAL CONVENTION

At meetings of this Council, held at the Arundel Coffee House, Strand, on Monday and Tuesday the 5th and 6th August, the following resolutions have been unanimously agreed to:—

Moved by Mr. Bronterre O'Brien, seconded by Mr. Feargus O'Connor:—

1. Resolved, That from the evidence which has reached this Council from various parts of the country, we are unanimously of opinion, that the people are not prepared to carry out the "Sacred Month" on the 12th of August. The same evidence, however, convinces us that the great body of the working people, including most of the Trades, may be induced to cease work on the 12th instant, for two or three days, in order to devote the whole of that time to Solemn Processions and Solemn Meetings, for deliberating on the present awful state of the country, and devising the best means of averting the hideous despotism with which the industrious orders are menaced by the murderous

[1] See especially I. Prothero, 'William Benbow and the Concept of the "General Strike",' *Past and Present*, No. 63, 1974, pp. 132–71.

majority of the upper and middle classes, who prey upon their labour. We, at the same time, beg to announce to the country that it is the deliberate opinion of this Council that unless the Trades of Great Britain shall cooperate, as united bodies, with their more distressed brethren, in making a Grand National Moral Demonstration, on the twelfth instant, it will be impossible to save the country from a revolution of blood, which, after enormous sacrifices of life and property, will terminate in the utter subjection of the working people to the monied murderers of society. Under these circumstances we implore all our brother Chartists to abandon the project of a Sacred Month, as being for the present utterly impracticable, and to prepare themselves forthwith to carry into effect the aforesaid constitutional object on the 12th inst. We also implore the United Trades if they would save the country from convulsion, and themselves and families from ruin, to render their distressed brethren all the aid in their power, on or before the 12th inst., towards realising the great and beneficent object of the holiday.

Men of the Trades! the salvation of the empire is in your hands!'

(The second resolution was concerned with the business which should be transacted at the 'Solemn Meetings').

(*The Northern Star*, 10 August 1839)

4. *The Trades and Chartist Organization: Dr. McDouall's Plan*
(Peter Murray McDouall was one of the most extreme physical-force leaders in 1839, when, according to Alexander Somerville, he cast himself for the role of commander-in-chief of the Chartist forces. He was outstandingly quick to grasp the importance of sound organization. Early in July, when keen to begin the 'sacred month' as soon as possible to precipitate a revolution, he wished the Convention to create 'a more perfect co-operation amongst the people', including the trade unions.[1] After the failure of the insurrections at Newport and in Yorkshire during the winter of 1839–40 physical force was soft-pedalled in the movement. Attention was transferred to plans of organization for peaceful and propagandist purposes. Of these the most fruitful was that of the National Charter Association adopted at a Conference in Manchester on 20 July 1840. The new association had a central executive and branches in the various towns. At first, however, it was slow to take root, partly because it was believed to be illegal under the terms of the 1799 Act against the Corresponding Societies. By February 1841 only 80 localities had registered. McDouall's scheme, announced two months later, was

[1] A. Plummer, *Bronterre*, pp. 98, 108 & 130.

put forward as a method of extending Chartist organization at ground-floor level. Formation upon the trades was seen as an alternative to winning middle-class support, as proposed by the movements which O'Connor had just condemned—Church Chartism, Teetotal Chartism, Knowledge Chartism and Household Suffrage Chartism. An article in the following issue of the *Journal* reveals, however, that McDouall still entertained the design of a general strike, and intended the new organization to provide it with direction when the opportunity arose. 'Accident, tomorrow,' he wrote, 'may create a most furious outbreak. If it did, where is the organization to give rise to courage?.. let me tell you that if you were good calculators, you would learn not only when to play a good card, but manage to have that in your hand at the proper time.' This was followed by an allusion to the secession of the plebs, the myth associated with the 'sacred month'.[1]

'WHAT HAVE WE DONE, AND WHAT HAVE WE TO DO?
To the Working men of every kind within Great Britain.

I HAVE in the two previous numbers of the Journal, contented myself with simply recommending union, energy, perseverance, and continued agitation at the present crisis. I have now to lay before you a plan by which to organize your numbers, and centralize your intelligence.

Recollect that no body of workmen, whether included under the names of trades, agricultural, mining, or factory workmen can be socially prosperous or independent unless they are also politically free.

In placing the following plan before you for your consideration and adoption, I have no intention of interfering with the working of that plan which has been recommended by the Manchester delegates. It appears to me that the Manchester plan is a good one; and, notwithstanding the cry of "illegality," I, for one, will never practise or recommend *over caution*, because I fear the law, the law-giver, or the law's instruments of tyranny or torture. ... We must pursue the sure plan *as long as we are weak*. The moment we are powerful enough, then the petty trammels of the law will be like a thistle under the foot of an elephant.

When I was in Dundee, I found that the trades there had declared for the Charter, and had organized themselves into chartist associations. I wrote out a plan for them, which the council printed, and which is now in the hands of Mr. Heywood of Manchester. The price is only one penny; by reading it every workman will at once perceive that I merely put, as it were, a more secure foundation under the frame-work so

---

[1] *McDouall's Chartist and Republican Journal,* 24 April 1841.

wisely recommended by the Manchester delegates. I propose the following, not to destroy, but to amend; not to pull down, but to build up; not to confuse, but to unite and consolidate.

The Manchester plan is one where the roof of the house, in my opinion, is too heavy for the side walls. I want to put solidity beneath, and a buttress against their system for the purpose of strengthening and upholding it; and, far from humbugging myself with useless fears of the law, I will take a part in rearing up a substantial stronghold for the protection of labour; and I will run any risk, as I have done hitherto, being perfectly satisfied courage alone can enable the labourer to gain his rights.

A changeable man, like a restive horse, always sees boggles in the way; and a coward, like the sloth, believes there is always a lion at the corner of the street. It appears to me, that to marshal the Trades under this movement, would imply the speedy emancipation of labour from political bondage and social tyranny. We have been told that we cannot gain the Charter without we first gain the middle class. We have as much use for them as a cart has for a third wheel, or a pig has for an umbrella. Why? Have they not the Suffrage already? Very well. Do you think they will assist you in getting it, unless you can prove to them that it is their interest to join you? If you could prove that to them, you would in the first place, have a three hundred horse power of persuasian; and in the second place, you would after all your labour *demonstrate clearly that what was their interest was your injury.* Any working man knows that who knows what a shop is, what profit is, and what the wrongs of labour are …

LABOURERS, LOOK AT THIS NEW FOUNDATION CAREFULLY.

1. I recommend all workmen known as the trades or mechanics to form Chartist Associations, to be called, for example, the Shoemakers', Masons', Carpenters', Chartist Associations, &c., &c.

2. I recommend all workmen known as miners and agricultural labourers to form Chartist Associations, to be called, for example, the Miners', Gardeners', and Field Labourers' Chartist Associations, &c., &c.

3. I recommend all workmen known as the manufacturing class to form Chartist Associations, to be called, for example, the Spinners', Weavers', and Gunmakers' Chartist Associations, &c., &c.

In forming these Associations, three things must be observed. In the first place, whether forming an Engineers', Miners', or Gunmakers'

Chartist Association, take care that each Association shall only be composed of avowed Chartists.

In the second place, take care that each Association shall be composed of only one *kind* of workmen, that is to say in a Shoemakers' Association take care that none but *resident* shoemakers be admitted; in a Weavers' Association, none save *resident* weavers; in a Carpenters', none save *resident* carpenters.

Lastly, take care that your Chartist Associations are distinct from your Trades' Unions. Mark here, the latter bodies, I predict, will come to their senses in time; in the interim, let them alone, or you will meddle with men of very conflicting ideas, with corn-law repealers, socialists, teetotallers, &c., &c., and involve yourselves in a maze of endless discussion. If a Trades' Union be unanimous to adopt the Charter, then form your Association out of the whole Union. If these preceeding rules are attended to, you will secure the following immediate advantages by the very fact of establishing Chartist Associations composed of members belonging to one craft, and holding only one sentiment on politics:

1st. Every man will know his neighbour.

2nd. No strangers will be permitted to employ the arts of deception amongst you.

3rd. No police agent can be harboured in your meetings undiscovered.

4th. If he did assume the trade and the garb of a workman, your proceedings are as public as if they were transacted on the highway, and at the same time the wall of brotherhood must make them as private as if only one man *thought* at his fireside.

5th. The fraternal feelings naturally belonging to all associated workmen would render the association more binding, more sacred, and more enduring than any other system I have yet seen tried.

6th. When the political movement was perfected, the same organization could be imitated for trades purposes, and at no time could the elements of the organization be destroyed, unless the various crafts could be abolished, and with them all signs of industry and every vestige of civilization.

Let us suppose that these reasons have been sufficient to influence the associated workmen of all classes and kinds to organize. The organization of every separate body of workman would be legal, if it had no branches within itself. All classes of tens, twenties, or fifties are illegal. Are they beneficial or not? Argue that well. If you decide upon the adoption of sub-divisions, then abolish the name class, have no stated number, no elected leaders. On the other hand, to be safe from the fangs

of the law, sub-divide your association into reading clubs of any number, or of every number, of subscribers to papers, pamphlets, &c.; and above all, *profess only to aim at the spread of knowledge.* I suggest the name reading club only for the purpose of screening yourselves from the law, which does not take cognizance of societies professing the spread of *any kind of knowledge.*'
(*McDouall's Chartist and Republican Journal*, 17 April 1841)

5. *Consolidation at Work*
(In the early 1840s the *Northern Star* and other Chartist periodicals recorded swift progress in planting Chartist associations among the trades. Though the preceding extract might tempt the historian to view the development as the implementation of a preconceived plan, this impression would be misleading. The initiative came mainly from the localities, where Chartists who were already trade unionists had a vital part to play. These were active in forming delegate committees or trades councils to propagandize among the trades of a district, and the gospel was often carried by a deputation from one trade to a meeting of another. The Executive of the National Charter Association did, however, encourage the process after McDouall joined it in June 1841. The doctor and his colleague James Leach were active in lecturing to the trades on the inadequacy of trade union action alone, unaccompanied by political reform, to uphold the standard of living of working men. Early in June 1842 John Campbell, the Secretary of the Executive, issued an appeal to the trades to unite with the Chartists. These exertions produced an uneven response. They were more successful in some places than in others, especially in Scotland, in London, and in Manchester. Moreover, the response of the weaker, locally organized trades, such as the shoemakers, was greater than that of the nationally–integrated skilled craftsmen. The extent to which the N.C.A. trade 'localities' were representative of the corresponding trade union branches also varied a good deal from instance to instance, but in London in 1841–43 about a third of these 'localities' were confined to a single trade, several of them meeting at a house of call of the trade.[1] In Manchester about that time, as the following extract shows, skilled metal workers resolved to join the N.C.A. 'as a body'.)

'MANCHESTER.—A general meeting of the hammermens' body to take into consideration the principles of the People's Charter, and the propriety of their joining the National Charter Association, was held in the large room of the Olympic Tavern, Stevenson's square, on Tuesday

---

[1] I. J. Prothero, 'London Chartism and the Trades', *Econ.H.R.*, 2 ser., XXIV, 1971, pp. 202–19.

evening; one of their own men was called to the chair. Deputations from the mechanics and smiths of Manchester, who attended on behalf of their respective trades, were introduced, and laid before the meeting their views on the subject, and informed them, that their trades, after maturely examining the subject, had found that the trades' unions had not accomplished that for which they had been formed, namely, the protection of the labour of the working man; and, therefore, they had come to the conclusion that nothing short of a participation in the making of the laws by which they were governed, would effectually protect their labour. Having come to this conclusion, they had joined the National Charter Association. The Chairman then introduced Mr. James Leach, who was received with repeated rounds of applause; and in a masterly manner, unmasked the monster, class legislation. Mr. Dixon then read to the meeting the Six Points of the Charter, after which Mr. Littlewood moved the following resolution:— "That we, the hammermen of Manchester, being convinced of the truth and justice of the People's Charter, do forthwith join the National Charter Association as a body; and elect a committee of nine, with power to add to their number, to carry out the above resolution." The resolution was seconded by Mr. Bate, and was carried unanimously. The following gentlemen were chosen as a committee to carry out the resolution, viz:— Mr. P. Clark, Mr. D. Grundy, Mr. G. Bate, Mr. H. O'Neil, Mr. H. Cummings, Mr. M. Lowe, M. J. Gladstone, Mr. C. Lowe, and Mr. Thomas Scowcroft. After thanks were voted to the Chairman, the meeting dissolved, highly delighted with the evening's proceedings.

MECHANICS BODY.—Mr. Wm. Dixon lectured to the above body, in their meeting room, Brown street, Manchester, on Thursday evening last. The meeting was well attended. This body is going on well, increasing in numbers every time they meet. They have a meeting every Thursday evening, in the Chartist Room, Brown-street, Travis street. The public are admitted.'

(*The Northern Star*, 16 July 1842)

6. *The Manchester Trades and the 'Plug Plot'*
(The wave of insurrectionary strikes, which spread across the manufacturing districts in August 1842, has been portrayed by most historians as a spontaneous reaction to wage-cutting, which the Chartists tried, belatedly and unsuccessfully, to control. It is true that the national leaders of Chartism merely displayed their divisions at and after a Chartist delegate conference in Manchester on 16 and 17 August, when the crisis had already reached its peak. At an earlier and more

formative stage, however, a temporary conjunction of trade unionists with the Chartists in Southern Lancashire, the base of the rising, threw up an organization, which gave direction to the strikes and strengthened their political complexion. From the first week of the outbreak a sequence of trades conferences drawn from that region assembled in Manchester and passed resolutions to cease work until the People's Charter became the law of the land. Motions to this effect were carried at two separate gatherings on 12 August. The ensuing extract describes the proceedings of a further conference on the 15th, at which a large majority of the delegates were of the same mind. These assemblies marked the acme of trade-union enthusiasm for Chartism, but the fusion was far from perfect. Despite the screening of delegates mentioned in the first paragraph, very few of the 131 participants listed by the *Manchester Guardian*[1] as being present when the chair was taken, can with confidence be assigned to organized trade societies. The vast majority could well have been chosen arbitrarily by groups of workers in special meetings.[2] Though some trade-union leaders and officials like Alexander Hutchinson, a smith from Messrs. Sharp and Roberts' engineering works, who chaired the meeting on the 15th, Benjamin Stott of the Bookbinders Society, and Robert Robinson and John Tear, secretaries respectively of the Old Mechanics and the Operative Dyers, took an active part in the strike movement, their exertions sometimes incurred the censure of the craft unions of the aristocracy of labour.[3])

'GREAT DELEGATE MEETING OF THE TRADES OF MANCHESTER, AND THE WHOLE SURROUNDING DISTRICT. MONDAY EVENING, HALF-PAST NINE.

This important meeting resumed its sittings at ten o'clock a.m., at the Sheardown Inn, Tib-street, Mr. Hutchinson in the chair. A committee was appointed to scrutinize the credentials of delegates for ascertaining that all were legally elected, and that all were *bona fide* representatives of trades ...

There was exhibited, as might have been expected, a difference of opinion amongst the thousands who were represented by the several members of this important meeting as to the precise object to be

---

[1] 17 August 1842.

[2] The best account of the Manchester trade conferences is contained in a Southampton University undergraduate dissertation by Dr. A. J. Peacock entitled 'The Organized Working Class Movements and the Great Strike in South Lancashire, August 1842', to which I am indebted.

[3] e.g. Robinson was censured by the Manchester No. 1 Branch of the Old Mechanics. J. B. Jefferys, *The Story of the Engineers* (London, 1945), p. 22. Tear, on the other hand, claimed to have taken part in the disturbances in pursuit of his duties as union secretary. J. M. Bellamy & J. Saville, *Dictionary of Labour Biography*, Vol. IV (London, 1977), p. 176.

recognised as the distinct purport of the strike. Some, and those the majority, were instructed on the part of their constituents, to disclaim all minor and secondary objects of contention, and to declare that their resolution was fixed to uphold the strike on no other ground than as a means to obtain the Charter, for which purpose they were resolved to maintain it to the last extremity.

Others, and those principally from Stalybridge and the other localities in which the strike began, were instructed that their constituents regarded it merely as a trades' strike, a question of wages, and trades' rights; while a considerable number of places, without giving any opinion of their own, expressed by their delegates their readiness to uphold their brethren in any struggle that might be deemed advisable, and to abide therefore upon the decision of that meeting, be the same what it might. During the day eighty-five delegates thus delivered their instructions, representing all the respective trades of Manchester, and of most if not all the towns and villages within twenty miles thereof. ... Of the eighty-five delegates, fifty-eight declared for the Charter; seven for making it a trades' contest; nineteen to abide the decision of the meeting; and one, the representative of the stone masons of Manchester, stated that his constituents were individually for the Charter, but that he had no instruction from them as a body, and could not therefore pledge them to any precise course of action.'

(*The Northern Star*, 20 August 1842)

7. *The National Association of United Trades, the Labour League and the New Trades' Organization, 1848*

(The National Association of United Trades, launched in 1845, was one manifestation of trade-union recovery in the middle 1840s. It has been variously assessed: by G. D. H. Cole and A. W. Filson as a revival of the idea of general union on a national scale, and by Henry Pelling as a limited device to enable autonomous unions to combine for parliamentary lobbying. Ambiguity was present from the start.[1] The Association, centred on London, was an amalgam of higher trades bestirred by the legal challenge of the 1844 Master and Servant Bill and weaker societies, such as those of the tailors, shoemakers and silk weavers, whose prime concern was to arrest the consequences of endemic surplus of labour by the regulation of wages and hours of labour and the settlement of unemployed artisans in agriculture and

---

[1] Cf. G. D. H. Cole & A. W. Filson, *British Working Class Movements: Select Documents 1789–1875* (London, 1965) p. 469; H. Pelling, *A History of British Trade Unionism* (Middlesex, 1953) p. 44.

manufactures. Although the secretaries of aristocratic trades, notably T. J. Dunning of the Bookbinders, played a prominent part in establishing the Association, they lost interest in it as the political threat to the unions receded, leaving it in the hands of officers of the humbler trades.[1] These looked increasingly to the state for the achievement of their purposes. With the Chartists, whose programme held the key to a more sympathetic government policy, the N.A.U.T. enjoyed close relations through T. S. Duncombe and the *Northern Star*. But the Association was not itself a Chartist body, and when the European revolutionary movement of 1848 produced a spur to activity, the Central Committee preferred to let subsidiary and lateral organizations agitate for social and political reforms. The Labour League, which became a journal of the whole N.A.U.T., was planned as a separate department. Its own initial objectives did not embrace parliamentary reform. This was left to meetings of delegates, whose exertions the Association, to a limited extent, encouraged. It seems likely that the body as a whole could not be brought to embrace the Six Points.)

(a) The Labour League

The C.C. have had under their serious consideration the propriety of extending the machinery and objects of the Association, to enable it to advocate and promote the passing of such legislative measures as are necessary to improve the condition of the labouring classes, and which require legislative sanction for their fulfillment, with this view they propose to add another department to the Association under the title of

THE LABOUR LEAGUE

The objects of which are proposed to be:

1st, The formation of local Boards of Trade, composed of an equal number of employers and workmen, with a president appointed by the government to regulate all trade matters and disputes in their several localities.

2nd, To cause the employers in all trades to provide properly lighted and ventilated workshops for those employed by them, in order to do away with the middleman and sweating system, and prevent the numerous evils arising from work being done at private houses.

3rd, Regulation of the hours of labour in all trades, with a view to equalize and diffuse employment among the working classes, so that some shall not be overworked, while others are starving for want of employment.

4th, The employment of the surplus labour of the country by the

[1] I. J. Prothero, 'London Chartism and the Trades', *Econ.H.R.*, 2 ser., XXIV, 1971, pp. 202–19.

government in useful government works, such as the reclamation of waste lands, improvement of harbours, deepening of rivers, etc.

5th, The establishment of a minimum rate of wages by Act of Parliament, below which no employer shall be permitted to set any one to work; such minimum to be regulated by the price of corn for the time being.

6th, Sanatory regulations of a general and comprehensive character.

7th, The appointment of a minister of labour to superintend the carrying out and practical operation of these various measures, for the improvement of the condition of the industrious classes.'

(Extract from Business Paper Containing Proposals for Revising the Constitution of the National Association of United Trades to be submitted by the Central Committee to the Conference of the Association. '*The National United Trades' Association Report and Labour's Advocate*' 13 May, 1848. Bishopsgate Institute)

(b) Trade Delegates and the Marriage of Political Reform and Social Change

(This article opens with a discussion of the contemporary revolutionary movements on the European continent and of Great Britain's part in them. Having suggested that political freedom must be conceded at no distant date and that social freedom should next receive attention, it proceeds.)

'Heretofore the movement party has been divided into two great sections, one having in view purely political reforms, and the other advocating social changes. Perhaps this "division of labour," to use the language of the political economists, has been in past times mutually advantageous to both parties, and the great cause of progress been materially served thereby. We have always said that there ought to be no dissention or jealousy between these two parties. The possession of power, and the ability to use it rightly, are two separate and distinct things. One party have been most laudably and beneficially occupied in endeavouring to secure for the whole people the right of managing their own affairs; the other has been not less usefully or less worthily engaged in educating the public mind as to the nature of the objects to which these powers when attained should be directed, and thus fitting the people properly to exercise these rights.

There are, however, symptoms of a new phase of the movement. In Manchester a new association has been proposed by the trades of that important city, which puts forth as its objects a series of measures which combine both the political and social questions upon which the public mind has been so long agitated. We believe that similar views are entertained by several trades in London, delegates from whom have lately had several meetings at the Bell, Old Bailey.

The list of measures put forth by the Manchester delegates is the following:—

1. Limitation of the hours of labour in all departments of industry.

2. Sanitary regulations of a general and comprehensive character.

3. Abolition of the middle-man system, viz., undertakers, squeezers, sweaters, &c., &c.

4. The establishment of a permanent industrial board of trade, with local boards in all cities, towns, or boroughs.

5. Abolition of the laws of entail and primogeniture.

6. Application of crown and waste lands by government grants, for the absorption of surplus labour.

7. Abolition of property qualification for civil and political representatives.

8. A national system of education, free from sectarian and political prejudice.

9. The necessity of a full, free, and complete representation of the entire people in the Commons' House of Parliament.

We look upon such movements as the natural offspring of the times in which we live. They prove that the events which are passing abroad have been carefully watched by the thoughtful and intelligent operatives of England, and that the true moral of these events is understood by the people, however little the Government appreciate it. The time has come for raising the standard of political and social regeneration in the full sense of these terms. If it be boldly raised, and manfully supported, it will ere long rally around it such an array of moral force, resting upon enlightened public opinion, as will secure for all classes the blessings of a national, just, and equitable state of society.

But in order to secure this great and glorious consummation, there should be as few divisions, and as little sectional agitation among the movement party as possible. Every advantage should be taken of existing organizations, where these are at all capable of being made to advance the cause. The time, labour, and expense which are necessarily required to form new organizations will be thereby saved, and made applicable to the promotion of the main object. We are most anxious that the working classes of this country should fully appreciate and act in the spirit of the sound philosophy embodied in the words of the immortal poet which form the motto to these cursory observations. We are earnestly desirous that while the stirring impulse of liberty vibrates alike on the shores of the Tiber, the Danube, the Rhine, and the Adriatic, and the tide of freedom pours onwards, fertilizing many a thirsty land, the trades of this country should take that tide at the flood. If they do so, and make an enlightened and simultaneous effort, immense advantages may be realized for themselves and for posterity.

The organization of the National Trades' Association is sufficiently expansive and simple to allow of its being made the medium for a universal movement of the working classes of this country. It already embodies in its ranks tens of thousands of the trades, and though simple in its organization, provides for a full, complete, and satisfactory registration and direction of the energies of its members. Why should advantage of these circumstances not be taken by those trades who have not hitherto joined it, as well as by those who, holding identical views with ourselves, are seeking to form new Societies? The Central Committee have for some time had under consideration the propriety of adding to the existing machinery of the association for the protection of industry and the employment of labour, a third department by which the social and political privileges of the working classes which are dependent upon the action of the Legislature may be watched over and secured. We shall probably in our next Report, state in detail the nature of the provisions proposed for that purpose. In the mean time we content ourselves with stating that we desire to see a LABOUR LEAGUE established with the most comprehensive and practical objects, and that it will be our earnest endeavour at the earliest possible moment to give practical force to these desires.

We have the high gratification to state, in conclusion, that by recent advices from our honourable and highly respected President, T. S. Duncombe, Esq., we may expect in a short time to have his presence and assistance again, his health having greatly improved of late. Rally, then, working men of England, around so noble, so well tried, and so honourable a champion of the People's Rights! Let us march forward under one banner, and be guided by the voice of a leader who not only possesses—what he most worthily deserves—the confidence of the trades and the Chartists, but also enjoys the respect and confidence of the liberal and enlightened men of all classes of the community, as the most independent, honest, able and successful representative of the people that ever sat in the House of Commons.'

(Extract from article headed 'Labour League'. *The National United Trades' Association Report and Labour's Advocate*, 13 May 1848)

(c) The New Trades Organization

'ADDRESS OF THE LONDON TRADES' DELEGATES TO THE TRADES OF GREAT BRITAIN AND IRELAND

"Awake, arise, or be for ever fallen"

FELLOW-MEN,—Having been delegated by the trades of London to frame a constitution for a National Organization of Trades, for the industrial, social, and political emancipation of labour, we now submit, for your approval, the following fundamental principles, which we have adopted after long and serious deliberation, as being best calculated to extricate all classes of the community who live by industry, from their present degraded and prostrate condition; and we earnestly recommend the trades throughout the empire, to lose no time in concentrating the intelligence, the energies, and the means they possess, to carry out those great and important principles which we propose as the basis of a great National Trades' Union.

1. That the land being the gift of the Almighty to the people universally, ought to be held in sacred trust by the State for their benefit, and not be exclusively possessed by a fractional part of the community.

2. That the elective franchise should be extended to every man twenty-one years of age, of sound mind and uncontaminated by crime.

3. That education should be secured by the Government for the people; and that such education, on the part of the State, should be of a strictly scientific and secular character, without in any way interfering with the rights of parents to give such religious instruction to their children as they may think fit.

4. That those laws which restrict the expansion of the circulating medium should be repealed, and a representative currency forthwith issued by the Government, equal to the amount of wealth offered in exchange.

5. That as Great Britain and Ireland contain a super-abundance of land, skill, and capital, to profitably employ and comfortably support more than double the present population, the Government should introduce a bill establishing self-supporting home colonies, to give immediate employment to the numerous but compulsory unemployed of our population.

6. That the application of machinery should be made available to the interests of the whole community; and that foreign manufactures, as

also goods made in prisons and work-houses, ought not to be introduced into the home market except upon such conditions as will secure the tradesman and artizan from the ruinous consequences of unequal competition.

7. That for the just protection of labour, local boards of trade should be established, composed of an equal number of masters and men, under the superintendence of a minister of labour, whose office would be to give an impetus to the industrial operations of the nation, and act as an impartial arbitrator between employers and employed.

8. That taxation should be equalized, by substituting for all other taxes a graduated property tax.

These are the principles which, in our opinion, ought to form the basis of a great National Union; and we now call upon the trades of Great Britain and Ireland to unite in one firm and indissoluble bond, and carry out the objects propounded in the foregoing constitution. ... Unite then, without delay, and you may rely upon the energies and devotion of the Trades' Delegates.

Signed on their behalf,

JAMES O'LEARY, Chairman

A. E. DELAFORCE, Secretary, *pro tem.*'

(*The Labour League*, 25 November 1848)

(In its next issue *The Labour League* announced the completion of this project under the heading 'The New Trades Organisation'. Its own attitude to the new body was not uncritical. While recognizing the value of an association for political agitation, it emphasized the things which working men could do for themselves by trade-union action. *The Labour League, or Journal of the National Association of United Trades*, 2 December 1848)

8 *Chartist Distrust of the 'Aristocracy of Labour'*

(The more powerful unions in the country generally held aloof from the N.A.U.T. Between them and the Chartists a great gulf was fixed. During his brief tenure of power in Chartism in 1850–51 Julian Harney made an effort to bridge it, succeeding in establishing good relations with individual leaders of the skilled trades like the engineer William Newton. When Ernest Jones superseded Harney as the head of Chartism in 1852, the policy was reversed. The newly founded Amalgamated Society of Engineers challenged the practices by which overtime working and dilution of labour were being introduced into the engineering workshops. For this its members were locked out by the masters in January 1852, and after three months forced to capitulate. While the struggle was still in progress, Jones attacked the policy of trade unions. After pleading the necessity for honesty he proceeded.)

'... Now, it being an established and admitted fact—a fact that its cleverest advocates have not been able to refute, that Trades' Unions are a perfect fallacy, and that no co-operative movement can raise the working classes under our present system, and since it therefore follows that the people exhaust their strength, and play into the hands of their enemies by running after such delusions, I ask, "Is it the best policy to let them do so?"

No! common sense says, "It is the duty of every right-thinking and honest man to warn the victim running blindfold to destruction."

Let us now come to the more immediate question of the hour—the case of the Iron trades. It is said: "By following out the same policy here, you estrange from them public support. It is a struggle of labor against capital. Without public support, labor cannot stand—will you therefore assist the victory of capital?"

This is a very specious way of putting the case. My answer is as follows: The victory of capital is certain; it don't want my assistance: it needs nothing but itself. The course the Iron-trades are pursuing, must end in defeat. Consequently, all their efforts will be wasted. The more assistance they receive, the greater the waste of popular resources. If after being warned and cautioned, as they have been, they STILL WILL go on, and destroy themselves, on their own heads be the responsibility. I refuse to share it, by supporting them, or by the guilt of a TACIT CONNIVANCE. But, if they have a right to ruin themselves they have not a right to ruin others. If they choose to leap down the Curtian gulf, (without, like Curtius, closing it), they have no business to make other trades the horse [t]hey ride.

Now, unquestionably, the decree of the employers is one of the most barefaced acts of social tyranny ever attempted. But, because the employers of the Iron-trades are KNAVES, is that any reason why their leaders should make the men FOOLS?

What do I want, then? Do I propose that the men should submit to such tyranny without resistance? Nothing of the sort. What I want is, *that they should resist in the right way*, in the way likely of obtaining a *successful issue*.

Suppose the Iron-trades met together, and said: "We are determined no longer to submit to the tyranny of our masters. To argue with them is of no use. To compete with them is hopeless—they have too much money. To combine against them is vain, for between combination—law, hunger-law, and surplus-law, they will beat us down. Therefore, we must change the whole system. This we can do only by changing the system-makers; therefore we will join the political union of the working classes."

Suppose they had done this—suppose their meetings had been for the Charter—suppose their subscription, (not the £25,000, leave that untouched if you like, but the subscription wasted in maintaining the non-employed), had been devoted to the Charter fund; a shower that would have raised up crops of Democracy from one end of the country to the other! Suppose one shout had burst from their great gatherings— "Political power—the sovereignty of the People!" Suppose the human machinery they command in Lancashire and London had been set in motion simultaneously for this great purpose; and at this crisis of Parliamentary "Reform"—what a reverberation it would have caused throughout the land! What terror it would have striken in employers! Why, men! "over-time", and "piece-work", (trifles in comparison!) would have been joyfully conceded by the masters—anything to knock up the movement, anything to stifle the great cry which should burst the death-knell of monopoly upon the ear of Time!

And all this you have foregone!—all this you have wrecked and wasted by your most egregious folly! And will you tell me, I am to stand silent by, in cowardly connivance?—and that this is the best policy?

Perhaps you may say—"But, would not the masters have turned you off the same for the political combination as for the social one?" I tell you THEY DARE NOT! In the one case, you would have had the people at your back,—in the other, you find yourselves alone. The low-paid trades sympathise not with the haughty aristocracy of labour that has spurned them. The other high-paid trades, like yourselves, are too selfish to extend a hand, where they do not feel the pain direct. I repeat, the masters DARED NOT have braved the war. Strikes and co-operations they can meet; because you have not the money for it they have, but political combination they cannot resist, because they have not the numbers for it, and you have. It would take millions upon millions to wage a social war with them—a few thousands can carry a political movement through its wildest ramification. They dared not have turned you adrift for political organization, for the very weapon, poverty, that beats you now, in your social struggle, would have been your strength, and they know it. The very appearance of 30,000 political martyrs in the streets would have shaken the Reaction Bill of Russell, and roused the dormant mind of every working-man! Oh! how you have played into the hands of the Government, ye co-operators, unionists and Amalgamated Iron-trades!

Of course, I know that abuse is the reward for trying to couch politically the eyes of the socially blind! But what then? I know that it may, possibly, set one portion of the working classes against the other. But, THAT BATTLE WILL HAVE TO BE FOUGHT, AND THE SOONER IT IS FOUGHT THE BETTER.

By raising the discussion—truth cannot lose, and democracy must gain. Those that are not with us ARE against us. The high-paid Trades recruited the constabulary ranks of 1848;—within their meetings and councils, political topics are forbidden; if we remain silent, how can we hope to change them? Their barrier of class-prejudice and ignorance must be broken down—(for the low-paid trades are by far the best educated portion of the working-classes)—and how can you hope to break it down, if you don't batter it in breach? The ordinary course of public meetings, tracts and lectures has been tried, and failed. They won't attend the one, or read the other. We have kept aloof from them for years? and what have we gained? Are they one jot nearer to us than before? No! they are further off. They won't come to us. What then remains? To FORCE OURSELVES IN AMONG THEM. Like the early Christians, go, unbidden, in their midst, carrying the gospel of truth right in face of their lurid torch of opposition, and speak its message through the savage yells of their arena. We have stood aloof in timid modesty too long. Truth is not merely a garrison, she is a storming force as well. In and at them—to rout them out of errors, and to lead them nobly captive to the truth.

A gentleman from Leeds asks:—"Why attack working-men's movements? Are there no capitalists' tyrannies and governmental wrongs worth assailing?"

I answer: Plenty—and we assail them, too. But *there are no evils so dangerous to working-men, as those which spring among themselves*—and from this simple reason; because the others they can be roused against easily—but to those which originate in their own ranks, they are wedded by partiality, prejudice, and a mistaken notion of self interest, and it is useless to assail the corruption that is without, until we have eradicated the corruption that is within. Therefore, every sincere reformer ought to war, as his *first* duty, against the mistakes in the popular ranks ere he assails the evils inflicted on it by others.

One point more: it is said I am setting the laborers against the skilled mechanics—the low-paid trades against the high-paid.

Do we fight against class-government? Well, then? there is class-government in our own ranks, and we ought to fight against it too. Do

we fight against aristocratic privilege? Well then—there is aristocratic
privilege of the vilest die among the high-paid trades, and we ought to
fight against it too. Truth is the best policy. THE ARISTOCRACY OF
LABOUR MUST BE BROKEN DOWN, the same as an[y] other
aristocracies. *If you don't,* when you have established democracy, *these
men will carry the Re-action. ...*'
(*Notes to the People,* Vol. II, London, 1852, pp. 860–2)

9. *Chartism: A Parent of the Co-operative Movement*

(The story of the origins of the Co-operative Movement has been told
with reference to Owenite Socialism rather than to Chartism. Though
there were precursors in the 1820s and 1830s, the beginnings of practical
success have been traced to the Rochdale Pioneers, a group of working
men, who, in 1844, without abandoning the communitarian aspirations
of Robert Owen as an ultimate goal, concentrated upon establishing a
retail store, selling at market prices and distributing a portion of the
profits to their members in proportion to their purchases. After that,
consumers' co-operatives multiplied, though Chartism, while it lasted,
proved something of a counter-attraction. Recent researches have
shown, however, that Chartist co-operative stores were founded several
years before the Rochdale pioneers made their famous move. This was
partly because Chartism breathed the spirit of artisan self-improvement
which also activated the early co-operators. But, as Dr. Alexander
Wilson has demonstrated,[1] in 1839 Chartist provision stores were
established in many parts of Scotland to further the Convention's
boycott of non-Chartist shopkeepers. The following extract from the
Scottish *Chartist Circular* likewise aimed to provide a specifically
Chartist justification for forming co-operatives. The article began by
exhorting the masses to unite behind a device by which 'the rampant
power of the master class—of the millocrat and shopocrat—may be
broken and destroyed.' Social power was presented as a means to
winning political power, though Chartists usually argued the converse.
The case proceeded as follows.)

'CO-OPERATIVE STORES.

... Before perfect freedom can be enjoyed, the social system must be
remodelled. Those inequalities in the condition of men, the source
whence originally sprung class legislation, with its numerous train of
ills, must be removed. It is those inequalities by whose operation the fair
form of society is blurred and defaced,—that separate class from class,
and man from man—that foster jealousy and hatred,—that beget pride
and a lust for power and dominion: in short, the fecund parent of misery

[1] *The Chartist Movement in Scotland* (Manchester, 1970), pp. 126–32.

and crime. From these premises it should follow, that, in as much as the Chartists succeed in obliterating the cause of the evils specified, in so much will they sap the foundation of exclusive political privileges, and thus hasten the accomplishment of their wishes.

I will instance a way in which something of this sort might be successfully attempted. In every considerable locality, let Chartist stores be established for the sale of commodities in most general demand, and let the profits resulting therefrom be applied to the furtherance of the Chartist movement. In this way funds may be created to an extent hitherto unapproachable, and private generosity remain untaxed. The profits realised from the sale of groceries and provisions are usually set down at ten per cent, while upon cloth and some other articles, they vary from fifteen to fifty per cent. Why should not the Chartists embrace this method of raising the sums necessary for effectually carrying on the agitation? Surely it is less objectionable than the one in general use; besides, this is not a bare suggestion for the application of funds assumed to be at the disposal of Chartists to certain purposes; it is to them a positive creation of means; created, too, as has already been stated, at the expense of their bitterest opponents. In the large towns, the difficulty of starting these stores is not be thought of. The committees of the different Charter Unions, of course, to controul their management. The experience of such parties in the details of business, is, doubtless, far from being extensive; but this I esteem a strong argument for their setting prudently about gaining practical knowledge of these matters, seeing it may be turned to such good account. The plan of dealing exclusively with professed friends was recommended to the Chartists by the first General Convention. The delegates, it may be presumed, knew well that such friends among the shopocracy were "few and far between"; but it was thought this advice would have the effect of driving not a few of their number into the ranks of the people, purely from motives of self-interest. The result proved one of two things to be true,— either the Chartists lacked union and energy sufficient to carry out the plan properly, or class prejudices were too strong to be subdued, even by the love of self.

Chartist stores have also, in some places, been attempted successfully; but these stores rested on too narrow a basis. They were never meant to benefit the cause of Chartism in the common acceptation of that term, being merely joint-stock companies, carrying on trade for behoof of a Chartist co-partenery. Whether these consisted of a hundred or a thousand individuals is of no consequence; the profits were divided equally amongst them, instead of being employed in the payment of missionaries and other like purposes, or allowed to accumulate to that extent necessary for fully employing themselves. Hence the distinction that exists between these stores and the ones indicated in this paper. The sum required to commence these need not be large; say from fifty to one hundred pounds for each, to be raised in small donations, or, if need be, as money, to be repaid after a certain period, with interest. These stores, once established, being the joint property of every member of the Union, of whom neither entry-money nor any stated payments need henceforth be exacted, they will stimulate members who have hitherto stood aloof from all active exertion, to enrol their names as members; because, in addition to the prospect of ultimate gain, present advantages are offered. There is a remark for ever on the lips of the one-sided, to which I shall briefly advert, and then conclude. Such persons will say "Oh! we dare say these things are all good enough, if we had them; but is it not better and surer policy in us to continue to agitate, agitate, agitate for our glorious charter instead of bothering our brains about secondary measures? The main object once secured, all things right and proper will follow—the abolition of the law of primogeniture, among the rest". To this sage argument it is summarily replied, that these stores, if prudently and faithfully managed, will prove the most effectual means of agitation yet tried. With their aid organisation may be *pushed far beyond* its present narrow boundaries.

Aberdeen, August 30th, 1841. G.R.'

(*The English Chartist Circular*, Vol. I, No. 35)

10. *A Chartist Critique of Co-operation*

(As Philip Backstrom has pointed out, there was not in early co-operation 'much of anything to be called a Movement'.[1] At mid-century the working-class consumers' co-operatives jangled with the old Owenite Redemption Societies, still emphasizing co-operation for production on the land and in self-governing workshops, and with the experiments launched by the upper-class Christian Socialists after their coming together in 1848. The last group was itself divided. The majority followed J. M. F. Ludlow, an orthodox Christian layman, in establishing associations for co-operative production among the artisans of the metropolis, e.g. the tailors' association of February 1850. Edward Vansittart Neale, however, a wealthy barrister, influenced more by the French Socialists than by Christian doctrine, while prepared to support and finance these activities, forged links with the northern co-operative

[1] *Christian Socialism and Co-operation in Victorian England* (London, 1974), p. 41.

stores and was converted to a belief in the primacy of consumers' co-operation as the best first step on the pathway to the co-operative commonwealth. His life's work was to unify the British Co-operative Movement, and he began by founding in 1851 the Central Co-operative Agency, as a wholesale agency for the consumers' stores, which would also serve as an exchange for the products of societies of producers. He endeavoured to interest the trade-union leaders in the project, and encountered some initial success. William Allan and William Newton of the Amalgamated Society of Engineers served on the committee. It was perhaps because he saw in Neale's system the most serious challenge yet to Chartism's position as a national working-class movement that Ernest Jones devoted so much space in *Notes to the People*, from the spring of 1851 onwards, to attacking the co-operative movement as it was then organized. As the following example shows, his criticisms were sometimes well-founded, especially with regard to co-operative production, but his repugnance towards profit making, on which the distributed dividend system rested, caused him to belittle the potential of consumers' co-operation. Jones was not against co-operation in principle, but he wished it to be organized on a national basis and underpinned by state credit.[1] His animus against existing schemes, like his opposition to the trade unions, was a function of his mistrust of the 'aristocracy of labour', which seemed likely to be enlarged by them.[2])

'A letter to the Advocates of the Co-operative Principle,
AND TO
THE MEMBERS OF CO-OPERATIVE SOCIETIES
(The article begins with an explanation of the aims and methods of co-operation in general terms. It then proceeds to the consideration of specific projects.)

... This brings me to the consideration of the co-operative plan by which you endeavour to effect the regeneration of society.

The co-operative power you have evoked can be applied to only three objects :—

    1. To the purchase of land;
    2. To the purchase of machinery, for the purpose of manufacture;
    3. To the establishment of stores, for the purposes of distribution.

    1. *The Land.* Consider, firstly, the enormous amount you must subscribe for the purchase of land in sufficient quantity to relieve the labour market of its competitive surplus. Secondly, remember that the more an article is in demand, the more it rises in price. The more land you want, the dearer it will become, and the more unattainable it will be

---

[1] *Notes to the People*, Vol. I, (London, 1851), pp. 84–5.
[2] See Part VII, 8.

by your means. Thirdly, recollect that your wages have been falling for years, and that they will continue to fall; consequently, while the land is rising in price on the one hand, your means of purchase are diminishing on the other. Fourthly, two parties are required in every bargain—the purchaser and seller. If the rich class find that the poor are buying up the land, they won't sell it to them—we have had sufficient instances of this already. They have sagacity enough not to let it pass out of their hands, even by these means. Fifthly, never lose sight of this fact: only a restricted portion of the land ever *does* come into the market—the *laws of primogeniture, settlement, and entail* lock up the remainder; a *political* law intervenes, that *political power* alone can abrogate.

It may, however, be urged, in answer to the first objection, that the capital invested in the purchase of land would reproduce itself. I answer, reflect on how our forefathers lost the land—by unequal legislation. It was not taken from them by force of arms, but by force of laws—not by direct legal confiscation, but they were TAXED out of it. The same causes will produce the same effects. If you re-purchase a portion of the land, you would re-commence precisely the same struggle fought by your ancestors of yore—you would wrestle for a time with adversity, growing poorer every year, till holding after holding was sold, and you reverted to your old condition. This can be obviated only by a re-adjustment of taxation—a measure that can be enforced by political power alone.

2. *Machinery and manufacture*. The second object to which co-operation is directed, consists in the purchase of machinery for purposes of manufacture. It is argued, "we shall shut up the factories, and competing with the employer, deprive him of his workmen, who will flock to us to be partakers of the fruits of their own industry." It is impossible for you to shut up the factories, because the great manufacturer is not dependent on home-trade—he can live on foreign markets; and in all markets, both home and foreign, he can undersell you. His capital and resources, his command of machinery, enables him to do so. Is it not an undeniable fact, that the working-men's associations—the co-operative tailors, printers, &c., are *dearer than their monopolising rivals*? And must they not remain so, if their labour is to have a fair remuneration? It is impossible to deprive the employer of workmen to such an extent as to ruin him—the labour surplus is too great; and were it even smaller, the constantly developed power of machinery, which he can always command the readiest, would more than balance the deficiency you caused.

If, then, we do not shut up the factories, we only increase the evil by still more overglutting the market. It is a market for that which *is* manufactured, far more than a deficiency of manufacture under which we labour. If we add to manufacture we cheapen prices; if we cheapen prices we cheapen wages (these generally sink disproportionately)—and thus add to the misery and poverty of the toiling population. "But," you may argue, "we shall *make* a market—create home-trade, by rendering the working classes prosperous." You fail a leverage: the prosperity of the working classes is necessary to enable your co-operation to succeed; and, according to your own argument, the success of your co-operation is necessary to make the working classes prosperous! Do you not see you are reasoning in a circle? You are beating the air. You want some third power to ensure success. In fine, you want political power to reconstruct the bases of society. Under the present system, *on your present plan*, all your efforts must prove vain—have proved vain—towards the production of a *national* result.

3. *Co-operative Stores.*—By these you undertake to make the working man his own shopkeeper, and to enable him to keep in his own pocket the profits which the shopkeeper formerly extracted from his custom.

These stores must be directed towards the distribution of manufactures or of food. If the former, you must either manufacture your goods yourselves, or else buy them of the rich manufacturer. If you manufacture them yourselves, the evil consequences alluded to in the previous paragraph, meet you at the outset. If you buy them, the manufacturer can undersell you, because the first-hand can afford to sell cheaper than the second—and recollect the wholesale dealer is every year absorbing more and more the retailing channels of trade.

We then suppose your stores to be for the retailing of provisions. Under this aspect, their power, as a national remedy, is very limited. Food is wealth—money is but its representative; to increase the real prosperity of a country, you must increase its wealth, whereas these storers do not create additional food, but merely distribute that which is created already. ...

(The remainder of the article is devoted to showing that the co-operative movement fails to achieve its basic social aspirations and to asserting the need to nationalize co-operation.)

                                                      Ernest Jones.'

(*Notes To The People*, Vol. I, London, 1851, pp. 28–9.)

11. *Chartism and Owenite Socialism*

(Robert Owen (1771–1858), the philanthropic millowner turned Socialist, was one of the great seminal minds of English working-class movements in the early nineteenth century. He supplied the cause with an armoury of ideas, but, as the studies by Professors J. F. C. Harrison and W. H. Oliver and others have reminded us,[1] he was never completely absorbed by it. Having come closest to being so in the period 1829–34, he moved away in the next ten years to head sectarian bodies, constituted on a cross class basis, which combined the advocacy of a Utopian Socialism with that of education and rationalist beliefs. Hence, while many Chartists had Owenite backgrounds, Owenism was, by the time of Chartism, a separate movement under organizations like the Association of All Classes of All Nations and (from 1839) the Universal Community Society of Rational Religionists. It proceeded not by political agitation but by despatching social missionaries, who delivered lectures, and by founding halls of science. The relationship of the Owenites to the Chartists was generally one of friendly disagreement about priorities.)

'SOCIALISM

LAMBETH.—on Tuesday evening, Mrs. Chappell-smith (late Miss Reynolds) delivered the first of three lectures, at the Social Institution, Westminster-Road to a crowded audience. The subject of the lecture was the present condition of the country, and the proposed remedies of the Chartists and of Mr. Owen. The lecturer traced, in a very livid and impressive manner, the progress of poverty amongst the industrious classes, and showed that, in proportion to the augmentation of the national wealth, its producers had deteriorated in their condition and comforts. The changes proposed by the Chartists she admitted to be good and desirable, but valuable only as means to an end—that being, the annihilation of the demon of competition. Supposing the Chartists obtained all they sought for, still, she argued, Mr. Owen's principles would have to be adopted, before any beneficial and permanent change could be effected in the social condition of the community; and inasmuch as it must be many, many years, before the Charter could be obtained, it was impossible to make up our minds to await its issue. She therefore gave the preference to Socialism as a present remedy, although we cannot think that she succeeded in showing how this could be realised without a preliminary change in the government and legislature, after the manner proposed by the Chartists.'

(*The Charter*, 13 October 1839)

[1] J. F. C. Harrison, *Robert Owen and the Owenites in Britain and America* (London, 1969); W. H. Oliver, 'The Consolidated Trades' Union of 1834', *Econ.H.R.*, 2 ser., XVII, No. 1, 1964, pp. 77–95.

PART VIII

Chartism and the Churches

1. *The English Established Church through Chartist Eyes*
(Of all the country's religious institutions the Church of England drew most of the Chartists' fire. The charges made against it were partly of repressiveness and intolerance but chiefly of subservience to the class interests of the aristocracy, as the following extract from a 'moderate' Chartist journal shows. The special hostility to the Established clergy, far exceeding that displayed towards Nonconformist ministers, was partly an inheritance from an earlier radical tradition, typified by Paine and Richard Carlile, which had linked priestcraft with kingcraft and lordcraft as the essence of 'Old Corruption'. It was also fed by such present realities as the oligarchical system of lay patronage and the authoritative status of the clergy in society, manifested by the fact that in the early 1830s nearly a quarter of the magistrates were drawn from the clerical order.[1] The attack, as framed below, exaggerated the shortcomings of the Church, but can be understood sympathetically. It drew examples from an earlier and less sensitive period, while ignoring or denigrating the reforms and reforming movements, which had quickened in the 1830s. Prime ministers since Spencer Perceval had studied the credentials, academic and theological, of candidates for high preferment, and the proportion of nominees to bishoprics connected with the peerage and the landed gentry by birth fell sharply in the generation after 1830.[2] In the Northern towns a significant number of parochial clergy involved themselves in such working-class causes as the Ten Hours movement and the agitation against the New Poor Law. Even among the Tractarians, 'those wretched crawling creatures', were men like Keble and Hurrell Froude, keen to sever the Church from the gentry and to associate it with the poor. The Chartists, however, could not know all this. They stood, moreover, near the beginning of the principal phase of administrative reformation in the Church of England, and in their day ecclesiastical abuses remained widespread. At no time, during the first half of the nineteenth century, did less than a half of the presentments to sees fall to persons related to the aristocracy by family or by marriage.[2])

[1] E. J. Evans, *The Contentious Tithe* (London, 1976), p. 11.
[2] R. A. Soloway, *Prelates and People: Ecclesiastical Social Thought in England, 1783–1852* (London, 1969), pp. 8–16.

'The Church of England: the Church of a Selfish Aristocracy

In polite and episcopal circles it is customary to talk of and believe in the poor man's church. From every other corner of society this falsehood has been driven; but in the bosoms of peers and bishops, and their subordinates, it still finds refuge, animating them to holy zeal and if necessary to holy persecution. "For what means are not justifiable in order to maintain so inestimable a blessing?" says some rosy and rubicund parson.

Unhappily, as we have hinted, the bulk of society do not look upon this poor man's church in any other light than that of a gross and crying evil. Of all the institutions which are maintained in opposition to the spirit of the age she is regarded as the most useless. Enlightened men recognise her as the incubus of civilisation and the most unenlightened perceive in the application of her immense revenues, the distortion of national wealth for the lowest party purposes. This general sentiment of hostility to the church of England is generated by the prevalent feeling in favour of democratic principles. The popular eye has become too keen to mistake the form for the substance of religion. And even if the vision of men were more blunted than it is, the dark ages of the world's history have passed away, and they now gaze upon our church establishment as laid bare by that flood of light, which the spirit of inquiry has poured into every crevice of the vast and unsightly building.

The most prominent shape which the opinion thus created has assumed is the conviction of the narrow and oligarchical basis upon which the church is constructed. With all the pretensions of nationality she is in truth nothing but a refuge for aristocratic destitution. Her constitution and entire history exhibit this fact in the strongest colours. We will glance rapidly at the one and the other.

Without going back to the days of Henry the Eighth, the greatest ornament of which the church of England can boast, every man is aware that the major part of church livings is in the gift of the aristocracy. Those wretched crawling creatures, the Oxford papists, plume themselves, in common with their brethren, on their direct descent from the Apostles; when the nominee of the owner of the advowson can be forced upon a bishop by the vulgar process of an action at law, as though the matter in dispute were a common nuisance or public obstruction. In consequence of this hopeful state of things the most bare-faced and unblushing simony is openly practised, and the nearest road to the apostolical seats of the Anglican church is through an advertisement in the newspapers offering a round sum for the enviable

privilege. Whatever power an oligarchy possesses is invariably used without the remotest reference to the general welfare. Accordingly we find that the younger sons or private tutors of the nobility, or the relations of their mistresses, are the persons who become, under their patronage, the ministers of our law-endowed faith. The idea of fitness never comes into the head of the patron or the presentee. But the considerations that guide the one, and which it would astonish the other to depart from, are "what are his connexions? Is he a staunch partisan? Are his politics of the right sort? Has he stoutly abused the dissenters? Can he worry a widow for church rates without flinching?" and many more of an equally amiable character. But whether he is likely to be obnoxious to those over whom he is appointed pastor—whether his temper and qualifications have been fashioned after the precepts of the gospel, are enquiries never made by the depositaries of ecclesiastical property in this country. As to the examination before the bishop, it is in most cases like the interview with the parochial clergyman on the eve of confirmation, a mere farce; and even where it is stringent it consists only by theological and philological trifles, which might have been adequate to the thirteenth, but are wholly inadequate to the wants of the nineteenth century. Need we in addition speak of the unequal distribution of church revenues—of the lordly income of her prelates, and the beggarly stipend of her curates? Need we expose the hypocrisy of such a man as Bishop Blomfield, prating about church extension with his mansion in Saint James' Square, his palace at Fulham and his fifteen thousand by the year? No! We feel that we have already advanced enough to show that the constitution of the church of England is formed upon the most approved method of a worldly and grasping aristocracy.

And if such be her constitution what do we gather from her history? Let her career during the last half century give the response to this pregnant question. At every attempt made in that period to reform and improve, the Anglican clergy have revealed themselves as the unswerving foes of popular rights and popular happiness. When the indignant voice of the nation uplifted itself against slave traffic, Anglican bishops recorded their votes in favour of its continuance. When our blood-stained penal code imposed the punishment of death for the most trivial offences, so that judges on the circuit left men to be strung up like onions, Anglican bishops, the high priests of a God of mercy, interposed to thwart alteration. The fetters of intolerance were struck off by the abolition of the Test and Corporation acts, and the Emancipation of the Catholics amid the discordant yells of a baffled priesthood: the Reform

Bill was carried despite not only the power of the aristocracy but the almost frantic efforts of the clergy; popular education was first contemptuously derided, then vehemently opposed, and finally stifled by the church in her miserable parish schools; and now wherever there is a parson, there, with some exceptions, are the synonyms of everything that is bigotted, everything that is hostile to human progress and human good.

The poor man's church forsooth! Rather the tool of the hereditary peers of England, who barter her apostolical seats like cattle in the market, and at whose selfish bidding she has ever been the willing instrument or instigator of aristocratic crime and aristocratic folly.

PRO-CHARTIST'

(*The English Chartist Circular*, Vol. I, No. 45, c. November 1841)

2. *The Chartists at Church, 1839*

(In July-August 1839, after Parliament's rejection of the National Petition, the Chartists of many provincial towns resorted to the practice of occupying the parish churches at the time of Sunday service. On 11 August about 500 of them walked in procession from West Smithfield to St. Paul's Cathedral, and Norwich Cathedral was similarly invaded on the following Sunday. Three provincial examples are given below. These demonstrations were part of a protest against the anti-Chartist conduct of the middle and upper classes, who constituted the habitual worshippers in these buildings. There was also, however, a claim that the churches rightfully belonged to the people. This was implicit in the instructions which the Chartists often sent to the officiating clergyman to preach from a certain text, and was explicitly stated by the rationalist Richard Carlile in the episode at Bolton described in (b). At Blackburn, also, it was made clear that the Chartist objective was 'to claim the church as the people's property'.[1] The application of the political doctrine of popular sovereignty to the affairs of the parish church reflects a lingering assumption of the identity of the civil and the ecclesiastical communities. It was shared, curiously, by William Lovett, who wanted not disestablishment but 'a Church truly National, governed *by the whole people* through Parliament'.[2] But the Convention of 1851 drew into line with advanced Dissenting opinion by endorsing the 'complete separation of Church and State'.)

(a) 'ASHTON, SUNDAY.—According to previous arrangement, the chartists of Ashton and neighbourhood assembled to the amount of

---

[1] Rushton's Collections 6. Manchester Central Reference Library. Manuscript Department, Ms. F. 942. 72. R. 121. p. 19.

[2] *Life and Struggles* (London, 1920). Vol. II. p. 405.

upwards of 2,000 and marched to the parish church. On the previous Friday evening a communication was sent by them to the Rev. Mr. Handforth politely informing him that they were coming to church, and requesting that he would be good enough to take his text from the first [i.e. fifth] chapter of the general epistle of St. James, beginning with the first and ending with the sixth verse, "Go to now, ye rich men, weep and howl for your miseries shall come upon you. Your riches are corrupted, and your garments are moth-eaten. Your gold and silver is cankered, and the rust of them shall be a witness against you, and shall eat your flesh as it were fire. Ye have heaped treasures together for the last days. Behold the hire of the labourers, who have reaped down your fields, which is of you kept back by fraud and cruelty; and the cries of them which have reaped are entered into the ears of the Lord of Sabbath [sic]. Ye have lived in pleasure on the earth, and been wanton; ye have nourished your hearts, as in a day of slaughter. Ye have condemned and killed the just; and he doth not resist you." During the reading of the first part of the service, the chartists paid every attention to the minister. It being the Rev. Mr. Bowden's turn to preach, he ascended the pulpit when every eye was fixed upon him, and to the utter astonishment of the chartists, he took his text from Mark xi., v. 17—"And he taught, saying unto them, is it not written my house shall be called of all nations the house of prayer: but ye have made it into a den of thieves?" No sooner had the rev. gentleman finished reading his text, than they got up to a man and peaceably walked out of the church. The Rev. Mr. Handforth, to whom the communication was sent on the Friday previous, is said to have been much hurt on the occasion; and we are informed, that to-morrow morning he will preach from the text which the chartists had pointed out from Saint James. There is little doubt but that they will again attend in thousands to hear him.'
(*The Manchester and Salford Advertiser*, 17 August 1839)

(b) 'THE BOLTON CHARTISTS—On Sunday morning last at an early hour, the chartists mustered on the New Market Place, for the purpose of again proceeding to the parish church. The morning being exceedingly fine, great crowds of persons were attracted into the principal streets to witness the proceedings. The chartists seemed rather disconcerted towards ten o'clock, as their numbers by no means answered their anticipations. After the bells had commenced ringing, however, they formed themselves; and, on moving off the square, their numbers, on being counted, were found to be little more than six

hundred, a large proportion of them being boys. On arriving at the church, they found the police and others busily engaged in making way for them through the crowd, and inviting them forward; but, on entering the church, they were somewhat disappointed in finding it about half filled with the usual members of the congregation. They were, therefore, obliged to procure seats where they could. Their conduct during the service was unusually decorous, probably owing to the sprinkling of other parties amongst them. The Rev. Mr. Robin, the curate, delivered an impressive sermon, though not particularly appropriate to the occasion. At the close of the service, they returned to the New Market Place; and, in the afternoon, a local preacher from Bury, of their own creed in politics, delivered a short sermon. In the evening Richard Carlile delivered a lecture, exposing some of their follies, but recommending them to continue their attendance at the church, which he said belonged to the people; and, if they were not satisfied with the minister provided for them, to elect one of their own, and place him in a pulpit in the church. He then proceeded to read over the 6th chapter of Timothy, and grounded his text on the same verse as that selected by the curate on last Sunday but one, and at the conclusion of his harangue appealed to them as to which had made the best sermon; as much as to say, "If the clergyman does not suit you, appoint me in his stead." The day passed off without the slightest disturbance, although many persons were in great fear that such extraordinary proceedings were calculated to end in nothing but a desecration of the Sabbath.'
(*The Manchester Guardian*, 7 August 1839)

(c)   'LEIGH

THE CHARTISTS AT CHURCH—On Sunday last, August 3rd, the chartists of Leigh and neighbourhood, in order that they might not be behind hand with their brother chartists in Bolton and other places, resolved upon paying a visit to the parish church. Several days previous to Sunday ample notice was sent to the surrounding towns and villages to attend early on Sunday morning at the church to secure themselves all the best seats, and by that means show the aristocracy and middle-class men, that by their unity and strength they were resolved to carry out the charter. The event, however, proved an utter failure, as out of Tildesley, Atherton, Westhoughton, Westleigh, Pennington, Lowton, Astley, and Bedford, the total amount did not exceed 2,000. The church, however, was nearly filled, and to the credit of the chartists be it said, they behaved themselves with becoming propriety, with one or two slight exceptions

scarcely worth notice. The Rev. Mr. Jackson, curate, delivered an excellent address from the 39th Psalm, 9th verse—"I was dumb, I opened not my mouth; because thou didst it." He was listened to throughout with the greatest attention: and after the service was over the multitude quietly dispersed. It is worthy of notice that on this occasion the whole congregation gave up their seats, and with the greatest good humour imaginable assisted the authorities in showing the chartists to seats, and in keeping order, and many expressed a warm desire that they would come every Sunday; to which we may add (if the motive be good), we should be glad to see all the churches in the kingdom filled with chartists every Sunday.'
(*The Manchester Times*, 10 August 1839)

3. *Some Anglican Responses to Chartism*
(With occasional exceptions, such as Dr. A. S. Wade, vicar of Warwick, who was elected to the 1839 Convention, the Anglican clergy were hostile to Chartism (though not to working-class interests in the broader sense), and preached many sermons against it. Emphases varied, however, between the different parties into which the Established Church was divided.)

(a) *A High Church View*
(*The British Critic* was the organ of the Tractarians, at that time edited by John Henry Newman. The article from which the extract is taken is a lengthy review of two published parliamentary papers, dealing with the Whig government's efforts to promote armed associations of the 'principal inhabitants of a disturbed district', to control Chartist unrest (See Part IV, 4). The argument is directed primarily against the millowners and the Whigs, not against the Chartists. The master manufacturers are accused of diverting economic discontents, against themselves and the new industrial order, into political channels; the Whigs, of aiming at a national guard, which would eventually direct the country, and of fomenting civil war. Incidental references to the Chartists are hostile. Later in the article it is urged that the 'one or two Chartist leaders' who threaten or intend the use of arms should be sentenced to the treadmill. But the extract below is sensitive to the distinction between radical political agitation of all kinds and 'genuine' trade grievances.)

'ART. V.—1. *Letters from Lord John Russell to the Lords Lieutenants and to the Magistrates in Sessions, and to Mayors in Boroughs, in certain Counties.* 1839

2. *Return to an Address of the Hon. the House of Commons, dated 20th August 1839; for a Return of all Associations formed and armed for the Protection of Life and Property, under the Authority of Letters from Lord John Russell to Lords Lieutenant of Counties and to Magistrates, dated the 7th day of May, 1839*

... While, therefore, discontent is a constant product of the social system in our great towns, its form and pretence will be found to vary according to very accidental circumstances; and it will be also found that the employers are not the last to give it, if possible, a political turn. We have known master manufacturers, persons of a certain amount of honesty and respectability, advocate on public grounds, without any disguise, this very line of conduct for its own sake, without any reference to the question whether there did exist national grievances which were proper grounds of discontent, and whose removal would be either an act of justice, or any real benefit. It was much insisted on by these persons, that, not the Reform Bill, but the *popular demand* for the Reform Bill, was the salvation of the country, inasmuch as it happily diverted the minds of the people from certain dangerous projects, foremost among which were some obnoxious schemes for extorting by conspiracy or by violence higher wages than the state of the market allowed. We also remember, that the Birmingham Political Union was much, and we will not say undeservedly, extolled by its wealthy members and friends, on the ground that it furnished method, union, and a political aim, to an excitement which might else have been directed to local objects, and found a vent in personal outrages and desultory agitation. They *avowed* it to be a salutary thing, that a political union menacing and controlling the state should have swallowed up trades unions, operative societies, and a host of private quarrels, which were directly dangerous only to individuals.

We have on one occasion seen the chief authorities of a manufacturing town attempt, though the attempt was vain, to divert a mob engaged in the *indiscriminate* destruction of property, by calling a public meeting for the purpose of resolutions, &c., in favour of the Reform Bill, and when that plan had miscarried, by exposing for signature drafts of petitions to the same purport in the market place, which however turned out equally unsuccessful. ...

It is as much the policy of these gentlemen to transfer the interest and expectations of the people from local to political questions, as it was the policy of the ancient kings of England to save their tottering thrones by setting their turbulent barons upon schemes of foreign conquest, or as it was the policy of the popes to stir up and gather against the Saracen distracted and rebellious Christendom. And we are disposed to believe that such is the natural leaning of the English character on the authority of rank and wealth, that the working classes would never take up political objects to any formidable extent, without some countenance from their employers, who are driven, as we have described, by the instinct of self defence, to be the chief political agitators. Now this influence may be considered as *external* to the populace, as the *suggestion* of another class, giving only form and pretence to the spirit of dissatisfaction. So also may be considered all the other rebellious influences at work,—the press, and the living agents of revolution pervading the country,—the thousands of miserable men in London, including not a few foreign refugees, who, like vultures, watch from afar the progress of discontent, and eagerly snuff the first scent of rebellion. All these influences act on the working population from without. The same may be said of Spenceanism, the reform mania, socialism, chartism, and all the other schemes for the renovation of our country, produced in such quick succession that time can scarcely keep pace with them; they are devised and propagated by men of other classes and professions than those whose benefit they pretend;—by men who do but cast the shadows of their own visionary systems on the surface of the unthinking multitude, just as eastern conjurors can throw the vivid forms of men and beasts upon the shapeless vapour and the midnight gloom. But nothing shows more plainly that the shape and colour of the public discontent is something impressed, by extrinsic means, upon the minds of the mass, and should be treated separately from the discontent itself, than the well known fact, that they who suffer most are not they who most complain and who are the most ready for deeds of violence. The secretaries of councils, the presidents and vice-presidents of union-lodges, the delegates and emissaries and all this sort of gentry, are universally men in the superior and more profitable branches of manufacture, or in some still higher profession—men, who either are receiving, or have received comparatively ample incomes: but whose undisciplined tempers, lawless ambition, and utter want of principle, have either thrown them out of employ, or suggested the hope of rising above their present rank by agitation. Whatever they have been, many of them are now living in luxury, seeing the world, and playing the great man, on infamous wages wrung from the trembling grasp of the poor wretches whom they are suffered partly to deceive and partly to oppress.

We do not deny that political excitement once created is apt to swallow up other grievances. If it had not this tendency it would not answer the employer's purpose to create it. Nor do we deny that it will sometimes continue much longer and go to much further lengths than its promoters anticipated or desired; nor do we deny that the promoters are themselves sometimes carried away by the passions they desire to excite in others, till they are at last in that ambiguous state between deceiving and being deceived which philosophers delight to imagine. Yet we maintain that the question of wages lies at the root of all manufacturing, as much as at the root of all agricultural, commotions; that, from the fluctuating character of trade, such commotions must be always expected; and that their political aspects are always adventitious, given to them, in the first instance at least, by the masters themselves.

We repeat, that what feeds and stimulates discontent in our large towns is nothing else than the mere want of higher remuneration for labour, whether that want be reasonable or otherwise. This want must always exist in more or less degree, and so also must that discontent. Any measures to satisfy or alleviate it, or to check its unruliness, must be regular, constant measures, consistent with the spirit of the constitution of English usage; and calculated rather to unite all classes, than to widen breaches and aggravate differences. ...'

(*The British Critic*, Vol. XXVI, July 1839, pp. 400–4)

(b) *A Low Church View*

(*The Christian Observer*, founded in 1802, was the chief magazine of the Evangelicals, who, though they were not the dominant party in the Established Church, occupied a more solid and respected position than the rebel Tractarians. Between one fifth and one ninth of the clergy adhered to the party in the 1840s,[1] and it had representatives on the bench of bishops and among heads of houses in Oxford University. The *Observer's* treatment of the Chartist visits to churches in 1839 breathed the cant and pietism which often marred the social witness of the group in those days, but its comment did not lack appreciation of the distress factor underlying Chartism. Evangelicals like Ashley and Parson Bull were in the forefront of the campaign against long hours of labour in textile factories.)

'... To take the case of the tumultuous invasion of churches; ought such an outrage to be permitted in any country which boasts of its laws,

---

[1] Owen Chadwick, *The Victorian Church Part I* (London, 1966), p. 446. The percentages have been calculated on a figure of nearly 15,000 clergy for England and Wales. If the Irish Protestant clergy were included in the total the proportions would be slightly lower. R. Currie, A. Gilbert & Lee Horsley, *Churches and Churchgoers* (Oxford, 1977), pp. 196–202.

liberties, and municipal regulations? Why are peaceable and devout worshippers to be put to flight by a revolutionary mob, which is only more dangerous because trained to obey the word of command, and to be silent and orderly till the signal is given for simultaneous attack? Assuredly such outrages might be easily and legally prevented, if the well-disposed inhabitants of every town and parish where they are likely to occur would resolutely address themselves to their duty. At first such proceedings are only laughed at as ridiculous; but they afford portentous precedents and examples. It is absurd to say that Chartists have as much right to go to church as other people; and that if they proceed thither in an orderly manner they cannot be legally dispersed, any more than a school or a benefit club. It is thus that, under the technical phrases of liberty, true liberty is violated. Chartists have a right to go to church, but not as Chartists; as worshippers, but not as invaders; nay, even in the strictest technicality of law, any person dispossessed of his legal right of pew or sitting, by force or terror, in consequence of their incursion, may indict the whole body present, or abetting, for a conspiracy. But we speak not of such technicalities; but of the undoubted right and duty of every body politic to preserve its own peace, and to punish wrong-doers. There has been too much laughing at riot, coquetting with sedition, and tampering with treason. We trust that the nation is at length aroused to a sense of its danger and its duty. Some of the sermons addressed to the Chartists have contained excellent instruction and advice; and we think that much more might be done than has been attempted, to show the misguided portion of the confederacy—the victims, not the ringleaders—the sinfulness and the folly of their conduct.* When we

---

* We do not however recommend political sermons. Some of the discourses delivered at churches into which Chartists have intruded, or in places where they are rife, have been very ill-judged. One clergyman so far forgot discretion and good feeling as to display his wit in taking for his text, 'My house shall be called the house of prayer, but ye have made it a den of thieves.' The Chartists quitted the church in a body upon its announcement; and thus far he triumphed; but he lost an excellent opportunity of addressing to them what might have benefited their souls. In most cases we believe that most good would be done by preaching as though no Chartist was present; avoiding all topics of secular strife; speaking to men as fallen, guilty, and sorrowing creatures; guilty and needing pardon and cleansing; sorrowing and needing consolation; and showing how the Gospel of Christ, the glad tidings of salvation, meet these exigencies. Many of the religious poor endure severe privations yet they do not become Socialists or Chartists; for they find in the instructions and comforts of religion that which guides and consoles them amidst their difficulties. Of the Chartists many probably are avowed and hardened infidels; and many more are utterly ignorant upon the subject of religion; a word spoken in season might, by the Divine blessing, be of great utility to the latter if not to the former: some who came to scoff, might remain to pray; a countenance more in sorrow than anger might soften down hostile feelings; and the hope set before men in the Gospel be seen to be a brighter prize than the delusive phantoms of political perfectionism.

think of the physical wretchedness of vast masses of our dense population, we cannot wonder that they are open to the seductions of designing men, who take advantage of their necessities to inflame their minds with anti-social principles, under the preposterous fancy that a revolution would better their condition; more especially when we consider that for want of churches and adequate means of religious training they have been allowed to grow up in a state of vice and ignorance, which prepares them to be the tools of infidels and political demagogues. Let it be remembered also how much these evil doers have been encouraged by some who, to say the least, ought to have known better. The recent presentation of Mr. Owen, the Socialist, to the Queen—a young and maiden Queen—by the prime minister, as the bearer to the royal ear and eye of an address from "The Congress of the Universal Community Society of Rational Religionists"—the abettors of a system which inculcates republicanism, levelism, avowed deism, and the most brutal licentiousness—even to the extinction of marriage, and the substitution of concubinage in its place, was an offence against public decency and national feeling, so gross and unpardonable that Talleyrand would have told Lord Melbourne that it is worse than a crime—that it is a blunder. And this when Chartists are parading our streets; and Unionists, invested with municipal authority, are seeing the dire conclusion of their own schemes; and the riotous scenes in Birmingham, Manchester, Newcastle, and elsewhere, are preluding the too natural results of that tampering with evil instead of repressing it, which has been among the most marked features of the policy of her Majesty's present advisers. These things are very distressing and very alarming; our best hope, under the merciful over ruling of the Most High, is that the nation is becoming sensible of the impending perils, and is arousing itself to avert them.'

(View of Public Affairs, *The Christian Observer*, N.s. Vol. XXXVIII, September 1839, pp. 574–5)

(c) *A Christian Socialist View*

(The Christian Socialist movement in England was first offered to the working classes as an Anglican alternative to Chartism. The Kennington Common demonstration of 10 April 1848 brought together Frederick Denison Maurice and Charles Kingsley, who were clergymen, and J. M. F. Ludlow, a devout layman, for this purpose. Two days after the great Chartist meeting the placard printed below, which Kingsley had drafted, was posted on the walls of London. Kingsley was the most rhetorical, though not the most radical of the group. He often managed to make the

Christian Socialist cause sound almost identical with Chartism. At a meeting in a London tavern he proclaimed: 'I am a Church of England parson and a Chartist'. Three years later, in the summer of 1851, he praised freedom, equality and brotherhood from the pulpit of St. John's, Charlotte St., with such enthusiasm that the incumbent was drawn to make a public protest. Nevertheless, he used the words in a different sense from the Chartists. As the placard shows, he prized moral reform more highly than political change, and his approach, like that of Maurice, who supported the union of church and state, and opposed the extension of the franchise[1], was thoroughly paternalistic. The movement launched by these men was not even Socialist in any *étatiste* sense. It was a mild advocacy of voluntary co-operation (See VII, 10), though Ludlow would also have brought in the state as an equalizer.)

'WORKMEN OF ENGLAND!

You say that you are wronged. Many of you are wronged; and many besides yourselves know it. Almost all men who have heads and hearts know it—above all, the working clergy know it. They go into your houses, they see the shameful filth and darkness* in which you are forced to live crowded together; they see your children growing up in ignorance and temptation, for want of fit education; they see intelligent and well-read men among you, shut out from a Freeman's just right of voting; and they see too the noble patience and self-control with which you have as yet borne these evils. They see it, and God sees it.

WORKMEN OF ENGLAND! You have more friends than you think for. Friends who expect nothing from you, but who love you, because you are their brothers, and who fear God, and therefore dare not neglect you, His children; men who are drudging and sacrificing themselves to get you your rights; men who know what your rights are, better than you know yourselves, who are trying to get for you something nobler than charters and dozens of Acts of Parliament—more useful than this "fifty thousandth share in a Talker in the National Palaver at Westminster"† can give you. You may disbelieve them, insult them— you cannot stop their working for you, beseeching you as you love yourselves, to turn back from the precipice of riot, which ends in the gulf of universal distrust, stagnation, starvation.

You think the Charter would make you free—would to God it would! The Charter is not bad; *if the men who use it are not bad!* But will the Charter make you free? Will it free you from slavery to ten-pound

---

[1] E. R. Norman, *Church and Society in England 1770–1970* (Oxford, 1976), p. 170.
* The Window tax was not then taken off. [footnote from text]
† Carlyle. [footnote from text]

bribes? Slavery to beer and gin? Slavery to every spouter who flatters your self-conceit, and stirs up bitterness and headlong rage in you? That, I guess, is real slavery; to be a slave to one's own stomach, one's own pocket, one's own temper. Will the Charter cure *that*? Friends, you want more than Acts of Parliament can give.

Englishmen! Saxons! Workers of the great, cool-headed, strong-handed nation of England, the workshop of the world, the leader of freedom for 700 years, men say you have common-sense! then do not humbug yourselves into meaning "licence", when you cry for "liberty"; who would dare refuse you freedom? for the Almighty God, and Jesus Christ, the poor Man who died for poor men, will bring it about for you, though all the Mammonites of the earth were against you. A nobler day is dawning for England, a day of freedom, science, industry!

But there will be no true freedom without virtue, no true science without religion, no true industry without the fear of God, and love to your fellow-citizens.

Workers of England, be wise, and then you *must* be free, for you will be *fit* to be free.

A WORKING PARSON'

(Charles Kingsley: His Letters and Memories of His Life, ed. by His Wife (London, 1877), Vol. I, pp. 156–7.

4. *The Chartists and the Nonconformist Churches*
(Nonconformity was, on balance, more favourable to Chartist political aspirations than was the Church of England. But it is unsafe to generalize about the attitudes of Dissent. An advanced group, mainly of Congregationalists and Baptists headed by Edward Miall, which campaigned against government interference with education, and for disestablishment, through the Anti-State Church Association founded in 1844, was willing to concede universal suffrage and, under pressure, the other five points of the People's Charter (see Part VI, 4 & 7). The position of the majority is more difficult to gauge. Debate has turned principally on the role of Methodism. Some historians, notably E. Halévy and E. P. Thompson, have stressed the debilitating effect of Wesleyan conservatism and other-worldliness on the economic independence and political radicalism of working men. But Eric Hobsbawm has refuted Halévy's view that Methodism saved England from revolution in the late eighteenth and early nineteenth centuries, and others, like R. F. Wearmouth, have charted the contribution of Methodism to the leadership and organization of working-class movements. The following documents have been chosen to illustrate both the negative and the positive impacts of evangelical Nonconformity, notably Methodism, on the Chartist movement. Probably Methodism was more a brake than a

booster, but the judgment that it saved England from revolution is a vast exaggeration.)

(a) Wesleyan Discouragement:

(After Wesley's death in 1791 the Wesleyan Methodist Connexion was governed by an oligarchical Conference drawn from the ministers and, at a regional level, by District Meetings composed of all the preachers within the district. Jabez Bunting, a strong Tory, was four times President of the Conference in the years 1820–44, and a dominant figure. Conference imposed upon the preachers a 'No Politics Rule', inhibiting them from involving the denomination in political agitation by their words and actions. According to the ensuing newspaper report, a District Meeting at Bath endeavoured to go further and to control the laity. Such action was often ineffective. It was stated in 1841 that, while the preachers were to a large extent under the direction of a party devoted to Toryism, fifteen out of twenty Methodists were favourable to a liberal government[1].)

'We are able to state, on the very best authority, that at a recent meeting of the Wesleyan preachers of the Bath district, consisting of between thirty and forty individuals, it was unanimously resolved that any member of the Methodist connexion who should join himself with the Chartists, should be excluded from their body. This decision we cannot but regard as honourable to the parties, and in accordance with the sacred volume, and one which should be known in every part of the kingdom.—*Bath Post.*'

(*The Chartist*, 26 May 1839)

(b) A Methodist Rebel:

(The term 'Methodist' comprehended, as well as the Wesleyans, a number of secession churches and offshoot denominations, e.g.—New Connexion Methodists, Primitives, the Wesleyan Methodist Association and eventually the United Methodist Free Churches. These were less conservative in both the ecclesiastical and the political sense than the Wesleyans, and more likely to throw up Chartist leaders. Joseph Barker of Wortley, the radical preacher and journalist, who was active in Chartism in 1848, had been a prominent figure in the Methodist New Connexion, the oldest of the schismatic bodies, formed in 1797. He was expelled, however, in 1841, ostensibly for denying the divine appointment of Baptism, and drifted through Unitarianism into free-thought. On leaving the New Connexion, he took with him about a fifth of the membership, including 29 chapels, a number of which became

[1] R. Currie, *Methodism Divided* (London, 1968), p. 49.

virtually Chartist institutions.[1] His case, like those of Thomas Cooper the renegade Wesleyan, Editor Hill the Swedenborgian minister, the Rev. James Scholefield the Manchester Bible Christian, and Joseph Rayner Stephens, who had resigned from the official Methodist ministry before he became a Chartist, makes the point that Nonconformists, conspicuous in Chartism, were often out on the fringes of the main Dissenting denominations. They, nevertheless, drew inspiration from the religious traditions of Nonconformity, as the extract from one of Barker's journals reveals.)

'Methodism

To C.W.—I have no doubt that Methodism has done a great deal of good in the world. It is doing a little good still, though its best days are long since past. It is doing good in teaching children to read, and training them to some degree of respect for decency and morality. It is doing good by keeping some individuals from drunkenness, from gambling, and from open, unrestrained indulgence in forbidden pleasures. It is, at the same time, doing a great deal of harm, in checking freedom of thought, freedom of speech, and freedom of action. It is doing a great deal of harm in instilling error into the minds of the young, and thus unfitting them for the discovery of truth in after life. It is doing a great deal of harm by upholding the tyranny of our national government, and by supporting mis-government in our various colonies. It is doing great harm by prejudicing its members against Reformers; against the advocates of truth and righteousness; and by representing the friends of truth, of justice, and of liberty, as infidels and anarchists.

Methodism now, is a very different thing from what it was in the early days of Wesley. Methodism *then*, was, to a great extent, the friend of liberty and truth, of justice and humanity. Wesley, though exceedingly ignorant on many important subjects, both in Theology and Politics, was still a Reformer. He was a terrible opponent of the horrible doctrines of Calvinism, and a determined foe of certain forms of intolerance and sectarianism. His great object was to make people good. He had more of religious and benevolent feeling than he had of intelligence or judgment, though he was far from being destitute of knowledge or cleverness on many subjects. He did a great deal towards promoting the comfort and welfare of the poorer members of the Methodist Society, as well as of other individuals. He formed an institution for the support of destitute widows. He formed another for the support of neglected orphans. And

---

[1] H. U. Faulkner, *Chartism and the Churches* (London, 1970), pp. 19 & 95; Currie, Gilbert & Horsley, *op. cit.*, pp. 141 & 146; D. Jones, *op. cit.*, p. 54.

he established a fund for the relief of the poor members of his society. And the penny a week subscription which now is taken by the travelling preachers, was originally collected for the relief of the poor. He established a dispensary and infirmary also for the relief of the poor. He also instituted a number of schools. He was a very economical and frugal man himself, and employed the whole of his income in relieving the wants of the needy, and in doing good in other ways as he had opportunity. He did a great deal in the way of publishing cheap tracts and cheap books: by this means he led thousands and scores of thousands to think and read. And though much that he taught, both in his sermons and his publications, was erroneous and injurious, there was much, both in his sermons and writings, that was true and good, and that was calculated to promote the illumination and improvement of mankind. The erroneous portions of Wesley's doctrines did much towards making men superstitious, enthusiastic, and mad; but the better portions did much towards making people virtuous, benevolent, and religious. And many of the parties that *co-operated* with Wesley were truthful, honest, and benevolent men. But the Methodist preachers of the present day are pursuing a very different course, from that pursued by Wesley and the Methodist preachers of his day. Still, there is no remedy but for those who see that the Methodist preachers are wanting in their duty, to be all the more faithful in the discharge of their duties themselves. We cannot destroy the influence of the Methodist Conference; but we can take care to use our own influence faithfully, in doing what the Methodist Conference neglects to do; or in opposing what the Methodist Conference may happen to do amiss. We cannot annihilate the Methodist organization; but we can publish truth,—we can fill the country with books and tracts adapted to expose prevailing errors, and to unfold and inculcate neglected truth. We cannot compel the Methodist preachers to advocate the rights of the people, or to labour for national reform; but we can advocate the rights of the people ourselves. And we can set such an example of patriotism and benevolence, as shall tend to secure the co-operation of the masses of our countrymen, and even draw away multitudes from under the influence of those faithless or ignorant priesthoods, who sacrifice the interests of their countrymen and of their kind, to the selfish interests of their order.' (*The Reformer's Companion to the Almanacs*, No. 12, October 1848)

(c) Reformers' Chapels:
(In addition to the churches which they established themselves in the

Christian Chartist movement (see VIII, 7), the Chartists found available in various towns of the North of England ready-made chapels where they could meet. These usually belonged to rationalist or millenialist sects, to vegetarians, to the adherents of a freelance radical preacher, or to splinter groups from the regular Nonconformist churches, rather than to those churches themselves. Thus Rayner Stephens had chapels at Ashton and Stalybridge supported by dissident proletarian Wesleyans.[1] The Bible Christians, a Swedenborgian sect not to be confused with the Methodists of that name, had a chapel in Every Street, Manchester, where ministered the Rev. James Scholefield, a vegetarian and radical. The Chartists held their conference there at the height of the Plug Plot.[2] The same sect also established in 1823 the 'Beefsteak Chapel' at Brinksway, Stockport, nicknamed because of its vegetarian emphasis. Rowland Detrosier, its minister during the early years, preached working-class independence.[3] At Middleton, too, a chapel was freely available for use by the Chartists.)

'MIDDLETON.—On Sunday a delegate meeting was held in Ebenezer Chapel, on the subject of the national holiday, when delegates were appointed to visit on the morrow the various towns, and report progress. At a very early hour on Monday the chartists began to assemble in Middleton and at eight o'clock hundreds of persons were opposite the Reformers' Chapel; from whence they proceeded to the Market-place, where a procession was formed, consisting of 1,071 men, and three flags. The procession proceeded up Market-street, down Chapel-street, past Messrs. Burtons' cotton mills, where part of the hands were working at the time. At noon, however, the whole of the hands in both mills left. The procession, on arriving at the print works of Messrs. Lewis Schwabe and Co., was joined by the whole of the workmen in the works. It then proceeded, with this augmentation, through [? Bexler] and Birch, where the numbers were 1,682, nearly all men. It then moved on towards Heywood, and on arriving at Heady-hill, on their way to Bury, they were informed by the Heywood procession, whom they met at this place, that the Bury chartists had been dispersed, and the riot act read. Upon this information the Middleton people returned home. At eight o'clock in the evening a public meeting was held in the Market-place, consisting of 5,000 persons. Mr. Robert Ward

[1] J. T. Ward, 'Revolutionary Tory: The Life of Joseph Rayner Stephens of Ashton-under-Lyne (1805–1879)', *Transactions of the Lancashire and Cheshire Antiquarian Society*, Vol. LXVIII, 1958, pp. 93–116.

[2] W. E. A. Axon, *The Annals of Manchester* (Manchester, 1886), p. 267.

[3] Gwyn A. Williams, 'Rowland Detrosier. A Working Class Infidel 1800–34'. *University of York Borthwick Papers*, No. 28 (York, 1965), p. 11.

was called to the chair. He gave an account of the proceedings at Ashton and Oldham; and Mr. John Hunt gave a description of Manchester. Delegates who had been to other places also stated the proceedings in each town, &c.

TUESDAY.—At eight o'clock in the morning a meeting was held in the Market-place, when it was agreed to abide by the orders of the convention. At noon the women held a meeting in the chapel above mentioned, but they came to no determination respecting the money deposited in the sick clubs.

WEDNESDAY.—A meeting was again held in the Market-place, after which nearly all the people retired home to their various employments. All has been very peaceable during the whole of the week, although the cessation from work was general.

FRIDAY EVENING.—All is perfectly quiet, and the people have resumed their employment.'

(*The Manchester and Salford Advertiser*, 17 August 1839)

5. *A Friendly Roman Catholic Gesture*

(As H. U. Faulkner wrote, 'the participation of Catholicism in the Chartist movement was always casual and incidental, never in any way general or official'.[1] The liberal bourgeois outlook of Daniel O'Connell, the lay chieftain of Irish Catholics, helped to turn the sympathies of immigrants towards the Anti-Corn Law League and away from Chartism. (See Part VI, 2). At Norwich, however, a note of affinity was struck. In 1848 an Irish priest, Fr. Thaddeus O'Malley, was elected from Nottingham to the Chartist National Assembly.)

'A ROMAN CATHOLIC PRIEST—THE CHARTISTS.

On Sunday morning the Radical Reformers of Norwich assembled in the Catholic chapel to the number of many thousands. They had been previously invited by the priest, who feeling for the want and misery to which the people have been reduced, has taken up their cause with the spirit of Christianity which would ere now have pervaded the whole Catholic hierarchy, were it not for the bloated Whig lawyer, O'Connell. The reverend gentleman preached from Luke III, 1—"Let him that hath two coats impart to him that hath none".[2] In a powerful and luminous discourse, he denounced the robbery of the poor, as well as the Church by that royal monster, Henry VIII.; and the conduct of the present tyrants in following up these robberies and oppressions, in a spirit at

[1] *op. cit.* p. 105.

[2] Presumably a confusion with Luke, VI, 29, or Matthew, X, 10, or some kindred text.

once setting humanity and the Christian religion at defiance. "The discourse was (says a hireling of the oppressors) the most inflammatory and dangerous we have ever heard." God send them more such discourses both in Ireland and England say we, and more they shall have, as it will be impossible for even Mokanna himself to keep up the delusion.'

(*The Northern Liberator*, 14 September 1839)

6. *Chartism and Sabbatarianism*

(During the 1830s, and again in the early 'fifties, great exertions were made to ensure a stricter observance of Sunday. In 1833 Sir Andrew Agnew, head of a Scottish landed family, introduced a bill to outlaw a wide range of Sunday sports and pastimes, to prohibit public lectures or speeches on the Sabbath day, and to forbid the hiring of carriages or the opening of turnpike gates on the same. This failed to pass, despite renewed attempts to carry it on three subsequent occasions in William IV's reign, but much was done on the private initiative of influential magnates like Lord Francis Egerton, who stopped all Sunday travelling between Worsley and Manchester on the Duke of Bridgewater's Canal in 1837. The Lord's Day Observance Society, founded in 1831, kept a vigilant eye on all desecration of the Sabbath. Professor Owen Chadwick has described this as 'a wave' of 'what later in the century was called the Nonconformist conscience'.[1] It seems, however, that the L.D.O.S. was an Anglican body, using clergymen as its recruiting sergeants,[2] though the Wesleyans, who stood nearest to the Church, lent enthusiastic support. As the extract shows, the Chartists opposed it vigorously. This was partly because of the 'strain of social paternalism', which was deemed patronizing, but also because the working classes of the great towns, with their Sunday markets and excursions, were peculiarly vulnerable to restrictive legislation. The Sabbatarians tried to show that, by banning Sunday work and by allied exertions, they were protecting the workers from exploitation. Up to a point this was true, as the popularity with the postmen of Lord Ashley's successful move to stop Sunday deliveries and collections of mail in 1850 clearly shows. Later in the century many working men rallied to the L.D.O.S. for economic reasons, but, except for Lowery, the Chartists remained unconvinced by the argument. They viewed the question as what Dr. Brian Harrison has called a 'culture conflict'. But the clash with Sabbatarianism was not a simple one. William Lovett, the skilled-artisan Chartist, supported the National Sunday League of 1855, dedicated to producing a secularized improvement culture by freeing the museums and art galleries from

[1] *The Victorian Church Part I* (London, 1966), p. 464.
[2] B. Harrison, 'Religion and Recreation in Nineteenth-Century England', *Past and Present*, 1967, No. 38, pp. 98–125.

Sunday closure.[1] The poor of Carlisle, for whom Dr. Taylor spoke, wished merely to defend their traditional way of life against the assaults of a mistrusted puritan *élite*. In this respect, as in others, there was more than one working class.)

'IMPORTANT PUBLIC MEETING AT CARLISLE.
DEFEAT OF THE "SAINTS" AND TRIUMPH OF THE CHARTISTS

On Monday evening last, a public meeting took place in the Coffee House Assembly Room, for the purpose of taking into consideration the best means of promoting a better observance of the Sabbath. Long before the hour announced, the large room (which will hold 1,200 or 1,400 persons) was literally crammed to suffocation. We have attended many missionary and other religious meetings, but never before did we see so immense an assembly congregated, consisting principally of the working classes. They seemed to have assembled *en masse*, for the purpose of putting an extinguisher on the cant and humbug which are generally put forth on such occasions. The priests and their friends appeared to be conscious of their proceedings being upset, for they consulted with each other as to the propriety of dissolving the meeting; however, the Rev. Mr. Fawcett determined on the meeting proceeding, though, from his observations, he clearly anticipated the results which finally took place; and there is no wonder, from the aspects of the assembly, and more especially as he observed some of the leading Chartists present; moreover, near the platform were observed, and almost cheek by jowl with the parsons, Dr. John Taylor, Mr. Cardo (who had been lately arrested in Wales), and George Julian Harney. Their dismay was complete when Dr. Taylor stepped on to the platform, with the Bible and other books of reference under his arm, evidently for the purpose of controversy. Well, the first step was taken, that of choosing a chairman. Mr. Fawcett, barrister, moved that Thomas Henry Grahame, Esq., of Edmond Castle, take the chair; when an amendment was made by Mr. John Armstrong, chairman of the Radical Association, that Mr. W. HALL take the chair, which was instantly carried. The object of the Chartists in having a Radical chairman was, that the resolutions they had to propose might be put.

Mr. W. HALL called upon the meeting to keep good order, and not to interrupt any gentleman who might wish to address them, nor attempt to put anyone down by clamour.

The REV. MR. ROGERS, secretary of the London Association, came

[1] *Ibid.*

forward and addressed the meeting at some length, stating the objects of
the society, and the great good they had achieved with the aid of the
clergy and others in the country. He spoke particularly of the
ironmasters of Wolverhampton, Cornwall, and other places, who had,
previous to the exertions of the Society, employed some thousands of
persons on the Lord's-day, but who had, in a great measure, given up
Sunday work, except that portion which was required for keeping up the
blast furnaces; further, they had achieved much good to the working
classes, in various parts, by having prevailed on their employers to pay
their wages on the Friday evening, in place of the Saturday evening; so
that the poor man was allowed to lay out his eight or ten shillings to
great advantage.[1] (Cries of "We cannot earn more than three shillings".)
Well; he (Mr. R) was sorry for them, but they could not alter these
things. He then told several silly and improbable stories. Two about a
butcher and a bargeman, who had carried on Sunday trading, but who
had declined; and though they suffered severely in the first instance, yet
they finally succeeded in a short time in getting rich. Surely, said Mr. R.,
the hand of God was upon them. He contended that not only did their
temporal happiness depend on keeping the sabbath, but also their eternal
welfare.

Mr. Fawcett, Mr. Ferguson and Mr. Grahame severally addressed the
meeting.

The CHAIRMAN enquired if they had any resolutions to put; and
being answered in the negative—

Mr. J. ARMSTRONG came forward and moved the following
resolution, making some severe strictures on the observations of Mr.
Rogers, which he considered anything but Christian.

That all interference with the consciences of men, either by Government
or societies, is a crime against the liberty of the subject; and that any
attempt to extort funds to support a particular form of worship, or any
attempt to compel the observance of any particular day, is an act of gross
tyranny, inconsistent with the principles of Christianity, and which
ought to be resisted to the utmost.

Carried unanimously.

DR. JOHN TAYLOR then rose, and in a speech of great length,

[1] The payment of wages late on Saturday evening, which remained quite common in
London at mid-century was an anathema to Sabbatarians because it encouraged workmen
to indulge in a late-night drinking spree, the effects of which lingered till Sunday morning.
B. Harrison, 'The Sunday Trading Riots of 1855'. *The Historical Journal*, Vol. VIII,
No. 2, 1965, pp. 219–45.

combated the views of the Rev. gentleman, and showed them to be completely erroneous. He believed Mr. Rogers had become the tool of a party to destroy the happiness of the people; and that he and his party had swindled the people.

As soon as the Doctor had finished, the Sunday observance gentlemen requested the Chairman to endeavour to make a road for them, as they wished to retire. This was readily complied with, after which the following resolution was moved and carried:

That this meeting cannot approve of the conduct, and believe in the honesty of those who have pretended to interest themselves in favour of a stricter observance of the Sabbath for the sake of the poor, because on all occasions they are found opposed to the fondest wishes and best interests of the poor, and have never assisted in any attempt to better their condition, or to regain their lost political rights.
Carried.

MR. CARDO and MR. HARNEY next addressed the meeting; but while the latter was speaking, the Superintendent of Police made his way to the chairman, and intimated that Mr. Gray, the landlord, wished the room to be cleared immediately, which was, in a great measure, complied with ...'

(*The Northern Liberator*, 21 December 1839)

7. *Church Chartism*
(Christian Chartism, an authentic expression of the sentiments of the people, began in Scotland in the spring of 1839, growing out of the idea of 'exclusive dealing against clergymen' who would not support the Charter. At first the Chartists sometimes worshipped in the open air, then they met in halls, and eventually, as in Arbroath and Glasgow, they built or acquired chapels, conducting marriages and baptisms. By the end of 1840 about twenty permanent Chartist congregations had been established in Scotland.[1] The movement spread to England, where churches were founded in Birmingham, Bath and elsewhere, but they sometimes lacked the independence and institutional maturity of their Scottish counterparts. The Birmingham church was largely an offshoot of the Baptists, and Arthur O'Neill conducted the services at West Bromwich in a room lent by one of the ironmasters. Besides being protest movements against orthodox Christian denominations, the Chartist churches were partly an affirmation of the social gospel, which was vigorously preached in them, and partly a bid to clear Chartism of the stigma of infidelity. Feargus O'Connor denounced them as divisive in an open letter to the *Northern Star* on 3 April 1841, but did not succeed

[1] A. Wilson, *The Chartist Movement in Scotland* (Manchester, 1970), pp. 124–5, 142–50.

in eliminating them. The *Chartist Circular*, from which the extracts are drawn, was the main advocate of Christian Chartism in Scotland.)

(a) The Blue Print of the Chartist Church

'Christian Chartist Churches.

As the Institution of Christian Chartist Churches ought to be a subject of deep interest to every man who values pure civil, and religious liberty, the following suggestions, by one of the People's sincere friends, may be advantageous to those engaged in the—

FORMATION AND GOVERNMENT OF CHRISTIAN CHARTIST CHURCHES

"This is the mild religion Jesus taught—
Peace—mercy—love—benevolence to man."
The Weaver's Saturday

In every well organised society it is necessary that equitable rules and wise regulations be framed for its formation and government, and that these shall always be honoured and obeyed by every member of the association, otherwise confusion and anarchy may disturb the order and harmony of the establishment, and finally overthrow it.

In the formation and government of Christian Chartist Churches, it requires mature wisdom and sound judgment to frame wise and useful laws for their government, safety, and happiness; more especially as Chartists are assailed by enemies on every side, who would rejoice to see them and their churches involved in anarchy and ruin. But in order to prevent such unhappy occurrences, and secure them from discord and disunion, we beg to suggest a few rules and regulations for immediate adoption; and although they may be in some cases modified to make them meet the peculiar circumstances of every separate Christian Chartist Church, yet they may nevertheless serve for a general guide, and preserve unity and harmony in all:—

Let every thousand Chartists, more or less, in every district, legally and cordially unite and form a Church, in which they and their families will assemble on Sabbaths, and worship God with good consciences, according to the command of Jesus Christ—unconnected with every other religious sect. All persons, male and female, of mature age, unconvicted of crime, and of sound minds, who subscribe to support the said Church, and no other, and who pay no church-seats elsewhere, and have not given due warning to the Chartist body of their intention to withdraw, shall be considered members, and be eligible to enjoy the privileges, and partake the ordinances, of the Christian Chartist Church in godliness and honesty.

Let all religious, social, and political meetings be held in the said Church, and every Chartist subscriber is to have access to the Sabbath and other meetings held in it, at pleasure; likewise every other person shall be welcome to attend, if he comes with honest intentions, and does not disturb the harmony of the meetings.

Let twenty-four honest intelligent men be chosen half-yearly, by the votes of the majority of all the subscribers, and these twenty-four shall be elders and managers during the term of their election. A chairman, secretary, and treasurer, shall also be chosen from out of the twenty-four, by the majority of all the subscribers, for one half-year only; but one half of the committee may be eligible for re-election, if the majority of the subscribers desire it.

Let an honest, wise, intelligent, temperate, prudent, zealous, and well-educated Chartist, who has been duly trained in religious, literary, political and philosophical societies, and is endued with sound judgment and fluency of language, be elected for their preacher and teacher, by the majority of the whole members, for one half-year only. The said preacher shall regularly preach the Christian Gospel, and legally dispense Christian ordinances every Sabbath; and also, if a teacher, instruct the children on week-days, honestly, without cant, hypocrisy, or superstition, under pain of instant dismissal from all further services in the congregation and school, or for three years at least.

Let no fixed salary be allowed the preacher for his ministerial labours; but the teacher shall be paid weekly, and in advance, for all the children he educates, and also enjoy a free school. Yet, if any or all of the subscribers wish, at any time, to reward their minister, they shall not be restrained from doing so; yet the said reward shall not, on any account, be abstracted from the Church funds, but be voluntarily collected, privately, for that purpose only. Wherever it can be conveniently done, it is desirable, especially in the infancy of the Church, that the offices of preacher and teacher be united in one person. Yet, when this cannot be easily done, they may be chosen separately. But the teacher is always to be able perfectly to teach the children reading, writing, arithmetic, music, political, philological, ethical and philosophical sciences, and soundly instruct them in the honest principles and legal duties of

Chartists, and teach them to become useful members and officials in the Christian Chartist Church. Every Chartist is requested to patronise the Chartist teacher and no other; and (if he has children at school) to pay him a reasonable sum weekly for his educational labours. The teacher may also be re-elected every half-year, or dismissed, as the subscribers shall consider him fit or unfit for his office, and according to his behaviour.

Let a full meeting of all the subscribers, male and female, be held on the last Saturday evening of every month, in the Church, at which meeting the committee shall lay before them an honest statement of all their monthly transactions, especially in pecuniary matters, which shall be approved or disapproved by the whole meeting, from the majority of whose votes there shall be no appeal. The committee shall then receive fresh instructions for their next month's procedure, from the majority of the votes of the meeting. But if, on any occasion, the committee shall fail, peaceably and constitutionally, to comply with the rules of the Church, or shall transact its business on their own responsibility, without the Society's concurrence, the said committee, any or all of them, who shall thus violate these rules, shall be immediately dismissed from office, and be ineligible for re-election for three years. The same penal law shall also be applied to delinquent and refractory preachers, teachers, and all other officials chosen in the Church.

Let no seat-rents be exacted from the sitters and members of the Church,—all are equally free to enjoy the ordinances of God, without any fixed extravagant payment for the same; but it is expected that every person shall leave his voluntary offering in the plate at the church door (under the care and inspection of four members of committee) every Sabbath day, and all collections shall be lodged in a secure bank every Monday by the treasurer, secretary and chairman (in name of the Church), and no part thereof shall on any account be withdrawn by any person or persons, except legally, and to defray the necessary expenses of the Church, and only by the command of the majority of the whole subscribers, as voted at their last monthly meeting, (and not otherwise, under penalty of fraud and felony). A proper precentor and beadle may also be chosen by the majority of the subscribers every half-year, and shall be liable to a three years' dismissal at any time for improper conduct, the same as the preacher, the committee, and other officials, if they displease the majority of the subscribers; but may be re-elected if the subscribers shall consider them worthy.

It would be desirable that literary, political, and philosophical associations, with good libraries, be connected with every Christian Chartist Church and School wherever they can be formed with ease, utility, and harmony.

Let all disputes be amicably settled by the congregational majority every monthly meeting; the minority, in every instance, to submit to the legalized majority, and be in obedience to the Society's rules.

Every monthly transaction to be honestly exposed, and freely discussed, approved, or disapproved, without malice, envy, or strife, but with kindness and affection, by all. No clique, subtlety, no hole-and-corner darkness, no secret coteries, shall be allowed, under pain of a three years' dismissal from office, and ineligibility for re-election during that time.

Let Christian Socialism, founded on brotherly love and Chartist unity, be encouraged, taught, and practised by the members of each and every Christian Chartist Church; let peace, liberty, knowledge, and equality cover the whole earth; let universal harmony and happiness be diffused in every society, enjoyed in every family,—and may God bless and prosper "THE CHRISTIAN CHARTIST CHURCH".'
(*The Chartist Circular*, 17 October 1840)

(b) The Scottish Churches and their Raison D'Etre

'Chartist Churches.

THE CHRISTIAN EDUCATION OF THE PEOPLE.

In every district there ought to be a Chartist Church planted for the benefit of Chartist families. It may be a private house, a school, or a public hall, rented by an association, for public meetings, education, and religious worship; and every Sabbath day the gospel should be preached in it by a religious, honest missionary, chosen by the Chartists. The duty may be executed in rotation by any members of the body who bear an irreproachable character, and are capable of performing it.

It is also necessary that baptism and marriage should be regularly dispensed by Chartist missionaries, and likewise the ordinance of the Lord's Supper, otherwise the parish and voluntary clergymen will keep a tenacious hold of Chartist families, if they are obliged to apply to them for any of these benefits, and will leave no means untried to draw the wanderers (as they shall call them) back to the God they have left. Hypocrisy and cunning of every description may in some cases be also practised by the wolves in sheep's clothing, to wile the Chartist flock back to the church. But in planting Chartist churches and schools for the people, it is necessary to examine the matter well, and resolutely to persevere in it, for the sake of the good cause, after having begun it. "He that puts his hand to the plough, and looks back, is not fit for the kingdom of God."

A marriage, according to the law of Scotland, is obligatory on the contracting parties, if it be performed in the presence of two honest witnesses, or if a free man and woman, in the presence of two veritable witnesses, acknowledge each other to be lawful husband and wife. It will be necessary that Chartist marriages be performed in a legal manner, and that a record be kept of them by the missionary and witnesses, as a reference, in case of disputes. These marriages will be perfectly binding on the contracting parties, and acknowledged by the law of the land, and recognized by the Church of Scotland, if the parties pay only a small fine to the kirk session for the poor of the parish. But so long as the married parties do not need to ask any privileges from any other sect than Chartist churches, they are under no obligation to pay fines to the establishment; and as for the voluntaries, until their clergymen declare themselves Chartists, the less you trouble them the better. Baptism is as sacred when performed by a Chartist missionary as by any clergyman in the kingdom. The holy sacrament of the Lord's Supper is also as sacred when dispensed by a lay preacher as by a bishop; and by you partaking of it in a Chartist church, you will commemorate the death of Christ as religiously, (if you do it with a Christian spirit) as if you were to take the symbols from the hands of the most Reverend Doctor of the land. This was the practice of the Primitive Christians.

If Chartist churches and schools were thus established in every district, voluntary clergymen would soon be obliged to declare their political opinion, and join the Chartist cause, to prevent starvation. Some of them, perhaps, might be mean enough even to agitate the expediency of petitioning parliament for endowments; for there is nothing, in my opinion, too inconsistent for a selfish truckling Whig to do. But let the people only mind themselves, and commence the good work in every district immediately. In many localities you have already begun Chartist churches, and even Chartist schools are not now an anomaly. They are also begun, and may God prosper his own work, and raise up Chartist Whitefields and Wesleys in His church, and Cockers, Ruddimans, and Lancasters, in his schools, until knowledge shall cover the whole earth

as the waters cover the channel of the great sea; and then the barren
places will sing, and the wilderness blossom as the rose; liberty will
flourish; and the gates of hell will not be able to prevail against us.'
(*The Chartist Circular*, 28 March 1840)

8. *Other Chartist Religious Observances*

(The motives underlying 'Church Chartism' also prompted other
attempts, which did not incur the censure of O'Connor, to impart a
Christian flavour to Chartist activities. In Leicestershire, where the
Baptists were strong, and some Chartist leaders had links with the
Primitive Methodists, Thomas Cooper commissioned two sympathetic
poets, John Bramwich and William Jones, to write Chartist hymns, with
which the public meetings of the local movement were enlivened. His
disciple Jonathan Bairstow conducted a memorial service at Derby for a
deceased follower, and camp meetings on the model of the Primitive
Methodists were a popular device for summoning large gatherings away
from the crowded town centres.)

(a) A Chartist Funeral Service at Derby

'It having been announced by hand Bills distributed through the
Town that Mr. Barstow would preach a Funeral Sermon upon the Death
of John Clayton a Chartist, who had died whilst incarcerated in
Northallerton Goal (sic), about ½ past Ten the leading Chartists
accompanied him into the centre of the Market Place where a chair
being placed he was speedily surrounded by about 3 or 400 principally
working men with not a few women, the time selected being just when
all the public houses are closed for Divine Service. The preacher on
ascending the chair first requested his audience to make no signs of
approbation or disapprobation but to listen in order and silence to his
address.

The preacher then gave out 2 verses from Watts' hymn Book, psalm
the 90, "Praise the Lord from whom all Blessings flow etc.". This ended
he put up an extempore prayer. The Burthen of the supplication
contained in which, was to pray for the assistance of the almighty in
bringing about the adoption of the principals (sic) of Chartism and the
removal of all Tyrants and persecutors of Chartists, calling upon
almighty God to bear witness to the Sufferings and deprivations of the
poor which the preacher attributed to the Bad government of our rulers
or as he designated them Tyrants. The preacher concluded a prayer of
Considerable length by calling upon our Lord Jesus Christ to intercede
for the liberation of all persecuted Chartists, instancing the sufferings of

the Lord's faithful departed servant John Clayton whose death had been accelerated by the persecution of our unjust rulers while he was endeavouring to bring about that, (as he the preacher expressed it) only cure for all the evils under which we are labouring, the people's Charter, which the preacher averred was moulded entirely agreeably to the rules laid down by our Savior (sic) himself while on Earth and given to us in his Book the New Testament. The preacher then selected for his Text the following portion of the 6th verse of the 19th Chapter of St. John— "When the Chief Priests therefore and Officers saw him they cried out saying, Crucify him, Crucify him".

The preacher commenced by describing our Saviour as a great reformer in religion and that in consequence of his being so he met with great persecution while on Earth ending in his crucifixion by the Chief priest[s] of that day, whom the preacher described as having become so corrupt and so debased that they lost sight of all the Best practices of their religion, looking only to profit, persecuting the poor, turning the house of God into a Den of Thieves, so much so that our Saviour found it necessary to take upon himself manhood for the purpose of eradicating those numerous corruptions which the Scribes and pharisees of that day had suffered to enter their practice of religion and which indeed had rendered that religion subservient only to their secular profit. To such an extent was it carried that our Saviour during his Earthly career found it necessary to overturn the Tables of the Money changers even in the Temple itself. The preacher then proceeded to contrast the practice of religion in the present day with that which he had described as existing amongst the Jews when our Saviour came on Earth amongst them as a great reformer of religion; drawing a conclusion from all this that the professors of religion in this day were equally Bad and corrupt with the Scribes and pharisees of that day, denouncing as Hypocrites all Bishops, Priests, Wesleyans and in fact all professors, ascribing to them persecution of the poor whose only object was to wring from the hard earnings of the poor as much as they could, describing the established Church as wringing annually from the people 1 million of money in order that its prelates and priests might live in sumptuous Palaces and fatten in the land, the only cure for which was as he averred the people's Charter. The preacher then went on to shew that all great reformers of abuses in all ages whether political or religious had uniformly met with persecution and cruelty from the Tyrant rulers of their Several times, pointing out Socrates, Cicero and Demosthenes as examples of his assertions. The preacher then proceeded by Scripture references to shew that our Saviour was himself poor and the Friend of the poor and that he uniformly denounced riches and advocated equality in all things, enforcing these principals (sic) continually, both by precept and example. The preacher continued at Great length in much the same strain, the general tendency of his observations having for their object the description of the evils under which he averred the poor were made to suffer by their unjust rulers, whom he frequently styled Tyrants, always concluding every long catalogue of evils, by pointing out what he asserted was the only cure for all evils whether political or religious, the people's Charter, concluding a lengthened address by warning our rulers to concede in time the Charter which he asserted the people would have, asserting in emphatic language that the lion of popular opinion already nashed (sic) its Teeth and whisked its Tail and unless these concessions were made in time its rage could not much longer be enchained and that should it be driven to take vengence on its oppressors, the dreadful effects of such a step were awful to contemplate. The preacher then called upon his hearers to make a collection to enable the Widow of the deceased John Clayton to have the last sad consolation of Burying her husband and removing his remains from the prison where he died.

The service concluded by a prayer in much the same strain as at the commencement and the singing of 2 more verses from Watts' hymn. The meeting then separated.

Amt. of collection 1.15.8¼'

(Report obtained by the magistrates. Ms. Volume, 'The Chartist Movement in Derby, 1841: Original Correspondence'. Derby Public Library)

(b) Chartist Camp Meetings

'ROCHDALE

SUNDAY—There have been three camp meetings on Cronkeyshaw today, at ten o'clock in the morning, half-past two in the afternoon, and six in the evening. The morning service commenced by singing a chartist hymn, to the tune of the old hundredth psalm. The nature of the hymn may be known by the two following lines, referring to the aristocracy, which formed a part of it—

"They call the earth and land their own,
And all they give us back's a stone."

The chairman, James Mills, of Whitworth, opened the business of the day, by stating, that every chapter in the Bible breathed nothing but freedom and liberty; while the paid expounders of it—the state priesthood—had been the greatest supporters of tyranny and oppression, in all ages of the world. They were the blind leading the blind, and a type of the very men that called out, "Away with him! away with him!" While the next speaker (Joseph Wood) was addressing the meeting, a respectable looking woman, nearly sixty years of age, dressed as a methodist, or one of the society of friends, was handed into the waggon. She sat down, put on her spectacles, and began to peruse a small Testament which she held in her hand. When Wood had concluded, she rose up, pulled off her bonnet, and read from Saint Luke's gospel the parable of the great supper—"But when thou makest a feast (Luke XIV, 13), call the poor, the maimed, the lame, the blind; and thou shall (sic) be blessed; for they cannot recompense thee". After commenting on this text, she informed the meeting she was a native of Oldham, and had seen the person who had fired the blunder-buss from the factory at Oldham upon the people, fetch garbage from her swill tub to satisfy the cravings of hunger. She concluded by exhorting the multitude to stand firm like the Israelites of old, and drive Pharaoh and his host into the red sea. After a short prayer, the meeting was dismissed.—By far the most important gathering was in the evening, when there were 8,000 or 9,000 persons present. The charter had been the theme of most of the speakers during the evening, and every thing was to be merged in that great question.'

(*The Halifax Guardian*, 20 August 1842)

Further Reading

To include in this book a full bibliography of works on Chartism would be unnecessary, as J. F. C. Harrison's and Dorothy Thompson's *Bibliography of the Chartist Movement 1837–1976* (Hassocks, 1978) is available; to append a representative bibliography of the social context of the movement would be impossible. The following are merely suggestions for further reading, mainly in secondary sources, on topics related to the documents.

THE CHARTIST MOVEMENT
The most recent narrative of the movement is J. T. Ward, *Chartism* (London, 1973), but M. Hovell, *The Chartist Movement* (3rd edition, Manchester, 1966, with a Bibliographical Introduction by W. H. Chaloner) remains a classic.

The latest revisions are in article form, of which the more important include: J. A. Epstein, 'Feargus O'Connor and the Northern Star' (*International Review of Social History*, Vol. XXI, 1976, pp. 51–97); Kenneth Judge, 'Early Chartist Organization and the Convention of 1839' (*Ibid.*, XX, 1975, pp. 370–97); T. M. Kemnitz and Fleurange Jacques, 'J. R. Stephens and the Chartist Movement' (*Ibid.*, XIX, 1974, pp. 211–27); C. Godfrey, 'The Chartist Prisoners, 1839–41' (*Ibid.*, XXIV, 1979, Pt. II, pp. 189–236); D. J. Rowe's 'The London Working Men's Association and the People's Charter' (*Past and Present*, No. 36, 1967, pp. 73–86) and his exchange with I. J. Prothero (*Ibid.*, No. 38, 1967, pp. 169–76).

General assessments of the movement are by Asa Briggs, *Chartist Studies* (London, 1959), Chaps. I and IX; David Jones, *Chartism and the Chartists* (London, 1975); F. C. Mather, *Chartism* (Historical Association G. Pamphlet, No. 61, repr. 1972, with extended postscript);

Dorothy Thompson, *The Early Chartists* (Macmillan History in Depth Series, London and Basingstoke, 1971).

R. G. Gammage's *History of the Chartist Movement* (repr. London, 1969) is the most complete of the contemporary accounts, which also include the autobiographies of Thomas Cooper, William Lovett and Thomas Frost.

CHARTISM AND THE CONSTITUTION

The political tradition from which Chartism sprang has been explored in John Cannon, *Parliamentary Reform, 1640–1832* (Cambridge, 1973); J. W. Derry, *The Radical Tradition: Tom Paine to Lloyd George* (London 1967); E. P. Thompson, *The Making of the English Working Class* (Harmondsworth, 1968). A. Goodwin, *The Friends of Liberty* (London, 1979) is an important new study of the formative period of English radicalism during the French Revolution.

Not less important for interpreting the tradition are certain mono-graphs and articles, notably Patricia Hollis, *The Pauper Press: A Study in Working-Class Radicalism of the 1830s* (Oxford, 1970); T. M. Parssinen, 'Association, convention and anti-parliament in British radical politics, 1771–1848.' (*The English Historical Review*, Vol. LXXXVIII, July 1973, pp. 504–33); A. Plummer, *Bronterre: A Political Biography of Bronterre O'Brien 1804–1864* (London, 1971); I. Prothero, 'William Benbow and the Concept of the "General Strike" ' (*Past and Present*, No. 63, 1974, pp. 132–71); Caroline Robbins, *The Eighteenth-Century Commonwealthman* (Cambridge, Mass., 1959); D. J. Rowe, 'Class and Political Radicalism in London, 1831–32' (*The Historical Journal*, Vol. XIII, 1970, pp. 31–47); G. Rudé, *The Crowd in History, 1730–1848* (New York etc., 1964); E. P. Thompson, 'The Moral Economy of the English Crowd in the Eighteenth Century' (*Past and Present*, No. 50, 1971, pp. 76–136).

The best study of English electoral politics in Chartist times is Norman Gash, *Politics in the Age of Peel* (London etc., 1953). John Prest, *Politics in the Age of Cobden* (London, 1977) is focused on the registration of electors, while E. P. Hennock, *Fit and Proper Persons* (London, 1973) provides the context of Chartist attempts to enter local government. Administrative changes which incensed the Chartists are examined in N. C. Edsall, *The Anti-Poor Law Movement* (Manchester, 1971) and in R. D. Storch, 'The Plague of the Blue Locusts. Police Reform and Popular Resistance in Northern England, 1840–57' (*International Review of Social History*, Vol. XX, 1975, pp. 61–90), which should be read in conjunction with other works listed under 'Law and Order'. English republicanism is surveyed by N. J. Gossman in 'Republicanism in Nineteenth-Century England' (*Ibid.*, Vol. VII, 1962, pp. 47–60).

CHARTISM AND SOCIAL REFORM

For the ideological taproots of the Socialist component in Chartism, see especially G. D. H. Cole, *History of Socialist Thought: Vol. I. The Forerunners, 1789–1850* (London, 1953); also H. L. Beales, *The Early English Socialists* (London, 1933); Max Beer, *A History of British Socialism* (repr. London, 1953); E. Lowenthal, *The Ricardian Socialists* (New York, 1911); T. M. Parssinen, 'Thomas Spence and the Origins of English Land Nationalization' (*Journal of the History of Ideas*, Vol. XXXIV, 1973, pp. 135–41); also works on Robert Owen listed under 'Chartism and the Labour Movement'. Patricia Hollis, *The Pauper Press* (see above) has a clear treatment of this theme.

Chartist Socialism itself may be studied in biographies: Alfred Plummer, *Bronterre* (see above); John Saville, *Ernest Jones: Chartist* (London, 1952); A. R. Schoyen, *The Chartist Challenge. A Portrait of George Julian Harney* (London etc., 1958). In an older school T. A. Rothstein, *From Chartism to Labourism* (London, 1929) remains useful.

The best studies of the Land Plan are Joy MacAskill's in Asa Briggs ed. *Chartist Studies* (see above) and A. M. Hadfield, *The Chartist Land Company* (Newton Abbot, 1970).

Social reforms generally are treated in D. Roberts, *Victorian Origins of the British Welfare State* (New Haven, 1960) and in Ursula Henriques, *Before the Welfare State* (London, 1979); factories and short-time movement in J. T. Ward, *The Factory Movement 1830–1855* (London, 1962); poor-law administration after 1834 in D. Fraser ed., *The New Poor Law in the Nineteenth Century* (London, 1976) and S. E. Finer, *The Life and Times of Sir Edwin Chadwick* (London, 1952), which also deals with public-health reform. S. D. Chapman, *The History of Working-Class Housing: A Symposium*, (Newton Abbot, 1971) surveys housing conditions. Keith Evans, *The Development and Structure of the English Educational System* (London, 1975) provides the essentials on educational reform, while J. F. C. Harrison, *Learning and Living 1770–1960: A Study in the History of the English Adult Education Movement* (London, 1961) is relevant to the self-taught culture of the artisans. W. Lovett and J. Collins, *Chartism: A New Organization of the People*, with an introduction by Asa Briggs (Leicester, 1969), a contemporary treatise, should be read by all.

An authoritative study of the temperance movement is Brian Harrison's *Drink and the Victorians* (London, 1971); his 'Teetotal Chartism' (*History*, Vol. LVIII, June 1973, pp. 193–217) is related to the present theme.

Among recent contributions to women's history the following are useful: R. J. Evans, *The Feminists. Women's Emancipation Movements in Europe, America and Australasia* (London, 1977); Dorothy Thompson, 'Women and Nineteenth-Century Radical Politics: A Last Dimension' in J. Mitchell and A. Oakley ed., *The Rights and Wrongs of Women* (Harmondsworth, 1976).

CHARTISM AND EXTERNAL AFFAIRS

H. Weisser, *British Working-Class Movements and Europe, 1815–48* (Manchester 1975) is a recent general survey. It should be supplemented by J. H. Gleason, *The Genesis of Russophobia in Great Britain* (London etc., 1950) and by the above-mentioned biographies of Harney and Ernest Jones. See also H. Collins and C. Abramsky, *Karl Marx and the British Labour Movement* (London, 1965) and A. Müller-Lehning, 'The International Association, 1855–59' (*International Review for Social History*, Vol. III, 1938, pp. 185–286).

The *Life and Struggles of William Lovett* (London, 1920 edn.) is the best source for the international interests of the moral-force Chartists.

The Irish connections of the Chartists are examined in D. Read and E. Glasgow, *Feargus O'Connor. Irishman and Chartist* (London, 1961), in Rachel O'Higgins, 'The Irish Influence in the Chartist Movement' (*Past and Present*, No. 20, November 1961, pp. 83–96), and in J. H. Treble, 'O'Connor, O'Connell and Attitudes of Irish Immigrants towards Chartism in the North of England' in J. Butt and I. F. Clarke, *The Victorians and Social Protest* (Newton Abbot, 1973).

For the background of the British India Society see E. Stokes, *The English Utilitarians and India* (Oxford, 1959). Attitudes towards empire in mid-nineteenth century Britain are surveyed in C. A. Bodelsen, *Studies in Mid-Victorian Imperialism* (2nd ed., London, 1960), but see also R. Robinson and J. Gallagher, 'The Imperialism of Free Trade' (*The Economic History Review*, 2. Ser., Vol. VI, 1953–54, pp. 1–15) for the seeds of a new approach.

LAW AND ORDER

A few studies of Chartist risings and physical-force potential exist. They include David Goodway's evocative Conference paper on

'Chartism in London' (*Labour History Society Bulletin*, No. 20, Spring 1970, pp. 13–15), F. C. Mather, 'The General Strike of 1842' in R. Quinault and J. Stevenson ed., *Popular Protest and Public Order* (London, 1974); W. H. Maehl, 'Chartist Disturbances in North-Eastern England' (*International Review of Social History*, Vol. VIII, 1963, pp. 389–414); A. Peacock, *Bradford Chartism, 1838–40* (University of York Borthwick Papers, No. 36, 1969), which has wide implications for the Newport rising; D. J. Rowe, 'Some Aspects of Chartism on Tyneside' (*International Review of Social History*, Vol. XVI, 1971, pp. 17–39); T. Tholfsen, 'The Chartist Crisis in Birmingham' (*Ibid.*, III, 1958, pp. 461–80); David Williams', *John Frost: A Study in Chartism* (Cardiff, 1939), supplemented by his 'Chartism in Wales' in Asa Briggs ed., *Chartist Studies* (see above).

The evolution of the state's machinery for controlling disturbances has been explored more systematically in its own right. General approaches are: F. C. Mather, *Public Order in the Age of the Chartists* (Manchester, 1959); L. Radzinowicz's *A History of English Criminal Law and its Administration from 1750*, especially Vol. IV, *Grappling for Control* (London, 1968), and his 'New Departures in Maintaining Public Order in the face of Chartist Disturbances' (*Cambridge Law Journal*, April 1960, pp. 51–80); R. Quinault, 'The Warwickshire County Magistracy and Public Order, c.1830–70' in Quinault and Stevenson ed., *Popular Protest* (see above), is a useful study of the magistrates. There are many relevant histories of police, notably T. A. Critchley, *A History of Police in England and Wales 900–1966* (London, 1967), and C. Reith, *British Police and the Democratic Ideal* (London, 1943). G. Harries-Jenkins, *The Army in Victorian Society* (London, 1977) reflects on the role of the military in the maintenance of public order.

CHARTISM AND SOCIAL CLASS

The most useful account of the social composition of the movement is in David Jones, *Chartism and the Chartists* (London, 1975). Local studies amplify the picture, e.g. A. V. John, 'The Chartist endurance: Industrial South Wales, 1840–68' (*Morgannwg: The Journal of Glamorgan History*, Vol. XV, 1971, pp. 23–49); I. Prothero, 'Chartism in London' (*Past and Present*, No. 44, 1969, pp. 76–105), as well as the studies by Rowe, of Tyneside, and by Peacock, of Bradford, mentioned above, and the contributions to Asa Briggs' *Chartist Studies*. Much valuable background information about lesser Chartists is embodied in J.

M. Bellamy and J. Saville, *Dictionary of Labour Biography*, 4 Vols., (London etc., 1972–77).

Class and class conflict have been discussed by historians, writing from different viewpoints. The following bear on Chartism and its background: Asa Briggs, 'The Language of Class in Early Nineteenth-Century England' in A. Briggs and J. Saville ed., *Essays in Labour History, in Memory of G. D. H. Cole* (London, 1960), also Briggs, *Chartist Studies*, Chap. IX; G. D. H. Cole, *Studies in Class Structure* (London, 1955); J. Foster's *Class Struggle and the Industrial Revolution* (London, 1974) and also his 'Discussion' with A. E. Musson, 'Class Struggle and the labour Aristocracy, 1830–60' (*Social History*, 3 October 1976); E. J. Hobsbawm, 'The Labour Aristocracy in Nineteenth-century Britain', in his *Labouring Men* (London, 1965); R. S. Neale, 'Class and Class-Consciousness in Early Nineteenth-Century England: Three Classes or Five' (*Victorian Studies*, Vol. XII, No. 1, September 1968, pp. 4–32); H. Perkin, *The Origins of Modern English Society 1780–1880* (London, 1969); I. Prothero, 'Chartism in London' (see above); D. J. Rowe, 'The London Working Men's Association etc.' (see above); R. N. Soffner, 'Attitudes and Allegiances in the Unskilled North 1830–1850' (*International Review of Social History*, Vol. X, 1965, pp. 429–54); T. R. Tholfsen, *Working Class Radicalism in Mid-Victorian England* (London, 1976); E. P. Thompson, *The Making etc.* (see above); A. Tyrrell, 'Class Consciousness in Early Victorian Britain: Samuel Smiles, Leeds Politics and the Self Help Creed' (*Journal of British Studies*, Vol. IX, May 1970, pp. 102–25).

CHARTISM AND CONTEMPORARY POLITICAL MOVEMENTS AND PARTIES

D. E. D. Beales, *The Political Parties of Nineteenth-Century Britain* (Historical Association Appreciations in History Series, No. 2, 1971) is a good, brief introduction to modern views of the development of the party system. For the principal parties see Norman Gash and others, *The Conservatives. A History from their Origins to 1965* (London 1977) and Donald Southgate, *The Passing of the Whigs, 1832–1886* (London etc., 1962). S. Maccoby, *English Radicalism, 1832–52* (London, 1935) is a useful reference book, but readers in search of guidance through the meshes of non-Chartist Radicalism will turn to the chapters by Alexander Wilson on 'The Suffrage Movement' and by D. M. Thompson on 'The Liberation Society' in Patricia Hollis ed., *Pressure from Without in Early Victorian England* (London, 1974). N. McCord,

The Anti-Corn Law League 1838–1846 (London 1958) is the standard work on its theme, but W. H. Chaloner's essay, 'The Agitation against the Corn Laws' in J. T. Ward ed., *Popular Movements c.1830–1850* (London, 1970) is an important contribution. So also is Donald Read, *Cobden and Bright: A Victorian Political Partnership* (London, 1967), which ranges over all aspects of radicalism. Lucy Brown, 'The Chartists And The Anti-Corn Law League' in A. Briggs ed., *Chartist Studies* (see above), is a seminal link study. B. Harrison and P. Hollis, 'Chartism, Liberalism and the Life of Robert Lowery' (*The English Historical Review*, Vol. LXXXII, July 1967, pp. 503–35) raises the question of Chartism's relationship to the emerging Liberal party of Mr. Gladstone.

CHARTISM AND THE LABOUR MOVEMENT

For this period G. D. H. Cole, *A Short History of the British Working Class Movement 1789–1847* (rev. London, 1948) remains the best history of labour movements as a whole, and the same writer's *A Century of Co-operation* (London, 1944) has not been superseded. Much has been learned, however, about the history of trade-unionism, and the most useful surveys are A. E. Musson, *Trade Union and Social History* (London, 1974) and H. Pelling, *A History of British Trade Unionism* (Harmondsworth, 1963). A different emphasis regarding the political interests of the unions appears in R. Challinor and B. Ripley, *The Miners' Association in the Age of the Chartists* (London, 1968) and in I. J. Prothero, 'London Chartism and the Trades' (*Economic History Review*, 2 ser., Vol. XXIV, 1971, pp. 202–19). The perspective of labour history during this period has been changed by a revised assessment of the role of Robert Owen. On this see J. F. C. Harrison, *Robert Owen and the Owenites in Britain and America* (London, 1969); S. Pollard and J. Salt ed., *Robert Owen: Prophet of the Poor* (London 1971); W. H. Oliver's 'Robert Owen and the English Working-Class Movements' (*History Today*, Vol. VIII, 1958, pp. 787–96) and his 'The Consolidated Trades Union of '34' (*Economic History Review*, 2 ser., Vol. XVII, 1964–65, pp. 77–95).

CHARTISM AND THE CHURCHES

H. U. Faulkner, *Chartism and the Churches* (repr. London, 1970) is a pioneer study. It should be read in the light of important recent contributions to the social history of religion. These include A. D. Gilbert, *Religion and Society in Industrial England* (London etc., 1976), a path-making book; K. S. Inglis, *Churches and the Working Classes in*

Victorian England (London, 1963); E. R. Norman, *Church and Society in England 1770–1970* (Oxford 1976); R. A. Soloway, *Prelates and People* (London, 1969). J. D. Gay, *The Geography of Religion in England* (London, 1971) and R. Currie, A. Gilbert and L. Horsley, *Churches and Churchgoers* (Oxford, 1977) are useful works of reference. E. Hobsbawm, 'Methodism and the threat of Revolution in Britain' in *Labouring Men* (London, 1965) opens a controversy on which much has since been written. A recent study of the political involvements of the Christian denominations is G. I. T. Machin's *Politics and the Churches in Great Britain 1832 to 1868* (Oxford, 1977). P. N. Backstrom, *Christian Socialism and Co-operation in Victorian England* (London, 1974) touches on Chartism's relations with the Christian Socialists; Edward Royle, *Victorian Infidels* (Manchester, 1974) on its affinities with rationalists. Owen Chadwick's *The Victorian Church Part I* (London, 1966) is the best general history of English Christianity during the Chartist period.

INDEX

312   CHARTISM AND SOCIETY

Bolton, 16, 161, 182, 190, 201, 202, 206, 211, 212, 274, 275–6
Bolton Free Press, 199–202
Bolton Reform Association, 207–9, 211–12
Bolton Working Men's Association, 212, 214
Boot and Shoemakers, the Friendly Institution of, 243
Booth, Dr. (Birmingham magistrate), 150–2
Bottomley, Samuel, 141, 145
Bowden, The Rev. Mr., 275
Bowers, (of Dukinfield), 143, 144
Bowring, Dr. John, M.P., 129, 232
Bradford, 42, 110, 157–9, 175
Bramwich, John, 299
Brandt, (barrister), 56
Bridport, 222
Briggs, Lord, 29, 45
Bright, John, 109–10, 137, 223–4
Bright, P. C., 140
Brighton, 55
British and Foreign Anti-Slavery Society, 135
British Co-operative Movement, 266
British Critic, 277–80
Broadbent, William, 141
Brooks, John, 136, 218
Brotherton, Joseph, M.P., 135–6
Brougham and Vaux, Baron, 105, 201
Buchanan, ?Robert, 69
Bull, The Rev. George Stringer, 280
Bunbury, Maj. Gen. Sir Henry Edward, 146–50
Bunting, The Rev. Jabez, 285
Buonarroti, Filippo, 92
Burgh, James, 48
Burn, W. L., 29
Burnett, Bishop Gilbert, 63
Burnley, 158
Burns, W. G., 66
Bury, 18, 62, 182, 183, 201, 276, 288
Bussey, Peter, 37
Bute, 2nd Marquess of, 76
Bythell, Dr. Duncan, 18

Campbell, ?Alexander, 69
Campbell, John, 250; ?136
Campbell, Sir John, 51
Canada, 41, 149
Cardiff, 178–80
Cardo, William, 66, 120–6, 291–3
Cargill, William, 120
Carlile, Richard, 40, 271, 274, 276
Carlisle, 61, 291–3
Carmarthen Working Men's Association, 31
Carpenter, William, 62, 89, 130
Cartwright, Major John, 21, 44, 48, 63, 66
Castlereagh, Viscount, (2nd Marquis of Londonderry), 58, 219n
Central Co-operative Agency, 266
Centralization, 26, 58–9, 83–5
Chadwick, Professor W. O., 290
Chadwick, (of Ashton), 145
Chance, (Birmingham magistrate), 151
Chappell-Smith, Mrs, (née Reynolds), 269
Charles I, King of England, 155
Charles Albert, King of Piedmont-Sardinia, 132–3
Charter, People's, 10, 12, 21, 34, 43, 47–8, 91, 106, 116, 121, 126, 195, 207, 208, 212–3, 221, 222, 224, 235–9, 242, 247, 248, 252, 283–4, 299–301; six points of, 9, 10, 22, 132, 224, 241–3, 251, 254, 284;

supposed antiquity of, 21, 44, 47–8, 53–4; see also Universal suffrage
Charter, 57, 89, 194, 199–202
Chartism: A New Organization of the People, 42
Chartist, 83, 194
Chartist Circular, 23, 263
Chartist Co-operative Land Society, 110
Chartist Co-operative Stores, 263–5
Chartist meetings: contentious subjects barred, 115
Chatham, 187
Child, Henry, 169
Christian Chartism, 11, 42, 247; Chartist Camp Meetings, 40; Chartist Churches, 40, 293–9; Chartist funerals 40, 299–301; Chartist hymns, 116, 299, 301
Christian Observer, 280–2
Christian Socialists, 265, 282–4
Church of England, 36, 40–1, 181, 221, 223, 271–84, 301–2
Church of Scotland, 298
Church, Chartist demonstrations at, 41, 274–7, 280–2, 289–90
Circassians, 119, 124, 125
Clarendon, 4th Earl of, 134
Clark, P., 251
Clark, Thomas, 231–5
Classical Economists, 39, 44, 89, 95
Clay, (Manchester carpenter), 243
Cleave, John, 48
Clisset, Isaac, 83
Cobbett, R. B. B., 153–6
Cobbett, William, 35, 63, 105, 137, 153
Cobden, Richard, 42, 137, 218–9, 227
Cochrane, Charles, 232
Cocker, Edward, 298
Coke, Sir Edward (Lord), 53, 63
Colchester, 226
Cole, G. D. H., 29, 35–6, 253
Collins, John, 31, 34, 42, 43, 66, 76, 106, 121–6, 222
Colne, 25
Colonies, 137
Combination Laws, 244
Communist League, 131
Communist Manifesto, 131
Complete Suffrage Movement, 12, 31, 41, 68–9, 91, 221–5
Condorcet, Marquis de, 43
Conspiracy, Chartist, 37–8, 140–6, 167–9
Constantine, Joseph, 141–4
Connor, ?Charles, 218
Conventions, Chartist, 9,
  1839—10, 10–11, 25, 28, 38, 56, 57–62, 63–7, 72–5, 96–9, 114, 120, 139, 179, 184, 207, 246, 263, 277
  1841—215
  1846—79–80
  1848—14, 187
  1851—93–4, 103, 274
Cooke, The Rev. Mr., (Barnsley magistrate), 153
Cooper, Thomas, 37, 68–9, 129, 130, 219, 286, 299
Cornwall, 292
Co-operative Movement, 263–8
Corn Laws and Free Trade, 16, 39, 41, 43, 111–2, 114, 131–2, 194–5, 196, 199, 202, 207, 208, 211, 212, 227–31; Anti-Corn Law League, 40, 77, 121, 188, 211, 214–19, 221, 229; see also Manchester Operative Anti-Corn Law Association
Corresponding societies, 176, 246
Cottam, (of Ashton), 145
Cotton Spinners, Friendly Society of, 241

318   CHARTISM AND SOCIETY

Stamp duty on newspapers, 9, 42, 87, 177–80
Stanley, Lord (later 14th Earl of Derby), 58, 233
Stansfeld, J. 130
Stephens, The Rev. Joseph Rayner, 10, 11, 20, 25, 28, 37,
     55–7, 63, 96, 98, 172, 184, 199, 209, 222, 286, 288
Sterndale, (Ashton Chartist), 143, 144
Stevenson, Dr. John, 150
Stewart, Dr. Gilbert, 63
Stockport, 14, 18, 26, 34, 110, 172–3, 189, 190, 191, 288
Stott, Benjamin, 244, 252
Stott, James, 142, 143
Straddling, (Halifax Chartist), 83
Sturge, Joseph, 221–4, 236
Suffolk, 146
Sunday Observance, 290–3
Sunday schools, 97
Sunderland, 61, 184, 185
Surrey, 26, 232
Sutton-in-Ashfield, 61
Swedenborgians, 286

Talleyrand-Perigord, C. M. de, Prince of Benevento, 122,
     282
Tariffs and trade, 120
Taylor, James, 142
Taylor, Dr. John, 37, 60–1, 62, 74, 139–40, 181, 291–3
Taylor, Joseph, 141
Taylor, P. A., 130
Taylor, P. A., jun., 130, 236
Taylor, R., 130
Taylor, William, 239
Tear, John, 252
Teetotal Chartism, 11, 67, 99, 247
Temperance, 40–1, 42, 45, 99–102, 112, 185, 292 & n.1
Ten Hours Bill, 9, 28, 113, 189, 211, 271
Thiers, Adolphe, 123
Tholfsen, Dr. Trygve, 28, 29, 40, 42
Thomason, (Foreign Policy Chartist), 125, 126
Thomasson, Thomas, 207–9, 212
Thompson, Mrs. Dorothy, 30
Thompson, Mr. E. P., 21, 29–30, 140, 284
Thompson, (Bradford magistrate), 158
Thompson, George, 135, 232
Thompson, Colonel Thomas Perronet, M.P., 48, 77, 232
Thompson, William, 91, 117
Thomson, Edwin, 120, 121, 125
Thornley, J., J.P., 153
Thorpe, (of Skircoat Green), 82
Times, 188
Toryism, 13, 28, 125, 170, 182, 183, 200, 211, 219–20,
     227; Peelites, 39; Young England Movement, 28,
     225–7
Toynbee, Joseph, 130
Tractarians,—see Oxford Movement
Training and drilling, Chartist, 146, 152–3
Trenchard, John, 63
Trevelyan, Sir Charles Edward, 134–5
Turkey, 119–20
Turner, (drink-seller at Derby), 220
Tyldesley, 276

Unemployment, 16, 90–1, 93, 95–6
Universal Community Society of Rational Religionists
     (Owenite), 269, 282
Universal suffrage, 183, 195, 208, 209–10, 213, 236, 284
Urquhart, David, 119–20

Venetia, 132
Victoria, Queen of Great Britain, 12, 23–4, 70–2, 282
Villiers, Charles Pelham, 194
Vincent, Henry, 27, 42, 45, 48, 76, 99, 129, 130, 171 n.1,
     178, 223
'Vixen', The, 119–20
Volney, C. F., Comte de, 245
Voluntaries, Scottish, 298
Volunteers, 146, 149

Waddington, H., 176–7
Wade, The Rev. Arthur S., LL.D, 277
Wages, 14–15, 96–7, 116–17, 184, 186, 188–92, 255
Wagstaff, (Clerk of Bradford Union), 157–8
Wagstaff, C. E., 235
Wainhouse, Robert, 81
Wakefield, 33
Wakley, Thomas, M.P., 41, 231–2
Wales, 20, 40, 178–80; see also under separate towns and
     districts
Walker, (Ashton Chartist), 141
Walpole, Horace, 117
Walsall, 201
Walson, (Birmingham Chartist), 121
Walter, John, 219, 220
Ward, Professor J. T., 9
Warden, John, 120–6, 214
Warren, (Manchester Anti-Corn Law supporter), 218
Warrington, 190
Warwick, 106, 150
Waterhouse, Solomon, 192
Watkin, Edward William, 214–19
Watkins, The Rev. Mr., (Barnsley magistrate), 153
Watson, James, 40, 48, 130
Wearmouth, Dr. R. F., 284
Webb, Sidney and Beatrice, 39
Wellington, 1st Duke of, 28, 58, 157
Wentworth, Martin G., J.P., 153
Wesley, John, 285, 286–7, 298
West Indies, 98
West, Julius, 12
Western Vindicator, 178–80
Westhoughton, 276
Westleigh, 276
Wheeler, T. M., 86, 88, 187, 235, 239
Wheelwrights' and Blacksmiths' Society, 243
Whigs, 29, 85, 103, 152, 170, 175, 183, 199, 211, 217,
     219, 220, 229, 230, 277
Whitefield, George, 298
Whitehead, (Ashton Chartist), 144
Whittle, James, 60
Wigan, 190
Wigton, 61
Wild, (Mottram Chartist), 80
Wilkes, John, 51
Wilkins, Charles, 214, 217, 218
Wilkins, David, 63
Willcox, James, 142, 143, 144
Williams, Joseph, 163, 165, 166
Williams, Morgan, 187
Williams, W., M.P., 232
Williamson, Superintendent, 164
Wilson, Dr. Alexander, 263
Wilson, Benjamin, 80–3
Wiltshire, 14, 176
Winlaton, 61
Winterbottom, Thomas, 146